David C. Humphrey

The
Extraordinary
Mr. Morris

The
Extraordinary
Mr. Morris

BY HOWARD SWIGGETT

Garden City, New York

DOUBLEDAY & COMPANY, INC.

Library of Congress Catalog Card Number: 52-5540

to
THE ABIDING MEMORY
of
MY MOTHER

Foreword

THERE CAN BE no question that the writing of biography is the greatest intellectual fun in the world.

No editor or critic can say, "That coincidence will never do," or "The plot is too complex to be credible." A novelist must be sure of the motives of his characters. God knows the motives of real men, or of Gouverneur Morris, when he wrote Washington "indispensable circumstances" required him to leave London for the Continent by way of Hamburg (1796).

If this book were fiction, I should receive a note from a publisher's reader saying, "All of us here feel your imagination has run away with you in allowing one of your principal female characters three simultaneous lovers; we feel it is excessive to have two of the three cripples; none of us is happy about your failure to build up to the marriage of Morris and Miss Randolph. As you have it, she simply appears as a result of implausible chance, and to have her accused of two murders and almost unmentionable other crimes is, to put it mildly, melodrama at its worst. We attach a list of similar items. . . ."

As to the story of Morris's life, I have told it without surmise, except where it is plainly labeled.

I have tried to avoid—and not always succeeded—arguing with other writers to "prove" that Morris was always right and his adversaries wrong. I hope I have imbibed some of his magnanimity.

I find it very trying if a biographer does not continually specify how old his people are. Human behavior can hardly be judged without relative ages. I have supplied them. It was particularly interesting to find that, in an age when women were traditionally finished if unmarried at twenty, two of the most charming of their time, Kitty Livingston and Fanny Burney, were spinsters to thirty-six and forty-one respectively, and that Lady Bessborough had four men in love with her at fifty-one.

As to Morris's falling in love at fifty-seven, readers may remember what the novelist Trollope said about middle-aged love, on which "subject men of one age are thoroughly ignorant of what is the very nature of mankind of another age . . . for real true love, love at first sight, love to devotion, love that robs a man of his sleep . . . love that is 'like a Hercules, still climbing trees in the Hesperides'—we believe the best age is from 45 to 70; up to that, men are generally given to mere flirting."

My text does not contain two incidents in Morris's life, and two comments about him, cited as gospel in almost everything written elsewhere about him. I am sure the incidents never occurred and that the inferences drawn from the comments are mistaken.

The incidents are: on a wager, after the Constitutional Convention, Morris slapped Washington on the back in a large company but was overcome with shame by Washington's frozen silence. The action is utterly out of keeping with his reverence for Washington, twenty years his senior, his own manners and general sense of fitness. However, even Professor Farrand includes it in a footnote in *The Records of the Federal Convention* with Parton's *Life of Thomas Jefferson* as the source. There we find that Martin Van Buren is *said* to have told it as having been told him by a man named "Fine of Ogdensburgh," who *said* Hamilton told him.

The next is that Morris, surrounded by a mob in France during the Terror, "quietly opening the door of his carriage, thrust out his wooden leg and said 'an aristocrat! Yes, truly, who has lost his leg in the cause of American liberty' whereat followed great applause from the mob." In several books, "Morris threatened with being hanged . . . unfastened his wooden leg, [and] brandishing it above his head, proclaimed . . ."

The authority for either version is the *Diary and Letters*, in the Anne Cary Morris edition, Vol. 1, p. 14, and it may be said that a granddaughter is better authority than the present writer. But such an action is completely alien to Morris. The wooden leg was a sensitive humiliation to him, and to suppose, with his pride and resource in handling mobs, that to save himself he had to resort to clowning about his affliction is ridiculous.

Why does his granddaughter tell it? It must be remembered that she never saw her grandfather and that he died when her father was three years old. I suggest the story was invented by one of the French family servants, or Martin Bromeline, long the steward, to pacify grandchildren's demands for stories. That is what it sounds like and the fact that Jared Sparks (1832) does not mention it makes that more likely. It is the sort of thing he would have liked, and if it had been true, or told to Mrs. Morris by her husband, she would have been likely to tell Sparks.

As to the comments: Hamilton called Morris "an exotic." It was not said as a considered judgment, as its citation *ad nauseam* implies. It was made by Hamilton in a fit of depression about himself when he thought all America was against him and he wanted company. An American happier in his environment than Morris would be hard to find.

Finally the timeworn tale that Madame de Staël and her circle were "too brilliant" for Morris. So the *Diary* for November 4, 1789, says, "I am not sufficiently brilliant for this constellation." It is quite obvious from the context that he believed the contrary. The "brilliance" of the De Staël circle is dubious enough, but as will be seen—and not greatly to his credit—he had no trouble competing in it.

The four items are what mathematicians describe as "the second degree of smalls."

Now to the pleasant task of acknowledgments. I owe a debt to exactly twice as many people, societies or libraries as are here mentioned. In the whole research only three requests for help went unanswered. As every writer knows, the slightest hint of a lead or clue is often as valuable as a whole sheaf of letters. So in my case with F. Abbot Goodhue, Chloe French, Wilmarth S. Lewis, and Lawrence Tower.

I have long felt that all people have to do, to live in peace and pleasantness, is to acquire the good manners, alertness of mind and level of intelligence of professional librarians and archivists. Conspicuous among them are: Mr. Ivor Avellino, Mr. Sylvester Vigilante and Miss Shirley Barker, author of *Rivers Parting*, of the American History Room of the New York Public Library. I suppose Ivor Avellino is not a clairvoyant, but he could make a fortune reading people's minds. You go to his desk and before you can put your jumbled needs into a request, he says, "Suppose you sit down quietly with Mathews' *Diaries Written Prior to the Year 1861. Then* you may have the index volume of Stevens' *Facsimiles.*" So it is with Mr. Robert W. Hill, Keeper of Manuscripts, N.Y.P.L., Miss Jean R. McNiece and Mr. Edward B. Morrison, his assistants. Their services and kindnesses to me have been enormous. With what perfection of library science the John W. Francis letter and the copies of the infamous John Randolph letter were produced.

I am very grateful to Mrs. Walter B. Thomson, librarian of the Hewlett-Woodmere Public Library, Hewlett, L.I. A word to Mrs. Thomson, and in three days, books arrive on loan from Yale, Harvard, the State Library at Albany, N.Y., or anyplace else which has them.

Mr. R. W. G. Vail, director of the New-York Historical Society, let me examine the Robert R. Livingston Papers, before they had been unpacked and recorded, and through his good offices, Mr. Goodhue Livingston most graciously agreed that I might quote them. Mr. Wilmer Leech advised me, as he had done twenty years before with my *War Out of Niagara.*

Mr. Roland Baughman of the Butler Library, Columbia University, gave me every facility in examining the De Witt Clinton Papers and much more time with the microfilm machine on the Robert Morris *Day Book* and *Letters* than I was entitled to.

In the delightful Alumni Room in the Low Library, Dr. M. Halsey Thomas, curator of Columbiana, produced a "folder" on Gouverneur Morris with copies of the letters Anne Cary Morris had sent *The Columbian* in 1818.

Mr. S. T. Riley, librarian of the Massachusetts Historical Society, told me of, and allowed me to use, the forty-seven Morris letters in their collection and solved a mystery for me.

Mr. Francis L. Berkeley, of the Alderman Library, University of Virginia, Dr. Clayton Torrence of the Virginia Historical Society, Mr. R. N. Williams, II, of the Historical Society of Pennsylvania, Mr. Herbert L. Ganter, Curator of Manuscripts, The Library, William and Mary College, allowed me to use the material of those libraries and, like Mrs. H. W. Howell, Jr., of the Frick Art Reference Library, replied to letters, special deliveries and telegrams the day they were received. So with Mrs. Elizabeth F. Sammis of the Stratford (Conn.) Historical Society.

On a very hot and humid day I found shelter in the cool, thick-walled library of the Long Island Historical Society where Miss Huntington and the staff produced material I did not know of. Like Dr. Thomas's room, this old high-ceilinged, dark-paneled library, with its delightful bays, should be seen by those who believe in functional architecture.

The chief and staff of the Manuscript Division of the Library of Congress could not have been kinder or more helpful to a troublesome fellow.

Dr. E. C. Russell, rector of St. Ann's Church, the Bronx, built in memory of Mrs. Gouverneur Morris, gave a whole morning to showing and telling me about it. There I saw my daughter, Courtney Gibb, like a Mohammedan at prayer, brushing the dust from the slab under the grating in the aisle, to reveal at last the date of Mrs. Morris's death which I found nowhere else recorded.

I can refer only mysteriously to the help of three close friends: Mrs. Russell Paris of Brookline, Mass., who paid a visit for me; Dailey L. Bugg, O.B.E., of Dayton, O., who replied to a telegram; George Seward of New York, who made a telephone call.

Cassius M. Clay of Paris, Kentucky, saved me from bad blunders on the Federal Convention. Gertrude Kelly, Grace T. Buchanan of Ambler, Pa., and her brother, my lifelong friend and classmate Henry Tetlow, were great stimulants. A special acknowledgment to McVickar Snow appears in the notes to Chapter Thirty-two.

Neighborliness is known to be a thing of the past. Therefore it cannot be that my neighbors, Catherine and John Finerty, let me come to talk about Morris, hours on end, without yawning; and Dr. Benjamin R. Allison told me about Dr. Hosack and Dr. Bard, and reviewed the medical histories of my principal characters; William and Valentine Edgar, he a grandson of Rufus King, "delivered and called" for books from their superb library and handed over the William Edgar Papers, 1773–1820, to be used as I pleased. For that matter I telephoned James and Gertrude Horan in New Jersey at ten o'clock one night to borrow two books. At seven in the morning they arrived first class and special delivery.

While in Washington, a complete stranger to them, I telephoned Jay and Audrey Walz, authors of the remarkable novel, *The Bizarre Sisters* (New York, 1950). Without a question, in simple declarative sentences, they gave me a wealth of references. Ian Hamilton of Washington, a descendant of Alexander Hamilton, put me heavily in his debt for help on letters of Angelica Church.

Though they have read none of the book, I am greatly indebted to Professor Allan Nevins of Columbia, Professor Samuel Flagg Bemis of Yale, and my friend, Bernhard Knollenberg, for their interest and the sources suggested.

Chapter notes refer more fully to advice from Gordon Aymar and from Theodore Sizer, of the Yale Department of Fine Arts, Professors Talbot Hamlin and Gilbert Highet of Columbia, and Frederick A. Pottle, editor of the Boswell Papers.

Katharine Anthony (*Dolly Madison: Her Life and Times*) and David Loth (*The People's General*) gave me a lead and a correction of great value. I am indebted to Lewis G. Morris for word as to Gouverneur Morris's coloring in a miniature and for permission to reproduce his Simitière engraving if the Emmet Collection's print did not suffice.

In England, four friends and colleagues of mine from the British Missions in Washington (1940–45) were of the greatest help. In view of Morris's post-Revolution acquaintances and activities in the City of London, it was very fitting that three of these friends should have returned to the direction of their respective banks. Through interlocking friendships came the lore of Bowood, the picture of it and Lord Wycombe—and photostats, records, charts, pictures of bombed Altona and Altona, 1795, and the find in ruined Hamburg by the Regierungsamtmann of Hansestadt Hamburg-Altona. All this material arrived with the wonderful English finish and the air of having been held for years just for me. These friends and the new one they brought in are: Colonel Reginald Benson, D.S.O., M.C., M.V.O.; the Hon. Thomas Brand, C.M.G.; Sir Charles Hambro, K.B.E.; M.C.; the Eighth Marquis of Lansdowne and Lord Strathcona and Mount Royal. How fitting to please them all by saying only, *Floreat Etona!*

I am deeply indebted to Monsieur de Heurtaumont, Château de Beauvrigny, Manche, France, not only for the generously proffered letters of Madame de Flahaut to Monsieur Le Roi, but for the review of all her unpublished letters in his possession for references to Morris.

Dr. William E. Rappard, director of the Institute of Higher International Studies at Geneva, and Mr. Roy Hunziker, counselor of the Swiss Legation, Washington, D.C., responded at once and most cordially to my questions as to Morris and Bremgarten (1794).

For research in distant places I have frequently had to employ men students. Actually I have never felt quite safe or sure about the product, but there is something alert and incorruptible about women. Perhaps it is not incorruptibility but a deep suspicion that men, or their writings, are never to be trusted, so that they go to wonderful extremes to satisfy themselves of the facts. It was therefore with complete confidence that I appealed to Miss Christiane Baron, then with ECA, Paris, for help on Madame de Flahaut. Within a few days of my first inquiry reaching Miss Baron, a stream of notes and suggestions from French sources began to arrive and continued on from Ankara, Turkey, where she had been transferred. I should have needed another year without her help. After my own stay in Washington, requests to Mrs. Virginia Freund, of the Folger Shakespeare Library staff—"in a spare moment could you please go next door . . . (Library of Congress)"—were all complied with and my debt for the results is very great.

When my daughter, Bonnie Kerner, wrote me that no Virginia newspaper in the Congressional Library for April–June 1793 mentioned the trial of Richard and Nancy Randolph, I knew it was true. Mrs. Aline Kent, at the expense of her own work in the sixteenth century, gave me great assistance. Mrs. John Kean, the present chatelaine of Liberty Hall, asked me there, showed me its treasures of Livingston and Kean lore—and drove me to the mouth of the river out of which Morris so often sailed and where British spies and the cartel commissioners (1782) landed. A stranger has seldom been so received.

I must add, with deep affection and recollection, that it brought to mind my first meeting with the late Robert W. Chambers, at his great house in Broadalbin, when I was writing *War Out of Niagara.*

Perhaps I am most indebted to Mrs. Elinor Henry, who typed the manuscript without protest at my penmanship.

I owe a very great deal to Miss Alverta Seeley, who has done so much to make this book possible.

It is a pleasure to record that Lee Barker, of Doubleday and Co., Inc., and Willis Kingsley Wing are, like Morris, "happy, sensible men," and that my debt to Mrs. Kathryn Tebbel of Doubleday's editorial staff is enormous.

Finally to F.B.S., as always, the words from the end of Cloten's Song in *Cymbeline.*

H.S.

October, 1951
Hewlett, L.I., N.Y.

Gouverneur Morris, 1780, by Pierre de Simitière

By permission of the Print Room, New York Public Library

Talleyrand by Mlle. Godefroy

Musée de Versailles

Adélaide de Flahaut

Drawn by G. Staal and engraved by Massard from a drawing by Chrétien.
By permission of the Bibliothèque Nationale

Bowood

By permission of the 8th Marquis of Lansdowne

Lord Wycombe, 2nd Marquis of Lansdowne

By permission of the 8th Marquis of Lansdowne

The Old Town Hall, Altona. Contemporary print

Evening he gives a sad Account of Things. The Weather continues very warm or rather extremely hot.

Saturday 11 August.

A Sleepless Night renders me heavy during this Day. The King's Speech remains yet at the Assembly which goes on rapidly under the Notice of the Tribunes. We are quiet here. Things are taking on their new order. The Weather continues to be very hot. M. de St. Pardou calls in the Evening and seems torn to Pieces by Affliction. I desire him if he sees the royal Family to tell them that Relief must soon arrive.

Sunday 12 August

This Morning Monsieur de Monciel and his Wife come before I am up. I have my House full all Day and am heartily fatigued this Evening. I called in the Morning on Lady Sutherland who is en pleine abbatue. The Venetian Ambassador was abroad and so was Madame d'Albanie. She & the Count Alfieri come about three o'Clock. She is violently affected and afflicted. The Weather is very warm still and even oppressive. The State of the Air is evidenced by some Perch which alive in the Morning at six o'Clock are spoiled at Dinner. So rapid a State of putrefaction I never yet saw.

Monday 13 August

Bright this Morning. Mr. Constable calls and Mr. Flynn and Mr. Swan with

with Mr. Ingram Mr Gore and Mr Jarvis and a naturalized frenchman. These four want Passports. Mr. Amory calls for the same purpose and Mr. mount florence to get a Passport for Mr Blagden. Madame d'allanis dines with me and requests me to ask a Passport for her from the british Embassador. I go after dinner and he as I expected refuses to grant it. The Weather is somewhat cooler this Evening having had Rain.

Tuesday 14 August

Write this morning. But I have many Interruptions. Among others Mr call on me. Mr francis gives a dreadful Account of what he said on the tenth and says that he shall not dare to tell it in America. Genl du Portail calls on me. He wishes to get away from hence should things grow more serious. Mr Chaumont comes just before Dinner. Mr Constable and Mr Shyn dine with me and so does Mr Chaumont. The Weather is more pleasant than it was but still it is very warm.

Wednesday 15 August

This Morning Mr Chaumont comes and we at length get thro our Business but in the middle of many Interruptions. L Rowes and Mr the british Minister call on me respecting some Points which he wishes to elucidate and to obtain my opinion without formally asking

Matoax May 12th 93

When I last saw my dear friend, I was in such
a state of mind, that I was incapable of feeling, or
expressing, any thing like pleasure, otherwise the sight
of her after so long an absence, could not fail of exciting
the most joyful emotions. for better than a week before
I met you at Cumberland Court house, my mind had
been in the most perfect state of misery, which humani
-ty is capable of enduring. I scarce know whether I should
have suffered so much, had I doubted my husband's
innocence, for then, I confess my esteem for him would
have been so diminished, that I should not have felt
what I did on his account. but perfectly conscious of that,
as I have ever been, & still dreading the diabolical
machinations of his, & Nancy's unprovoked, (but not less
rancourous) enemies, words are inadequate to express
what my weak mind endured. but let us quit a

Letter of Judith Randolph to Mary Harrison, May 12, 1793

With the permission of the Virginia Historical Society

Letter of Anne Randolph, 1800

By permission of the Alderman Library, University of Virginia

Morrisania Feb. 7th 1815

Dear Sir

I wrote to Mr. Sypes a few days ago
requesting him to call on you and read the packet
which I took the liberty of forwarding, to your care,
last week. By this day's mail I send in three packages
a copy of my answer to Mr. Randolph's letter. I
am anxious that it should be seen in Richmond with
the certified copy of his.

I should indeed be a Monster
were it possible for me to commit any impropriety
as the wife of such a Husband, the Mother of such
a Child as Heaven has blessed me with.

Poor Saint George has recently
written me a most affectionate letter. Such only
did I ever get from him.

Most respectfully I am your
humble Servant
Ann C. Morris

Letter of Anne Morris, February 7, 1815
By permission of the Virginia Historical Society

je suis arrivée de la campagne depuis 2. jours et je repars aussitôt
ce qui m'empechera d'avoir le plaisir de vous voir; je vous prie
d'être assez bon pour m'envoyer ~~~~ ce qu'il peut vous rester d'argent
à moi, car j'ai des centièmes dîners a payer qui me tourmentent
beaucoup. —

je joins ici une quittance avec la somme en blanc car
je l'ignore exactement — je vous prie Monsieur de
croire à tous les sentiments que je vous ai voués,

le 23 ~~~~~~ an 8   A. Flahaut

je vous prie d'être assez bon pour m'envoyer les billets sous
enveloppe cachetée. — Si je puis avoir une minute avant
d'aller dans ma petite terre ce sera pour aller vous
remercier et vous demander pardon de mon importunité

Letter of Adèle de Flahaut to her publisher
By permission of Bibliothèque Nationale

Mrs. Perez Morton by Gilbert Stuart

By permission of the Worcester Art Museum

David B. Ogden by John Trumbull

By courtesy of Yale University Art Gallery

Gouverneur Morris, 1810, by Sharples

By permission of John Turnbull and the Frick Art Reference Library

Nancy Randolph (Mrs. Gouverneur Morris), 1810, by Sharples

By permission of Miss Beatrix Cary Davenport and the Frick Art Reference Library

Contents

Illustrations
following Foreword

The
Extraordinary
Mr. Morris

A Whole Entirely Different

THIS IS A BOOK about a lighthearted gentleman who was one of the patriot leaders. His adversaries conceded the brilliance of his genius and the friends who were closest to him, like Washington and John Jay, deplored his foibles.

To understand Gouverneur Morris, man of the world and its affairs, stylist of the Constitution, minister to France, and "the great lover with the wooden leg," we do not have to reconstruct an antique way of life nor reflect on problems which are dead today.

During his lifetime two of the three paramount issues were how men could be governed yet left with their liberty, and how Europe could live in peace, undominated by a single power. These have yet to be solved.

Only the third, which seemed perhaps the greatest at the time, has been solved. It was the sovereignty of "the Western Waters."

There was an enormous variety to life in eighteenth-century America. Social classes were clearly defined, and localities had their own unimitative customs and cultures.

No one, not even any of the great patriots, was the typical colonial American.

There was, however, a well-to-do, educated, landowning

class, with mercantile affiliations, of whom Gouverneur Morris is typical.

These people are human and familiar today. There was a great deal of fun and gusto about them, and almost a complete absence of that mixture of pious prudery and "refinement" which appeared sixty-odd years later.

Many of them knew, visited, entertained and wrote to each other. Their letters from New York manors, Virginia plantations, or the Upper Posts, like Detroit or Michilimackinac, are from men and women "longing to hear" ordinary, familiar news, "how you passed the Winter and how you were divided, I mean the little card-parties etc., etc." They want clothes of the newest fashions, luxuries for the table, and "next summer" they plan to visit each other though five hundred miles away. They worry about "academies" for their boys and girls. The men send kisses by a friend to other men's wives or a beauty in New York or Fort Niagara. They are sure the "ladies conversation in the afternoon is a scandle broth or Detroit [then a stockade of log huts] is much altered." Four swanskins are sent from St. Joe twelve hundred miles by canoes and batteaux to a merchant's wife in New York with a request for some olives and twenty-four packs of playing cards "by some opportunity" in return.

The writers are concerned with money-making from lands, house rents, "adventures," banking, insurance, cattle and fur sales. Almost their deepest apologies come when they "cannot send newspapers and magazines," particularly if "peltery" or tobacco quotations are being awaited.

Their fertility and mortality are perhaps their most striking human differences from today. Patrick Henry was one of nineteen children, John Marshall of fifteen. But though Cotton Mather had fifteen children only two survived him.

Ships brought fevers like a Black Plague as far north as Philadelphia and New York almost every summer, though at their height country districts like Greenwich Village and Long Island were untouched. "Cholera Morbus," diphtheria and consumption were terrible scourges. "Measles with sore throat, is causing great havoc, Major Ancrum's two boys, young Alex

Macomb and Sally . . . twenty odd dead" one Christmas week in a dozen families in Detroit, a commonplace throughout the colonies.

Yet often those who survived lived to a great age, Jefferson to eighty-three, John Trumbull to eighty-seven, William Short to ninety, John Adams to ninety-one, William Johnson, first president of Columbia, to ninety-two, and Charles Thomson, secretary of all the Continental Congresses, to ninety-five. Morris said once it would be that way with the nation, "assured of a long and vigorous life if it survived to any age at all."

In Morris himself, what, if anything, seems archaic is that a man so immersed in public affairs should have had a temper of such sunny magnanimity and have been equipped with so enormous a knowledge of human history

Unlike a few of the patriot planners, he did not have to contend with the dark terrors of Calvinism, the sense of sin, fear of the Hereafter, and that truth, as they believed, that only some are foreordained to everlasting life . . . none of that touched Morris in the slightest. "Whatever is, is," he was fond of saying and was quite sure in the long run it was all for the best, the act of the forgiving and loving Parent of Mankind.

He was a great many people in one. Faced with a problem of practical reality, he was as dependable and sensible as the banker in *The Tale of Two Cities,* who said, "This is business. . . . If business is to be done, I'd better do it." Like James Boswell, he felt himself "able and undaunted to engage in the wars of the Paphian Queen." He had the liberal culture of the great Whig lords, their love of books and the advancement of knowledge, houses and the land, but he was totally different in lacking their most flagrant vice. He looked on gambling with contempt, refusing ever to play for high stakes, in spite of his wealth, and giving his small winnings to the servants.

When America's friend, Lord Shelburne, reflecting on the enormous enrichment, at the cost of the state, of English ministers like Robert Walpole, the first Lord Holland, Sandwich and Grafton, said political corruption was inevitable, Morris told him, with truth, that it was not so then in America.

There was much of Charles James Fox's gay and brilliant

precocity about him but neither drink nor gaming was a problem to Morris. He was ahead of Edmund Burke in foreseeing that a Napoleonic despotism would follow the French Revolution. Burke's *Reflections* contain much that Morris had already written to Washington and Jay, but without Burke's mysticism and sentiment. Nor could the sensible Morris have ever thrown a dagger around the floor of Congress, as Burke did in the House, to the titters of the members.

One of the many ladies who at different times found refuge from the Terror in his legation in France wrote a long tribute to him—he was "habitually serene and ever at peace with himself"; he had a great love of order; he was always "ready for abstruse inquiry or the trifles of social amusement."

Physically he was magnificent, well over six feet tall, a strong, athletic figure without the lankness of Jefferson or Monroe. In an early miniature his eyes are blue and his hair light brown. Admirers and adversaries agreed on the ring and appeal in his voice. Even after the loss of a leg his bearing was so splendid that the French sculptor, Houdon, had him pose for his figure of Washington. The amputation had affected his physical activities very slightly. He was an outdoors man to the end of his life, a fisherman, horse breeder and farmer, a great walker, camper in the wild lands, and halfway through his fifties he shot the St. Lawrence rapids in a canoe.

Although he lived in a time when the well to do were said to use more perfume than soap he had the present-day taste for cleanness of clothes and body. At the end of a day's journey there is always a bath and "fair linen" and a search for a laundress for "foul linen." There was a bathroom at Morrisania in 1800 and in the ill-smelling Louvre even his lady bathed daily, "washing herself to the arm pits with Hungary Water." She and Morris visited their dentists regularly. He regarded snuff as a disgusting habit and did not smoke.

With his great talents why does he come short of absolute greatness? The answer is probably the absence of the Roman *gravitas* in his nature. He has balance of mind, the habit of hard work, great outward emotional control, at times almost to the point of callousness, but underneath it all is a charming levity

and an indifference to what people say. If, however, the interests of his country are at stake, he is second to no one in
sacrificial devotion to duty. Above all, though, there is the
question of the appeal of Eve.

It can hardly be that he alone of the patriot leaders was
devoted to the pursuit of love. He was, however, until he was
fifty-seven, one of the few bachelors among them and the
stories of his "gallantries" were talked about in America and
accompanied him to Europe. Certainly he made no effort to
suppress them, and in his *Diary* for the ten years in Europe
recorded them in detail.

Jared Sparks, writing the *Life* in 1831, with the *Diaries* before him, could not have been expected to record such amorous
frivolity. He expurgated so carefully that the unwary reader
would suppose that Morris's life in Europe, though occasionally
gay, was never unchaste. In 1888, when fuller excerpts from the
Diaries were published, the same impression was left and in the
circumstances this was inevitable. It sufficed to persuade
French writers, as late as 1935, that Morris had at most been an
unsuccessful aspirant for the favors of the ladies he knew.
American writers on Morris followed Sparks. Biographies of
his adversaries portrayed him as a butterfly and a social climber
though not a libertine. In part the false picture arose from the
lack of sources now available, but even more from the mythmaking process which made of the Founding Fathers men
utterly deaf to the uproar of sexual life.

Lives and Letters published in the nineteenth and early
twentieth centuries are dull reading, because they pride themselves on omitting "anything of a purely personal interest." So
Charles King, a great physician, wrote in the foreword to the
six-volume life of his ancestor, Rufus King, "a luminary of the
age." We know from such books everything these men thought
about politics and public affairs, but of course almost nothing
of them as men.

Writers of wisdom and experience of life seem still to be
shocked and shaken if they discover that a founder of America
ever behaved as an errant human being. A writer of great reputation, himself a veteran diplomat, says, "It was [Harrison

Gray] Otis who wrote of Hamilton's liquorish flirtation with a married woman at a fashionable dinner-party," as though such a thing had never happened before, and "proved" that Jefferson's views on the value of a French alliance were right and Hamilton's wrong.

This attitude of mind, D. H. Lawrence once suggested, has to do with some deep sense of guilt in the American soul. Fortunately we do not have to look for it in the soul of Gouverneur Morris, who thought women were wonderful creatures, to whose pursuit a man could happily devote all the time he could possibly spare from statecraft and finance.

Reference has been made to his resemblance to Boswell in liking "the wars of the Paphian Queen," a euphemism both of them used for the acts of love. There was, however, an enormous difference between them. Fundamentally it was of fastidiousness. Morris's eye was caught as quickly as Boswell's by "beauty begging in the streets," or by the Cinderella appeal of someone's governess or young female relative. Boswell of course was utterly promiscuous with women of every class. Not so Morris. No Pamela for him, no Temperance Ray, the servant-girl mother of John Trumbull's son. Except for a curious interlude with a landlord's daughters, his affairs were with a few women of rank, beauty and unusual intellectual gifts and, sensual in the extreme as his great affair was, it and the other principal ones were acted out as though they were a long, engrossing play. All of the ladies would have graced Morrisania. He had a sense for the grace of life.

In a general way the men who disliked or distrusted him most were James Lovell and Joseph Reed, in the Continental Congress years, and Tom Paine, John Adams, Thomas Jefferson, James Monroe and Lafayette thereafter.

We do not know enough of the full lives of Lovell and Reed to assess the value of their judgments. But their letters seem to indicate they were both gloomy, fretful, petty-minded men to whom Morris's exuberance must have been exasperating.

It was also quite natural that John Adams should distrust Morris. There is a strain of hypochondria, foreboding and premature old age in Adams. At thirty-seven, the age when Morris went to France, Adams had written, "For the remainder of my days, I shall decline in sense, spirit, activity." Of course it was not true even of Adams, but the man who could think about it could hardly have been expected to like Morris, who at sixty-four wrote a friend that he still felt "the enthusiasms of inexperience and the gaiety of youth."

Even so, it is interesting to find two almost identical entries in the *Diaries* of these dissimilar men. "Still, calm, happy Braintree," Adams wrote at a journey's end, and there is an entry by Morris at Morrisania forty years later, "Return home in the evening. Dear, quiet, happy home."

Monroe and Jefferson had this same love of their houses, so marked in the patriot leaders. Morris died in his house before Monroe and Jefferson had lost theirs to their creditors. In a way this was an aspect of the differences in them. Monroe, for all his great titles, was a most unlucky man and both he and Jefferson lacked in everyday life the sensible, methodical regard for money which Morris had and which has nothing to do with avarice.

Morris was born amidst wealth but inherited only a small patrimony. To live as he wanted to, he saw that money was essential and set himself to make and keep a fortune, which he did.

He wrote William Carmichael in 1789 that he wished not to accumulate money but to enjoy his possessions in peace. "I want to live properly, farming *cum dignitate* and to this end it is essential to possess a modest share of fortune's favours." The man to whom he was writing, then our minister in Spain, died bankrupt and Jefferson, Monroe and Hamilton almost so. There is something of austere magnificence, though, in the fact that men of such "opportunities" could have died so poor. It was not the *politique* of Europe, as the wealth of a Lord Holland or a Talleyrand bears witness.

Tom Paine and his biographers are, with those of John Paul Jones and Lafayette, Morris's most bitter enemies.

For years Morris did Paine many kindnesses but if it was impossible for John Adams to like Morris, it was inevitable that Morris should have contempt for Paine, so antagonistic were their qualities. For one thing Paine seems to have been physically dirty. He appears frequently through Morris's life and the reader must judge between them. It may be noted here, however, that Paine's biographers find and applaud, as something noble, a sexlessness in him, not only during his brief marriage but for the rest of his life. For that matter so after 1784 do many admirers of Jefferson.

Morris regarded celibacy as "an impious and unnatural doctrine." Small wonder that twisted men, like Paine and the impotent John Randolph of Roanoke, should have borne him such malice.

This generalization can be made of his adversaries. They included some "great men" and their reasons for opposing Morris were often well founded. None of them, however, possessed his quality of sunny magnanimity or surpassed him in that blend of vision and moderation which is wisdom.

What did Morris believe in? First and most passionately in the abolition of slavery. It is a shock, even across the years, to realize that that horror was not then confined to the South. It was to a Northern branch of a great New York firm of international merchant bankers that letters went saying:

I send you a little Pawnee wench to sell this winter. . . . She is past danger of her first sickness, sell her for 27 or £28.

The negro wench who speaks good English and French with her child and one on the stocks is worth £120 York.

He believed in a republican form of government for this country, and that it should provide personal liberty, safeguard free enterprise and be supported by heavy taxation. He was born into a family who, like the Van Rensselaers and the Livingstons, lived in a species of feudalism, as lords of their manors. Yet all recognized when the old order had passed away and made small effort to prolong it. He considered that governments were better run by aristocrats than by democracy, but no one required of aristocrats more sacrifice for the public good than he, and no one was more intolerant or contemptuous of an aristocracy without brains, vigor or the ideal of human welfare.

He was still a youth when he wrote the verses defining a gentleman

> Whose generous tongue disdains to speak
> The things his heart disproves
>
> Who never did a slander forge
> His neighbor's fame to wound
> Nor hearken to a false report
> By malice whispered round.
>
> Who vice in all its pomp and power
> Can treat with just neglect
> And piety, though clothed in rags
> Religiously respect.
>
> Who to his plighted words and trust
> Has ever firmly stood
> And, though he promise to his loss
> He makes his promise good. . . .

Much of what he lived by is in this boyish jingle. He was, at various times in his life, intolerant, wrongheaded, immoral, shocking and outwardly callous. He was never fantastic nor grotesque. Few men, however, have been as free of hatred, envy, malice and all uncharitableness as he. No man was freer of lamentation over life's sorrows. To the world he took the loss of his leg at twenty-eight as though it were a careless trifle. The terrible charges brought against his wife thirty-four years later disturbed him not a whit except as they made her unhappy.

"He has virtues, defects and talents," Madame de Damas wrote, "but their nature, their use, mixture and results form a whole entirely different from anything I have seen."

It is that something "entirely different" which is his fascination. Financier, statesman, diplomat, thinker, sinner, faithful husband, farmer, trustee, flâneur, patriot and American—he plays each part with protean zest and skill, and draws to him publicly and privately a great company of actors.

His theatrical life is like a five-act play where the major and minor characters constantly return, drawn by links and coincidences in the complex plot. Some of them come on for a scene or a single speech and hurry off to another theater where their own lives are playing.

In Europe the "guest appearances" go on with even James Boswell in character in a coffeehouse. Hardly a celebrity of the time fails to appear, except Horace Walpole and Edward Gibbon, and they both are in the wings and the latter's voice is heard "off." It would have taxed even Morris's receptive mind to understand if his friend, Madame de Staël, had tried to explain how she and her mother linked Boswell and Gibbon together.

Virgil, so familiar to the patriot classicists, wrote, "*Quisque suos patimur manes* [Each of us suffers his own fate]." So it is with all these lives. They go to inevitable ends, developing but never changing. As the invention of a novelist they would be unbelievable.

The characters of Washington, Jay, Hamilton and Robert Morris led inevitably to their contrasting ends. That Jefferson's family life should be linked to Gouverneur Morris's seems an implausible device of a writer, as does the private debt Morris unknowingly owed patriots as unalike as Patrick Henry and John Marshall.

All Morris's long relations with Lafayette follow naturally from their first meeting that cold night at Valley Forge. Tom Paine and he are never out of character from the day Morris recklessly denounces him in the Continental Congress, later gets him a job, loans him money in Europe and leaves him a prisoner of Robespierre. From the moment John Paul Jones calls at the Office of Finance in Philadelphia in 1781, it is necessary to the plot that he should die one summer afternoon in Paris in a brief interval between two visits from Morris.

Three other characters, a man and two women, played the leading roles opposite Morris. In the moralist's eyes each was very sinful. What happened to each of them, not once, but repeatedly, would have utterly destroyed the ordinary person. Hardly a human vicissitude escaped them—poverty, sickness, disgrace, the threat of death, homeless exile were the lot of each. Over all this each triumphed, the two greatest sinners to live the longest lives, into their seventy-sixth and eighty-fourth years.

An extraordinary will to survive was common to each of them and, despite all the differences between them, arose in large measure from the utter lack of that conviction of sin which is said to be the basis of all psychoses. Like Morris, each possessed that attractive, healthy-minded quality which prevents people sitting down by the waters of Babylon to weep.

These people were Talleyrand, Adélaide de Flahaut, Morris's mistress, and Nancy Randolph, his wife.

CHAPTER TWO

The Trifles
of Social Amusement

(1752–74)

At the manor of Morrisania, Gouverneur Morris was born at one-thirty in the morning of January 31, 1752. His father was fifty-four years old and his mother, Sarah Gouverneur, thirty-eight. He was his father's seventh child and fourth son and his mother's first child and only son. His father died when Gouverneur was ten years old, leaving instructions that he should have the best possible education provided it was not at Yale, of which two of his half-brothers were graduates.

Theoretically so sunny and healthy-minded an individual as Morris, almost wholly free from complexes, must have had a happy childhood of love and security. But this broad conclusion should not be drawn too quickly in his case. There were curious cleavages in the family.

Sparks was evidently allowed to say that Morris's half-brothers, the youngest thirty-two years older than he, resented and disliked their stepmother. It would then seem to follow that his mother, much older, somewhat embittered, made her own gifted son the object of a special devotion and let him be aware of her hostility to his half-brothers.

His later lack of intimacy with, if not indifference to, them fits the picture. On the other hand, the feeling between his mother and himself, twenty-five years later, appears almost casual. This is followed by the fact that, while he and his half-brothers who lived in America were patriots, his mother at best was a passive Loyalist. His full sister, Isabella, married a Loyalist and Euphemia's husband was of dubious attachment to the patriot cause and his father a Tory refugee. Toward his sisters Morris later assumed practically the responsibility of a father.

There is another current psychological theory to consider—that his later search for love arose from inner needs not met in childhood.

Whatever the validity of these theories, they plainly caused not the least introspection on Morris's part. He achieved an amazing mental maturity at an early age and combined it with a delightful gaiety and zest for life.

We can also be sure that, whatever tensions there were in the manor house, they did not affect the healthy, outdoor pursuits of a normal boy. It is clear that the only period in which Morris could have acquired his knowledge and love of farming, fishing and sailing was as a boy at Morrisania.

He was prepared for King's College, later Columbia, at a Huguenot academy in New Rochelle where, Sparks says, "he acquired the basis of the French language, which in after life he wrote and spoke with nearly as much fluency and correctness as his native tongue." This is more or less true—it was of great advantage to him as early as the French Alliance in '78—though if Sparks had not turned his eyes in shame from the *Diaries,* he would have seen that Morris's French mistress was often *moqueuse* about his fluency and correctness and said to him of a plan he had written in French for the King that it was good but not French.

He went to King's College, then bounded by what are now Church, Greenwich, Barclay and Murray streets, and received his B.A. in 1768, at sixteen. It was the June that Massachusetts sent letters to all the colonies asking their support against the Townshend duties. In October British troops commanded by a Colonel Dalrymple began landing in Boston. For his Commencement Address Morris, appropriately for him—spoke on Wit and Beauty, and even more appropriately, when he got his

M.A. two years later, on Love, "the bright and steady lode-star of the moral World."

When Talleyrand, two years Morris's junior, got his B.A. at the Sorbonne in '74 his address was entitled *Tentative,* and he asked whether "science must guard the lips of the priest."

It is safe to say that no commencement orator in '68 or in '70 at William and Mary, Harvard, Yale, King's, New Jersey, Queen's or Pennsylvania discussed separation from Great Britain, and only a handful of men on the whole continent thought of it as happening.

The New York Bar was the natural career for a young man like Morris. He was very much a younger son, with a legacy of ten thousand dollars from his father's estate somewhere in the future. The idea of "amounting to something," "making a career for yourself," was already in the air of America, and who, with his talents and his presence, his family connections and friends, was likely to make a better one than this tall young man who entered the law office of William Smith, a former partner of one of the Livingstons?

The great Livingston family were spread from Albany down the Hudson to Clermont, where the patroon Robert R. Livingston, twenty-four, lived, and now over to Elizabeth Town, New Jersey.

While an undergraduate at Yale in 1740, William Livingston had described the house he wanted to live in. In 1760 he had acquired the land for it in New Jersey and now was drawing the plans for what was to be Liberty Hall.

He was then forty-seven, a tall, gaunt Calvinist whose appearance, religion and nickname, "The Whipping Post," were in contrast to his happy, exuberant nature. In his large family were two of the most delicious young girls in North America.

Katherine, "La Kitty," his fifth child, was born in 1751, the year before Morris, and Sally, the eighth, in 1756.

Morris's letters to them began when he was nineteen, Kitty twenty and Sally fifteen. They "prove," as writers like to say, that young men and maidens have changed very slightly in one hundred and eighty years. If such youthful, "important," "misunderstood," pleading, occasionally "daring" letters are not written today, it is only because song recordings have taken their place.

There is one aspect of them, however, which has gone forever. The penmanship is beautifully legible. Examination of many patriots' letters seems to indicate that only two of them had not been taught to write a decent hand. Knox's script, as big and shapeless as himself, is almost illegible and William Livingston wrote so badly that Washington always had his whole staff in to decipher his dispatches. Morris wrote as clearly in 1816 as he did to Kitty Livingston in 1770.

The first of the letters are lines to Kitty written in "Colonel Morris's Library Friday morning at Ten O'Clock" in May:

> Know then, dearest Kitty, thy note I received
> And that sooner you came not would sorely have grieved,
> Had Lewis not told me that your short Delay
> By continuing longer you richly would pay.
> To welcome you hither each tree shall appear
> In the gayest apparel he wears thro the year,
> And the fragrance of May shall invite you to rove
> And join with the songsters which people each grove
> For thee every Beauty more fair shall be seen
> More blooming the Blossoms, more verdant the green

—and so on.

There is also a poem written at "Princetown April Tuesday Morn," evidently to his brother-in-law, Samuel Ogden, six years older than he. It urges "Samuel dear" to return

> . . . to the living God
> From whom so deeply you've revolted
> And that without a cause, you Jolt Head

ending, after fifty-six lines,

> O dont despise, the Blood Christ spilt
> For thine and for thy Fellow's Guilt.

The first letter to Kitty is from Morrisania in November '71, the month after he had been admitted to the Bar. She had "lost the two or three verses I began when I last (no it was not the last time) I saw you. . . ." So he sends new ones to be sung,

which she and "Sally can sit in judgment on." She may take to
herself "any part of me you think proper"—

> Love, thou tender Foe, to Rest
> Soft Disturber of the Mind
> Ease at length my Troubled Breast
> Sweet Tormenter now be kind. . . .

There is another verse and "should be more by rights but I have
no time. Adieu."

The question of public finance had a way all Morris's life of
intruding on his lighter interests. And it was that, even then,
which gave him no time for the rest of the song.

The colony of New York was still heavily in debt for the
French and Indian Wars and the Assembly proposed to meet it
with interest-bearing bills of credit, a proposal enthusiastically
received by the people as making money more plentiful. Morris's hatred of any form of paper money was so deep-rooted that
one almost thinks he had been frightened by it in the cradle.

Twenty years old, he wrote a powerful attack on the evil
of putting off payment with a new indebtedness, instead of
meeting it by taxation. How it happened that he had the wisdom and effrontery to write the profound and unpopular paper
he did is not clear, except as part of his special genius.

On top of it rather as James Boswell had done, he wrote to
William Smith that he would like to go to Europe for a year "to
rub off in the gay circle a few of the many barbarisms which
characterize a provincial education and to curb the vain self-
sufficiency which arises from comparing ourselves with com-
panions who are inferior to us." He did not see Europe for
twenty years, by which time his worst enemy could find no
"barbarisms" in him, whatever other reservations they may
have had.

Meantime Liberty Hall was ready for occupancy. Downstairs was the Great Parlor, thirty-six feet by twenty, Livingston's library, a small parlor, a dining room and another room,
with the kitchen in the basement. Upstairs were six bedrooms.

Fruit trees from England and France were being set out and
a great horse chestnut, still standing, was planted by the door.

There was a trout pond and the Elizabeth River ran three miles unvexed to the Kills. The beaux from New York could sail to the Livingston garden.

On May 24, 1772, Morris wrote Kitty, sending her "crowquills" to sharpen into pens to write him "which will relieve my mind too much disposed to wish and wish the hours away, a sensation which, dear Kitty, you are by no means unacquainted with," and then, in immemorial fashion, he renews "to you my frequent request that you would favour me with a small lock of your hair which indeed I shall wear devoutly as a sacred relick. . . . All nature is now beautiful but I have a very small relish for its appearance."

There was no answer for some weeks, when the little flirt in Elizabeth Town wrote him that she had not replied sooner because she had hurt her ankle! "Had you written me," he replied, "that you had a pain in your ankle I should on that principle have been satisfied (as to why you could not write). You cannot guess how happy I am from the consideration that for one month I have been the subject of your meditation. Indeed, my dear Kitty, you can form no conception of the variety of emotions I felt on reading this part of your letter nor can I possibly describe them. . . . In the dreaming way I generally converse with you at least once in every three days or rather nights. [In your letter] you tell a great big lie. . . ."

There follows the classic expostulation of youth. Why should she say the better he knows her, the less he likes her? Or that he thinks her "imprudent"? "You impudent baggage [you must learn] not to bear false witness against yourself." Then, from the summit of the years, he closes "after all you are a good ~~gal~~ girl Kate (mark the erasure) and I love you heartily that I do—Farewell—May the great Parent abundantly bless you wishes most sincerely, Yours, Gouverneur Morris." Usually, in the cryptic anonymity of the young lover, they are not signed.

All this brought an invitation to Elizabeth Town, and when he left August 16, he of course wrote that "my amusements at Newark after I left you, tho' lively enough in themselves, were sufficiently dull to me." A fine burst of masculine exhibitionism naturally follows. He walked three miles in the woods with a gun; he rowed himself four miles in a heavy boat to the ferry; crabbed and caught a dozen sturgeon, all the while "almost naked" and up to his knees in water, his "hands torn," his "feet cut"—"at the time I thought myself exceedingly happy." He would like to tell the "vexations" fortune has tantalized him with, if he could do so in confidence—and not have Sally and Susan read it, but no, since she had said she "once warmly loved [someone else] (Susan [an elder sister] says five times)" it is clear that he is a fool, and she can judge how "uncomfortable and hopeless a passion of [his] kind is." His opinion of her is so good and of himself so humble that he "will be

> "Whatever you please
> Gouverneur Morris."

At the end of August he heard she had gone to visit the Albany Livingstons "to be smitten with a Dutch beau." He had "literally conveyed" her message to Polly Morris who was ill, "unwell I mean," and had a languid smile, but he certainly *never* wrote to her or anybody, on his honour—and he has his letter to Polly before him—that he was not happy at Elizabeth Town! In fact he had said he was so sure he would be happy that he would "not have given *even* thanks as a premium to insure my bliss." He is very sorry to have insinuated anything to anyone by any inadvertence that Kitty doesn't like. "What it is which you dislike I know not [but] I would do anything" to explain. Then, masculine pride reborn, he says, "You threaten me much but I fear you are only a bully." "With great propriety," he subscribes himself "Very affectionately yours."

By January 1773, having reached man's estate, he put off these boyish vaporings and wrote, without salutation, "What do you think, Kitty? I have adopted Sally [seventeen] for my daughter. Never was a little creature so admired. As to her heart when in the midst of her admirers it singeth with joy. The rosy fingers of pleasure paint her cheeks." Morris goes on to describe the "gentle Strephons" who hang about her, "bending forward . . . rolling [their eyes] sighing most piteously . . . another sitting sidelong on her chair with melancholic and despondent phiz prolonged unto the seventh button of his

waistcoat . . . another his elbows fastened to his short ribs
. . . in the midst of all this sits Miss with seeming unconscious-
ness of the whole. . . . I shall dispose of her before the winter
is out, I believe, provided Mamma has no objection." As to
Kitty, he is "very sincerely, your friend," and John Jay with his
tall stooping figure and his wonderful eyes would be the husband of Sally.

In June, back at home, Sally sent him some "ruffles" for his
wristbands. This aroused him to heights of eloquence: "Man
indeed draws his plan of happiness but by woman is it executed.
All our joys are cemented and secured by those fine threads of
affection [like those in the ruffles] which by the softer sex are
so interwoven into life. . . ."

The letter also says that William Duer has arrived, and
Morris wishes he could see the meeting of "two tender hearts."
Duer, twenty-six, was to be in the Continental Congress with
Morris and the "tender heart" he was meeting was another
Kitty, daughter of Lord Stirling, whose wife was a New York
Livingston. They would not be married for six years, when
Washington would give the bride away.

On August 30, though now her "sincere friend" only, Morris
writes Kitty of the press of business he has been under, which
is why he has not written. Still they are sure to meet at Lord
Stirling's in the fall and meantime he would like to know "in
minute detail" how she is.

He is sure that "what will come will be right whether or not
agreeable to him." He went to Lord Stirling's and down to
Philadelphia, where he was "up all night making merry," as the
tea was dumped into Boston Harbor on December 16.

In March '74 he was elected to the Moot, the famous club of
which William Livingston was then president. The club dined
in winter at Fraunces' Tavern and had their own summer club-
house at Kip's Bay on East River. Twenty-seven men were
members, his lifelong friends John Jay and Robert R. Livingston, both a little older than he, among them.

A month later John Jay married Sally Livingston in the Great
Parlor at Liberty Hall, while another later author of the *Federalist Papers*, Alexander Hamilton, was a guest.

On May 10, 1774, word reached Boston that the port would be blockaded in June and on May 17 Gage, the new commander-in-chief, landed there. It may almost be said that until that moment only the grim but great Puritans in Boston foresaw that war and even independence would follow. But all the colonies, though New York perhaps least, responded to the call for help from Massachusetts.

No British troops were quartered on New York and the tea ships there had been sent home without violence. Certainly no one of prominence in New York, however he might feel about his ancient English privileges, shared the righteous and turbulent anger of the Adamses. All the traditions of New York, the landed gentry, the Anglican Church, the idea of pleasure were opposed to New England. Small wonder that the first revolutionists from Boston never liked the New Yorkers or the reverse.

But in response to the letters from Boston, the New York Sons of Liberty called a great public meeting on May 19. Morris was there and wrote Penn in Philadelphia his often-quoted letter the next day. He was twenty-two and the letter is not one of exalted ideals of liberty and independence. While he agrees that shutting of the port of Boston is intolerable, "it is the interest of all men to seek for reunion with the parent state —[since otherwise] we shall be under the domination of a riotous mob. . . ." A safe compact could be made, leaving internal taxation to America and the regulating of trade to Britain, since only she can protect it. "We ourselves are competent" to regulate our internal peace, and to refuse taxes, laid on us, for government or defense. In assigning the regulation of trade to England we do no more than "place [it] in the hands of one part of the Empire," where it can be protected. "And what danger is in the trust? She cannot destroy our trade and still derive a profit from it." His views are not wholly mercantile. He says "men are by nature as free as air [and] have an antecedent right to the utmost liberty, which can be enjoyed consistent with the general safety."

It is held against him that he referred to the populace that day as "Poor Reptiles," which he did, though somewhat rhetorically, as basking "in a vernal spring, struggling to cast off the winter's slough." But it may also be noted that he saw very clearly, young as he was, that not all virtue was on one side. He went on, "Their committee [that of the gentry] will be appointed, they will deceive the people and again forfeit a share of their confidence, and if these instances . . . of perfidy shall continue to increase . . . farewell aristocracy."

A New York Committee of Fifty-one was appointed, twenty-three by the Sons of Liberty, twenty-seven by the Moderates, and "by mutual consent" Francis Lewis was added.

On June 17, Boston sent out its resolution for a General Congress to meet in Philadelphia and John Jay, James Duane and Philip Livingston, fifty-eight, the eldest, were named as delegates by New York.

On August 20 the Massachusetts delegation, the two Adamses, Cushing and Robert Treat Paine, reached New York for a week's entertainment before going on to Philadelphia.

In his *Diary*, John Adams does not mention meeting Gouverneur Morris, though from what he told Marbois five years later he probably did and even heard with some contempt of his levity and versifying. He of course saw a great deal of Jay, the Livingstons and William Smith, in whose law office Morris was still working.

He was much impressed by New York, though he did not like it. "The streets are more regular and elegant than those in Boston and the houses are more grand, as well as neat." Still, "with all the opulence and splendor of this city there is very little good breeding to be found. We have been treated with an assiduous respect but I have not seen one real gentleman, one well-bred man since I came to town." There was "nothing genteel," he said, even about William Livingston, surely an extreme statement even for a Bostonian. One of his criticisms was that everyone interrupted him and "talked very fast." They probably did, for their fears in Banquo stuck deep. Even Alexander McDougall, Son of Liberty, later a general in Washington's army, warned Adams of the fears "of the levelling spirit of the New England colonies" and the Episcopalian prejudice against them. Still, all were patriots and even Adams concluded that, though ungentlemanly, the New Yorkers were "modest, decent, sensible men."

Perhaps the New Englanders' visit sobered New York more than they thought. Shortly after they were gone a commercial traveler from Detroit wrote back, "I am in the land of good wine, good oysters and pretty girls . . . though the [New York] people in general discourage all kinds of dissipation as conforming to the wishes of the Congress. On this account we have no plays and decency prevents any dancing. I hope my poor friend Billy has some favoured she to pass his evenings with."

The First Continental Congress sat until October 26, issued its appeals, agreed to meet the next year, to stand by Massachusetts, but its address to the Throne, for redress of wrongs, was still from loyal subjects of a King who was reminded in it that he had "the distinction of reigning over free men."

The King had read such words before. In 1770 the Livery Company of London had told him, "We owe to Your Majesty an obedience under the restrictions of the laws *and* Your Majesty owes to us that our representatives, free from the force of arms and corruption, should be preserved to us in Parliament."

Few men in America, except Sam Adams, believed it was best to have no king at all.

CHAPTER THREE

Half of New York
Was Disaffected

(1775–76)

O₂N JANUARY 6, 1775, the Moot held its last meeting at Fraunces' Tavern. It was the last meeting by acquiescence, brought about by the cleavage in opinion between these intimates over the First Continental Congress.

The division in the club is a microcosm of that in the province of New York. Of the twenty-two men then members, nine became Loyalists, ten Patriots, two were doubtful and one "turned out badly," but the nineteen had already made up their minds. Many like the nine of the Moot remained loyal to the King, but there was not a man of first-rate ability among them.

The manner in which the happy, wealthy gentlemen of America flocked like the zealots to the patriot standard is a phenomenon still not fully explained. None of them had had the personal experience of interference with liberty which the Bostonians knew. Washington, Charles Carroll, the Livingstons, the Morrises, the Laurenses, the Lees, to name but a few, had nothing to gain, all to lose and no burning hatred of England to sustain them.

It had been only thirty years since the Scottish lords had gone to the block after Culloden, and they had been drawn to the cause of the Young Pretender by deep and ancient sentiments.

Originally it was "proved" that the patriot leaders wanted a new nation where men would be "free" and foreign lackeyism be unknown. Subsequently it was "proved" that restrictions on American trade drove them to revolution. Each conclusion is sound in part but neither can be the whole answer.

Underneath, intangible feelings must have been at work, turbulent feelings of vigor and self-confidence, like those of the Virginia commissioners talking to the Western tribes at Fort Pitt: "We are not afraid these people will conquer us. They can't fight in our country and you know we can."

Massachusetts, the conspicuous victim of oppression, was unpopular with the other colonies. Many felt her troubles were of her own making. But there seems to have been the moral feeling, unconnected with self-preservation, that not to stand by her would be the betrayal of that which is near to that which is far, which is the definition of treason.

To his half-brother Lewis, Morris wrote: "As to myself you well know that the offers of my service were merely for the benefit of the general cause considering that my little abilities were more adapted to the deliberations of the Cabinet than the glorious labors of the field."

Why this large, splendid-looking young man of twenty-three felt he was not called upon to fight may not be the mystery which as late as 1938 puzzled one of the wisest of his descendants. But in any event it was to the congresses and cabinets and not the field he went.

Word of Lexington reached New York April 23, a month after Burke's speech on Conciliation, and "the Tories turn Wigg so fast it will soon be like Massachusetts Bay," R. R. Livingston wrote his wife, adding that he would be home "as soon as I can but I must endeavor to get some cash first."

"At all corners," William Smith wrote in his *Journal* on April 29, "people inquire for news . . . tales of all kinds invented, believed, denied, discredited . . . taverns full with men talking politics at night . . . few jurors and witnesses attend court . . . Wilkins and Parson Seabury disappeared. Their wives betake themselves to Mrs. Morris at Morrisania as I learn from Richard and Gouverneur Morris."

A month later Morris was sitting as a delegate from West-chester in the Provincial Congress. His election, in fact that of any Westchester delegate to a Provincial Congress, had been bitterly opposed by his brother-in-law, Isaac Wilkins, among others.

Wilkins is far from an appealing character in Morris's life, but this must be said for him. He was no "snivelling Tory." With Samuel Seabury and Colonel Philipse he came to the caucus and shouted his "abhorrence of all unlawful congresses and committees," on his own behalf and that of 480 other free-holders of Westchester. He could make no headway but there is something fine and funny in the spectacle of his stamping out, with Seabury and Philipse, all three singing, "God Save the King."

Although the gaiety of inexperience never left Morris, he came almost overnight to a maturity of political knowledge and wisdom that is amazing. Both Hamilton and he appear to have had at their finger tips everything that had ever been written on the art of government. For all Morris's frivolity there must have been as many hours spent in study "in Colonel Morris's library" as Adams spent in Boston and Braintree—and the notes and verses to Kitty and Sally have been only brief interruptions.

Perhaps the youngest delegate, he was at once one of the most active. Like most men, he still hoped there might be a sufficient redress of grievances to prevent war, but he moved a resolution of implicit obedience by the Provincial to the Con-tinental Congress, the first example of his desire for a strong central government. That concept of governing, and taxation to the uttermost, were from the start his deepest political views.

It was obvious that money could not be raised in time by taxation and there were two alternatives: every colony should strike [print] for itself a sum set by the Continental Congress; the Continental Congress should strike the whole, issue it pro-portionately to the colonies, each being responsible for "sink-ing" (redeeming) its share.

Morris was on his feet at once with an amendment to the second. Let it be done but with the proviso that "all colonies will discharge that which one cannot pay." This wise move was

his first congressional success and after it he was elected to his
first chairmanship, of the Committee of Correspondence. His
ability to think in national terms, his ability to persuade by debate, his ability to write at twenty-three were as a whole exceeded by none of the patriot leaders.

His amendment to the Plan of Accommodation a month later
is an example of that accommodation within himself to which
Madison later referred. The plan was a long and good one, but
Morris moved and secured an amendment that "no one article
should be considered so essential to the others, as to *exclude*
the idea of accommodations without such article." It was in this
speech that he pointed out the vital need of an "independent
American navy," a piece of advice he later gave to three Presidents of the United States with the additional proviso that it be
powerful. It is not evident that anyone else had previously
proposed it.

On the twenty-eighth of June, New York sent his letter to the
Continental Congress, urging them still "to use every effort for
the compromising of this unnatural quarrel between the Parent
and the Child, *and if we fail*, we may stand fair and unre-
proachable by our own consciences in the last solemn appeal
to the God of Battles."

One of the great occasions of Morris's life occurred that summer. Washington came through New York on the way to command the army around Boston and Morris was of the committee
of two to receive him.

Silas Deane, about at the time, described the man Morris
saw and to whom he was to be so unceasingly devoted (until
the actual day of Washington's death). Deane said, "Washington is almost as tall as Colonel Fitch and almost as hard a countenance yet with a very young look and an easy soldier-like air
and gesture."

In the contrast and conflict between John Adams and Gouverneur Morris it is interesting to see how similar were their
ideas of justice toward those whom they opposed. Adams had
defended the British officer and men accused in the Boston
Massacre. In May '75, Rivington, the Loyalist editor in New
York, was arrested and his press destroyed by the Sons of Lib-

erty. He appealed to Morris for help and Morris wrote to Richard Henry Lee, twenty years older than he, and later so much
his adversary:

The history of his case is simply this: his company, his acquaintances, his friends were warm advocates for the power of [British]
government; indifferent wise, his mind took a wrong bias from interest, deference for the sentiments of others, and opposition. A tool
in prosperity, a cast-off in adversity he solicits the assistance of that
body which his press has aspersed. Magnanimity will dictate to that
body the true line of conduct.

Rivington was not a worthy character, but magnanimity in
such times for a tool and castoff is a rare thing.

Lee wrote back, "the Friends of virtuous Liberty in New
York have certainly effected a most important change in the
political system of that flourishing city. I congratulate you, sir,
and your worthy associates. As to Mr. Rivington, he repents
and should be forgiven."

When Charles Lee shortly left New York for the command
in South Carolina, Morris urged him "to [try] to prevent any
mischievous resolution against this unfortunate printer. . . . I
plead the cause of humanity to a gentleman," he concluded.

It was the absence of this sort of easy and assured generosity
which most horrified Morris in the French Revolution.

All this was a fine start and may have turned the young man's
head, for on July 1, 1776, as Howe's fleet was coming to anchor
in Sandy Hook, Jay wrote to Livingston, "To my great mortification our Convention influenced by one of G. Morris's vagrant
plans have adjourned to the White Plains. This precipitate, ill-
advised stroke of Morrisania politics quite confounds me."

To move the convention away from the encircling British
arms may not have been "vagrant" or "ill-advised" but Jay,
though Morris's close friend, was often his critic. They were all
quite candid with each other. Morris airily told Robert Livingston, "You're too lazy. Jay is too proud. He is too hasty. You're
too inattentive to public affairs."

The Third Provincial Congress now became "the Convention
of the Representation of the State of New York" and in part a
convention to make a state constitution. The committee to draft

the constitution was, in order of seniority, Jay thirty-one, Livingston thirty, Morris twenty-four, and the first and last were the bold leaders. Its work lasted almost nine months and the central ideas animating Morris, and set forth by him with persuasive clarity, largely prevailed then or thereafter.

Against his desire for a strong executive, the opposition favored a "Board," not a governor. The trouble, he said, "with the royal governors lay not in the power that they held but in the source from which that power came," and a man, the source of whose power was the suffrages of freeholders, could be trusted with a great deal.

With an ardor not surpassed by the immigrant Tom Paine's pamphlet on slavery of March the previous year, Morris demanded immediate abolition. Then with an enlightenment at the Jefferson-Franklin level, he demanded complete religious toleration, something which in its full meaning probably existed *de jure* nowhere in the world. Jay himself, with his Huguenot family traditions still too bitter, opposed this. Morris, again with that sensible "accommodation" within his healthy mind, won by proposing a qualification that "toleration shall not hold to justify practices inconsistent with the peace and safety of the state." To hold at once views so far to the right on the actual governing of men, and to the then benign left on their personal freedom, and to do so with effective force and without ambivalence was a remarkable quality of spirit.

There was an everyday side to his good will to men. He wrote to Washington saying that the Committee of Safety had ordered sick soldiers moved to the Loyalist Colonel Montresor's property at Little Barn Island. The choice of the places induces him to suspect that it was "actuated by those illiberal prejudices which have great weight in little souls," for it is certainly wrong to "place the sick on an island nine miles from the army." It would be more rational to erect buildings on high ground near Hudson River or "if an insular position is indispensable on Blackwell's Island much better adapted and nearer the city."

The New York Convention was not meeting in cloistered seclusion. The night of June 22, one David Gray galloped into White Plains to wake Morris, Jay and Philip Livingston, the

Committee of Safety, with word that the British were landing at Huntington, Long Island. Not true, as it turned out, but the awakened planners had to act swiftly to send out the alarm.

And almost the next day the daughter of Samuel Fraunces, in whose tavern the club had met, discovered the plot to poison Washington at the Mortier House in Richmond Hill, where she was now the housekeeper. Hickey of the Life Guards was hanged for it on the twenty-seventh, implicating a civilian, Mathews, in it.

The Committee of Safety, which might so easily have been swept into hysteria, held there was no martial nor extraordinary jurisdiction over Mathews and that in effect he could not be charged except by civil due process. Mathews wrote Morris July 2 that he had a wife and ten children dependent on him. What happened to his "earthly tabernacle would not be of any consequence" but for their sake he asked a hearing.

James Coggeshall wrote Morris the same day from the same New Jail:

> Residing peaceably on Long Island I was taken prisoner, brought to town and put in jail. I flatter myself that for merely being a servant of His Majesty, it cannot be the intention of Congress to keep me in this situation. In a bad state of health I am unable to bear the dismal and weary hours of a prison.

It is rather agreeable to think that the men who were leading a great revolution did not feel that every little man's un-American activities warranted condign punishment.

These merciful New Yorkers, however, did not favor a milk-and-water war. Jay wrote Morris that if he were vested with absolute power "he would destroy Long Island, Staten Island, the City and County of New York and all Westchester below the mountains" rather than have them fall to Howe's army.

On July 9, Hancock's letter with the Declaration reached White Plains and was accepted with a shout. The New York Signers were Philip Livingston, William Floyd, Francis Lewis and Lewis Morris, Gouverneur's half-brother, the last Lord of the Manor.

It is an example of how men regarded what might well have been their death warrant that William Livingston was in a fury

against his "political enemies," who took advantage of his having accepted the command of the New Jersey Militia to send
another Signer to Philadelphia. And Robert Morris signed the
Declaration against which he had voted.

At the end of the month in London, Lord Shelburne said the
Address from the Throne, on the rebellion in North America,
was "a string of sophisms no less wretched in their texture than
insolent in their tenor."

The events of the last week of August, however, made it
likely that, whatever its virtues and valor, the patriot cause was
lost.

Howe's army began landing at Gravesend on Long Island on
the twenty-second, won a stunning victory over Washington on
the twenty-seventh but allowed his army to get across to New
York on the night of August 29/30. Every mistake possible in
war, except cowardice, was committed by both sides.

The great Jehovah must have been as shocked as the Continental Congress at Washington's ineptitude. The cause was
saved by luck or destiny and the fact that Washington recognized his blunders in time and tried to rectify them. By that
time the British held all the area John Jay would have destroyed.

Morris stayed with the army on the retreat across the Jerseys
and from Boonton in November wrote the New York Convention at Fishkill one of those light-minded letters which did him
so much harm.

The truth is, a series of accidents, too trifling for recital, have
prevented me the pleasure of attending the convention for upwards
of a month past. Among the last, let me mention the loss of all my
horses. As soon as I can find any of them, or purchase another, I
shall hasten to Fishkills.

It seems apparent that he wanted to stay with the army as
long as possible, and the loss of horses and the difficulty of getting other ones in a retreat are to be expected. But perhaps no
legislative body has ever received a more flippant excuse and
such levity did him no good, though there is no evidence that
it mattered to him.

At Newark during the retreat Paine was writing, "These are

the times that try men's souls," published the week before the dash on Trenton.

On the last day of the year Morris asked Governor Clinton for "a pass to Hackensack for Mrs. Haward, housekeeper in the family of my sister. I have given her a letter to Mr. Wilkins in reply to one I received praying me to come in and accept a pardon."

CHAPTER FOUR

We Are Hellishly Frightened

(1777)

THERE IS SURELY a touch of impudent comedy in the spectacle of the Continental Congress, the Continental Army of perhaps 2000 men, and the so-called state governments and their militia pretending to carry on the war in December 1776.

Howe, with the main British force, was out in the Jerseys, cleared to the Delaware. Sir Henry Clinton held New York City and presumably the Hudson as far north as he cared to go. Burgoyne was in Canada ready to join hands. Execution or deportation awaited at least two hundred of the patriot leaders.

In the face of this, the civilian element was busy on Articles of Confederation and state constitutions. The Committee of Secret Correspondence of the Congress had become the Committee of Foreign Affairs dealing with its missions abroad, particularly that of Dr. Franklin in Paris seeking French aid and alliance.

In Fishkill, New York, Morris, Jay and Robert Livingston were writing the New York Constitution. It did not contain the abolition of slavery, which Morris sought, but on his motion "a freehold of value of £20," instead of £40 in colonial times, qualified a man to vote.

Word of Washington's strike at Trenton on Christmas Night, followed by the little victory at Princeton, January 3, 1777,

reached Fishkill on the sixth. As though nothing else had ever
been expected, Morris wrote calmly, either to Washington or
Schuyler—the letter is addressed "Dear General":

We intend publishing an account of the various successes since
crossing the Delaware and therefore wish you would send us all the
intelligence in your power for that purpose. *But let us take care to
say* nothing by *authority but what is strictly true.*

These sensible men were very careful never to mislead the
people with false hopes, though Morris privately was often
overoptimistic. "I will lose two beaver hats if [our] army is not
in New York by July 1st," he wrote Hamilton in the spring. In
later years he forecast the exact day that Napoleon would quit
Moscow, three months in advance, but here he was off by six
years.

In mid-January Morris had a silent part in a controversial
incident that has become famous in American history and been
the subject of controversy as recently as 1951.

During the Battle of Long Island, General Woodhull, a member of the convention, then commanding the Suffolk County
Militia, was taken prisoner and died of wounds, said to have
been inflicted after his surrender. He had been brought "in a
shocking, mangled condition" aboard a cattle scow where Lieutenant Robert Troup and other American officers were prisoner.
All had been barbarously treated.

Morris was appointed to take a deposition from Troup, who
had been exchanged. "Upon the Holy Evangels of Almighty
God" Troup swore to the atrocities and Morris was directed "to
prepare a narrative of the conduct of British officers and troops
toward the American prisoners."

It would be pleasant to say that research indicates this was a
familiar atrocity myth. Unfortunately, and almost unquestionably, it and the whole story of shocking treatment of prisoners
by the British command appears true.

Troup is one of those minor characters we have spoken of
who walk on for brief scenes. He was then twenty years old
and had been a friend of Hamilton at King's College. In 1780
when he was secretary to the Continental Board of Treasury,

he drew $9500 against a salary, for the period, of $500. He was allowed to resign without punishment or restitution.

It was he who in 1800 found Morris's funeral oration for Washington so disappointing and that year he succeeded the incredible Charles Williamson as agent for the Genesee Lands, which Robert Morris had sold the British Pulteney Associates in 1791.

In May, Morris was elected to the Continental Congress but because of the growing menace on the northern frontiers of New York did not attend until 1778.

Whipple, a New Hampshire Signer elected at the same time, and later one of Morris's adversaries, came through Fishkill that summer and left notes of the living conditions.

He stayed at "Week's House" there, which he had been told was "good." "It may be so sometimes but we could get no meat to eat. They had some indifferent wine upon which and some bread and cheese we dined. We drank tea and ate bread and butter for our dinner. This might have been put up with if it had been accompanied by good humor but our landlady was the most ill-natured and unmannerly vixen that ever a poor traveller was plagued with. She refused to broil a slice of pork or toast a bit of bread." And then, this early Duncan Hines, aged forty-seven, warns, *This house should be avoided.*

By June 17, Burgoyne was moving toward Ticonderoga with almost 8000 British and Hessian troops, their women and children, their Indian allies, and that large, delightful, indomitable person, the Baroness de Riedesel.

Two months before a merchant in Montreal had written William Edgar in Detroit: "Our campaign is to begin early in June [with] nothing to oppose them from this to Albany except Ticonderoga." He said, "The factious subjects below are now in the greatest disaster and put to flight wherever the King's Army appears." It was "melancholy," he said, to think that it would take "60 or perhaps 100 years" to restore the colonies to their "former flourishing state."

A "man with a blind left eye," wearing "a speckled under jackoat," came in with word that St. Leger and the Butlers, a thousand strong, had left Niagara for Oswego. There were "private villeins" in every hamlet and to face them all Schuyler had 2000 militia, "500 men to the westward" and 2600 Continentals, and even the latter rebelled at digging trenches which would have to be abandoned to Burgoyne.

Morris, with the "brass" of which he was later accused, proposed violent action, scorched earth, as it was called a hundred fifty years later.

I shall give it as my opinion to the general whenever he asks it [Morris wrote George Clinton, the new governor] to break up all the settlements upon our northern frontier, to drive off the cattle, secure or destroy the forage and also to destroy the saw mills. These measures, harsh as they may seem, are, I am confident, absolutely necessary. They ought undoubtedly to be taken with prudence and temperately carried into execution but I will venture to say that if we lay it down as a maxim never to contend for ground but in the last necessity, and to leave nothing but a wilderness to the enemy their progress must be impeded by obstacles which it is not in human nature to surmount, and then, unless we have, with our usual good nature, built posts for *their* defense they must at the approach of winter return to the places from whence they first set out.

The finish and style of this dispatch, written in the hurlyburly of an anxious headquarters, is in a way as remarkable as its proposals.

To Clinton, July 16, he wrote:

If the enemy give us time I imagine the roads will be so obstructed that with the help of a few brave fellows in the woods we should be able so to annoy General Burgoyne as to prevent him from penetrating far into the country. . . . Upon the whole I think we shall do very well.

To this, Jay, on behalf of the Committee of Safety, replied:

DEAR MORRIS
We could wish your letters might contain paragraphs for the public . . . the people suspect the worst because we say nothing. Their curiosity must be constantly gratified or they will be uneasy.

Jay, of course, had the problem of public opinion to face, as Morris did not, but Morris was annoyed at the idea of gratifying "curiosity," and he wrote back, Abraham Yates being a cosigner, that they ". . . had been afforded great pleasure by the suggestion since we are enabled in some measure to collect from it our errand to the northward [has as one of its most important objects] in the opinion of your honorable board the collecting of news." They thought, he goes on, they were to confer with General Schuyler "on measures for the aid and support of the Northern command." They go on then to say acerbly that they will return for questioning, "But, sir, Burgoyne cannot flee" and if 3000 militia from New England can come up and Washington spare "1500 good troops we may laugh at Mr. Burgoyne and Mr. Howe."

It is interesting to see this early in American history the supremacy of the civil power. It was not then supposed that all wisdom lay with the army commanders.

On July 29, John McKesson, secretary to Governor Clinton, wrote him:

Mr. Morris is returned from General Schuyler. He had told the Council that Burgoyne has undoubtedly 10000 men. . . . But, sir, this has only been communicated to the Committee of Safety.

Mr. Jay and Mr. Morris are by the Council appointed to repair to head quarters and confer with His Excellency, General Washington, about the state of the Northern Army. These gentlemen are expected to sett out 6 or 8 hours hence.

Then, in a postscript, he asks the faithful civil servant's rhetorical question, Won't they call to visit their governor?

Sally Livingston, now Mrs. Jay, went as far with them as the Ogdens' at Persippiney, twenty miles from Liberty Hall, and there she read "from breakfast till noon" the books Morris had gotten out of Morrisania, particularly the memoirs of Madame de Maintenon. It is interesting that both Morris and Talleyrand took their books to exile.

The New York emissaries did not go like frightened men at their wits' ends. The New York Council gave them a "memorial" to the Continental Congress: they were to discuss there the importance of New York from the military and food-supply point of view; they were to explain "why reinforcements are wanted" with reference to the Indian rising; they were to urge that Washington be reinforced by the militia of Maryland, Pennsylvania and New Jersey, thus allowing him to send two Continental brigades and one regiment of riflemen to Schuyler.

Howe's fleet, with his army aboard, had been seen off the Delaware Capes on July 30, the day Schuyler abandoned Fort Edward, and it was high up the Chesapeake by August 21 with Philadelphia as the army's objective.

It is quite easy now to see what Washington should have done on July 30: march with his whole force to overwhelm Burgoyne, march them back, flushed with victory, to meet Howe. At the time it may not have been so evident, or so possible.

It is said the campaigns of Frederick the Great, known to Washington, should have been his guide. On the other hand, Frederick had neither Congress nor public opinion to consider. Few commanders, even today, would enjoy facing the "opportunity" Washington did then.

In any event the brigade and the rifle regiment were sent north.

But Congress had decided, the day before Morris and Jay arrived, that Schuyler would be relieved in favor of General Gates. Schuyler was held responsible for the loss of Ticonderoga and Fort Edward. Additionally Schuyler's personal unpopularity with New Englanders made the change a political necessity if the New England Militia were to be under the Northern Command.

Morris and Jay preferred Schuyler but with a quick sense of the realities agreed. They talked to Gates, as he was preparing to leave with his staff, and among them Morris saw a man named Clajon, whose face he remembered. He asked Gates in effect if Clajon had been cleared as a security risk and told him something he knew of him. Three years later Clajon suddenly brought up the matter in a series of unusual letters to Morris.

At the time Morris wrote at once to Schuyler "with that incautiousness natural to me" that, after Schuyler had done all he could to help Gates in the take-over, "you will find it in honour to resign," adding if, before Gates arrived, "an unexpected attack with fixed bayonets without firing a shot" were made on Burgoyne "it would provoke a rout."

Schuyler replied with a natural sense of injury. If Gates defeated Burgoyne it would only be because he had the reinforcements Schuyler had asked for. His own only demerit was that New Englanders did not like him. It is wonderful to see Morris soothing the feelings of a man old enough to be his father. He gives him lessons in how to take disappointments. He points out that the safety of New York is all that matters and that "the season closes fast and if Burgoyne cannot get to Albany, he must at least retire to Ticonderoga." In September, knowing that misery loves company, he informs him of Washington's defeat at the Brandywine "with a loss far from inconsiderable."

With even the small forces sent to the north Washington might have won the Brandywine action, but on his part there was marvelously little lamentation over it. The reinforcements made Saratoga possible and as it turned out that was the greater prize.

Morris was back in Kingston, New York, on October 8 as Fort Montgomery on the Hudson fell to the British.

"We are hellishly frightened," he wrote Robert Livingston, "but don't say a word of that for we shall get our spirits again . . . the militia behaved as well as men would do. We shall beat them." He wrote it not knowing that Burgoyne's surrender of his whole army was in the making at Saratoga as of the day before.

Three days later came that theatrical incident in American history, The Silver Bullet. Daniel Taylor, Sir Henry Clinton's courier to Burgoyne, was captured. He carried "a small silver ball of oval shape about the size of a fusee bullet and shut with a screw in the middle." When he was taken and brought before Governor Clinton, he opened the bullet and swallowed the paper hidden in it. He was given an emetic and purgative in one but even after its action was able to secure and conceal the paper. Then he was told in familiar fashion that its contents were known because "Captain Campbell, another messenger who he knew was out on the same business," had been taken.

Facing execution, Taylor produced the letter. It was from Sir Henry Clinton in New York to Burgoyne. It told Burgoyne that "Clinton had made himself master of the key of America," but, as *Governor* Clinton laconically advised the Committee of Safety, "you will observe [he] is in no way confident of their

being able to form a junction of their armies though there are
nothing but bars between them."

Five days later, October 16, Burgoyne signed the capitulation. On October 25, Todd and McGill, the Montreal traders,
wrote Edgar in Detroit that "General Bourgoyne [had] been
under the necessity of agreeing with General Gates that his
troops should pile up their arms and march to Boston there to
embark for England. . . ."

There is ancient authority for the fact that men more easily
believe that which they desire. Only four days before they had
written Edgar that "Bourgoyne will come back with his army
to this country and are now near Fort George."

Now they comforted themselves that Burgoyne was reduced
"to about 3500 men, two thirds Germans who refused to fight.
The Yankees had 25000 of their regulars"!

On the thirteenth Morris had written gaily to R. R. Livingston:

Last evening the great city of Esopus was alarmed by one schooner
and one little brig under the command of Captain Wallace who
hath graced the British Army by firing two or three [flour] mills.
The alarm exhibited more of the drolerie than the pathos of distress.
The good domimie and his "ye frow" laded upon my wagon [their
whole family and furniture]. . . . Willy squealed. Sally bawled.
Addam played tricks and ye frow [was] like Hecuba at the taking
of Troy. . . . The eldest daughter of Low at all times sufficiently
affecting to the sight but now bedewed with pearly drops stood a
second Medusa. . . .

Beauty, however, was not always in distress. Near Philadelphia, at the time, Sally Wister, fifteen,

heard a great noise about 7 o'clock in the morning. To the door we
all went. . . . There were a large number of waggons with about
300 of the Philadelphia militia begging for drink and several pushed
into the house. . . . One of those that entered was a little tipsy and
had a mind to be saucy. I then thought it time for me to retreat, so
figure me, (mightily scared) running in at one door and out another,
all in a shake with fear, but after a little, seeing the officers appear
gentlemanly and the soldiers civil I called reason to my aid . . .
though my teeth rattled and my hands shook like an aspen. . . .
Several officers called to get refreshments but none of consequence

till afternoon [when] two genteel men of the military order rode up to the door . . . and asked if they could have quarters for General Smallwood. Aunt F. thought she could accommodate them [and] one of the officers wrote "Smallwoods Quarters" over the door which saved us from straggling soldiers. When we were alone, our dress and lips were put in order for conquest and the hopes of adventure gave brightness to each before passive countenance.

The week after the surrender Morris with his friend Blatchley Webb, two years younger, rode out to Stony Ridge and then crossed the Hudson to Rhinebeck where they spent the evening with "two very pretty daughters" of Captain Sheldon's.

On November 15, with Duer, Duane, and Francis Lewis, Morris signed the Articles of Confederation on behalf of New York, and left to take his seat in the Continental Congress.

From Boonton, New Jersey, where his brother-in-law, Ogden, had an ironworks making munitions for the army, he wrote Livingston:

I suffered as much from not being able to see you and my other friends at the manor as from any other circumstance attending my jaunt toward Congress.

Tell Ned to read Chesterfield and for God's sake cure him of sensibility [the opposite of common sense in eighteenth-century idiom]. It is certainly as dangerous to be under the control of the soft as the rough emotions.

CHAPTER FIVE

For God's Sake,
My Dear Morris

(1778)

LATE IN 1777, as a result of the surrender at Saratoga and the American defeats at the Brandywine and Germantown, General Gates had been made president of the Board of War and Conway, his friend, inspector general.

Both appointments struck at the prestige and power of Washington and in a measure represented the first split of Congress into two groups.

With Burgoyne and his army prisoners, the possibility of all the patriots being hanged together had passed. Men's natural differences and preferences could now be expressed.

Furthermore, there were compelling reasons why men should question what John Adams called "the superstitious veneration that is sometimes paid to General Washington." He had bungled like an amateur, he had been indecisive, he had shown "the extreme unwisdom of allowing clergymen, politicians, editors and citizens" to have views on military strategy, a phrase of Charles Francis Adams, the younger. As to the last, there is much evidence that Washington recognized from the start that such conference was the price of republican government and that the subservience of the military to the civil arm must be complete.

Still, he had been defeated at Long Island, Brandywine, Paoli

and Germantown and, as Adams puts it, had had to crawl into
Valley Forge on December 9. In Montreal, Todd and McGill
were "assured that General Howe's success at Philadelpia will
forever ballance the capture of General Burgoyne." Lacking
Adams's omniscient hindsight, their only comment to Edgar was
"God lend it may."

"I always contended for Gates," John Adams wrote later, and
congressional veneration now began to gather round that head,
with small regard to such matters as the two weeks' delay by
Gates after Burgoyne's surrender in starting Morgan's riflemen
back to Washington or the five weeks before the main reinforcements arrived, going only twelve miles a day in the autumn weather. Four years later, going down to Yorktown,
Washington's army went 492 miles in the summer heat at an
average of twenty miles a day.

Washington's blunders were those of inexperience. The will
to learn and rectify was there. It is hard to escape the conclusion that those of Gates were either willful or basically incompetent. The division in Congress between supporters of Gates
and Washington was not between good men and bad men. All
were patriots and all were somehow now sure of ultimate victory, so that the terms of peace with Great Britain shortly became the dominant problem in their minds. Independence was
a thing taken for granted.

Although the division was not between bad men and good,
it does seem that on Washington's side were the more assured,
the more vigorous, the more experienced and the more likable.
There was a good deal of littleness and vindictiveness among
his adversaries. "What a lot of damned scoundrels we had in
that Second Congress," Morris wrote later to John Jay, and Jay
replied, "Yes we had." While this is an excessive judgment, it
was aimed at men like James Lovell of Massachusetts, who in
November had written, "I have reason to think the battle of
Germantown was the day of salvation [from General Washing-
ton] offered by Heaven to us."

The principal opponents of Washington in Congress were a
group of New Englanders (John Adams had just gone to Paris)
—the fussy but often amusing Lovell, forty-one, a year after

John Adams at Harvard, his lieutenant, and, like him, "of per-
fervid devotion to Gates"; Sam Adams, fifty-six, and William
Whipple of New Hampshire—with Henry Laurens, fifty-four,
from South Carolina and the Lees of Virginia. Joseph Reed of
Pennsylvania, thirty-seven, fresh from Washington's staff, was
with them.

It would be easy to say they were all of a piece, sober, dull
and censorious, but Henry Laurens wrote the governor of New
Jersey, Kitty Livingston's father, that April: "Will you say you
have not more than once toyed away an hour talking nonsense
with the pretty girl above stairs and sometimes below stairs?"

With the British Army holding Philadelphia, Northern delegates to the Congress sitting at York had to cross the Delaware
into Pennsylvania near Bethlehem.

There, on January 3, Morris had learned that "the mad-
headed Governor of Pennsylvania" was so harassing the Quakers "that they have serious thoughts of shifting their quarters."
His "love of mankind and [his] attention to the interests of the
state which gave [him] birth" led him to sit down and write to
Livingston a characteristic letter. It says that the religious opinion of the Quakers is a matter of indifference to him and Livingston, who "consider mankind from their relation to us by the
same common Parent and not from the similitude of their ecclesiastical tenets." It is not to be contested that Quakers are
good and industrious people, even though "by an Act of Parliament sometime in the end of the year 1748 they are averse to
bearing arms and taking baths. That they are Whigs in principle I believe. Could we [in New York] obtain these men who
are excellent husbandmen and mechanicals with their wealth
which is not small at the trifling expense of an act of the legislature I think we should make a good purchase."

It is well to weigh the practical broad-mindedness of this
suggestion, about a religious minority, against the charges that
Morris was an "aristocrat" in the worst meaning of the word.
America was sparsely settled. No more should be asked of men
than that they be "good" and industrious. They came of one
Parent.

Morris rode on to York where Congress was sitting in the little courthouse in Center Square and took his seat on January 20. There was a degeneracy of representation there, Hamilton wrote later to Governor Clinton, "[the councils of Congress] having been beggared to enrich the administration of the several members." Jefferson was absent in Virginia, Franklin and John Adams in France, and the New York delegation, Hamilton said, was "outstanding."

It has long been the habit to portray the Continental Congress as a group of weak, timid, if not indeed frightened, men setting themselves with a sort of inept malice to thwart the cause. Some of them were like that. But it must be remembered that it was they who set the pattern of the supremacy of the civil power and in however stumbling a fashion carried on the executive and legislative powers of a new government.

The immediate crisis, as Morris took his seat, had to do with what has since been called the Conway Cabal. Whatever conspiracy there may have been to dismiss Washington altogether, it is now agreed that General Conway with all his faults did not deserve to have it named for him.

He was an officer in the French service, with a long and evidently successful career under Frederick the Great. Like most of the foreigners, he supposed that the Continental officers would rejoice to serve under him, and when one of them, General Varnum, cockily told him "there were some men in this continent who know more about manoeuvres than the King of Prussia this made me dumb." He wrote Washington that his appointment as inspector general was opposed only by him and "you cannot bear the sight of me in your camp."

It was evident that the army at Valley Forge did not want Conway around and for that and other reasons he was under orders to go as second in command to Lafayette on an invasion of Canada, a plan opposed by Washington.

The day of his arrival at York Morris was appointed to the committee which was to go to Valley Forge "to regulate the Army." Washington had written him in November on hearing that he was coming, "I am exceedingly happy in your appointment . . . [and about your views on unity] for I am a great

friend to harmony at all times and especially in public councils."

On the Army Committee with Morris were Charles Carroll,
forty-one, pro-Washington, with Dana (Mass.), Folsom (N.H.)
and Joseph Reed (Pa.) against. They were going, James Lovell
said that day, "to rap a Demi-G—— over the knuckles."

The following day Lovell found himself on another committee, with Morris and Dr. Witherspoon, to write a Manifesto
Against the Injurious Treatment of Prisoners by the British.

It was the beginning of the long employment of Morris's pen
in national service.

Burnett, the great authority on the Continental Congress,
writes, "With the simple quill of a goose, a little ink and the
English language [Morris] could do ofttimes marvels in bringing the minds of men into unison."

Making all allowance for the personal inadequacies and inexperience of the majority of Congress, it is obvious from these
two immediate appointments that Morris's brilliance and talents were well known in York. Nor can there be any question
that he did not propose to hide them under a bushel. His
"brass" and assurance at twenty-six must have been very trying
to his seniors.

The average age of the seven men in Congress most critical
of him was forty-six. Only two men in York were younger than
he, Charles Pinckney, twenty-one, and Frelinghuysen, twenty-
five. Neither compared with him either in prominence or in attendance.

The Army Committee arrived at Valley Forge on January 26.

That night, in a dramatic setting, Morris met Lafayette for
the first time. The marquis had arrived in camp three days before with a letter to Washington from the Board of War.
Washington read it and handed it to him without a word. It
was the appointment of Lafayette by Congress to command
the expedition against Canada to be mobilized in Albany with
Conway second in command. His orders, thereafter, would
come from Gates.

Lafayette exploded in a letter to President Laurens: "how
can I support the society of a man [Conway] who has spoeken

of my friend [Washington] in the most insolent and abusive terms, who tried to spread the fire in every part of the Army and the country?" He followed this by galloping off to Congress in York, evidently passing Morris en route, to say he would not be separated from General Washington. He had returned with their consent just before the committee arrived and Morris came into the room where he was writing.

Myth has probably left with most Americans a picture of Lafayette as a slim, dark and charming boy. Actually the man Morris saw was almost as tall as he. The surgeon Thacher described Lafayette that fall as "nearly six feet high, large but not corpulant . . . he is not very elegant in his form, his shoulders being broad and high nor is there a perfect symmetry in his features. His forehead is remarkably high, his nose large and long. Eyebrows prominent over a fine, animated hazel eye. He converses in broken English."

The novelist Stendhal saw him fifty years later and wrote, "A tall figure of a man . . . with an impassive, cold, insignificant face much like that of an old family portrait. He had the same faults as I had. He was chiefly interested in pinching the behind of some pretty girl."

Morris and the marquis were both great talkers and they evidently had a great deal to say to each other. When they had finished Morris wrote Henry Laurens, "I am deeply surprised at the mature judgment and solid understanding of this *young* man for such he certainly is" (Lafayette was twenty). The "solid understanding" had to do with what Lafayette told him of his objections to Conway, not only on personal grounds; he objected also to the policy of having two foreigners in command of an American expedition. Lafayette told Morris he favored the Continental, General McDougall, instead of Conway.

Morris favored this but, with his usual temerity, he added to Laurens that "it deserves the consideration of Congress [whether] it is prudent to trust a person [Lafayette] whose object is to push his fortunes in France where the Grande Monarque may probably like Canada as much as any of his predecessors."

This was a very early forecast of the aims of French policy

and a perception that French aid, if it came, was coming at a price and for an advantage. Washington of course realized this from the beginning, and may have talked to Morris about it that day. Or the voluble Lafayette may have said things, perhaps in French, which Morris understood more clearly than others did. Whichever it was, it illustrates the fact that, though sometimes mistaken, Morris was never dazzled nor fooled where the interests of his country were concerned.

Lafayette, gratified at Morris's support of the McDougall idea, added a postscript to the letter he was writing Laurens, saying, "When I had just finished, M. Morris came into headquarters and as I did know he was a friend of ours I have communicated to him almost all my letter."

Two days later Laurens replied, "Forgive me, my dear Marquis, for expressing some regret that you discussed any part [of the plan] with a gentleman who though very sensible appears to me, and has given some proof, to be guardless and incautious."

It was not only his adversaries who worried about Morris's guardlessness. Robert Livingston wrote from Clermont the same day complaining of Morris's silence. The press of official business does not seem to have occurred to him.

"Can you yet," he asks, "be wasting those precious moments in dissipation which your country requires you to employ in her service, moments that can never be recalled? . . . Forgive my freedom but friendship requires that I should speak its language. Your reputation suffers here most exceedingly."

Morris replied, "There are no fine women in York Town. Judge then of my situation. Worse still I am now in camp and Lady Kitty [Alexander] and Miss Brown within 3 miles of me. . . . I can't go to see them."

If there was ever a period in Morris's life when neither friends nor foes needed to worry about his foibles, it was the Valley Forge months.

Almost at once Charles Carroll and he brought Dana over to the idea that Washington's failures arose less from military incompetence than from shortages of supplies and money.

Wagon loads of food for the hungry army were spoiling in

York because Congress had not found money to hire teamsters. Further to drain the main army for the Canadian expedition would be suicidal. Arnold, who had been there with Montgomery's army, wrote Morris from Albany the whole plan was fantastic.

(Morris's reply to this letter was to cause him deep though brief anxiety four years later.)

The plan was no secret. William Edgar's Montreal correspondents wrote him: "Two men . . . say that on the 1st of January, Mr. Washington was killed and his army destroyed. Notwithstanding these disasters the Yankees are from desperation resolved to try their arms on this province."

At the moment, however, another letter came curiously to light, the first of the long string of evil omens for Morris, arising from the marriages of his sisters, Isabella and Euphemia. The former was married to Isaac Wilkins, a Loyalist, who would take her from New York to Nova Scotia for asylum, to return when Morris did, at the end of the century. Euphemia, two years Morris's junior, had married Samuel, the son of David Ogden of New Jersey, a Tory from the start and ultimately the Loyalist agent in London. No question arises of the father's right to stay with his King. He made no secret of his choice. As to Samuel Ogden, there is much question, though his ironworks at Boonton, New Jersey, made munitions for the Continental Army and he had a commission in the state militia.

But one night at Valley Forge, Joseph Reed showed Morris a letter captured with enemy mail.

It had been written by David Ogden in London to Morris in '75, crossed the ocean three times and been found on a British ship. In it Ogden noted with satisfaction Morris's loyalty to the King.

To a man of Morris's personal pride and "brass," the letter, coming at a time when he was sweepingly criticizing almost everyone but Washington and his army, must have been a severe shock.

His answer was that it had been written, two years before, in reply to one of his of 1774 when, like most men, he had been loyal to the King. Further, it was a letter to him, not by him, and anyhow, he was not responsible for the writer's opinion. Reed and his associates evidently accepted the explanation but it left them with reservations.

The "army, naked, starving, out of health, out of spirit," presented problems of immediate reality transcending those of French policy or Morris's Loyalist relatives.

On February 17 they had been four days without meat. That night Morris sent an express to Governor Clinton of New York with an appeal, wonderfully mingling patriotism and flattery, begging for supplies, and adroitly adding that if they were impossible, "at least help with the transport" from some other state.

It required national patriotism and provincial pride for Clinton to reply, "Notwithstanding the difficulties, 100 head of cattle and 150 barrels of pork are now on the way to headquarters."

It was not only lack of meat that weakened the army. The organization of the whole force was chaotic, less because Washington and others did not know how to organize an army than that Congress, as on far later occasions, felt that it knew more about establishments, regimental returns and promotions than the army did. It was not at all a question of the paramount subordination of the military to the civil government. Washington believed in that as completely as any man. It was rather that there seemed to be no one in Congress combining force with clarity of mind sufficient to help Congress understand and approve what he wanted to do.

The issues often seem minor. Who shall have the right to promote? Through what grades? How many majors to a regiment? How shall the artillery be integrated into the whole? If officers and men cannot be paid regularly and punctually, what future offset can be made? Half pay for life? Bounty at the peace? The *Journals* of Congress are filled with incredible trivia: "3 vests, 2 for winter, 1 for summer," to be issued to officers; "$40 due Colonel Livingston approved for payment; 15 day furlough for Chaplain Lane . . ."

It seems fair to say that in young Gouverneur Morris, with his flair and his sagacity, Washington found his best advocate.

We need not magnify the intimacy of the relationship between them nor dispute "the more confidential relationship of the great commander with Francis Dana." Certainly they became friends. To Morris, Washington was the one great American all his life. To Washington, Morris was a gifted, forceful man of whose defects he was entirely aware. Part of Washington's greatness lay in his extraordinary insight into men, which told him they were not all the same and not all perfect.

At "Moorhall Camp, Valley Forge," when Morris found time to write personal letters at all it was "with an argument at my elbow. Should bonds be taxed. Massachusetts [Dana] says yes, New Jersey no. Both may be right. I hate disputes."

Such letters to both Jay and Livingston break into cipher: "I intend to procure 13, 15, 17, 15, 20, 22, 8, 17, 15, 10. . . . There are a set of scoundrels at the head of whom are 19.2.10.16.3.13.- 15.20 . . . very busy in attempting to ruin the 19.7.3.16.2.13."

The Livingston-Morris-Jay group apparently had its private cipher for many years. Letters twenty-five years later occasionally use it.

All the grim Valley Forge winter and into the spring Morris was at headquarters, his tireless pen writing the reports to Congress on the army's necessities in supplies and organization and money. "For heaven's sake, my dear friend," he wrote to Jay, "excite yourself strenuously in the great leading business of taxation." April 10 "he is still at camp. We expect he will join us [at Yorktown] in a fortnight."

Then on the twelfth Duer, his colleague in Congress, wrote late in the evening to Robert Morris, "It is said Gouverneur Morris is at your chateau for the sake of our country, my dear Morris, entreat him to push on. For want of representation in the State of New York [we cannot get a quorum for the establishments of the army]."

Actually something far more serious was in the wind. The cabal, to oust if not actually to arrest Washington, and replace him with Gates, was within a single vote. But on the fifteenth Gates was sent to the Hudson River command at Fishkill and his orders were written by Morris, Francis Dana, now won to Washington's side, and William Duer.

Morris wrote Livingston, "To our worthy governor I have recommended Gates. He has sense enough to see that he has made some wrong steps and though I will not promise his amendment as a man I think I can venture to say that as a politician he will not be difficult." He is elated that "the French monarch [treated] with America as equals" and ends: "Bury a bottle of old Falernian for I intend when the storm abates to come and make a riot!"

It is interesting to note that Congress that week passed a resolution relieving the commissary agent of liability for mis-appropriations in his department. The only votes against it were those of Gerry and the three delegates who had lived at Valley Forge and seen with their own eyes the civil frauds and corruption—Morris, Charles Carroll and Dana.

Washington, brushing aside the whole Gates business, wrote Morris, "Our matter [the army establishment] requires immediate remedy" and then goes patiently on to say, "The resolution of Congress directs a Council of War to be formed of major generals and the chief engineer. . . . By this the commanding officer of the Artillery is negatively excluded [although] from the nature of his appointment [he] is more officially a member than the other. . . . Both or neither ought to be there . . . or if preference is due it is to the commanding officer of the Artillery. . . . Resignation after resignation is taking place."

A word to the wise was sufficient. Morris replied on May 1, "Knox [chief of Artillery] is to attend the council." There is an interesting aftermath to this insistence on having the valuable Knox in the Army Council. At Yorktown De Chastellux saw him laying the guns himself, "very corpulent but agile . . . we were amazed at the extraordinary progress of American artillery as well as of the capability and instruction of a great number of their officers."

To Washington, Morris went on, "The [other] affairs of the army are delayed for the French Alliance which has broken in upon us," but adds that on the half-pay measure they had done fairly well "in the hurry of business and the want of time."

The hurry of business, military and diplomatic, was enormous. It was known that Lord Carlisle, the friend of Charles Fox, and William Eden, British commissioners, were coming out to talk peace, and a committee of Dana and Drayton, headed by Morris, recommended to Congress that "the United States cannot hold a conference or treaty with any commissioners on the part of Great Britain unless they first withdraw their fleets and armies and acknowledge the independence of the United States." After debate Congress adopted it unanimously.

An Address to the Inhabitants of the United States on the Present Situation was drafted by Morris for the committee of Richard Henry Lee, Chase and himself. It was sent out, in Morris's draft, to be read from every pulpit, and closed with the words, "If you exert the means of defence which God and Nature have given you, the time will soon arrive when everyman shall sit under his own vine."

Morris and the two Lees wrote the manifesto to the inhabitants of Nova Scotia on the vital question of fishing rights, leaving to Ellery, McKean and Carroll a reply to the bishops of the United Brethren of Pennsylvania on the same day! Would a modern Congress have the breadth of vision to appoint two Catholics (McKean and Carroll) to such a committee?

On the night of the mischianza, when the British were dancing with the girls Morris had known in '75, he was writing Robert Morris a long, cogent letter on the difficulties with the New Englanders in Congress, but with it he sent "somewhat for your evening's amusement," though we know not what.

To Washington he was able to report that with James Lovell and Wolcott only against, a bounty of eighty dollars at the peace had been voted N.C.O.'s and soldiers and half-pay for seven years to officers "not holding any office of profit under the states."

Washington thanked him for "agreeable intelligence which (though not equal to wishes) exceeds expectations," but he went on ominously:

Evils will soon be manifested in the moving state of the army if the Departments of Quartermaster and Commissary [are to] enable us to keep face with the enemy who . . . are busy preparing for departure from Philadelphia . . . the sooner regimental regulations are set about the sooner they will be finished and for God's sake my dear Morris let me recommend it to you to urge the absolute necessity of the measure with all your might.

Morris replied to hurry the regimental returns and he would secure "the measure." He added that "Conway now says he didn't resign. Too late thank God." He reported that with Duer and Drayton he was on the Committee for Recruiting Continental Battalions for the Duration of the War.

Meantime Laurens had told Lafayette that "the arrangements for the French gentlemen," the Gerard Mission coming out, had been entrusted to Morris and Dana and to confer with them. Morris had blithely written John Jay, "I congratulate you on our alliance with France. Love to Sally, Adieu. Gouv. Morris."

Franklin had been in Paris since Christmas week, 1776. He had labored there a long year under "a storm of bills coming upon me . . . long humiliated with our running from court to court begging for money and friendship," until the news of Saratoga reached him and Vergennes pricked up his ears.

Franklin sent Austen over to London to talk to Lord Shelburne, whom we shall meet so frequently, and Pitt wrote to Shelburne: "though at dinner, I cannot suffer your lordship's servant to return without expressing . . . [my] sentiments of the conduct of the American colonists, full of nobleness, dignity and humanity, absurdly and unjustly distracted and alienated. . . . I rejoice that the Americans have behaved in victory like men who were actuated by principle."

And now Franklin had the French Alliance and Gerard was coming out as minister. It goes without saying that the French Alliance enormously shortened the war and was of incalculable benefit to America. It was not, however, made in the spirit of Lafayette's headlong gallantry. Franklin saw from the start it would not come without clear advantage to France, and Washington pointed out that "no nation is to be trusted further than it is bound by its interests."

France had been the enemy against whom Washington and the veterans had fought. France, repossessed of Canada, would be a menace. France in the West was an alien danger and though all hearts were lifted by the good fortune—"each officer and soldier is to have a nosegay in his hat," as it is announced to them—the shrewdest of them saw they had won it by their own efforts and not from charity.

The French and foreign volunteers who had, as one of them said to Hamilton, "overrun America like the sheep of Panurge" were not all so popular as Lafayette and Steuben, who, with little English, insisted to an astonished lady he had caught a whale in the Hudson and had a hard time grasping that the word was "eel."

Washington was already worried over the lavish manner in which the Laurens-Lee clique in Congress appointed foreigners to commands "from a little plausibility and unbounded pride and ambition." How familiar the steps of the *arriviste* he sketches. They want just the honor of serving; then, rank without pay; then an advance on their pay; then promotion. So he wrote to Morris. To which Morris replied: "The faith of Congress is in some measure pledged to De la Newille but his brevet is not going to get confirmed," and he added that even "Steuben will not get what I am told he requires. At least they won't if I can help it."

There was justification in all this, though the Francophiles were bitter about it. Brissot de Warville said later, "The French whom I have seen here are eternally opposing the manners and customs of the American, decrying their institution, exalting the favors rendered by the French Government to the American and diminishing those of Congress to the French." Foreign alliances are seldom happy.

The burden on the few capable men who remained in the small Congress was of course enormous. Laurens complained to Sam Adams of their inexperience in discussing treaties, and R. H. Lee wrote his brother Arthur, "The members of Congress are so perpetually changing it is of little use to give you their names," but he lists thirty-six of them with "Governeur Morris and Colonel Plater" (of Maryland) among them.

Perhaps the heavy and varied responsibilities were too much for even Morris's mental equilibrium. In any event on May 27 he wrote a reckless and unfortunate letter to Washington say-

ing, "I hear you expect soon to be in Philadelphia. The instant
the enemy evacuate in my opinion the best disciplined troops
in the army should be marched in to requisition goods necessary for the army, and to place a levy of one hundred thousand
pounds on the city."

This idea out of the Thirty Years' War perhaps only shows
that the most intelligent of men are capable of folly.

Washington replied from Valley Forge on the twenty-ninth,
with that capacity for tactful rebuke, that strong man's gift for
never saying the word that hurts too much. The letter is a long
one, reviewing first the British political situation, then saying
that he believes "they will march the flower of their army un-
encumbered with baggage through the Jerseys," lamenting that
with 3000 men still sick at Valley Forge he cannot follow with
a large detachment to risk "perhaps a capital stroke and loss."
At the end he says, "your idea of levying contributions on
Philadelphia widely differs from mine. . . . [I find it] inconsistent with sound policy . . . [it] would be looked upon as an
arbitrary stretch of military power . . . [would] inflame the
country and lay the foundation for much evil." Surely a
commander-in-chief of forty-six has never pointed out the folly
of a congressman of twenty-six more effectively and finally or
with less sting.

Whatever chagrin Morris felt was doubtless assuaged by
the fact that on June 8 Laurens himself wrote Washington that
"Lord Abingdon's protest [in the House of Lords] does honor
to Mr. Morris of New York, the merit of our resolution of April
22nd is fairly ascribed to him." John Jay wrote to Governor
Clinton in the same vein the next day of Laurens's speech in
Congress giving the honor to Morris. The resolution, Jay said,
"was too strikingly marked with Morris not to be known by his
friends to have been produced by his pen."

One can imagine the pride of this very proud young man,
and it would be fascinating to know with what lady he shared
it.

On the thirteenth Laurens started to read to Congress the
first letter from the young Lord Carlisle. "I oppose going on
with it," Morris called out, "and thereby we will strike convic-

tion to the souls even of Tories that Great Britain is reduced to
imploring a peace from America," which caused Bartlett, a
Massachusetts member, to write, "Mr. Gouverneur Morris is
an eternal speaker and for artifice a Duane and for brass equal
to any I am acquainted with."

It is amusing to consider what a blow to Morris's pride it
would have been to know that his name was omitted from
those of "the leading [New York] rebels," whom the Rev. John
Vardill considered worth the commission's while to win over.

Vardill, a former Episcopal clergyman from New York, then
living in England, wrote a brief for William Eden's guidance
which had good advice and good intelligence. He told Eden
it would be "prudent to maintain a gravity in your deportment
and to join as little as possible in convivial parties and public
diversions. . . . Loyalists are too obnoxious to the leading
rebels to be of any service in [conciliation] . . . Governor
Tryon vain, resentful . . . his secretary plausible, good-
natured, shallow . . . try to get Jay on your side by submitting
to be confuted by him [rather] than by a direct attempt to
convince him . . . a prospect of keeping his present office
of chief justice would probably weigh much. He is obstinate,
indefatigable and dogmatic [but has] courage, zeal and ability
. . . and is married to a daughter of Governor Livingston . . .
a man of genius and learning, a violent advocate for independence, a most inflexible enemy to reconciliation. . . .
Robert R. Livingston . . . the mainspring of the family . . .
talents more specious than solid, elegant, persuasive . . . desires honours and wealth chiefly to employ them in pleasures.
. . . James Duane . . . a plodding lawyer, capable of any
meanness. . . . These are the only persons of the province of
New York in the Congressional cause who are worthy of your
attention."

"I shall have little hope," he warns Eden, "[of your success]
unless Dr. Franklin has privately approved of the plan."

On June 16, the night the British evacuated Philadelphia,
Morris wrote Clinton that "our friend and my very worthy
colleague, Philip Livingston, had died." He was sixty-two, a
Signer of the Declaration, and had been ill almost since his

arrival at Congress. He was buried in York at the cemetery on Prospect Hill.

Morris went on that he realized that the Vermont claims had been neglected under the pressure of the British commissioner business, but that he had obtained a hundred thousand dollars for New York and hoped their Continental officers could now be paid. Robert Morris disturbed him by writing that day that he hoped to see Johnstone, of the Carlisle Commission, and propose to him a commercial alliance with Great Britain. Nothing, in Gouverneur's opinion, could be more ill advised. He was a protégé of, though not related to, Robert Morris. They were born on the same day eighteen years apart. He was later to be Robert's benefactor but there is much indication that he did not always approve Robert Morris's mingling of the commercial interests of his country with his own. Though unknown then to Morris, Johnstone had also approached Joseph Reed of Pennsylvania, who had received the Ogden letter earlier in the year, and offered him a bribe of ten thousand pounds for his disaffection.

The King's instructions to Carlisle and Eden were: "If you should at length despair of bringing such body or bodies of men to a treaty . . . publish a proclamation."

With the British Army safe in New York, Carlisle published an appeal to the people. Morris replied in his "An American" letters, ending one jocosely, "oh my Lord, my Lord, you have tried fleets, and armies and proclamations and you now threaten us with newspapers!" This light-mindedness Laurens found "puerile with a dash of insolence as unnecessary as it will be unavailing." But it put a number of people in good humor.

Governor Clinton now wrote Morris that he wanted to know more about the wherefores of the hundred thousand dollars secured for New York in May. Well, Morris writes him patiently, as a father to his son, the savages are about to irrupt on the New York frontiers; (news of Wyoming had already been received and what was to be at Cherry Valley); the British Army in New York will be likely to move up the Hudson; the state militia are unpaid and "money may be wanting in the Treasury." Those were some of the things the money could be used for. He also cautioned his governor that there must be no countenancing of Vermont independence, at that time. "No new independent state without the consent of the state in which they were governed at the first congressional election."

He was a little exasperated at both Robert Livingston and Governor Clinton for not realizing that he had more to do than look out for the local interests of New York. He read Livingston a sharp lesson on the machinery of the Continental Congress. "By resolution 3 days a week are set aside for Treasury and Finance business, and two days for Foreign Affairs. Remember that Congress is also an executive body. . . . I do not mean to apologize. . . . I cannot go to the New York Legislature. . . . Let me point out my situation." He is on the Committee of Treasury and Finance, on the Commissary and the Quartermaster committees. He must "prepare a Manifesto on the Cruelties of the British [to prisoners]. The minutiae are infinite. The heat is unbearable. I have had no exercise all week except to walk fifty yards to Congress."

This was in Philadelphia and shortly afterwards Thacher wrote in his *Journal*, "In company with Mr. Gouverneur Morris and our surgeon general I rode to camp near White Plains, waited on Colonel Scammel, the adjutant general, to inquire whether any regiment is destitute of a surgeon." Morris's mind always had its own effective follow-up system. He warned Governor Clinton to keep a careful accounting of the "lend-lease" of Continental and state cannon and the next day urged on him heavier taxation to counteract the rise in prices in Continental money. The same day he wrote Washington that he was reluctant, even under the necessity of stimulating recruiting, to offer a bonus of ten dollars specie. "I fear to influence the rapacity of soldiers with the love, by the possession of, a metal of which we have such a plenteous lack." But if you do not agree, he concludes, I will reopen the matter.

When he was at his best, and he usually was, he had a wonderful sense of when to press and when to accommodate. He was never reluctant to advise his elders but the advice was seldom bad. He heard four days after his accounting and taxation advice to Clinton that a new and difficult oath of loyalty was being required in New York. "Bend the spirit of the legislature at times even to the prejudices of the people" (by making the oath easier to swear) and then, with wise provincialism calculated to please Clinton, he pointed out that New York, though fifth in population, was only eleventh in the Continental contributions she had had to have.

"You must feel a greater modesty of disposition than the language [of my letters] may indicate," he told Washington.

He was called back to Congress in mid-September to act as chairman of the committee drafting instructions to Franklin as the first American minister. Chase, Drayton, Sam Adams and Richard Henry Lee served under him. In October it was decided that Lafayette should take out Franklin's credentials and instructions as well as Morris's own observation on finance to show the French Government, and Morris, Lee, Sam Adams, Drayton and "Wederpurn," as the Marquis de Chastellux called Dr. John Witherspoon of Princeton, were appointed "to cause an elegant sword to be made and presented" to the marquis.

A Congress which could supply such a galaxy of ability for one small committee would seem to have had enough to satisfy even Morris but he said to Jay that idleness, dissipation and peculation were rife among most of them. He said Schuyler would make the best president Congress ever had. "His wife would be worth the gold of Ophir—she would out-intrigue Sam Adams." Livingston was urging him to come "to see the state and see the Jays on the way." He says he is "a little hurt by [Morris's] dogmatic manner and uncommunicableness."

To which Morris replied, "You have given me very excellent reasons why I should be at Poughkeepsie. Jay has given me a very good reason why I should not. I am no longer a member of your legislature [but of the Continental Congress]. You say that I have my *Soulagements* and I thank you for your wish. I have experienced much pain during my short life from being said to be happier than I was. . . . Tell the women they must all love me for I love them all."

Outwardly of course, and away from the army, affairs looked bright but, on October 4, Washington asked Morris, "Can *we*

carry on the war?" Not unless the states as a whole rallied to
the nation. There was a species of army soviets of mixed civil
and military personnel in the army lines, and the rifle strength
was still desperately low. There is an appealing human letter
by the weary Washington of October 8 to Morris. He says he
cannot remember whether, when it was agreed not to enlist
prisoners and deserters, it was to apply to Pulaski's corps. And
wasn't the reason for letting Pulaski raise his corps to induce
him to give up the command of the cavalry?

The *Journals* of Congress have an entry on November 3 of
amusing interest: "The Committee on French Promotions
ordered that Mr. Lovell be added to the committee. Ordered
that Mr. G. Morris be excused from attending."

But on November 10, realizing that without supplies and
money the army could not be held together, however bright the
future, Morris, Scudder and Whipple were appointed to regulate the Commissary and Quartermaster departments.

In twenty-four hours expresses were off to the thirteen governors with four dispatches of great breadth and vigor. The
first ordered a state inventory of "Flour, Wheat, Rye, Barley,
Oats, Corn, Rice, Beef, Pork, Working Oxen, Horses, Cyder,
Vinegar."

"It is impractical to continue the war, at least to advantage,
while we remain supremely ignorant of the supplies our
country can afford. Use industry and secrecy and all imaginable
speed . . . for the ensuing campaign."

The second demanded heavy taxes and price fixing and an
inventory of engrosses (paper money).

The third condemned distilling in New Jersey, Pennsylvania,
Maryland and Virginia. "Drunkenness at all times a crime is
almost self-murder now. Malt makes people stupid and useless
and enervates mind and body . . . prohibit the conversion of
bread into liquid poison. . . . Seize it for the use of the army's
sick and wounded *at a low price*."

The fourth demanded exemplary punishment for bribery
and corruption.

This was perhaps the first time on this continent that the

states had been ordered to do something by what was still the shadow of a central government.

The same night a rider went to Washington with a letter from Morris urging him to winter in Philadelphia near to Congress. It was previously noted that the make-up of the opposing groups in Congress was not of good men against bad men. As an example, on the vote, December 2, to carry out the sentence of the court-martial against Charles Lee, James Lovell and Sam Adams voted aye with Morris against noes from Duane and Lewis, Henry Laurens and Roger Sherman.

On December 1, to Morris's delight, in spite of what he had said about Schuyler, John Jay was elected to Congress and on the tenth to be its president. New York was shaken by the Cherry Valley massacre of three weeks before and even Governor Clinton was alarmed for the safety of the state.

Morris, never in a panic, wrote him calmly:

If the whole New York Brigade which is ordered to march to the defense of our frontiers is not thought a sufficient force . . . it shall be our care to obtain the aid you require.

Then, as a practical man, he added that he understood that out of the hundred thousand dollars each New York delegate had been voted a thousand dollars toward his salary and expenses. He would be glad to have the three dollars per diem due him since his arrival in Philadelphia eleven months before.

It seems evident he had earned it.

CHAPTER SIX

He Bears It with Becoming Fortitude

(1779–80)

THERE HAD BEEN a storm in Congress in the summer of '78 which did not reach its peak until the following winter, nor blow itself completely out in Morris's case in thirty years.

Morris had written Jay, "Your friend, Deane, who has rendered most essential services, stands as one accused. The storm increases and I think some of the tall trees must be torn up by the roots."

Silas Deane had returned from Paris with Gerard's mission. He had been sent out as American financial agent to raise money and supplies and the beginning of these had come through his arrangements with Beaumarchais.

The instructions to Deane provided, *inter alia*, a commission for him on certain purchases. The actual understanding under which Beaumarchais supplied the famous millions was not clear then and perhaps is not so even today.

Did that wealthy wit, the jester of Paris, the author of Figaro, though not a banker nor a merchant, supply them out of the goodness of his heart or was he acting secretly for the government of France? And were they a gift or a loan?

Arthur Lee, Franklin's colleague, said they were a free gift from France. Deane said they were a charge on the United States owed to Beaumarchais. There were further charges that

Deane had improperly enriched himself and as to the whole business, Deane, on July 28, 1778, had demanded a hearing from Congress and a vote of confidence or condemnation.

Familiar delays and partial hearings followed until Deane in exasperation in November published an Address to the People bitterly attacking his adversaries and demanding justice.

Thomas Paine, then forty years old, a violent, twisted, often valuable, more often uncontrollable, man, had, since the previous April, been acting as secretary *to* the Committee on Foreign Affairs and in his own mind the post seems to have become Secretary *of* Foreign Affairs. In either case he was unusually bound to official secrecy.

He chose, however, to reply to Deane's address, in the same paper, saying in effect that the Beaumarchais advances were not a personal loan, but given to America by the French King, at the time an ally of England by treaty. He concluded that if anyone would come to his office he would show him the verifying documents.

Whatever the facts were, this flagrant violation of official secrecy shook even a free-talking Congress and Gerard, the French minister, demanded a disavowal and Paine's dismissal.

On January 6, 1779, "Mr. Thomas Paine is called in [to Congress]. Is he the author of Common Sense on Mr. Deane's affairs? He answered he was the author of those pieces. He was then ordered to withdraw."

Except for his views on slavery, Paine represented most of the things Gouverneur Morris disliked in a man, and the next day he made a sensational speech in Congress, demanding that Paine be dismissed without a hearing, since the violation of secrecy was admitted and indefensible. The truth about Beaumarchais was neither an issue nor a defense. He said that Paine called himself Secretary of Foreign Affairs. If it were true, the post would require above all knowledge and discretion, but actually Paine was "a mere adventurer," never fit for the post in the first place, had abused it in the second and was undeserving of any further confidence. With this very damning invective, Morris then had the bad judgment to refer to Paine's humble origin and to allege, irrelevantly and with doubtful accuracy, that Paine could not even write grammatically. Some trivial example of the sort may have stuck in his mind and been let loose in the excitement of the moment. And Morris doubtless felt, on good evidence, that irreparable harm could be done by this wild man if he was not brought down finally and completely.

Duer of New York wrote Paine March 9, "Your objects are truly macchiavellian, your favorite object is to disgrace Pennsylvania, insult the president of its council and support general anarchy."

At the end of the speech seven states voted against giving Paine a hearing, four for, one divided, and one absent, R. H. Lee, Whipple and Sam Adams being among those for the hearing.

The next day Congress had a letter from Paine beginning: "Finding by the *Journal* of this House of yesterday that I am not to be heard . . ." and there was an uproar as to who had let him see the *Journal*. As a resolution was passed ordering "the President of Congress to ask members on their honor if they had told Thomas Paine," Henry Laurens himself rose to say he had told Paine and supposed Thomson (Secretary of Congress) would readily show him the *Journal*.

Reference has been made to the impression of littleness in the Laurens-Adams-Lee clique. Laurens had dragged into the debate on Washington the year before the fact that Congress had not received Burgoyne's flags. Now, making no defense of his informing Paine, he asked how it happened that Robert Morris had been able to ship fifty hogsheads of tobacco for his private account on "the ship *Farmer* chartered and insured on public account."

While this had no possible bearing on the business of Paine before the House, or Laurens's own indiscretion, it sufficed to push aside the vote on Paine, while a committee investigated Robert Morris.

There was some commingling of the affairs of Willing, Morris and Company with those of the country but the committee found that he had "acted with fidelity and integrity and an honorable zeal for the happiness of his country."

Paine was dismissed on January 16, and Gerard, with Gallic acumen, immediately offered him a retainer to hold his pen in readiness for the use of France, and wrote to Vergennes that he would understand the reason of the outlay for this purchasable man.

It is interesting to contrast the violence of Morris against Paine with the moderation of his counsel to Governor Clinton on the matter of Vermont and the New Hampshire grants, which had been troubling New York for thirty years.

New Hampshire had long asserted and exercised the right to grant lands in the country between the Connecticut River and Lake Champlain. Colonial New York had resisted this and even appealed to the King, getting a decision which gave them jurisdiction to the Connecticut. In New York's judgment this allowed them to annul the grants made there by New Hampshire. There was a catamount outside the inn in Bennington, Vermont, as there is today, with its teeth bared toward New York.

Ethan Allen and his Green Mountain Boys came out of the disputed country.

Congress in 1779 very naturally and wisely tried to avoid settling whether Vermont should be independent or the sovereignty go to New York or New Hampshire. Both Roger Sherman of Connecticut and Elbridge Gerry of Massachusetts felt independently that any decision by Congress "would give fresh discontent and increase the difficulty."

There was strong state pressure on Governor Clinton to secure a decision favorable to New York. And as governor he naturally wanted it, if only to be relieved of the trouble and dissension.

This was the sort of thing which inexperienced, emotional men insist "must be settled now," but which wiser men see must be left to time.

The New Yorkers, Jay and Morris, were able to take a national view of the issue and one which saw that compulsion was no settlement. "It is a mighty arduous business," Morris wrote Clinton, "to compel the submission of men to a political or religious government. It appears to me very doubtful whether Vermont, if independent, would not be more useful to

New York, than as the Eastern District." He went on (he was
now twenty-seven), "The security of a republic is the diffusion
of knowledge, and the vigor and *spirit of a common sentiment.*"
He continually pointed out to Clinton that it is easier to lead
than drive. "More is to be hoped from gentle and persuasive
measures than from force. Unanimity is very desirable," and
John Jay and he signed another letter telling their governor
"the more gentle, just and persuasive the Proceedings are, the
more likely they will be to succeed."

Had these powerful men taken the stand that right is right,
or might is right or "it must be settled now," the harm they
would have done the American cause could have been very
great. In effect they told Clinton to consider the beam in his
own eye. "For God's sake," Morris wrote him on February 20,
"tax and leave to a future period the equitable adjustment of
these things."

Morris, the previous year, had urged Clinton to make the
loyalty test more palatable, and when now Jay and he learned
that the property of Tories could be confiscated in New York
on the unsupported statement, without evidence, of one witness
they expressed their horror of such a policy.

On the sixteenth, in a letter to R. R. Livingston, Jay made
specific reference for the first time we know of to Morris's most
fascinating "foible." In one of the classic euphemisms they all
used, he wrote, "Gouverneur is daily employed in making
oblations to Venus."

To such oblations Morris devoted, as we shall see, a great
deal of his energies. But then and later his desires seldom interfered with his business. The day after Jay's letter Fell, in his
Diary, noted that in Congress "G.M. moved with many reasons,
well drawn up . . ." that a committee of the most divergent
views draw the new instruction to Arthur Lee. Witherspoon,
Sam Adams, Smith, Burke, with Morris as chairman, were appointed. Another great lover, and very great man, was in Paris
about to present his credentials as our first minister to a king,
and Fell reports that the business of Congress was held up "for
a long debate about Dr. Franklin's character."

The main interest of Congress that spring was to settle the

terms on which they would make peace. There is a good deal of
attractive cocksureness about such optimism, less, however,
than the still pitiful condition of the army at Middlebrook
warranted.

On April 7, Washington appealed to Morris on one of the
difficulties. "There are only two ways," he wrote, "to complete
the corps of Artillery, either by original express enlistments
(now forbidden) or by drafts from the infantry, which is most
discouraging to the infantry who lose thereby the most healthy
and robust men which the Artillery requires." Morris quickly
got a resolution through Congress permitting "original express
enlistments."

The Newfoundland fishing rights, so important to New England and to the country, were one of the main issues of any
peace, and about them there was violent disagreement in Congress. "Last Saturday we got all shook up together about our
Tomcod," James Lovell wrote Sam Adams. No one of course
wanted anything less than unrestricted right of Americans to
fish in any sea. What worried Morris, though not Jay, was that
the quick French offer to guarantee such rights set a precedent
of American submission to France which would later plague
us. Morris moved to the effect that America had "a commercial
right to take fish upon the fishing banks of North America and
elsewhere upon the high seas," that there then must be express
agreement to that in any treaty with Great Britain but that
America "will not consent that France shall guarantee the said
right unless it has had prior recognition from Great Britain."
In other words that the French guarantee should not be
brought up in the negotiations nor be a part of them. The point
may seem a small one but it was essential to make clear to the
ally, three times the size of the enemy, that America did not
propose to be their dependency in any sense.

Tom Paine took advantage of the fact that "no secret of
Congress was not known and talked of in every state" to publish a letter saying that an Impartial American had told him
there were "lurking foes" in Congress and that Gouverneur
Morris had written "thank God we of New York hold the keys

of the 13 states in our hands and in our power to give them
up to the King of England."

As with the Ogden letter the year before, Morris was able
to show that the letter was written by him before he had been
a delegate to either Congress or the Provincial Assembly and
that the quotation was out of context.

Though it was disposed of, or perhaps because it was, Joseph
Reed wrote Morris early in April, setting forth a number of
grave charges against him. No other delegate to Congress
seems to have aroused so much controversy and personal enmity and the reasons are not hard to understand. One of the
youngest of them, more brilliant by far than most, perhaps all,
opinionated, scathing, impatient of dullness and delay, shocking
doubtless to the New England Puritans and the Quakers, annoying to the very men he persuaded, unpopular because of his evident indispensability in all their larger affairs, his adversaries
naturally sought to find everything possible to bring against him.

Reed's letter to him is missing, but we have Morris's reply of
twelve pages, 3600 words, written with his usual incisive force
and felicity on April 9.

After a polite preamble he examines the charges seriatim:

As to the complaint that he intervened on behalf of British
officers in Lancaster under a flag, when their tavern bill was
raised because they were British: yes, he did since "the probity
of the United States was involved."

As to the complaint that he appeared as a lawyer before
the Pennsylvania House of Assembly: yes, he did, after Reed
himself told Robert Morris and Biddle that he approved.

As to the complaint that he showed a letter to General Washington but when Pennsylvania asked to see it he said it was
private: yes, he did. It needs no explanation but he is always
willing to explain his conduct.

As to the complaint of procrastinating public business, he
presumes there can be no objection to seeking amendments to
what his conscience cannot approve.

As to the complaint that he is "wrong in supporting the Army
as they are assuming enough without any encouragement," it
should be realized "the Army will never be dangerous to the

liberties of America unless from a groundless distrust of them."

As to the complaint of his having interfered in the Pennsylvania state constitution, "what was the interference except to bring *you,* Mr. Biddle and Robert Morris together at my house, being present at your request and faithfully keeping the secrets to which effect the honor of every person present was pledged."

As to Reed's "mentioning to a gentleman of New York that I kept company much with Tories," he does not like it, since it is untrue, but he bears Reed no resentment.

And then with his airy, agreeable assurance he tells Reed, "I am infinitely superior to littlenesses and much more to the abominable weaknesses which some have thought proper to charge me with." He then says that the idea that he was concerned with General Arnold in the purchase of a share of the (prize) sloop *Active* is preposterous. Actually he gave his legal services to the captors, though Arnold offered to be security for his fees. The charge that he supported "Mr. Deane from interested motives" is "a cruel insinuation," and he would like to know whether "support of a man who asks justice" is meant to imply "assistance in fraud or guilt."

It is hard to see what justification, unless seniority, there was for Reed to call him to account for such a variety of actions. But Morris, in his sunny, unmalicious way, closes the letter by telling Reed, "You must be convinced that I am by no means a hollow friend and I assure you that if compelled to be your enemy you shall find me a generous foe."

Reed replied by asking whether Morris's letter was public or private.

"I pray you to consider it," Morris answered, "in whatever light you shall think proper . . . that my enmity or friendship are indifferent to you I can readily believe because I have a juster sense of my own insignificance than the world is willing to allow me."

It was a month later that Charles Carroll wrote Carmichael: "the faction of the Lees is industriously propogating that their opponents are most of them engaged in mercantile connections with Deane and others. . . . I have heard it said that G. Morris is in trade. I hope the report is groundless. I have a high opinion of this gentleman's ability and integrity; the latter may be warped by the prospects of amassing a great fortune. *Ceci entre nous."*

The report may not have been wholly groundless and the fact that Carroll, Morris's friend, was plainly worried about it gives it serious weight.

It marks the entry on the stage of a man, just Morris's age, whose partner he is later to be. The man is William Constable and for the ten years from 1789 on he is one of the most important people in Morris's life and is revealed by his letters as a merchant banker of sound world credit, and a man of good will and common sense. In the decade of the nineties he stands for all that is best in big business: shrewdness, prudence, integrity and generosity. Robert Morris for much that is worst.

We know from the William Edgar Papers that as early as 1773, when Constable was twenty-one, his New York house was an important factor in the fur trade with the Upper Posts and with London.

We also know that he reached Philadelphia from England during the British occupation and, as Van Doren says of him, "saw that business was business" and made large profits.

After the evacuation and when Arnold was military governor he was involved with him in the improper business of the sloop *Active*, though not in treason.

In Montreal they heard and informed Edgar in Detroit that "William Constable was laid in limboe by the Philadelphians for some concerns found out with Arnold. What is become of him I know not. But some whisper the worst."

On March 2, a month before his letter to Reed, Morris wrote a letter to Governor Clinton which, read by itself, sounds like an amusing example of how even a man at the center of things in wartime may be puzzled by procedures.

It says that William Constable had been in the United Kingdom at the beginning of the war and had then come to Philadelphia where he had taken the oath. It does not say he was there during the occupation or that he took the oath after the American entry. It asks how he can "with propriety" reside in New York. Just let him come along, Clinton replied.

The coincidence of time and the inference that Constable wants to be away from Pennsylvania, with the extent of the surrounding suspicions, are such as to make it likely Morris was more "in trade" than he should have been and permitted himself associations he would have condemned in someone else.

On the other hand, the Letter Books of Morris and Constable at that period apparently do not exist. They might put a better light on it.

In May, Morris wrote by Gerard, who was going out to see Washington at Middlebrook, recommending plans for an attack on New York City. He told Washington that Gerard was bringing "good news," as to men and money coming, "it is and ought to be a secret even from Congress for which I need give you no reason as you are but too well acquainted with them."

It never seems to have occurred to Morris that, had his criticisms of Congress to the commander-in-chief gone astray, they would have done great damage. Washington was careful never to refer to them but does not appear to have warned Morris to stop them.

Washington replied, "I was desirous to convince the minister that we are willing to make every effort in our power for striking a decisive blow. Yet my judgment rather inclines [to the relief of the Southern states as of having] greater magnitude and still more important advantages."

He did not tell Morris nor the French minister that a Continental expedition under Sullivan was forming to lay waste the Indian lands of New York and Pennsylvania. It was a prior necessity if the army was to be fed.

Morris had now been continuously in Congress or with the army since his seating in January '78. It is a little difficult to realize that his services were dependent on votes at the election coming up in the fall.

He naturally felt that he ought to go to New York to mend his fences. Governor Clinton wrote him in June urging him to stay in Philadelphia, assuring him, "it will be attended with no consequences to your prejudice in the minds of your constituents." Livingston felt that "oblations" were keeping him away, for Morris wrote him, evidently from headquarters at Middlebrook:

Here in a dirty village where no society can be maintained you talk to me as familiarly of Bacchus and Ceres, Minerva and The Graces as if we had met on Mt. Ida. . . . Bacchus has not been seen here for some time. . . . The Graces abhor an abode where there is not one Venus to entertain them.

Back in Philadelphia, ten days later he sent Livingston a paper on the Newfoundland fisheries. Modern though he was, he did not believe international affairs should be conducted in a fish bowl. "It is particularly unfortunate for the people and for Congress should this be thus publicly stated."

He remained in Congress and on July 19, serving on the Marine Committee with Carmichael and Whipple, he made a proposal to Franklin in Paris.

As a result of British ravages in Connecticut, he proposed retaliation in Great Britain "by a few desperate, determined men under the promise of handsome rewards . . . under Captain Jones if [he] is in France." This brilliant commando concept speaks for itself but it is interesting to note that with its audacity went good sense. It expressly gives Franklin on-the-spot discretion in the matter and tells him not to discuss it with the French if he does not think well of it.

In August, Luzerne came out from France with word that Spain had entered the war as an ally of France. Governor Clinton in Poughkeepsie published the resolution of Morris, Gerry and Dickinson urging the states to redouble their efforts to offset the French criticism that "preparations were not made earlier." In England, Lord Shelburne noted that "in every Protestant and Dissenters home the established toast is success to America!"

There was a charming convention of the time by which, when something for the benefit or glory of their country occurred, they all wrote each other, as Morris did to Livingston, August 10, "I congratulate you on the news of Count d'Estaing's success in the West Indies," as though it were the other's own doing.

With the good news, Morris went off to New York State for "some days' leisure," to come quickly back on word that Jay was to go on mission to Spain.

Jay, perhaps forewarned that he might go as envoy, had written Governor Clinton on August twenty-seventh, "Several circumstances have come to my knowledge leading me to suspect that pains have been taken to injure Mr. Morris in the opinion of his constituents. Justice to him, as well as regard to truth, obliges me to say he deserves well of New York and America in general."

Shortly afterwards, now definitely appointed to Spain, to the weakening of the New York delegation, he wrote again: "Morris is again with us and I am glad of it. His constituents must either be infatuated or wretchedly misinformed if they omit continuing him in the delegation." On the twenty-ninth Jay wrote two very careful letters. To Clinton he said, "As a private, out of door counsellor Morris will be serviceable. His ability enables him to promote every cause he may advocate but if I may be permitted to advise, he should restrain himself from taking any part or pushing any measure respecting your dispositions without the previous concert with Livingston and Hobart." The letter seems to say that on national issues Morris could be left to himself, not on state issues to which he was more indifferent.

He then wrote a letter addressed jointly to Robert Livingston and Morris, saying, "my Dear Friends, I exceedingly regret Morris's not being sent to Europe where his ability would have done honor as well as service to his country. . . . Your manners and address will give New York great advantage in contested matters and if Morris governs his imagination he will conciliate friends. . . ."

On October 5 James Lovell was writing Whipple, "If Jay is taken or drowned we shall have a total suspension of negotiations for a time. . . . I have not yet seen the Tall Boy [Morris]."

He had not seen him because, in the New York election at

Poughkeepsie, Morris had been tied with L'Hommedieu and then defeated in the legislature's run-off.

L'Hommedieu, then forty-five, had graduated from Yale when Morris was two years old. He had an honorable political career, then and thereafter, dying in his seventy-eighth year as clerk of Suffolk County, a post he held continuously for his last twenty-seven years!

Clinton wrote Jay that "the imprudence of some of Mr. Morris's friends occasioned the loss of his election. However I am inclined to believe he will be appointed to fill up [your vacancy]."

Morris took the defeat well and generously. He wrote to Clinton that it was true he had lowered a Continental apportionment to New York for what he thought were sound reasons. "Perhaps I may not have thoroughly accorded with the views of my constituents. If so let me bear the blame singly and none of it fall on my worthy colleagues as I am the blameable. . . . If I thought the weak voice of their servant would weigh with those whom I represented . . . I would caution them against those palleative remedies [of finance] which have been so ineffective." And to Livingston he said no more than "I learn from your quarter that I am no longer to be that wretched creature a statesman." He had already written him, "I am a little sanguine (by natural temperament) and never look upon the dark side of objects unnecessarily."

John and Sally Jay were to sail October 20 and Morris reached Philadelphia the day before. "When I arrived the world (or at least such part of it as I warmly love) was on the wing," he wrote. The reference is of course to the Jays but doubtless also to "dearest Kitty" Livingston, still unmarried, there to see her sister off. She had been in Philadelphia during the summer and her father had written "Caty" not to be an immodest nor an unpatriotic flirt.

British raiders had descended on Liberty Hall earlier in the year looking for her father's state papers. They were in a chest in the parlor and the family tradition is that she told the British officer they were letters from her beaux and that if he would guard them she would get the state papers. From the library she brought an armful of old legal briefs, tied with red tape and sealed, and the ruse was successful. And one would like to have seen her in white nightrobe and cap standing as a "ghost" on the stairs later till the British patrol which had murdered the rector's wife saw her and fled, believing she was the ghost.

The boy-girl affair of six and seven years ago should, it would seem, have ended as Jay's and Duer's and Hamilton's did in marriage.

Sally Jay's letters to Kitty on the trip are addressed to "the Lady Abbess of The Nunnery of Persippeny," written no doubt facetiously since she sends her "pink lute-string negligees and silk stockings." Still, one wonders how much Morris's other "oblations" had to do with the end of the love affair. As will be seen, though, Kitty was not pining away.

On shipboard, the previous summer, "with the wind blowing out of Nantes," Marbois, coming out as consul, asked John Adams "in the evening" about Gouverneur Morris.

I said it was his christian name; that he was not a governor. The consul said he had heard of him as an able man. I said he was a young man chosen into Congress since I left it; that I had sat some years with his elder brother in Congress; that Gouverneur was a man of wit and made pretty verses; but of a character *très leger*. That the cause of America had not been sustained by such characters as that of Gourverneur Morris or his colleague Mr. Jay who was also a young man about 30 [actually thirty-four] and not quite so solid as his predecessor Mr. Laurens [fifty-five] upon whose resignation in the sudden heat Mr. Jay was chosen.

Whipple (forty-nine) wrote Peabody (Mass., thirty-eight): "The Tall Boy will not be here hereafter to trouble you as he no longer has a seat in a room where he has at least shown a disposition on some occasions to perplex business." Some sympathy must be extended these people. For two years Morris must have infuriated them by demanding the individual ayes and noes on almost every vote. It is also to be considered that the Adamses, the Lees, Whipple and Roger Sherman, as Signers, may have felt a special annoyance at the prominence and presumption of a man whose years were sixteen less than the average of the Signers, the youngest of whom, Edward Rutledge, was three years older than Morris.

Of course James Lovell rejoiced most of all. He had heard Morris criticize John Adams himself and said it was "low arts." A kind word must parenthetically be said for that terrific, joyless worker, Lovell. He sent copies of some papers to Jay in Madrid saying, "The weather is murderous hot and I can't go up and down stairs to the offices in search of those authenticated [documents] which regularly ought to go to you and other dignified officers abroad." To Oliver Pollock, who wanted some of the money he had given George Rogers Clark, Lovell was less apologetic, saying that there was such confusion he could not even find the drafts in the heat.

Now he heard that the defeated Morris, with his "low arts," was "making all smooth" to obtain the Paris post, as secretary to Franklin.

There was apparently a good deal of feeling about it and the nominations which followed are interesting.

"Mr. Mathews, South Carolina [thirty-five] named Gouverneur Morris." This seems straightforward. "Mr. Ellery, Rhode Island [fifty-two], named Lovell, Massachusetts [forty-three]." No service to his country was too much to ask of Lovell, even in Paris under a libertine like Franklin (seventy-three). "Lovell named Colonel Hamilton [twenty-six (twenty-two?)]." This nomination should split the Morris vote and no one could say New England congressmen were against youthful promise. "George Plater, Maryland [forty-four], named Colonel Stewart." Pause there, Morocco! Why did Plater, William and Mary '53, who had dined in London at the Temple with Charles Carroll in the sixties, married Elizabeth Rousby in '64, and who was to be sixth governor of Maryland, propose Colonel Stewart? Was it the act of a jealous husband? Plater's portrait is of a prissy, stupid man and Buchholz in his *Governors of Maryland* says, "to speak of one of the Chief Magistrates of Maryland as a commonplace man is perhaps to give offence," though thus he speaks of Plater!

As to his own nomination, Lovell hastily explained to Sam Adams (fifty-seven), "You must know that upon finding

Gov'eur was named and was solicitous to be with Dr. Franklin
. . . I did not insist upon my name being struck off."

He had written in considerable anxiety to Henry Laurens,
"Your son having declined to go to France it was determined
that tomorrow a secretary will be chosen. No nominations yet
made but Gouverneur Morris will be the man and I know your
opinion of him."

As Lovell was bracing himself for the supreme sacrifice of
going to Paris, the matter was settled by young Colonel Laurens
deciding to accept.

It is fascinating to consider that had Morris immediately
been chosen to go he might, on November 30, have been present at the Church of St. Jacques du Haut-Pas, when the Count
Alexandre Sebastien de Flahaut, Chevalier de la Billarderie,
aged fifty-one, married Adélaide Filleul, *sans naissance, sans
fortune*, aged eighteen.

Instead he ended the year with a defeat and a disappointment.

With the perplexer of business out of the way the New Year
opened with a marvelous letter from Lovell to Gates. How
familiar it is. "We are aiming at a curtailment of expense by in-
spectors to visit and break up unnecessary posts in the staff
departments and reduce the number of officers; and also to
lessen the number of horses and wagons in the army. In short
we are beginning to do many things that ought to have been
done a year ago."

On February 3 while practicing law in Philadelphia Morris
began his series of "An American" letters in the *Pennsylvania
Packet*. They were concerned with the country's finances,
lucidly and brilliantly done. In general they dealt with the
futility of hoping to make depreciated currency legal tender by
law. "Money is of too subtle and spiritual a nature to be caught
by the rude hand of the law. How will you find a man's money?"
Above all they pressed his invariable theme, heavy and still
heavier taxation without which price control was impossible.
Anything subversive in them would be caught by Lovell, who
assured Sam Adams, "I will always allow myself to stand as a
check upon Gouverneur Morris."

Early in April, Jay had arrived in Madrid, after many perils by land and sea but happily neither taken nor drowned as Lovell had feared. Plagued by Carmichael and Brockholst Livingston of his own household, arrogantly treated by the Spanish ministers, flooded with unpayable drafts from Congress, one of which, for $333, Florida Blanca paid, saying "no more," he wrote to Clinton: "Where is Morris? Keep him up. It is a pity that one so capable of serving his country should be unemployed but there are men who fear and envy his talents and take ungenerous advantage of his foibles."

That spring Morris sat to Pierre de Simitière, a Swiss artist, for a portrait. It is a right profile of an attractive face, the nose and chin strongly masculine, the eyes frank and good-humored. There is humor around the outer edge of the mouth, itself strong and sensual. The whole face is that of a man, challenging to a woman with strength and masculinity, intriguing with a hint of weakness or vulnerability and appealing in its obvious good-humored kindness. The picture was probably finished shortly before March 27 when William Clajon, of Gates's staff in '77, suddenly appeared.

He seems to have been one of those unlucky people who after a series of misfortunes tries to fix on one person as the source of all his trouble.

He now wrote that Morris had seen him with General Gates, as an A.D.C. in '77, and told Gates he "was no good because of a perjury conviction in New York." Gates, Clajon stated, did not believe it but had left him behind in Philadelphia. Clajon said the charge was untrue, as the records would reveal, and demanded satisfaction though expressly barring a duel.

Morris replied, "When I saw you near Gates person in '77—perhaps Mr. Jay was present as we all came on the same business—I am certain I did not report you had been convicted of perjury. . . . You will agree that in the very critical situation of things to the northward the point of faintest recollection of your being engaged in any manner in any such suit [as perjury] rendered it my duty as a public man to give the information. I could not have told him what you suppose because it is inconceivable, if I had, he should have kept you confidentially employed about his person without any enquiry [as you state to have been the case]."

The answer was not satisfactory to Clajon and he replied insisting on a public disavowal of the charge, adding, "you were generally considered at that period as one who was far from wishing well to General Gates" and elaborated on the point of Morris then being in the Continental Congress. Morris pointed out that though it was irrelevant he was not in that body until January '78. To this Clajon said, "Whether you sat in Congress in '77 or not your connections and your official consequence was the fame." Much was made of "attested copies for General Gates, etc., etc.," and on May 10, having found Morris's next reply unsatisfactory, Clajon wrote that he would "send for your final answer about noon tomorrow at Mrs. Ryves on Penn Street."

It is not clear what Clajon's exact relation to the perjury case being tried was. Morris saw him in court with the defendant, who was evidently convicted.

The next day Morris wrote patiently back, "Since [you say] fighting is out of the question I do not know what can be done more explanatory . . . [since you have my denial] that I said what General Gates alleged" and then he added with his felicitous usage and consideration: "On the whole [after carefully studying your letters] I really do not perceive your wishes but whatever they may be I imagine that a personal conference will better tend to convey and gratify them. I expect to leave today or tomorrow on a short excursion . . ."

The excursion was very short. William Bingham wrote John Jay how it ended.

An unlucky accident happened to Gouverneur Morris [on May 12, 1780]. In attempting to drive a pair of wild horses in a phaeton he was thrown and in the fall his left leg caught in a wheel and was greatly shattered. He was under the necessity of having it amputated.

Livingston wrote Clinton, Houston wrote Schuyler, "you have heard of poor Morris's misfortune in the loss of his leg. He bears it with becoming fortitude."

This appears to be the substance of all that was said publicly at the time and may indeed have been all there was to say. Morris does not seem to have said any more. Ten years later he told Minette de Staël, in answer to her question, that he had not lost his leg in the service of his country. But about the same time the then Lord Palmerston, father of Victoria's minister, met him in Paris and recorded him in his *Diary* as "A charming, sensible man" who had lost his leg in escaping from a jealous husband. Morris's *Diary* makes no mention of Palmerston.

The Palmerston entry would then appear to be gossip or myth were it not that Jay himself, breaking through his Huguenot reserve, wrote gaily in consolation to Morris, "I have learned that a certain married woman after much use of your legs had occasioned your losing one." He wrote simultaneously to Robert Morris, "Gouverneur's leg has been a tax on my heart. I am almost tempted to wish he had lost *something else* [Jay's italics]."

From the scene of the accident Morris was taken to the home of Colonel George Plater.

There, as Jared Sparks characteristically expresses it, "he received every attention, which kindness and sympathy could dictate, and for which he ever manifested the strongest sense of gratitude."

Again this would seem to be all were it not for an entry of unparalleled emotion for Morris in his *Diary* for May 5, ten years later. He is dining with the Beckwiths in London and "Just as I am coming away from this place Mrs. Beckwith informs me that Mrs. Plater is dead. I get away as soon as possible that I may not discover emotions which I cannot conceal. Poor Eliza! My lovely friend; thou art then at peace and I shall behold thee no more. Never. Never. Never."

No more, except that on June 1, 1790, three weeks later, Mrs. Isaac Low, a Cuyler of Albany, "tells me many things respecting Mrs. Plater which I am surprized at her knowledge of."

Few men have been better equipped with the pride and assurance necessary to stand such a crippling blow. Except for a natural rage at the "cursed mud" in which he often fell and the malign luck that tumbled him down the staircase in the Louvre, tearing the knee out of his breeches, it seems to have made small difference to him, although he was always conscious of it. He was a great walker until his last years, three leagues then if the road was good, and he climbed to the top of the steeple at Bruges.

At the time, he is said to have told the attending surgeons, "The removal of my leg cannot add to your celebrity. Is there not one among you younger in your calling who might perform the cut and thus secure the fame [?] for his benefit?" Young Huchenson was pointed out, so Dr. John W. Francis said.

There was a long six months' convalescence and the beauties of Philadelphia must have done all they could to spoil him, though they showed De Chastellux twenty-two hundred shirts they had cut and sewn that summer for the army. Well though he masked his sense of loss, it must have contributed to his desire to show that he could still win any woman.

On November 25, Livingston wrote him:

I congratulate you in your restoration to the beau monde and I congratulate the Beau Monde on your restoration to them. I am told you are Master of the Ceremonies to La Belle Madame Bingham. I consider you as enlisted for the season as I am persuaded she will claim all the attention you can possibly spare.

. . . I have felt much for Mrs. Arnold if, as is supposed, she was ignorant of her husband's crime.

Morris replied:

My restoration to the Beau Monde, my dear friend, is like a resurrection from the grave. The vestments will smell of the earth they were laid in. Little then have the Beau Monde to rejoice, for they acquire an appendage useless at all times and umbruous now— a wooden member.

Eight years later Mrs. Bingham sent for another "manly and elegant youth" to be her Master of Ceremonies. His name was Richard Randolph.

CHAPTER SEVEN

I Do Not Think My Conduct Reprehensible

(1781)

ALTHOUGH the main fighting was far away in the Carolinas, Morris heard early in 1781 that Morrisania, where his mother was living, and De Lancey's Royal Refugee Corps was quartered, had been stormed and ravaged by the Continentals.

In March word reached him that his mother, whom he had not seen in five years, was dying.

The only tangible evidence of his attitude toward his mother is contained in a letter he wrote to her April 17, the previous year. Sparks quotes it in full, saying, as the custom of the period demanded, that it "bears strong testimony to the goodness of his heart and the strength of his filial affection."

The formality of the salutation, "Dear Madam," and the signature, "Yours, most affectionately, Gouverneur Morris," are doubtless no more than the good manners of the time. The letter is filial but suggests that his mother, at sixty-four, was unsympathetic to his patriotism and indifferent to his welfare.

He says, "I have heard of you, but not from you, since I left Morrisania; neither have I had the satisfaction to learn that, of the many letters I have written, you have ever received one. . . .

"I received great pain from being informed that you are distressed on my account." The distress apparently was caused by his sense "of a higher duty [which] has bound me to the service of my fellow creatures. . . .

"I know that for such sentiments I am called a rebel, and that such sentiments are not fashionable among the folks you see. It is possible, though I hope not, that your maternal tenderness may lead you to wish that I would resign these sentiments. . . ."

He says that he is "much distressed for ———. I sincerely love him and I fear that we are separated for a long season." The blank is Sparks's doing, the context making it clear that Morris referred to his brother-in-law, the Tory, Isaac Wilkins, who had fled to Nova Scotia.

"Let me again entreat you to make yourself happy. . . . There is enough of sorrow in the world without looking into futurity for it. Hope the best. If it happens, well; if not, it will then be time enough to be afflicted. . . ."

Now, a year later, hearing that she was dying, he had applied for a pass to visit her. Army Headquarters and Governor Clinton approved.

As he was about to leave, William Smith Livingston wrote Governor Clinton, "I have obtained a pass [of exit from New Jersey] through Mr. Ogden. He married a sister of Gouverneur Morris. Old Mrs. Morris is dying. Gouverneur goes into New York next Wednesday to see her (and I beg to accompany him)."[1]

Clinton's reply came quickly back. "The peculiar situation of the state exposed in almost every quarter renders it necessary to prevent as much as possible any intercourse with the enemy. [Request refused.]" Simultaneously Joseph Reed wisely or vindictively, who can say, refused Morris the exit pass from Pennsylvania "as improper for a person who had been in offices of high and responsible trusts." But it is possible, as two later events indicate, that if Samuel Ogden's name had not been included both W. S. Livingston and Morris could have visited New York.

It must be remembered that the Arnold treason was only a

[1] The letter from Princeton contains the familiar story of wartime housing shortage in the little town of seventy houses. "Dr. Witherspoon [president of Princeton, has rented] the house in which [my mother] lives over her head without previous notice because he could get a little more from some other persons."

few months old and the air was still full of rumors of subversion
—*Greene had gone over to Cornwallis. Silas Deane to London.
The Loyalists were up.* It is incredible that in every war rumors
should be snatched at and believed in by both sides. Believe it
or not, it is a fact that Todd and McGill on March 30, 1779,
wrote William Edgar that "12000 Russians are said to be landed
at New York."

The Freeman's Journal in Philadelphia published letters supporting Reed's decision, perhaps written by him, and in a very
temperate letter to the *Journal* Morris replied, saying in part:

It is true, I was for sometime honored by my countrymen, much
beyond my desert, and beyond my ambition. When our prospects
were very gloomy, I was deeply engaged in public business of an
intricate nature and placed in a variety of arduous and critical situations. I have thought much, labored much, suffered much. In return,
I have been censured, reproached, slandered, goaded by abuse,
blackened by calumny and oppressed by popular opinion. All this
has been borne without complaining and avenged only by forgiveness. . . .

I did not think that my conduct (in desiring to visit my mother
laboring under the pressure of sickness and age) was reprehensible;
but since, my countrymen, my intentions are disagreeable to you, I
shall persist no longer. Having already devoted the better part of my
life to your service, I will now sacrifice my feelings to your inclination.

So Joseph Reed had his way and in midsummer, three days
after his appointment to the Finance Office, Morris's pride had
another shock when he had to write "His Excellency, the President of Pennsylvania":

I am informed that a letter written by me to the late General
Arnold while I was on a committee at the Valley Forge is among the
papers which were taken at the discovery of his defection. Will you
permit me, sir, thro your Excellency to intreat of the Honorable
Council that either the letter or a certified copy of it may be sent to
me.

It had, of course, nothing to do with treason—but with the
aborted Lafayette campaign to Canada—but no one knew
what forgery might have been found there.

Reed's early death in 1785 at forty-four makes difficult a

balanced judgment of him. He had been Washington's military secretary around Boston, fought in the Battle of Long Island, and as president of Pennsylvania abolished slavery there. He had been head of the commission trying Arnold for alleged malfeasance as military governor of Philadelphia. He was bitterly suspicious of Silas Deane, both as "being in the British interests" and as partaking of the "profits of iniquity." In a scathing letter of November '81 to General Greene, he portrays Deane's supporters, including of course the Morrises, as using "money, expectation of office, entertainment and good wine" to further their ends. The same letter tellingly describes Robert Morris, as Superintendent of Finance. "Those who know him will also acknowledge that he is too much a man of the world to overlook certain private interests which his command of the paper and occasional speculations in that currency will enable him to promote . . . ever been a ruling principle with him to connect the public service with the private interest," and he adds that "censorious people say *his* director [is Gouverneur Morris]."

It is all very effective and persuasive until it becomes a little maudlin about his own breach with Washington, and how he himself could have been Secretary of War. On the whole the impression is of a narrow and suspicious man.

There were two new and important appointments, at a cabinet level, to be made by Congress that spring, a Secretary *of* Foreign Affairs and a Superintendent of Finance.

With characteristic assurance Morris wrote a brilliant but sprightly paper on the make-up of an effective Cabinet. Finance and foreign affairs interested him most. The man handling national finance must be "warmly and thoroughly attached to America, not bigoted to any particular state and his attachment founded not on whimsical caprice, resentment or weak compliance . . . but on a manly and rational conviction of the benefits of independence and unity."

A Secretary of State must have "a genius, quick, lively and penetrating. . . . He should write on all occasions with clearness and perspicuity . . . conveying strong sense and argument in easy and agreeable diction . . . [with a temperament] mild, cool and placid, festive, insinuating and pliant, yet obstinate . . . communicative yet reserved."

If in finance he was thinking of Robert Morris, the second sketch must be about what he thought of himself, with a good deal of reason. It would be interesting to know what would have been the effect on our affairs if one of our Secretaries of State, with their frequently great qualities, had ever been *festive*.

The choice was not easy. Even the patriot elite were running short of capable men. Franklin, John Adams and John Jay were in France, and Jefferson, as governor of Virginia, was being harried from his capitol and then from Monticello by Tarleton's cavalry.

From Clermont, Robert R. Livingston asked Morris, "Who is to be your Secretary of Foreign Affairs? James Lovell or Matlock, I am told. Yourself or Madison are the only persons I can think of but you are too well qualified to be appointed." He also asked who would succeed Franklin in France.

Livingston, though he said that all he was doing was "digging, planting, pruning, walking, talking and writing bad verse," must have been aware that he was not forgotten "in the great theater of politics and pleasure" at Philadelphia.

Morris wrote him that Foreign Affairs lay between Lee, Madison and Livingston himself. "I believe you will be appointed. As to Lawrence [young Laurens] as envoy to France, I really love him as an agreeable, sensible young man, but . . ."

It is wonderful in these old letters how often an apparently casual question lights up the whole background of rivalry and ambition. Livingston, like any man, wanted the Foreign Affairs post, but he deprecates the idea that he will get it though he thanks Morris "for remembering a man who [lives in] the depths of solitude." Then he asks, "Will Joseph Reed have to be provided for?"

In March, Robert Morris was appointed Superintendent of Finance. "If he accepts the office," Gouverneur wrote Governor Clinton, "which Congress against his will conferred on him, I shall hope to see some better mode of raising money . . . and I shall be morally certain of honesty in the expenditure."

Robert Morris accepted, though he asserted, "It will expose me to the resentment of disapproving and designing men and to the calumny and detraction of the envious and malicious."

Before considering the two Morrises in the Finance Office, mention must be made of a joint decision of theirs while Gouverneur was still acting as an unofficial adviser to Robert.

We have already had an insight into the sort of man James Lovell of Massachusetts was. He was nonetheless a patriot with the salt of New England in him. There were certain things he could do wonderfully well.

On April 10 the Morrises sent for him and asked him to act as receiver of continental taxes in Massachusetts. Nothing is more obvious than that Lovell was the incorruptible tax collector personified—but it was not the sort of thing that would be obvious to petty politicians. Nor was it an attempt to get him out of Congress. They wanted him to take both posts. They said if taxes were left to the Continental loan agents, as had been suggested, there would be favors and a commingling or offsetting of tax and loan receipts.

Lovell said he was not sure one man could legally have both posts. They showed him that statute allowing it, and finally the public-spirited patriot Lovell agreed with political opponents, also patriots, and accepted to the great benefit of his country.

We have seen the views of Joseph Reed on the Morrises in the Finance Office. In the person of Robert Morris a great deal of mythmaking long went on—the pure-minded patriot pledging his fortune for Washington's army "in the dark days of the Revolution," dying in poverty, after years of a debtors' prison, forgotten by an ungrateful country.

At the time, it must be realized, there were barely a dozen men in America with sufficient experience of trade and finance on a great scale to enable them even to understand the workings of a Finance Office. Then, as now, minor politicians, zealots, reformers protested against entrusting the country's finances to "big business" men who were at least capable of understanding how it worked.

Robert Morris's firm did a world-wide trading, shipping and

banking business with correspondents in both the Indies and Europe. Through his office and Bingham's in Philadelphia, or Constable's in New York—and only a few others in the entire country—came the documents of trade in the "wet fur skins" of Canada and the West, tea, and pepper from the Malabar Coast, cotton, tobacco, coffee, hardware, salt meat, fish, naval stores. The habit of such business, to say nothing of expertness in it, was necessary for the Superintendent of Finance.

Fifteen years later, bankrupt and pathetic, borrowing from Peter for Paul, Robert Morris is one of the typical semitragic figures of the 1920s. In 1781 he was a rock of experience and integrity.

Benjamin Rush in describing his fellow townsman said, "Robert Morris was bold, sensible and agreeable. His peculiar manners deprive him of much of that popularity usually following great exploits of public and private virtue. He was proud and passionate and he always had virulent enemies as well as affectionate friends."

"Don't let Alexander get fat," Angelica wrote her sister, Elizabeth Hamilton, "or he will be unable to flirt as Robert Morris." Either description fits Gouverneur equally well, and there is a description of Robert by John Adams quoted in *The Republican Court* which applies so well to Gouverneur that the reference in the index is to him.

Gouverneur Morris, after working with him unofficially during the spring, was appointed assistant superintendent on July 6. It was of course a great blessing to him to be back in the inner circles after his electoral defeat and the loss of his leg. There can be no question that he accepted at a financial sacrifice. One legal fee, four thousand dollars, that spring exceeded his salary. But it was also a blessing to his country and his chief.

The office kept an official *Day Book* erroneously referred to as Robert Morris's diary. Its unknown penman was a great artist and visually it is a thing of beauty. It records the daily conferences and correspondence of the office, so that congressional committees may be readily answered. But in its pages there is also much of human interest and entries made with a careful eye to later defense.

The revenues for which it was accountable were of a varied and complex nature: Continental taxes; contributions in kind from the states; Loan Certificate receipts; bills of exchange for export goods to be discounted at the new Bank of North America with its capital of four hundred thousand dollars; bills on Paris for tobacco, cotton and rice; French gold shipments—not many of them—and the French credits authorized in the discretion, within limits, of Luzerne, the French minister.

The disbursements were for all the expenses of the government, but they were not against a budget. The office was jammed with people wanting to be paid—contractors with notes of army commissary agents, Colonel Harrison for Washington's expenses, John Paul Jones for an installment on his shipbuilding in Boston, "even the express riders come to be paid" and,

Paulding and Williams who captured André applied for annuity ordered by Congress November 3, 1780 and Paulding brought a pass from the Secretary of the Governor of New York, the writing of which being known to Gouverneur Morris, I issued warrants for $200 each.

And Book A, Folio 17, has the famous entry:

Congress empowers General Washington to seize flour wherever he could find it. I determine to procure supplies and pledge my private credit.

In August the Foreign Affairs post went, as Morris had forecast, to Livingston. He wrote Gouverneur saying that he was "delicate about asking [the amount of] the emolument. Mrs. Livingston says there is nobody she would as soon chose to hire a house for her as you. Let it be in a good street, not a busy one —stables near." Then he adds, in very natural fashion, that he will need an advance or loan of five hundred dollars.

In late July the great coming event begins quietly in the *Day Book*. Robert Morris has been summoned to Army Headquarters at Dobbs Ferry. Before leaving he calls on Luzerne "to know the extent of credit he can give me on account of 6 million francs for the campaign. If the expedition goes on against New York he can venture to assist me with 1 million more."

Robert Morris was gone from August 7 to 21, leaving Gouverneur as acting superintendent.

It was in that interval that he first dealt with Haym Salomon, the paper broker. Salomon, then forty-one years old, had come to this country from Poland in 1772, and became, in all ways, a valuable and self-sacrificing American patriot.

A biographer of his states that Morris wrote him a "disagreeable letter . . . manifestly unwarranted [since] Gouverneur Morris knew nothing about conditions governing the bill market . . . couched in terms gallingly offensive to a sensitive man . . . many a man [on receiving it] would have quit the game in disgust."

The incident is of some importance because it has been represented as having to do with religious prejudice rather than the bill market, of which it is hardly likely Morris "knew nothing."

Although Salomon was a patriot, he was also a broker—an essential service to the Finance Office—and from the sale of bills received a discount or commission. He was a businessman and to call him a "sensitive man," who finds a business letter so "gallingly offensive" that he might "quit the game in disgust," is quite absurd.

Here is the letter:

I am much surprised at the information you gave me this morning of the sale of bills on such lax credit. Before you ventured in anything of that sort you should have given me notice of it. Though I permitted a certain sum to be sold on credit, I had no idea of any thing of that sort being carried to such an extent. However as you have done it I will not falsify your promise but in future you must not sell on credit at all, nor under six shillings for cash. I will write to Mr. Morris and should he think proper the directions may be altered but not otherwise. I must insist upon an account immediately of what bills you have sold.

To anyone of business experience the situation seems quite clear.

We know that Congress had transferred about fifty thousand dollars in bills of exchange on Franklin to the Finance Office on June 4. They had not been offered in the following sixty days, presumably because the office judged they would bring six shillings cash at the right moment.

Without impugning Salomon's motives, it appears he took advantage of Robert Morris's absence and the twelve-year juniority of his deputy (Salomon was forty-one, Gouverneur twenty-nine) to sell bills at four shillings, part for cash, part on time.

Gouverneur Morris tells him he is to go no further, says he will not repudiate what has been done, though he must have an immediate accounting, and says that he will write to Robert Morris, who can of course change the instructions in Salomon's favor if he wishes.

Salomon was a private individual, Gouverneur Morris a public servant accountable to Congress. There is nothing to indicate Salomon felt the way his biographer did about the incident. He came to Morris later for a letter of introduction to Robert R. Livingston which Morris gave the "broker to the Office of Finance" in pleasant terms.

The curt entry in the *Day Book* for August 27 implies the Superintendent agreed with his deputy.

No one can of course now say how many men were in the well-kept secret that the campaign was to be in Virginia and not against the British in New York. On July 17, four days before Robert Morris asked Luzerne for a million francs more "for New York," Beau Fersen, then twenty-six, rode "220 miles in 36 hours" to Rochambeau's headquarters in Newport to report the conference with Washington. He wrote the Swedish ambassador in Paris that night:

"*Nous devons marcher en suite en Virginie avec notre armée joindre a lui [Washington] et chasser les Anglais de cette partie.*"

Washington's *Diary* for July 21 reads:

"The enemy did not appear to have had the least intelligence of our movements [toward Yorktown the day before]." The army was moving by Saw Mill River, East Chester Road, "Sheldon's cavalry scouring Frog's Neck . . . [the infantry joining] with Lauzun's Legion for the purpose of scouring Morrisania to the Harlem River." Scour it they did and eight years later Morris drank with Lauzun in Paris to celebrate it.

Hamilton, torn between love, pride and "security," wrote his Betsy: "A part of the army, my dear girl, is going to Virginia. I must go without embracing you, alas. I must go. . . . Don't mention I am going to Virginia."

The *Day Book* of the Finance Office was written for any British spy to read. It said that at headquarters the Superintendent "talked economies and Colonel Tilghman took notes of such conclusions as we agreed, a copy whereof he gave me." Contractors were called in for Osnaburgs "for the intended siege of New York."

Then, on August 30, Washington, with his suite, arrived in Philadelphia and stayed at Robert Morris's house.

On September 3 the army was passing through on the way to the Head of Elk, as they had four years before, going down to the Brandywine.

Gouverneur Morris, a stump hanging from his magnificent body, had to watch them "in a dust like a smothering snowstorm," pouring through "in a column two miles long," with all the beauties "watching from the open windows of every house."

The French came through the next day "in white broadcloth faced with green," full bands and field music playing and the "effete aristocrats" he was later to know so well were "ruddy and handsome" after the long march from Newport.

Luzerne borrowed thirty cooks from the French Army to give a great entertainment for the populace. Outwardly all was glorious but from the head of the column on September 5 Washington sent back word that his troops must be paid. "Great symptoms of discontent had appeared on their passage thru' the city."

The *Day Book* reads:

I desired Mr. Gouverneur Morris to accompany me on account of his speaking fluently the French language. We set out at 3 for Chester. On the road an express arrived from General Washington at Head of Elk with news that DeGrasse was in the Chesapeake.

The Morrises reached Rochambeau's headquarters and the count let them have "20000 hard dollars to be repaid by October first."

The road coming back to Philadelphia was jammed "with the last division of the French Army, their artillery and baggage."

Another rider from Washington was in Philadelphia waiting for them. A month's pay for the troops was the absolute minimum. Colonel Pierce, the paymaster general, left with it that night and on the tenth word came that a French gold shipment had reached Boston, and the finance officers, heaving a great sigh of relief, wrote out the packing instructions for its movement.

It was that week the Morrises gave Tom Paine a sinecure as a "writer" and on the twenty-seventh, Gouverneur was down with "fever and ague." He was not recovered until October 17.

Awaiting him was a peremptory question from Washington. He had ordered fifty hogsheads of rum for the army. "Where is it?"

Twenty hogsheads and "30 casks of Taffia" were rolling that night and Robert Morris wrote John Jay in Paris, "Gouverneur is with me [again] and a most useful and able adjunct he is."

Competence was only part of his make-up. Magnanimity was another. He wrote the Board of War that night asking that a parole be accepted from a British officer, Captain James Watson. His privateer had been taken and American prisoners aboard all "commended his humanity." If "it is consistent with general line of conduct the Board have proscribed to themselves . . . I know it will give you pleasure to retaliate an act of humanity."

As Morris was writing, Beau Fersen wrote his father:

"We have just taken Cornwallis with 6 or 7000 men," and four days later Colonel Tilghman "arrived in the morning with the despatches of the surrender," and "to lay the colors of Cornwallis at the feet of Congress."

There was a Te Deum at "the Romish Church," which the finance officers attended, "impressed with ideas of the most solemn and awful nature."

Sure though they had all been that it would happen, the reality seemed incredible.

On November 27 George III went to tell his Lords and Commons:

> "It is with great concern that I inform you that the events of war have been very unfortunate to my armies in Virginia and have ended in the loss of my forces in that province."

Lord Shelburne, moving an amendment to the Address, said it was absolutely impossible to continue the struggle. "America could not be conquered by arms."

CHAPTER EIGHT

Often Wise, Sometimes
Out of His Senses

(1782)

YORKTOWN was but two weeks past when Robert Morris wrote the president of Congress: "When I say that I cannot command more than one twentieth of the sum necessary for the current services of the years, I am within the strictest bounds of truth." The victory tended to harden not only the French credits but their views on what terms America should be allowed to have in making peace with England.

Gouverneur Morris had written Jay, who was going from Madrid to Paris as a peace commissioner, "I am sure there is something in your bosom which will revolt at the servility [of obeying] the dictates of the French Ministry. No other Congress will surrender all, as this has, to an ally. I am more moved than I have ever been."

So many French individuals were greatly and generously attached to the American cause that it has been inferred the French Government was equally so. Their actual attitude is revealed in the amazing conversation between Jay and Lafayette in Paris, eight months after the surrender of Cornwallis. Jay's brief *Diary* records:

Lafayette said General Washington had the taking of New York much at heart and that he [Lafayette] had often applied to ministers here for aid. They seemed disinclined and said it was not worth

while forming expeditions for the taking of places which must be
given up at the peace.

As for Sir Henry Clinton in New York, the most he was prepared to negotiate about was an exchange of prisoners.

February 24, 1782, was Sunday and the Finance Office
closed, but in the tradition of wartime Sundays, the Morrises
both came down, "wrote some letters and then went in pursuit
of health on horseback."

It is pleasant to know that Gouverneur could still ride. Paine,
in his vulgar way, had described him to Bache, Franklin's son-
in-law, as "hopping around on one leg."

When they got back from the ride they found "General Knox
and Colonel Tilghman from General Washington to confer with
Gouverneur Morris and myself respecting negotiations with
commissioners from Sir Henry Clinton at Elizabeth Town regarding an exchange of prisoners." Past accounts for maintenance and future subsistence would have to be prepared.
"Colonel Tilghman took notes."

The commissioners on each side would have to be a soldier
and a financial civil servant. Clinton named General Dalrymple,
who as a colonel commanded the first landing at Boston, and
Mr. Andrew Elliott.

On March 11, Washington sent Knox and Gouverneur Morris
their powers. As he did so, Lord North's government fell and
Shelburne succeeded him, oddly dismissing Edward Gibbon,
the historian, from a sinecure as one of his first acts.

Their instructions set forth that "no one was to land from
New York except the commissioners and those immediately
connected. It is expedient not only to prevent new channels of
communication from being opened but to shut the former." The
person of Lord Cornwallis was to be offered for Henry Laurens,
a prisoner in London. But this was not a *sine qua non*. "It is
better that four or five gentlemen remain in captivity than that
a hundred should."

The importance and excitement of the mission was the sort
of thing to appeal to Morris. Few things are stranger than the
sensation of meeting the foe under a flag.

There appears to be no record of where the commissioners

met in Elizabeth Town. Liberty Hall, then as now, would have been the most suitable place. There was also the smaller but beautiful Boxwood Hall, the home of Elias Boudinot, the commissary general of prisoners. And of course the Samuel Ogden house where Morris presumably stayed.

On the night of the thirty-first, after the first meeting, Morris wrote to Robert Morris that he had "had some very free conversations with Dalrymple who wants to know how we avoided the [financial] convulsions apprehended. . . . [I gave him] details *with great candor* [his italics]. You may rely that Germain and Sandwich will give place to Shelburne and [Admiral] Howe." Dalrymple said that the loss of America would render British "more compact." Morris seemed to have learned more than he told.

He was unaware that the day before Washington had written General Knox from York Hutts, near Pompton, New Jersey (the writing in Colonel David Humphreys's hand):

You are too well acquainted with my opinion of certain characters in this state especially one who I am told is now in attendance on you at Elizabeth Town to need a repetition but I wish it were possible for you to guard your colleague [G. Morris] against the arts and the disadvantage which certainly will result from the free intercourse of sentiments, with the person I allude to, on points which can avail the British commissioners. I have every reason short of positive proof to believe the person is a traitor to this country in the pay of the enemy and that every piece of information he can extract from Mr. Morris will be communicated to the commissioners on the other side. You will readily perceive this is a confidential letter written for the best of purposes.

There can be no question the person was Samuel Ogden. Washington of course had many sources of military intelligence but Governor Clinton of New York had almost certainly informed him that, in the previous November, Ogden had been named to him as "a rendez vous" for an enemy courier.

A glance at the map of New York Harbor shows how critical a spot Elizabeth Town was, with Staten Island easy swimming distance away and the channel running up to Newark or the lower bay.

What caution Knox may have suggested to Morris we do not know, and the dramatic revelation by the British commissioner that Captain Joshua Huddy, of the New Jersey Line, had been hanged while a prisoner of war provoked a bitterness in the negotiations and broke them off on April 9.

Washington called a council of general and foreign officers to consider a reprisal. Their choice fell on a Captain Asgill, "a capitulation officer" from the surrender of Cornwallis. Washington was greatly concerned by the choice, writing Lincoln, Secretary of War, that an "unconditional prisoner" must be chosen.

The matter dragged on until in July Lady Asgill appealed to Marie Antoinette on her son's behalf, she to Vergennes, Vergennes to Washington, and Congress released Asgill.[1]

Meantime Washington's fears about Morris had died down and on August 7 he wrote him jocosely about Dalrymple's sailing home and sent his love to Kitty Livingston.

When Washington's letter was received Morris was writing his third letter, within the year, to Matthew Ridley in Paris.

Ridley, three years older than Morris, had come to America in 1770 and returned to England in '75. He had served on the Committee for the Relief of American Prisoners, gone to Nantes in the shipping business, revisited America and been sent back to France as agent for Maryland in November '81.

Morris wrote him first on December 3 asking him to send out "a very plain very good goldwatch and draw on me for the money." He implies that "the public letters to Doctor Franklin" would give Ridley something to keep him out of mischief in Paris.

In June a long, lighthearted letter followed. Ridley has told him Lafayette will bring out the watch and apparently said that his two young sons were averse to being kissed by French ladies.

[1] A further example of the extraordinary way in which all the actors in Morris's life-play appear and reappear is the fact that Genêt, then twenty years old, later to be so notorious as French minister to the United States in '94, was present at Lady Asgill's interview. The Queen was in bed "and appeared to me like a goddess," Genêt noted.

Morris, who had just written a profound and brilliant paper on the coinage system, replied to Ridley:

I am perfectly in opinion with the French ladies that however [the boys] may at present be disinclined to kissing, *cela viendra*. Should you in the absence of Mrs. Ridley meet some fair French woman so like her that when the accusing spirit is busy some cordial drop may obliterate the crime pray take pains to convince her that an aversion to kisses is not the endemic disease of America. Urge upon her this conviction with the fervor and enthusiasm of a man zealous to wash away a national aspersion. . . .

The letter goes on as to the political situation, pointing out that the war has enriched Spain "with a piece of Florida, Minorca and the Bahamas," thanks to the American Navy, and hopes that "the possession of a naval force" will be brought about without much difficulty.

It concludes with a line of romantic interest. Kitty Livingston, to whom Washington sent his love, "complains that you [Ridley] have said nothing."

A letter in August is very confident that the country, not having died young, "will grow up vigorous . . . though the Confederation has not given Congress sufficient authority . . . [still] Savannah is evacuated certainly, Charleston probably [and] Sir Guy Carleton [Sir H. Clinton's successor] is very polite. The several Assemblies passing high-toned resolutions."

The October letter says, "I presume you are perfectly domesticated *chez* Madame Jay and therefore I do not know how I can put into better hands the assurances of my love and esteem."

The last letter of the series encloses letters for each of the Ridley boys and asks to be presented "tho unknown to Mrs. Ridley who I hope has before this made you happy in her company."

In spite of Mrs. Ridley's presence he concludes, "I shewed the last clause of your letter to La Kitty but without urging at all your request. You sir may dare, I, you know am timid." Morris was evidently a gentleman who did not always kiss and tell.

As the letter was being written John Adams "went in search

of Ridley and found him. He lodges in Rue de Cléry 60." Adams had known him since '78 when in Paris. "Mr. Matthew Ridley of Maryland has made a present to the United States of a valuable manuscript upon Naval Affairs." Now both Jay and he found Ridley a valuable and well-informed adviser.

To the romantic, however, Ridley's appeal lies in the second marriage he was to make five years later.

The *Day Book* of the Finance Office provides a wonderful picture all year of the schemes of the great and greedy. Charles Thomson, secretary of Congress, Lincoln of the War Department and the two Morrises talked till 11 P.M. one May night with Thomas Fitzsimons, a director of the Bank of North America, who offered to supply money to all the prisoners in New York, if he was allowed to export tobacco. What lay back of it we do not know. "Assent refused," the *Day Book* says.

Rutledge and Livingston were called in but "Boudinot, the chairman not appearing we broke up."

Luzerne gave a great banquet to celebrate the birth of the Dauphin and the president and Council of Pennsylvania returned the honor. The Morrises went, getting back to the office at eight, to find that Congressmen Bland and Osgood, who disliked them, had been there at six, though "Lincoln was supposed to have told them" they would be delayed.

Then Robert Livingston came to see them, asking to be allowed to "collect the salaries of foreign ministers of Congress and remit to them after deducting his commission." This was too much even for his friends. Robert Morris said there should be no commission. The envoys should appoint their own agents of collection.

James Lovell came to question the amount of such salaries. Morris told him they should be paid quarterly in Philadelphia. "We cannot afford salaries sufficient to lay up fortunes but they should equal their expenses." They took advantage of the visit to get Lovell to agree that expresses should be hired to "bring remittances from the receivers of Continental taxes," and they told him of the increasing highway robbery of their riders.

One day after dealing with suppliers' bills, the outfitting of a schooner, the pay of a pilot, rations for enemy prisoners and the beginning of the semi-annual Investigation of Finances by Congress, they notified other bureaus they must "not let people in departments come to Robert or Gouverneur Morris for money."

The entry for June 24 reads, "Gouverneur Morris promised £2000 part cash part notes as absolutely necessary to keep Frasch furnace in blast for shot and shell." Livingston at Foreign Affairs told them Luzerne said his government said to pay no attention to the claims of Beaumarchais.

In July, Gouverneur Morris sent Knox a packet of "two weeks news papers for General Dalrymple. They are in consequence of an agreement we made at Elizabeth Town being a cartel of gazettes. He was to send out the New York papers. These we want for the use of the office and had in vain attempted to get through the commissioner of prisoners. He promised very fairly."

He wrote Knox further, "Our sovereign lords the Congress have at last assented to (not approved of) our conduct at Elizabeth Town. After the abusive letter of Sir H. Clinton it would have seemed . . . an approbation should have taken place." He encloses "copies of the accounts [of expenses] against the enemy."

They were hard pressed for money in August. Robert Morris had to ask William Bingham, "already a heavy creditor of the United States," for twenty thousand dollars on the twenty-eighth and "borrow $10000 on my own note from Holker as a standby."

The next day Arthur Lee, Osgood and Clarkson came around from Congress as an Investigating Committee. Of course such inquiries and checks on executive departments are an essential safeguard of democratic government. Still it is wonderful to see the day's operations stop, as the small staff is pulled off their work to give the committee "a complete statement of all money received and spent since the establishment of the office."

Why should there be a Continental receiver of taxes in each state? "Showed them the Act of Congress November 3, 1781." Why were the loan officers not used? How wise the Morrises had been to name Lovell a receiver. They explained to the committee: not all loan officers were fit to be receivers; if people paid taxes, for current expenditures, they would demand a deduction for interest due on Loan Certificates; in accounting you cannot properly commingle. "Tummults and revolts" would follow.

It has been remarked before that all the patriot elite not only knew each other but often were engaged in the same ventures.

Jeremiah Wadsworth had been commissary general of purchases for the Continental Army and later Rochambeau's. He would go to France in '83 to make his accounting on the latter post and do some profitable trading afterwards on his own in France. He was one of the founders of the Bank of North America.

He now wrote to Gouverneur from Hartford, Connecticut. Congress had apparently asked some questions about Robert Morris. The letter was a month on the way and appeared to have been opened.

If the orders from the Board of Treasury are designed to injure Mr. Morris, Gouverneur replied, "they will be disappointed. The notes will be paid and that they know full well. Such [personal] paper as he choses to circulate will be readily accepted by most people to whom it may be convenient because they believe in the value. So does the Board."

Then he adds, "Constable will correspond with you about the L'Orient Plan. . . . I am persuaded . . . that we are rendered almost certain of success." In mercantile ventures with Constable, Wadsworth, like him and Morris, acquired enormous wild lands in the Genesee Valley. His sixteen-year-old daughter Harriet was then in love with John Trumbull, the painter, four years Morris's junior.

The ripples run out and out. In '87, Morris delays writing Henry Knox until he sees Wadsworth. He writes later to Knox via Constable. From London four years later William Knox writes his brother Henry that Gouverneur has sold the McComb-Robert Morris lands in the Genesee, though Henry Knox had authorized William to sell his part.

Henry Knox writes to Colonel Smith, John Adams's son-in-law, to offer his St. Lawrence lands. "Governor Clinton can in-

form you of the lands 42000 acres." Gouverneur Morris's sale of
the Genesee lands at a crown an acre should make the St.
Lawrence very desirable.

The limitations of the best of men were described at the time
by Franklin. He said John Adams "means well for his country,
is always an honest man, often a wise one, but sometimes, and
in some things, absolutely out of his senses."

CHAPTER NINE

I Found He Meant G— M—

(1783–86)

T HERE WERE two other callers at the Finance Office in January 1783 who came on very different business.

In Paris, Franklin, Jay and Adams had signed the peace with Britain without consulting Vergennes, the French Foreign Minister. This was what Gouverneur Morris had hoped they would do but what Congress had expressly forbidden. Vergennes, when he was told, said they had "not been particularly civil to the King."

Now Franklin was coming home and Jefferson going out as minister. January 23 he came to be briefed on finances by Robert Morris. It was probably the first and only time until 1789 that he and Gouverneur Morris met.

More ominous at the time was the visit of General Mc-Dougall from Newburgh. There the army, now disciplined, fed and clothed, was unpaid and "the distresses" were very grave.

The best the Morrises could tell McDougall was that Congress had made "no settlements secured by competent funds" and the most they could do was one month's pay and it at the rate of half a dollar a week. Soldiers and non-commissioned officers would get cash and officers sixty-day notes.

Hamilton was in Congress and McDougall talked to him

and Madison, and then to Rutledge and Richard Henry Lee.

The small country had its independence but was without national credit, funds or policy—without a strong central government and with men like Sam Adams and Patrick Henry, who had taken a mighty part in separation, dubious of the wisdom of ever having one.

The army in general favored such a government if only to deal effectively with its grievances. Knowledge of what armies can do against a civil authority, from the Roman legions to Cromwell's Ironsides, was in the minds of all these well-read men. Madison wrote that there was "a peculiar awe and solemnity, and distress" in the air affecting them all.

General Greene, commanding in the South, wrote, "Plain dealing will soon become necessary . . . there is an awful suspense in the air. It is feared Robert Morris will resign."

General Knox at West Point wrote Morris his often-quoted letter of February 21 that the favorite toast of the army is "a Hoop to the Barrel or Cement to the Union." The letter came in the military bag to Lincoln at the War Department.

While it was en route, Rutledge and Mercer had moved in Congress that debts due the army should be the first charge on the proposed tariff. The discrimination was voted down with only Rutledge's state, South Carolina, where Greene's army was restless, supporting it. On February 25, Congress in desperation referred the problem to the individual states.

Gouverneur Morris had foreseen this ten days before and warned Greene that if the army made the mistake of appealing to the several states it would divide the army into thirteen parts. He advised both Knox and Greene that there would be no general debt assumption by the Confederation "unless the army be united and determined in the pursuit of it and unless they be firmly supported and as firmly support the other public creditors."

The question is whether Morris meant by this that a coup d'état by the army was the only solution. Were he and Hamilton, as a modern writer asserts, in favor of a Fascist march on Philadelphia?

If so, his letter of February 28 to Knox, two weeks before the denouement, is remarkably mild.

> . . . The same person who takes this letter will deliver to the general [Washington] copies of the Letters containing Mr. R. Morris's resignation. . . . I have three months more of hopeless slavery to encounter in this office. . . . It is hardly to be conceived what instruments there are here to work with. It is not in them to conceive great nor to pursue just ideas. Nature sparing in good gifts has been prodigal of littleness to them . . .

Then on March 12 two anonymous papers, called the Newburgh Addresses, were published, exhorting the officers of the army to compel Congress to do them justice. If their demands were not met "the army will resist disbandment to the death."

Washington, deeply shocked, sent the Addresses to Congress. To Hamilton he wrote: "to Mr. Gouverneur Morris is ascribed in a great degree the ground work of the superstructure which was intended to be raised in the army by the Anonymous Addresses."

At that moment Major John Armstrong, twenty-five, an aide to General Gates, came forward in manly fashion to say the Addresses were entirely his creation and in his words. Armstrong was later to sit as a senator from New York with Morris and, like him, to be a minister to France and we shall hear of another strange outburst of his in 1803.

His general, Gates, to his credit stood by Washington, who addressed the officers at Newburgh. When he was done they all subscribed to an Address to Washington saying that, while their grievances were great and just "the officers of the American Army view with abhorrence and reject with disdain the infamous proposals contained in a late anonymous address to the officers and resent with indignation the secret attempts of some unknown person to collect the officers together in a manner totally subversive of all discipline and good order."

Hatch, who has perhaps made the deepest study of the matter, believes that Morris favored a peaceful coup d'état, but that the scheme was "too violent for a person of orderly and conventional instincts like Morris." He is also inclined to feel that Hamilton was "willing to threaten what he thought it unsafe to attempt." But in all events, he concludes, "the utter collapse of national authority was making men desperate."

Possibly it was all a *ballon d'essai* and the end result was good. As to Morris's actual complicity, it seems most unlikely that it went further than believing some goad to action was necessary. Complicity would be contrary to his whole record, and apparently his record on important issues was consistent, except for one incredible shift in London, 1790. Finally it does not appear to have affected Washington's regard for him, as would likely have been the case if he was author or coadjutor.

There is one other circumstance which may bear on this, although whether for or against his complicity who can say?

Plans for the Society of the Cincinnati, the officers of Washington's army, with its hereditary, primogeniture laws, were shortly under way at Annapolis. There were a great number of honorary memberships, even to Franklin, who, though opposed to it like Jefferson, had accepted. Robert Morris, R. R. Livingston, James Duane, William Duer and John Dickinson, John Lansing and John Church, Schuyler's English son-in-law, were all shortly honorary members. Morris was not for twenty years, a fact to which he made pointed reference on several later occasions.

The society in its inception represented much that he most deeply believed in. Washington, Hamilton and Knox were his close friends, to say nothing of the honorary members. Who of any of them would not have wanted him in that inner circle from the start? His main adversaries except Monroe, or Gates, were outside of it. Could his omission have had to do with Newburgh? Or with the disclosure in Colonel Pierce's *Diary* at the Constitutional Convention? Or with what?

At the beginning of June he left the Finance Office and went back to "scoured" Morrisania where his mother's claims against the British for its use amounted to eight thousand pounds. There was twenty-year-old Cape wine still in the cellars and doubtless he raised the riot which he had once told Livingston he would do, when it was all over.

There is a Livingston letter to him from Clermont of August 15. It is exasperating that it should be the only one with some words elided. Perhaps if it were clear we should know more about Mrs. Plater.

> Is your friend . . . really dead or has he revived in pity to you. He must certainly know . . . his death by . . . the sin would lessen your pleasure in loving his wife. I will ask no more questions about my fair friend.

He was back in Philadelphia by January of 1784. Reaction to the long war had affected the country and the paradox of war prosperity and full employment produced a "luxury" whose ill fame disturbed Jay in Paris. Morris wrote him lightly not to grieve about it. "It is not so bad a thing as it is supposed to be." It is in this letter that he said:

> A national spirit is the natural result of national existence, and although some of the present generation may feel colonial opposition of opinion, yet this generation will die away and give place to a race of Americans.

Still, as Hamilton wrote Morris, "We are doing those things which we ought not to do. Instead of wholesome regulations for the improvement of our polity and commerce we are labouring to contrive methods to mortify and punish Tories and to explain away treaties."

The collapse of "prosperity" came by March, when there was a run on the Bank of North America and, with ominous warning of what was to come, bills of Robert Morris to a total of sixty thousand pounds went to protest.

Samuel Osgood wrote Elbridge Gerry that he was "disgusted with everything" and that Van Boeckell, the Dutch minister, "has a good opinion of R— M— but says he has very bad councillors. I found he meant G— M—. He has the same sentiments of him as I have." How much in keeping with later events it is that Osgood, who was to be a father-in-law of Genêt, Morris's adversary years later, should think badly of G— M—. And that, the week of Osgood's letter, Hamilton should write to ask Morris the "best mode of receiving and paying out gold" in a bank. And that Marbois, in spite of what Adams had told him, should ask his views "on the commerce between the United States and the French Islands."

To the latter went a particularly brilliant, farseeing reply on the importance of a low cost of living to the natives, if export— or import—trade was to flourish, and of as free a trade as possible in American vessels as a means, not of draining supplies from Europe, but by its very turnover creating an exportable surplus for the Continent.

In December that year De Chastellux wrote Morris that the paper had been read by the French Minister of Marine, who said, "and repeated it several times, that he had seen nothing superior or more full of powerful thought, on the subject of government and politics." That De Castries had given it to many friends to read so that "I have been congratulated on having such a friend in another hemisphere."

In July, John Jay came from France to succeed Livingston as Secretary of Foreign Affairs for Congress and Jefferson after a long delay went out as minister. Matthew Ridley came home that summer, doubtless on the same ship with the Jays. One may believe Morris drove La Kitty to the dock to meet them.

Morris had not finally decided what he was going to do. Even in September he was "not yet clear of the Office of Finance" and wrote Livingston: "whether I shall go extensively into the practice of law must depend on circumstances."

One thing he did do to his eternal glory. With Jay, he founded the New York Manumission Society for the abolition of slavery, with Aaron Burr, for once on the side of the angels, moving for immediate emancipation. It is pleasant to note that William Livingston, now sixty-two, came up to join the abolitionists.

The society was more than a propaganda or missionary agency. It performed definite services for slaves.

A man wrote William Edgar, now established in New York:

I have sold my negro boy [who] is to be set free when he arrives to the age of 25 years, September 29, 1804. Please either keep the agreement [to that effect] or lodge it with the Society for the Abolition of Slavery.

It is wonderful to see how much these New York aristocrats, disliking the mob, felt for the enslaved and oppressed. Hamil-

ton defended the Tory, Waddington, against what he felt was
an unjust suit under the wartime Trespass Act.

There is a letter from Morris to Livingston from Williamsburg, Virginia, in April '85. It says Livingston's letter "found
me engaged in a tedious, disagreeable business which I can't
foresee the end of. This circumstance precludes me from accepting your appointment (though I am grateful to you and
your colleagues for the honor). . . . I much regret that necessity which withholds from my fellow citizens the feeble aid of
an old servant."

Livingston's offer was probably to the New York-Massachu-
setts Boundary Commission of which Jay, Duane and he were
members. Morris doubtless felt he must devote himself to his
private affairs if he was to acquire the fortune he wanted. On
his mother's death Morrisania would go to his half-brother,
General Staats Morris, in England, and if Gouverneur wanted
it, a good deal of cash would be required.

Robert Morris had weathered the protests of the previous
year and secured an exclusive contract for 60,000 hogsheads
of tobacco from the French monopoly, the Farmers-General.
He had additional world-wide ventures and, like all who could,
was speculating in lands to the west and north. In much of this
Gouverneur Morris was closely associated, though particularly
at the time in the tobacco contract.

He evidently felt that it and the other ventures had a good
chance of success, but he had also seen enough of Robert
Morris's methods to have reservations. Robert Morris was now
fifty-one and probably "a financial wizard" to all but the friends
and foes of the inner circle who knew how far he carried optimism and opportunism. It is interesting to note that John
Adams thought very well of Robert Morris. He was, Adams
said, "of masterly understanding, an open temper and an honest
heart. He has vast designs in a mercantile way . . . but he is
an excellent member of our body."

The buoyant and often reckless qualities which made him so
valuable to his country made him a bad business partner. To
say that a man has a shrewd and calculating business sense has
become derogatory, but Gouverneur Morris must stand up

under it. Although closely associated with Robert Morris, his own capital and his day-by-day business were with the firm of William Constable and Company in New York.

The tobacco contract took the Morrises frequently to Virginia and Washington's *Diary* indicates the pleasure it gave him to have them both stay at Mount Vernon on their way.

Late in April Washington decided to sit for a portrait by the painter Robert Pine, on Gouverneur's recommendation. That week in Paris Adélaide, Countess de Flahaut, was delivered of a son, Auguste Charles Joseph, who was to have a long and incredibly theatrical life. His father was not his young mother's husband, but a priest, aged thirty-one, two years younger than Morris, whose name was Charles Maurice de Talleyrand-Périgord.

It was that spring that Gouverneur addressed the Assembly of Pennsylvania on their resolution to abolish the Bank of North America. Of all his speeches and writings, the twenty-nine pages of it quoted in Sparks are those which his biographers would most like to quote in full for its wisdom and its wit. To speak 10,000 words on the theory of money and banking and make it fascinating to a layman is a rare achievement.

Of course the target was made to order. The objections to the bank included such assertions as "that it enables men to trade to their utter ruin by giving them the temporary use of credit and money; that the punctuality required at the bank throws honest men into the hands of usurers; that the great dividend on bankstock induces monied men to buy stock rather than lend on interest . . . and tenthly that it is destructive of that equality which ought to take place in a free country."

On the first point, after examining it thoroughly, Morris said "it would be a marvelous thing indeed, if the use of water were prohibited, because some people chose to drown themselves." On the last point he asks "whether by equality is meant equality of property, or equality of rights. If it be the former then it may perhaps be doubtful whether the opposers of the bank would themselves agree to an equality, that is to say, a general division of property among all the citizens of Pennsylvania." If it is rights, any man is free to buy bank stock or a farm and he can buy stock for less than a freehold. "Neither ought to grumble at the right or possession of the other."

But, he says, what is most likely the objectors mean is, "under a plausible cry raised about equal rights, to cover the dictates of envy at superior fortune and success in the world."

Between his brilliant shots is a patient and penetrating explanation of the use of money and credit in building the industry of a new country.

On January 14, 1786, Mrs. Morris died at Morrisania in her seventy-third year. It is hard to know how her son, who revealed so much and yet so little of himself, felt. He bought Morrisania from his half-brother, the British general, and ultimately, like Jefferson, he fell in love with his house, that relationship so often more dangerous than love of women.

CHAPTER TEN

All the States
and Colonel Hamilton, Ay!

(*1787*)

A DELEGATE to a national political convention rises with proud provincialism to cast the vote of his *sovereign state*.

In 1787 the individual states were equal and sovereign indeed. Nine of them had their own navies. New Jersey had its customs service and Virginia had separately ratified the treaty with England. They were bound together by the Articles of Confederation, "a mere compact resting on the good faith of the parties," as Morris had said. Under it each state had one vote, and those of nine states were required for any major decision. In the Continental Congress the states voted as a unit, so that all the votes of dissenting minorities within a delegation were lost.

In February 1787, Congress adopted the resolution to call a convention whose sole and express purpose should be the *reporting* of the revisions in the Articles of Confederation necessary to "render the Federal Constitution adequate to the exigencies of the Government and the preservation of the Union."

At the height of the war sectional jealousies had, even under the impetus of self-preservation, almost brought defeat or dissolution to the cause. The wartime state legislatures and governors had had great power which they would not readily

HUNT LIBRARY
CARNEGIE-MELLON UNIVERSITY
PITTSBURGH, PENNSYLVANIA 15213

surrender to a federal government, as Washington from retirement at Mount Vernon wrote Knox.

The problem of how men can be governed yet left with their liberty was enormous and precedents were fewer than today. England since 1688 had achieved internally a reasonable success, but there were too many bitter memories in this country to permit copying her constitution, even without a king, much as men like Washington, Adams, Jay, Hamilton and Morris admired it. The British parliamentary system had long presented a spectacle of corruption and improper enrichment and its recent leaders, with notable exceptions, had been degraded or stupid men like Sandwich, Grafton, North and Germain. Only with the defeat in America had the ministry ceased to be the personal government of the King.

The fact was, as Morris said later, "it shows the boldness of the experiment in which we were engaged that we were forced to take all other nations, whether dead or living, as warnings not examples."

In writing the Declaration, Americans had been concerned with great ideas. Now they must be concerned with methods of implementing the ideas and of unifying thirteen states of differing interests, wealth, culture and products.

Montesquieu's *Spirit of the Laws*, with its elaborate, though not wholly novel, system of checks and balances was as much of a guide as there was.

The convention was to meet in Philadelphia in May and many of the great names of 1774–75 would be missing. Jefferson was in France as minister, John Adams in London, Patrick Henry was opposed to the convention, Samuel Adams was not a delegate and Tom Paine, perhaps fortunately, was in Europe. John Jay's nomination had not been confirmed by the New York Senate.

Morris was in Trenton, very early in January, when to his surprise he learned that Pennsylvania had "appointed [him] commissioner for the convention in May. Had the object been any other than it is I would have declined. The appointment [by Pennsylvania, where he was disliked] was the most unexpected thing that ever happened to me." The delegation was a strong one including four Signers, Franklin, then eighty-one, Robert Morris, James Wilson and George Clymer.

It was not certain that Washington would go as a delegate, though the Cincinnati were meeting in Philadelphia and it was hoped that would bring him. Colonel Humphreys wrote him: "Gouverneur Morris and some others have wished me to use whatever influence I might have to induce you to come."

He came and, unanimously chosen to preside, did so without participating in the debates but by his balance of mind, his superiority to sectional feeling—both qualities so equally characteristic of Franklin—held the fifty-five men together through the hot summer until thirty-nine signed a Constitution which Morris, speaking not for himself alone, said he would take with all its faults "as the best that was to be attained."

Here the great business of government must pause for an event in which surely all right-minded readers will rejoice.

Early in March, William Livingston, still governor of New Jersey, wrote his often-quoted letter in which he said his principal Secretary of State, "my daughter, Kitty," was off to New York "to kick up her heels at the balls and assemblies of a metropolis."

It is startling to realize, particularly in the eighteenth century, that La Kitty, the darling of them all, was now a spinster of thirty-six. What can have ailed the gallants of Washington's army?

In any event the English-born Mr. Matthew Ridley, now a widower, for whom Morris had been a go-between, was married to Kitty on the fourteenth of April in the Jays' house in New York. Unhappily there was no issue of the marriage and Ridley dies in '89, aged forty.

The Federal Convention opened on May 25. Three things were done the first day conducive to clear thinking and the frank expression of opinion with the right to change it.

Loose earth was spread in front of the State House to deaden the noise of passing traffic. A rule of secrecy, objected to by no one, was adopted. Nothing spoken in the house was to be "printed or otherwise published or communicated" without permission. "It was essential," Madison said, "to let uncertain men change their minds . . . much is to be gained by a yielding and accommodating spirit [so that men may be] open to the force of argument."

Finally these freedom-loving men subjected themselves to the following tyranny,

Every member rising to speak shall address the President and whilst he shall speak none shall pass between them *or hold discourse with another, or read a book, pamphlet, or paper, printed or manuscript.*

Colonel William Pierce from Georgia, an officer of Washington's army, wrote his impressions of all his fellow delegates in his *Diary:* "Madison, with his spirit of industry and application . . . always the best informed man on any point in debate . . . easy and unreserved." (De Warville said he had an air of fatigue and a censorious look.) Hamilton, "his language didactic like Bolingbroke [but again] as light and tripping as Sterne's, of small stature and lean. His manner tinctured with stiffness and sometimes with a degree of vanity." Corpulent James McHenry, the "dear Mac" of Hamilton's wartime letters; Gunning Bedford, "32, bold, nervous, very corpulent"; Dickinson, fifty-five, a Quaker "with an affected air of wisdom he labors to produce a trifle. His language irregular and incorrect, his flourishes like expiring flames"; Rufus King, Morris's close friend, "five feet ten, well-formed, handsome, with a sweet, high-toned voice. A luminary of the present age"; Daniel of St. Thomas Jenifer, "from his long continuance in single life no doubt but he has made the vow of celibacy. He speaks warmly of the ladies notwithstanding." He was sixty-four; Charles Pinckney, "twenty-four [thirty], neat and perspicacious"; Roger Sherman, sixty-six, "who was a shoemaker in early life and now on the Connecticut bench." And then he comes to a long entry about Gouverneur Morris:

He is one of those geniuses in whom every species of talent combine to render him conspicuous and flowing in public debate. He winds through all the mazes of rhetoric and throws round him such a glare that he charms, captivates and leads away the senses of all who hear him. With an infinite stretch of fancy he brings to view things, when he is engaged in deep argumentation that render all the labor of reasoning easy and pleasing.

Then, perhaps thinking he had been too impressed, he says, ". . . but he is fickle and inconstant, never pursuing one train of thinking nor ever regular." He adds that Morris "is engaged in some great mercantile matters with his namesake, R.M.," and finally tells us something about Morris, nowhere else recorded, which throws new light on his war record, possibly his absence from Masonry, and on other events of a different sort in France.

"He was unfortunate in losing one of his legs and *getting all the flesh taken off his right arm by a scalding when a youth.*"

This, at last, would seem to make clear why, with his youth and strength, Morris was not in the army and what he meant when he wrote his half-brother of his offer of services "you well know . . ."

The French Legation's observer wrote his government:

Gouverneur Morris; avocat célèbre; une des têtes les mieux organisées du continent, mais sans moeurs, et, si l'on en croit sans principes; infiniment intéressant dans ce conversation et ayant étudié avec un soin particulier la partie des finances. . . . On le craint encore plus ne l'admire mais peu de gens l'estiment.

In general the conflicting concepts of the delegates had to do with maintenance of the equal sovereignties of the thirteen states against a strong central government. State attachments and state importance, Morris said, have been the bane of this country. We cannot annihilate it but we can perhaps take out the teeth of the serpent (the jealousy of the states). "When the Confederation was formed," he went on, "the small states aware of the necessity of preventing anarchy, and taking advantage of the moment, extorted from large states an equality of votes." Did, he asked, small states honestly think that preservation of their suddenly precious rights would result in an effective form of government?

It was doubtless this art of biting phrasemaking such as "their suddenly precious rights" which contributed to Morris's unpopularity.

The small state of Rhode Island felt so strongly about her precious rights that she had not sent any delegates. Bedford, of Delaware, said a central government was an attempt of the big states to aggrandize at the expense of the small and that if the Confederation were dissolved in favor of a national government "the small states [would] find some foreign ally."

Yates and Lansing of New York, then fifth in population, abruptly quit the convention, leaving Hamilton alone and hence without a vote, because they were opposed to any new form of government. They said they had been appointed to revise the Articles of Confederation, not to draw up a new constitution. They went home like the militia some of their relatives commanded, saying they feared "sovereignty, oppression and expense"![1]

Morris, very strong for a national government, said that two supremes were inconceivable. State and federal governments could not both be supreme. Then he said contemptuously that they had not "assembled to truck and bargain for one particular state. This country must be united. If persuasion doesn't do it, the sword will." He made it clear, however, that he meant an outside sword or a tyrant's sword armed against them all, and in that wonderful spirit of accommodation and mutual respect which underlay all the bitter differences of opinion, Bedford and he apologized to each other for the threats with which they had spoken. Morris in his flowery, cocky way added that in addition to representing America he at least had come "in some degree as a representative of the whole human race."

Then came the question of how the executive and the Congress were to be chosen, granted that by some miracle the states could find a formula for equal sovereignty among themselves.

[1] Who could have foreseen that day that only Yates of the New York delegation would die a normal death?

In June 1831, when Jared Sparks was gathering information for his biography of Gouverneur Morris, Madison wrote him with an older man's normal pride, "I am the only living Signer [of the Constitution] since the death of Mr. Lansing who disappeared so mysteriously not long ago."

On a December morning in 1829, John Lansing, then seventy-five years old, left his hotel in New York at 9 P.M. to post some letters on the Albany boat at the foot of Cortlandt Street. He never returned and was never seen again. It was believed that he had been murdered. He had been a delegate to the Continental Congress, the Constitutional Convention and mayor of Albany. His disappearance and death are still a mystery.

Yates died normally in 1801, aged sixty-three, and Hamilton at Burr's hands in 1804.

There was wide agreement among these men that the blessings of liberty and independence would be lost if people were unconditionally allowed to vote.

Madison himself, the protégé of Jefferson, said the people were "subject to transient impressions." As the population increased "power will slide into the hands [of those who are under hardships] and [they will] vote for levelling."

Roger Sherman, a lifelong adversary of Morris, said the people lack information and are likely to be misled. Elbridge Gerry of Massachusetts, who was to sit in the first House of Representatives and be Vice-President under Madison, said, "The evils we experience flow from the excess of democracy." Hamilton put his views mildly for him in saying, "The people seldom judge or determine right."

Morris added that "people never act from reason alone. [They] are the dupes of those who have more knowledge."

Such was the confidence of the founders in "the people." But this did not mean they lacked any confidence in the ultimate greatness of their country or in the imperative rights of all men to life, liberty and the pursuit of happiness.

Yet there is a danger that these quotations, except in the case of Hamilton, do not fairly state the beliefs of these men, so subtle are the words "liberty" and "democracy." Madison, for example, said in discussing the manner of choosing the executive that he preferred "an election by the people, or rather by the qualified part of them at large. With all its imperfections, he liked this best." Sherman and Gerry favored an annual election to the House "because [they thought] representatives ought to return home and mix with the people." Madison, on the other hand, felt a congressional term of three years essential to acquire a national point of view.

None of them, however, shared Hamilton's extreme view that there should be a Senate limited to the landed gentry, serving for life, with a president, for whose election to a life term the poor had no vote, and that he should appoint the state governors.

Inextricably tangled in all these preliminary conflicts was the question of slavery.

A Southern proposal that the Senate be proportional to the state's wealth was supported by Morris, until he suddenly realized that slaves would be claimed by the South as wealth.

Whatever the limitations of his many prejudices, there is no question of the consuming moral hatred he felt for slavery. It was the curse of heaven, he said, on the states where it prevailed. Compare the free regime of the middle states where a rich and noble culture marks the prosperity and happiness of the people with the misery and poverty which overspreads the barren wastes of Virginia and other states having slaves. And he spoke in his most damning way of "the inhabitant of Georgia or South Carolina who goes to the coast of Africa and in defiance of the most sacred laws of humanity tears away his fellow creatures from their dearest connections and damns them to the most cruel bondages."

Abraham Lincoln remembered the speech when he was speaking at Cooper Union seventy-three years later, but John Rutledge of South Carolina, listening to it at the time, simply replied that "religion and humanity have nothing to do with the question."

Butler of South Carolina, with a premonition of the future, said that "the security the Southern states want is that their Negroes may not be taken from them which some gentlemen within or without these doors have a very good mind to do."

But those most opposed to slavery were wisely unwilling to divide the country further at that time. With Morris leading them, however, they refused the Southern states representation for all their Negroes—discouraging thereby the slave trade —and the vote went 6–4 against the South, with Georgia and South Carolina then threatening to go home.

Less noble and more insular fears disturbed Morris and other Northerners about the South. They were afraid of a push toward the Spanish settlements and the mouth of the Mississippi. Sixteen years later, against his own party, Morris supported Jefferson in the Louisiana Purchase, and told his fellow Federalists that the problems of government there were neither insoluble nor incompatible with American ideals. But in 1787 he saw that what his country most needed was such peace and stability as Walpole had given England after the Marlborough wars. Actually, as with Walpole's England, America did not have to fight for twenty-five years, to her inestimable advantage.

The fears Morris felt about the Northwest Territory were less justified. He seems to have been curiously blind to the greatness of our trans-Allegheny destiny until after his return from Europe in 1799.

He did not want the new states of the Ordinance of 1787 to come in, and to the Constitutional Convention he put his objections in rather silly terms for him. He said, among other things, that "the Western states will not be able to furnish men equally enlightened to share in the administration of our common interests. The busy haunts of men, not the remote wilderness are the proper school of political talents."

Madison, looking up from his privileged notes, said, "Apparently the gentleman determines the human character by the points of the compass."

The convention first heard Edmund Randolph propose the Virginia Plan for a Constitution. It was profound and powerful, largely the work of Madison, and proposed to do away entirely with the Confederation, putting a national government in its stead. This was far beyond what many delegates were prepared for.

It contained provisions, such as a triumvirate presidency, which discussion at once showed to be impracticable but opposition to it arose most violently over the clause giving Congress a veto of all laws passed by individual states. If this were done, Delaware said, she would withdraw and the other small states agreed with her.

"By the tact of Madison and Gouverneur Morris," as the historian John Fiske wrote, "the question was postponed." The debate gave the delegates an opportunity, for the first time on a national basis, to gauge the force and extent of their colleagues' views. Even so the opening weeks of the convention were not encouraging. Attendance was sporadic and Morris himself was absent during the last three weeks of June. It is interesting to realize that in this interval, far away in Switzerland, Edward Gibbon finished *The Decline and Fall* on a night when "the sky was clear and moonlight glittered across the lake." Morris returned on July 2 to find the delegates exhausted by the terrible heat and their apparently irreconcilable views, and an adjournment was taken until the fifth.

The impasse arose from the primary question of how the states were to remain equal and sovereign in the delegation of their powers to a central government. In general a Congress composed of Senate and House had been accepted but as to how and by whom and in what numbers they were to be elected there seemed no acceptable answer.

The delegates knew that, whatever they might want, their proceedings had to be ratified by the states and ultimately accepted by the people in whom so many had so little confidence, and they were not men to court an ultimate rejection. As Morris wrote twenty-four years later, "They did not sink into despondence because they could not form nor establish the best of all possible systems," and they were endowed, as surely few groups of men have been, not only with patriotism but with an amazing good sense that let them endlessly explore, adjust and compromise the extremity of their views.

Roger Sherman of Connecticut had earlier proposed a Senate of equal members for each state and a House based on proportional representation but the motion had not found a seconder.

On July 5, when they returned, Elbridge Gerry suggested the same compromise with a representative for every 40,000 people, counting three fifths of the slaves.

Morris, in general support of it, pointed out the practical lack of a census and suggested as a basis the use of the estimates of 1774, and his committee came up with a plan for an original House of 56 members. The plan went to a larger committee who changed it to 65 and Madison, dissenting from his fellow committeemen, proposed to double it, saying, "The majority of a quorum of 65 is too small to represent the whole United States." The motion was lost on the tenth.

Six days of terrible heat followed. A motion to adjourn *sine die* hung over the convention. Then something happened which was possible only in America. Out of the West came a cool wave, blowing the heat and humidity out of Philadelphia, leaving the sky blue and clear with elixir in the air.[2]

On the sixteenth, in a surge of energy and acumen, they adopted the great compromise of an equal Senate, a proportional House with money bills to originate in the House, and the small states, sure of an equal voice in the upper chamber, dropped their opposition to a strong national government. "Give New Jersey," one said, "an equal vote and she will dismiss her scruples."

Vexing and difficult as all the rest was, it was in effect only a problem of manageable detail. The cornerstone was laid and the principal building was up and the technical equipment could be installed.

In the relief and excitement that followed, it is wonderful to note that the original rule of secrecy was not forgotten by these prudent men. There were no leaks and Madison, writing to his close friend Jefferson in Paris the next day, did not even mention the vote.

There was quick agreement on many of the powers to be delegated to the national government, both express and implied.

The unit rule for state votes in the Continental Congress was swept away unanimously, leaving each senator and representative free to vote in his own name.

By July 26 so much progress had been made that a ten-day adjournment was taken to allow a committee as widely distributed geographically as possible to co-ordinate what had been done. Its members were Gorham (Mass.), Ellsworth (Conn.), Randolph (Va.), Rutledge (S. C.), and Wilson (Pa.).

They all knew the end was in sight and Washington gave Peale some time to paint his portrait. On the thirtieth comes the entry in Washington's *Diary* so delightful in its implications to those interested in Gouverneur Morris.

[2]In his years of study of the effects of climate on civilization Ellsworth Huntington concluded that the monotony of climate was the worst brake on progress and variability the greatest impetus. Certainly Americans, with their savage summers, are particularly responsive to the tonic west wind that can blow in, dropping the temperature twenty degrees in an hour and making us all feel like kings going forth to battle. So far as I know, Huntington missed this great example of his theory.

Both Morris and he were living in the house of Robert Morris,
at Lemon Hill (now in Fairmont Park). It is quite possible, of
course, that their mere propinquity brought about the day that
followed. Whatever the reason—and almost certainly it was
the pleasure each had in the other's company—Washington
"went with Gouverneur Morris in his phaeton, my horses, to
Valley Forge to get trout. . . ."

How familiar the desire to revisit the great scene of the past
and what reminiscence it must have provoked as they drove
along the road out which Howe had rushed the grenadiers in
'77 when only the fog saved his army. Up the road the Continentals had come in, only to go back with a victory missed by
the narrowest of margins. On out the pike where Howe had
gone in the winter of '78 to look hopelessly at what he mistak-
enly thought was the stronghold of Valley Forge and to turn
back.

And then at Valley Forge itself "while Morris was fishing
[Washington] rid over the old cantonment of the American
Army of the winter of 1777 and 8, visited all the works which
were in ruins."

The day was evidently a success as on August 3 they went
fishing "not very successfully" for perch in the Delaware at
Trenton.

There was twenty years' difference in their ages. Washington
was then fifty-five. Aside from all bonds of patriotism and
public service, one of the things which most strongly bound
them together was the passion of the eighteenth-century gentleman—so conspicuous in the English aristocracy, so almost generally absent in the French—for country life and its pleasures.
The land, the air, "a view," the goodness of the soil, of crops,
the betterment of flocks and herds, these were the things they
wanted to get back to when they had settled the affairs of men
and, in Morris's case, of certain ladies.

On August 6 the convention reconvened. The weather was
warm again but it mattered less. There were only five weeks
to go, five weeks with five to six hours a day of debate. During
them Morris was at his most voluble. He made altogether 173
speeches, the most of them all, except Madison. Measures he

supported were not all accepted. He said many unwise and prejudiced things but that he gave a ferment to it all there can be no doubt and as Madison wrote:

It is but due to Mr. Morris to remark that to the brilliance of his genius he added, what is too rare, a candid surrender of his opinion when the lights of discussion satisfied him that they had been too hastily formed and a readiness to aid in making the best of measures in which he had been overruled.

The final debates ran from August 6 to September 8. Morris's bankbook for this period is in existence. On the sixteenth he paid $3.60 for "political enquiries." The debate the day before had had to do with the question of money bills originating in the House which Morris opposed as "unnecessary and inconvenient." On the business coming up the next day he was trying to get a three-quarters vote in the Senate to repeal laws vetoed by the President. There was also a check to Dolly for $13.69. The last check in the book is to Dolly for $234.54, but she may have been his laundress or landlady.

There is of course an enormous literature, primary and secondary, on these days, and in citing here only the views of Morris it is not intended to suggest that they were the most important or the most accepted. But it is with him we are concerned.

It is interesting to note that while Morris opposed universal suffrage he was even more strongly opposed to the plan to have the President selected by Congress. The President must not be "the flunkey of Congress. It must not be able to say to him you owe your appointment to us."

Between the extremes of popular as against congressional selection, James Wilson (Pa.) brought forward the electoral college formula, and Morris supported it and was on the committee for its drafting.

He saw "the one great object of the executive [as the] control of the legislature. [The President] should be the guardian of the people, even," he added, "of the lower classes against legislative tyranny."

On the question of the tenure of the presidency the convention was greatly divided—for one term, for two, for a life term,

or to ineligibility after one. In this connection it has often been
remarked that the convention gave no thought to the existence
or effect of political parties. Morris, however, said early on,
"Some leader of a party will always covet [the President's]
seat, will perplex his Administration, will cabal with his legislature, till he succeeds in supplanting him." Morris favored
re-eligibility and two long terms, the second as a reward for
good behavior. On this he won, though the first draft provided
congressional election for seven years only. "We are acting a
very strange part," Morris said; "we first form a strong man to
protect us and at the same time wish to tie his hands behind
him."

There was much debate on the treaty-making powers of the
Senate, so at issue as this book is written, almost one hundred
and sixty-five years later. It was proposed, as late as August 22,
that "the Senate of the United States shall have powers to make
treaties and to appoint Ambassadors and Judges of the Supreme Court."

Madison rose at once to say that "as the Senate represents
states alone, for this as well as other reasons it is proper that
the President should be the agent in treaties."

"Mr. Morris," the record of the *Debates* continues, "did not
know that he should agree to refer the making of treaties to the
Senate at all but for the present would now be willing to add,
'but no treaty shall be binding on the United States which is
not ratified by law.' "

How far Madison looked across the years when "he suggested the inconvenience of requiring a legal ratification of
treaties of alliance for the purpose of war."

Morris said, as he had ten full years before, "he was not
solicitous to multiply treaties. He wished none [even of com-
merce] to be made with Great Britain till she be at war. Then,
a good bargain might be made with her." Washington and he
had frequently to remind their colleagues that nations did not
make treaties out of vague good will, and that a negotiator
needed to be more than "a charming fellow" in bargaining.

A clause was proposed giving the national government the
power "to subdue a rebellion in any state on the application

of its legislature." Young Pinckney moved to strike out "on the application etc.," and Morris seconded him.

Alexander Martin of North Carolina said "the consent of the state ought to precede the introduction of any extraterritorial force whatever," to which Morris replied, "The executive [of the state] may possibly be at the head of the rebellion. The general government should enforce obedience in all cases."

The point was finally discarded except as it is compromised in Article IV, Section 4, of the Constitution.

Had Martin's clause been adopted, Lincoln's hands, legally at least, would have been tied in 1861.

In one of his strong and hasty outbursts Morris demanded that the President not be impeachable, at which the venerable Franklin said well, he'd either be impeachable or he'd be assassinated. Morris looked at the great fount of wisdom and experience and said at once, "My opinion has changed."

Franklin and he were at one, however, in believing that senators should be possessed of "great personal prosperity" and receive no salaries.

On the question of large salaries for the Supreme Court, Morris felt strongly. The value of money, he said, may not only alter but the state of society may alter. The amount of salary must always be regulated by the manners and style of living in a country. The force of his opinion in this matter arose from his belief in the Supreme Court as "a strong barrier against the instability of legislative assemblies," a doctrine not accepted until John Marshall was Chief Justice, and voted down at the time on the grounds that "no court had any peculiar knowledge of the mere policy of public measures."

In spite of the growing unity, the question of states' rights was still not settled. Roger Sherman moved that "state governments be restricted to matters of internal police and those wherein the general welfare of the United States is not concerned."

With vivid memories of the finances of the Revolution, Morris rose. Even that gave them too much freedom, he said. "The internal police, as it would be called and understood by the states ought to be infringed in many cases, as in the case of paper money and other tricks by which citizens of other states may be affected." The mordant phrase "other tricks" was for once overlooked and Bedford moved, with Morris seconding, that Congress should legislate "in all cases to which the states are severally incompetent and for the general interests of the union or in which the harmony of the United States may be interrupted by the exercise of individual legislatures," and it passed unanimously.

It is interesting to consider how little Morris's anti-Southern views affected his friendship with Washington. We have seen what he said about the barren lands of Virginia and the inhumanity of Georgia and South Carolina. But he could also, when he wanted to, speak with a wise lightness of tone. He listened to Mason of Virginia expatiating, though an anti-slavery man, on Southern demands for "justice" in the counting of their slaves for suffrage. "In the dilemma" of doing justice to the Southern states or to human nature, Morris observed, "we must decide in favor of human nature."

He warned the convention of "the dangers of admitting strangers in our public councils"—that is, citizens too recently become such. One must wonder whether he was thinking in part of Tom Paine. Gerry agreed, citing the extent of European secret services in this country, and Mason referred to the danger of "persons attached to Great Britain [working] themselves into our councils." But Madison said he saw no need of being too strict.

To this the bachelor Morris made a reply in the sort of simile he often thought in. "We should not be polite at the expense of prudence" he began, going on, "It is said some tribes of Indians carry their hospitality so far as to offer to strangers their wives and daughters. Is this a proper model to us? I would invite them to my table, would provide for them comfortable lodgings but would not carry the complaisance so far as to bed them with my wife." He concluded, ". . . the lesson we are taught is that we should be governed as much by our reason and as little by our feelings as possible." He said this in sequence to the metaphor of "my wife." It is amusing that he asserted the same thing about "love," but in the choice of mistress or wife, forgot it with attractive gaiety.

Whether this farfetched simile was persuasive or not, Morris won his point. A congressman had to have been a citizen for seven years, a senator for nine. Rutledge, wanting to restrict the number of years' residence in a state, was shouted down by delegates who said, "We're now forming a national government."

Now they had all had their say and the end came quickly. On September 8 a Committee on Style was elected by ballot: Alexander Hamilton (N.Y.), William Johnson (Conn.), Rufus King (Mass.), James Madison (Va.), and Gouverneur Morris (Pa.). It is interesting to note that on this committee only one member was from south of the Potomac. The Ivy League did well. Hamilton and Morris were Columbia, King was Harvard, Madison Princeton and William Samuel Johnson, though the son of the first president of King's College and himself but recently elected president of Columbia, had had the wisdom to go to Yale!

The actual writing went to Gouverneur Morris, with the concurrence of all necessary for submission of the draft to the convention. "The finish given to the style and arrangement of the Constitution fairly belongs to Gouverneur Morris," Madison wrote to Jared Sparks in 1832.

Out of the awkward first draft beginning "We the people of New Hampshire, etc. etc. etc. do ordain, declare and establish the following Constitution," Morris made the marvelous, felicitous Preamble: "We the people of the United States, in Order to form a more perfect Union . . ."

On the twelfth he had done it all. On the fifteenth it was ordered engrossed, Madison with wonderful restraint recording the immortal event: "on the questions to agree to the Constitution all the states Ay."

Forty-two delegates were present for the signing on the seventeenth, and all but Gerry, Mason and Randolph were ready to sign. At that last moment Gorham of Massachusetts rose to say that, "if it was not too late," he would like to see "the number of representatives . . . one for every forty thousand" altered to "one for every thirty thousand . . . for the purpose of lessening objection." How easy it would have been for small-minded men to say, "You should have thought of that before. . . . Change one jot or tittle and you open the whole subject. It's all or nothing."

But apparently all recognized this as a wise afterthought, likely to be palatable to the people, and Washington, intervening for the only time, asked that the change be made. Article I, Section 2, was altered accordingly.

Most of those present were aware of the defects in the Constitution which even Mason trusted to posterity to amend. Most of them felt as Franklin did: "I confess there are several parts of this Constitution which I do not at present approve but I am not sure I shall never approve them. . . . In these sentiments, sir, I agree to this Constitution with all its faults, if they are such. . . . [I] wish that every member of the convention who may still have objections to it would, with me on this occasion, doubt a little of his infallibility and to make manifest our unanimity put his name to this instrument." They were all anxious that the assent be unanimous in effect, in spite of the absence of sixteen delegates, including the New York majority. How to achieve it in form?

Madison's notes read: "[Franklin] then moved that the Constitution be signed by the members and offered the following as a convenient form, viz 'Done in convention by the unanimous consent of the *states* present.' This ambiguous form had been drawn up by Mr. Gouverneur Morris in order to gain the dissenting members and put into the hands of the Doer Franklin that it might have the better chance of success."

Morris that night drafted the letter of submission for Washington to send to Congress in New York.

The Constitution which we now present is the result of a spirit of amity and of that mutual deference and concession which the peculiarity of our political situation rendered indispensable. It is not easy to be wise for all times not even for the present, much less for the future; and those who judge of the past, must recollect that, when it was present, the present was future.

So it was over with and William Jackson, aged twenty-eight, acting as secretary, that evening burned all the miscellaneous papers and left in the morning for New York.

The delegates behaved like men of good will and good cheer.

"When," Washington's *Diary* of that day records, "the Constitution received unanimous consent of eleven states and Colonel Hamilton from New York . . . the members adjourned to the City Tavern, dined together and took a cordial leave . . . [afterwards I] retired to mediate on the momentous work."

The next day he "finished what private business I had to do in the city, took my leave of those with whom I had been most intimate, dined early (one o'clock) with Robert Morris and Gouverneur" and set out for home, and Morris for Morrisania.

It is amusing to consider what a Congressional Investigating Committee of today's type might have made of certain papers of the time and what they might have said to Washington, Abigail Adams and James Madison if called upon to testify long afterwards. To Washington they might have begun, "Is it not a fact that during the entire convention you accepted the hospitality of Robert Morris, then engaged on 'great mercantile matters' with Gouverneur Morris with whom you went 'fishing'? Is it not a fact that you never once opposed the latter's views, often expressed, that the 'common people' were 'dupes'? And did you not appoint this very same Morris to be minister to France? . . ."

The next witness would be Abigail Adams, wife of the second President of the United States. They would ask her what she meant when she had written that Washington had appointed Morris to the legation in France because he was afraid of him. "Tell this committee, Mrs. Adams, what Morris had on the then President at whose house in that very same Mount Vernon he was known to have stayed."

And then James Madison would be called on to explain a sinister letter. "It is a fact, is it not, Mr. Madison, that you sat in the Constitutional Convention with a Gouverneur Morris?"

"Yes, there were some fifty other people there too."

"You were almost constantly in agreement with this Morris, were you not?"

"Not constantly. We differed on many points. I refer you to the *Debates.*"

"Yes, but you kept the records of those debates personally and you have had a great deal to say about what 'great services' this Morris rendered. What was your reason?"

"His services were very great."

"To whom?"

"To our country."

"Not to you personally?"

"Certainly not."

"Well then, perhaps you will tell this committee how it happens that as a representative of that sovereign state, the Mother of Presidents, Virginia, you chose to be dependent on the bounty of a resident of New York, not even acceptable as a delegate to the Senate of his own state, a man who deserted John Paul Jones, as he was dying, to dine with a notorious woman and who conspired with foreign radicals to secure the execution of Thomas Paine."

"I was certainly not 'dependent on his bounty.'"

"We show you this letter of January 20, 1788, to the Commonwealth of Virginia. It states that your expenses at the Constitutional Convention amounted to £165.12.0, and that you received from this Commonwealth £14, with the result that you assert a claim against them for £151.12.0. Now perhaps you will explain why your letter tells them to pay £30 to a certain John Blair *but* £121.12.0 to this very same Gouverneur Morris?"

CHAPTER ELEVEN

What Is Bob Morris and Governier About?

(1788)

WHAT IS Bob Morris and Governier about, with all their polished instruments? I hardly think they are idle," a New Englander wrote to a friend.

It was 1788 and the Constitution had gone to the states for ratification. Jefferson in Paris had received copies from Jay and Madison and wrote that he was "captivated by the composition of the opposing claim of the great and little states" and the letter goes on, "I like . . . I am pleased . . . ," lamenting only the omission of the Bill of Rights, on which all states had voted no, leaving it for the amendments which came two years later. But as more copies from Adams and Gerry reached him he found "things in it which stagger all my dispositions to subscribe to what such an assembly has proposed."

Nor were all other Virginians pleased. Richard Henry Lee wrote acidly to Edmund Randolph, "To say that a bad government must be established for fear of anarchy is really saying that we must kill ourselves for fear of dying," and Patrick Henry, "with a power of speech to stir men's blood," as Morris wrote Hamilton, was bitterly opposed to ratification.

From Morrisania, on October 30, 1787, Morris, sure that the states would ratify, had written Washington that he must accept the presidency. "The truth is that your great and decided superiority leads men willingly to put you in a place which will not add to your personal dignity, nor raise you higher than you already stand. But they would not readily put any other person in the same situation."

At the end of that November, Gouverneur, with Robert Morris, stayed two days and two nights at Mount Vernon, on their way to Richmond.

Washington hoped to see them on their way back, though part of the business taking them to Virginia was the lawsuit of his friend Carter Braxton against Robert Morris.

The Morrises had much to do in Virginia. Their friends, Hamilton and Jay in New York, were writing the *Federalist Papers* with Madison a contributor from Virginia.

"Robert Morris, the cofferer, with his aide-de-camp, Gouvero, has taken the field [for ratification] in Virginia," so the former wrote Gates.

Gouvero attended the Virginia debates, writing frequently to Hamilton about them, but his most pressing business was the "great mercantile matters" which Colonel Pierce had heard about. They were not all with Robert Morris. William Constable wrote him, "Will any of your Virginia friends adventure in [with us]? I long to hear of your safe arrival. My best to Robert Morris."

Two days later Constable wrote warningly: "I am perfectly safe on this subject [an unspecified venture]. I wish Mr. Robert Morris's business stood on as good a footing."

In his *Autobiography*, Jefferson said, "My duties at Paris were confined to a few objectives: the receipt [in France] of our whale-oils, salted fish and salted meats on favorable terms; the admission of our rice on equal terms with that of Piedmont, Egypt and the Levant; a mitigation of the monopolies of our tobacco by the Farmers General. . . ."

In seeking this mitigation the red-haired Jefferson was assisted by the red-haired Lafayette.

The fiscal agents of the Farmers-General were Le Couteulx and Company, bankers of Paris. With them Robert Morris had an exclusive contract, providing him with a cash advance, to buy American tobacco. The contract was so valuable that with it in his hands it was said he could even manipulate the discount rates of the Bank of North America when he was in the market.

The tobacco was not shipped to nor financed with France directly, but through London with additional charges and commissions profitable to those involved. All this is the familiar workings of "trusts" then and today.

It naturally occurred to various men in America and France that the shipments of tobacco should be made in some way to apply in part directly to the American debt to France, as was done with foreign raw materials through "reverse lend-lease" in World War II.

Acting for a French group, the brilliant Brissot de Warville came out to America proposing to offset part of the debt to France by tobacco purchases, from which the Farmers-General and Robert Morris would be excluded. In America he was associated with William Duer and Osgood, who had regarded Gouvero as "a bad councillor."

One would like to draw some wise and profound conclusion from the fact that men so unlike as Jefferson, Lafayette, Osgood and his later son-in-law Genêt—and others like Thomas Paine and James Monroe—should all be opponents of Gouverneur Morris but except that red-haired men seemed particularly allergic to him, there seems to be nothing more conclusive to say.

The Morrises had not failed to anticipate the plans of De Warville. They themselves planned to have deliveries of tobacco to the Farmers-General apply in part on the debt—and in France to sell shares in the purchase of ten square miles of Pennsylvania, opposite Trenton, as well as loan certificates and their "wild lands."

Into these grandiose schemes now came the commercial phrase "late in delivery" so familiar and full of anxiety to businessmen the world over. Robert Morris was heavily late on the last part of his contract and it was a question whether the Farmers-General would accept.

There could be no better nor more willing emissary than Gouverneur Morris to go to France.

It must have been plain to him that he could secure no elective office in the new government which he would want. In the executive branch Hamilton would have the Treasury, which Robert Morris later declined, and for all his genius Morris could not expect Foreign Affairs, even if the incumbent did not have to be from Virginia or Massachusetts. So it was agreed that he should go to France.

Madison wrote Jefferson: "The affairs of Robert Morris are still much deranged."

The *Diary and Letters* of Gouverneur Morris are so full of quotations from Swift, Chesterfield, Sterne and particularly Shakespeare that one wonders he never remarked how like the Merchant of Venice Robert Morris was:

> . . . all my fortunes are at sea;
> Neither have I money, Nor commodity
> To raise a present sum,

nor applied to himself the line from *Hamlet,*

> For every man has business and desire.

As he listened to the voice of Patrick Henry, stirring men's blood that spring, all but persuading Virginia not to ratify, he could not know that five years later the voice would save the life of a girl whom he had just met as a child of fourteen.

Nor could the young man, Richard Randolph, then eighteen, older brother of Theodorick and John Randolph of Roanoke, have known as he listened to the debates that the mighty voice would at the same time save his own life. It is part of all the tangled coincidences that Lafayette should then have been writing Washington, "Paul Jones [forty-one] has entered the Russian service and will command a squadron on the Black Sea." Jones left his mistress, Aimée de Tellison, natural daughter of Louis XV, to Jefferson's care. The lady he had wanted to marry, Dorothea Spottswood Dandridge, had been the wife of Patrick Henry for ten years.

Gouvero at the time was staying at Tuckahoe, the plantation of his friend, Colonel Thomas Mann Randolph, on the James River. The father of Jefferson had been this Randolph's guardian and Jefferson had lived at Tuckahoe for seven years.

Colonel Randolph was now forty-seven, the father of thirteen children. The fourth child, Thomas, would marry Jefferson's daughter and be governor of Virginia. The seventh child, Judith, now sixteen, would marry her cousin Richard Randolph the next year and her little sister Nancy, whom Morris saw, had been christened in St. James, Northan Parish, Anne Cary Randolph in September, two months after her birth in 1774.

From Richmond on June 13, Morris wrote Hamilton of Patrick Henry's "dark mode of operating on the minds of members" but said, "Be of good cheer. My religious belief [prevails] where my understanding falters and I feel faith as I lose confidence. Things will yet go right but where and how I dare not predicate. So much for this dull subject [of ratification]. . . ."

Then he goes on:

. . . a friend of mine in this country, Mr. Thomas Mann Randolph, a gentleman possessing one of the best fortunes in this country, and clear of any debt of his own has become unfortunately involved by being surety for another. His payments on that account are considerable already some ten or twelve thousand pounds sterling. The rest will follow in good season and in this country he has time enough particularly because the money is due in Britain and as yet the law is against British creditors and indeed the delays of the law here are against all creditors. His lady, an amiable woman (remember that) is not in much good health . . . and he is in the benevolent intention of taking her to New York. But the apprehension of a suit at such a distance and where he is so little known gives him pause . . . be all that as it may he has asked me whether he would be subject to such a suit in New York and I have answered in the affirmative under my general idea of our jurisprudence telling him at the same time that I recollect something of a law which permits the payment in suit in paper money. I have promised to write for information to a friend and have as you see performed my promise. Drop me a line in answer confined to this object direct to the care of Benjamin Harrison Jr. at Richmond to whom I will give directions to open it and communicate the contents to Mr. Randolph should I, as I hope, be on my return before yours can reach me.

Adieu

P.S. Mention also the value of the paper.

The amiable lady died. Colonel Randolph married again. His daughter Judith went to her bridegroom's plantation, Bizarre.

There, after Morris had succeeded Jefferson as minister to France, Nancy Randolph went to live and Theodorick Randolph, the bridegroom's young brother, came home to die.

On July 4 the ratification of the Constitution was celebrated in Philadelphia and in the parade "the rabbi of the Jews with a minister of the Gospel on each side was a most delightful sight."

Morris was at Morrisania, assembling his letters of introduction to France and arranging his affairs to leave for the long ten years of voluntary exile. In Boston lived a lady he was to meet when the exile ended. She was the lovely Sarah Wentworth Apthorp of Gilbert Stuart's portraits, then twenty-nine, married to Perez Morton, two years older than Morris, a brilliant Bostonian and a former Continental officer.

In that September, Morton seduced his wife's young sister Frances, who then committed suicide.

On October 9, John Adams, always so censorious of Morris, sitting with Governor Bowdoin as special judges, exonerated Perez Morton for complicity in the suicide. Morris, Randolph and Morton were linked by interlocking seductions. They were utterly dissimilar men, yet oddly enough each was an early and ardent abolitionist.

On December 21, 1775, Perez Morton attested that "a Negro man Salem Poor behaved like an experienced officer and an excellent soldier [in action]. . . . In the person of this Negro centres a brave and gallant soldier."

Richard Randolph's will, freeing his slaves, was written with that hatred of slavery which is in Morris's speeches in the convention.

It may not be irrelevant that, thirty days after his exoneration of Morton, Adams wrote his "dear child," Abigail, "General Knox will tell you how completely I am initiated into the Order of Cincinnati."

That day Morris wrote Washington, thanking him for his letters of introduction, and telling him of the Chinese pigs and geese he was sending him. "It would be degrading to the noble race of man should I introduce politics after hogs and geese."

Washington's letters of introduction were many—to Shelburne, and Arthur Young, the husbandman, to Rochambeau, "though you must be already personally acquainted and favorably impressed with Mr. Morris's character," to Lafayette and De Chastellux, "although you are well acquainted with Gouverneur Morris."

Morris particularly asked for one to Jefferson, "whom he had met one day at the Finance Office."

The week before Christmas the small ship *Delaware* passed Henlopen outward bound to France. Morris was aboard and during that wintry voyage he wrote a 3000-word paper on American finances. It canvasses methods by which the Union may secure the import duties then received by the several states without causing "Disgust among many friends of the new Constitution and [furnishing] weapons to its enemies." By the methods he proposes, the Union will be able to meet its interest, sinking fund obligations and current expenses by a tax of one fortieth of the people's annual products and industry and an ad valorem duty on imports of five per cent.

The labors he was to have in France were in general these: secure acceptance of the late tobacco deliveries; sell Robert Morris's Genesee and St. Lawrence lands; fund the American debt to France through private bankers paying in cash and kind; secure for Robert Morris's firm buying orders for flour, wheat and salt provisions for the French West Indies; cement and develop William Constable and Company's business through London banking houses such as Phyn, Ellice and Inglis; negotiate loans with the famous Dutch bankers in Amsterdam; have an eye for "new business."

Almost ten years before he had intimated to Ridley that he would sometime convince French ladies that all Americans were not averse to kissing. He must have had love's labors in mind for himself and he may well have expected that he would have the legation in London or Paris before he came back.

CHAPTER TWELVE

Atlantic World
of Enlightenment

FRANKLIN, Jefferson and Gouverneur Morris, in turn, sailed from Philadelphia, a city of somewhat more than 40,000 people, leaving a country of about 3,000,000 to go to Paris where 700,-000 of France's 24,000,000 subjects lived.

Their missions took them to England, which, with a third of the French population, though ringed with foes, had "fronted them with a grand courage. Only in America had the tide run too strongly to be turned."

How did it happen that these three men, with all the differences of environment and experience, were able to enter at once into easy intimacy with both the French and English ruling classes, with all the differences which lay also between them?

Dangerous as generalizations are, it would seem true to say that the basic amalgam consisted in their all being omnivorous readers. They had read the same books and were familiar with the same "enlightenment" whether or not they accepted it.

Love of books and their possession was the common passion of Lord Shelburne, Talleyrand, Franklin, Jefferson and Morris.

Their wives and women friends read and wrote. Germaine de Staël was publishing her *Letters on the Works and Character of Rousseau,* and Adèle de Flahaut was writing in a retreat in the

Louvre, "a chair, a harpsichord, a few books, a table with my writing things. A sort of ideal circle which separates me from the rest of the apartment."

Lord Shelburne's new bride had written that "he came up to me early and read some Thucydides *History of the Peloponnesian War*" and a few days later "after breakfast Lord Shelburne lent me a little book called *Le Siècle d'Alexandre* and I saw him no more till dinner."

In the library "two hundred feet long and thirty feet wide" Lady Holland, at twenty-seven, in six months had read "the Duchess of Marlborough's *Apology*, Burnet's *History*, *Ye XXII Satire* of Juvenal, Hearne's *Travels into North America*, Smith on *Human Species*, Bancroft on *Dying*, some desultory chemistry, *Roderick Random*, *Lazarillo de Tormes*, *The Life of Sixtus V*, and various German and French plays, novels and trash, Cook's *Third Way*, Wolf's *Ceylon*, part of Ulloa's *Voyage*, some paper in Ye Memoirs of Ye Exeter Society, frequently dipping into Bayle, Montaigne, La Fontaine, Ariosto, ye three first books of Tasso, Lord Orford's works." Her flock of young children and the suit for adultery against her by her former husband, Sir Godfray Webster, evidently prevented really serious reading.

In America we have seen Sally Jay reading Morris's copy of Madame de Maintenon's *Memoirs*. Abigail Adams had evidently read all that her husband had, and in Philadelphia there was Elizabeth Graeme Ferguson, "the most learned woman in North America," with whom Laurence Sterne had struck up a friendship as she picked a winner at Newmarket. The *Massachusetts Magazine* began publishing the lyrics of Sarah Wentworth Morton, the wife of Perez Morton, writing as Philenia in 1789, and there is later evidence that Nancy Randolph was precociously reading *Tom Jones* and *Pamela*. In '81, William Edgar had sent a friend's library to him by canoes from Detroit, including his dictionary. The friend had written him, "The large 4th volume dictionary belonging to General Hamilton [George Rogers Clark's prisoner at Vincennes] will be enough for the Post. I fear much [Hamilton] will never get back to enjoy it."

There were, however, two French novels which probably

few people in America had read, but which reflected by their contrasts much of the moral attitudes of the French court.

These were *The Princess of Cleves,* published in 1678, and *Les Liaisons Dangereuses* by Choderlos de Laclos, published in 1782. The first is the story of a great lady's loyalty to an ideal and to a husband she does not love, so that even when he is dead she cannot bring herself, because of "a phantom of duty," to marry the man she loves. The other is the story of its title, the pursuit of seduction, by a man and woman, whose rewards are satisfactions arising less from sensuality than from their cerebral examination of how they have achieved their conquests.

The people Morris knew in France behave in their private lives like the characters in these books and two of the women at times speak almost the very words.

If reading was the common bond of all these men and women, the absence of "gallantry" in America was what the French travelers viewed with their most witty perplexity. How was it possible for beautiful women and distinguished men to meet, in the luxury and gaiety the French saw, without seductions? Or so the French thought.

"The women," Brissot de Warville noted at dinner with the president of Congress before a ball, "had their bosoms very naked. I was scandalized at the indecency *in a republic.*" Considering that robes were so décolleté in France that *"le moindre mouvement faisait sortir du corsage le bout des seins,"* this indicates a good deal of reverence for republics.

The thing was, the Duke of Liancourt believed, that "unmarried women enjoy the same degree of liberty which married women do in France and which married women here do not like."

"American women," Rochambeau contributed, "once they have entered the state of matrimony give themselves to it and you seldom see, particularly in the rural districts, a woman of loose morals."

This conjugal fidelity puzzled them all. Talleyrand shortly found Madame de la Tour du Pin, a refugee near Albany, actually sleeping with her husband every night in all her famous

Dillon beauty. "It is essential," Talleyrand wrote his friends, "to have a good reputation in this country."

Claude Blanchard, a younger Frenchman, saw it as a consequence of Americans having no outside diversion. *"Pendant l'hiver ils sortent peu et passent des journées entières au coin de leur feu et à côté de leurs femmes* sans lire et sans rien faire!"

The French were all puzzled. At Newport, seven years before, Fersen had written his father, "You know the French, my dear father, or what are called men of the court to judge of the despair of all the young men of that class, obliged to pass the winter tranquilly in Newport far from their mistresses and the pleasures of Paris . . . *points soupers . . . point . . . point . . ."*

The English were less puzzled. Perhaps the common language helped them, as the lack of it distressed Edward Gibbon and Lord Sheffield, who found the Swiss girls "extremely shy of pawing or handling." There are those who believe "pawing or handling" was invented during the thirties or forties of the twentieth century.

While Americans in considering marriage naturally thought of the suitability of the spouse, and the position or money marriage might bring, there were no *moeurs de temps,* demanding, as with Adèle de Flahaut, that youth and innocence unconsulted and unwilling be sold for an old title and a fortune. Nor was there any such concept as that held even by the liberal Lord Shelburne who, according to Lady Holland, liked "a woman of rank [to] marry her equal whom she rather dislikes and [to have her] conquer a partiality to another [and] to fulfill all her duties scrupulously and punctually."

Actually there seems little evidence that there was not a high degree of marital happiness in America among the patriot leaders. Certainly with their beauty, youth and distinction, couples like the John Jays and the Rufus Kings should have had it. What face is lovelier than Sally Jay's in the profile by Pine with her long-lashed eyes and her smiling, slightly pouting lips? In '83 she looked so much like the then beautiful Marie Antoinette that a whole audience rose in a Paris theater to cheer, thinking she was the Queen.

Nor can any generalization of coldness be drawn from the

stilted form in which many but not all these wives and husbands usually wrote each other.

Sally Jay addressed her husband as

My dear Mr. Jay [apparently only Bingham called him Jack]
On Friday myself and the children had the pleasure of receiving your kind letters. . . .

Sincerely and affectionately yours
Sally Jay

and while Jay addressed her as "My dear Sally" he ordinarily signed "Yours sincerely, John Jay."

Hamilton, on the other hand, wrote his Betsy all his life with ardor. "Monday at furthest I embrace my angel. . . . Think of me—dream of me and love me, my Betsy. . . . Yours, my angel, with inviolable fidelity . . ." and so on to the last letter before Weehawken: "Adieu my darling, darling wife."

Of course the War of Independence, like all wars, had stimulated marriage and raised the birth rate. "An uncommon cheerfulness prevailed everywhere among the friends of the Revolution," the physician, Benjamin Rush, noted. "The population in the United States increased more rapidly from births during the war than ever in the same number of years. . . . Due to the extreme circulation of money . . ."

Former young officers of Washington's army saw another cause. Captain John Marshall, twenty-nine, later Chief Justice, had in 1784 in spite of the financial panic written Major James Monroe, twenty-six, later senator, governor of Virginia, minister of France, Secretary of State, of War, President of the United States:

"The excessive cold has operated like magic on our youth. They feel the necessity of artificial heat and quite wearied with lying alone are all treading the broad road to matrimony."

This Atlantic world may have had its different standards for married love or infidelity, but there is an enchanting identity in their attitude toward their children.

It is true that Abigail Adams found it "amiable" that the Marquise de Lafayette "adored her children [and] the more remarkable in a country where the least trait of such a disposition is scarce known." Talleyrand's lonely, unhappy childhood has been generally accepted as an example of the habit of the time.

Morris did not find this to be the case, either in England or in France. Can it be that his friends, those wicked and worthless people, abhorrent to Mrs. Adams, were so affectionate by nature that their sweetness extended even to their children? Certainly he had to hurry from Madame de Corny's because Madame de Chastellux was waiting to present her ten-day-old son. Certainly on St. Valentine's Day, the De Ségurs "collected the parents to a great number" to see their children's party. Certainly Beaujolais, the Orléans boy, had to be admired whenever Morris called. And the heartless Madame de Flahaut was prostrated after rescuing her five-year-old son from an angry dog. Did she and Morris not set aside Christmas afternoon to take him to *goutées,* children's parties?

Staying in London, during the French Revolution, Morris broke off his business to visit the De Ségur children at Shooter's Hill. As in later wars, the De Ségurs had sent their children away from the perils they stayed to face.

Angelica Church could not be interrupted by him or any caller "because she is engaged at cards with her children." And did not that "adulterous woman," Lady Holland, write, "Oh! My dear children fond as I am of ye all, I had sooner at this instant hear of your deaths than that you shall be gamesters and spendthrifts"? Lord Wycombe's mother, Lady Shelburne, "dressed him in garter blue, the color that becomes him best [to be] admired as he deserves." This great lady, and unnatural mother, goes on to say, "My dear little child takes notice of a watch [and] is much bigger than any of the princes had been." When he is five she goes to the nursery "to see Lord Fitzmaurice dine and teach him after to spell words." On Boxing Day, Fanny Burney tells De Narbonne, the depraved lover of Madame de Staël, "You will have a terrible dinner, alas—but your godson [six months old] comes in for dessert!"

The propaganda agent, Dr. Berkenhout, who had accompanied Lord Carlisle's mission, had said American legislators in general were "unpolished, illiterate, poor and of no character

. . . the lowest, most contemptible fellows I ever saw except at the Robin Hood. . . . Washington himself owes his abilities to his opponents' want of abilities, or to something worse. . . . His army is a contemptible band of vagrants, deserters and thieves. . . . When Britain once resolves to conquer America, the business is done."

The aristocratic William Eden, his superior, brother of Sir Morton Eden, who was later to present Morris to the Emperor in Vienna, wrote at the same time, "It is impossible to see even what I have seen of this magnificent country and not go nearly mad at the long train of misconduct and mischance by which we have lost it."

It was magnificent in spite of what Dr. Rush called some "rogue-minded zealots," and the few people who had "liberty, horse, donation, gambling and rambling manias." Magnificent and pleasant in houses like Morris's where an English lady had "a favorite dish (a nice little pig)" and "for the first time a good watermelon, which in hot weather tastes like sweetened snow."

Much of the magnificence lay in the character and influence of Washington, to whom, however, Benjamin Harrison had written of the washerwoman's daughter, "Kate, clean, trim, and rosy as the morning to unbend your mind from the cares of war," Washington, who referred to his butler as *Mr.* Hyde—for that matter the British commandant of Fort Niagara acknowledged a dispatch brought by "Mr. Raccoon, the savage"—Washington baffled young Blanchard, Rochambeau's commissary, who had been told "General Washington said grace when there was no clergyman at table as fathers of a family do in America. The first time I dined with him there was no clergyman at table and I did not perceive that he made this prayer. Yet I remember that on taking his place at table he made a gesture and said a word which I took for a piece of politeness and which perhaps was a religious action."

Taken for all in all, as Brooks Adams wrote in a wonderful passage, he was the greatest man of the eighteenth century . . . "his greatness chiefly consists in that balance of mind which enabled him to recognize when an old order had passed away. . . . [He] prevailed not only because of an intelligence and elevation of character which enabled him to comprehend and persuade others . . . but also because he was supported by a body of the most remarkable men whom America has ever produced."

How incredible it was then, and in the light of after history, that following Arnold's treason they did not all start accusing, purging and killing each other. And that, after the victory, there were no political executions, harried though the Tories may have been as to their property. Within a short time even Dr. Bancroft, the British spy in Franklin's home in Passy, was forgiven and in correspondence with many of them, collecting and publishing Franklin's Political and Miscellaneous Papers in London.

The fact was that, in spite of their human shortcomings, the leaders were, all but one, unpurchasable men and as a result possessed of an easy assurance. It was a simple matter for any of them to go anywhere as the equal of any personage in the world. If, after all they had achieved, they felt perhaps they were a little more competent than anyone else, it was not to be wondered at. Nor were the things they were most interested in politics and statecraft only.

Possibly the Englishman whom men as diverse as Washington, Jefferson and Morris would most like to have had at their houses was the husbandman, Arthur Young. Fertilizers, seeds, cattle and poultry strains were of enormous interest to them all. Shelburne sent Franklin gooseberry bushes, Morris sent Washington China geese, Jefferson brought home grass seeds from Ireland, and Rufus King, coming home from the London Legation, told the Secretary of State, "I should like to be allowed to carry [in the ship] a few sheep of the breeds most esteemed here," and being settled in Long Island, chartered a sloop to bring elms from Massachusetts for his estate. Nor was all such traffic westbound. A British officer returning to Ireland ordered "wild rice as grows in the Grande Manee, a small bag cost what it will . . . Illinois nuts for planting . . . pajotte lettuce seed."

What a renaissance, with what a commerce of both ideas and the fruits of the earth, might have been possible in that Atlantic world of enlightenment but for one thing.

In France the feudal nobility lived at court with the King. To be sent to their estates was a punishment.

The kings could go their silly ways without its mattering, Louis XVI to hunt, George III to bathe "with success. A machine follows the royal into the sea filled with fiddlers who play God Save The King as His Majesty takes the plunge."

Even the famine which threatened France was curable where, as Morris noted, "to see the extended harvests in summer we wonder how it can all be consumed."

All the scandal and illegitimacy in French society, where not to be a natural child of Louis XV was somewhat unique, did not result in a race of weaklings. Lauzun and De Noailles were among those who tramped "ruddy and handsome" 548 miles in thirty-seven days to Yorktown through the American summer.

Unfortunately for them, there did not exist what James Boswell called "the wide speculative field of English ambition" which America had inherited. The French nobles could find nothing to do, so chose to throw away in unaccountable fashion all their talents and graces and many of them their lives.

CHAPTER THIRTEEN

Mr. Jefferson, with Whom
I Have Only a Slight
Acquaintance

THE MEASURE of Jefferson's greatness is so plain, and the political division between him and Morris so marked, that it is hard to realize they were both "good English Whigs, cordial in their free principles and in their jealousy of executive majesty."

It would be far from the truth to suppose that a Jefferson, hostile to the French King, a zealot for the downtrodden peasants, a man without aristocratic or women friends, received Morris, a butterfly, a social climber and a man more royalist than the King.

Neither had then heard of Robespierre or Danton and no one can suppose either would have appealed to Jefferson any more than they did later to Morris.

The two Americans who had debated and finally written the Declaration and the Constitution were in complete agreement on the political folly of the nobles, "so furious that they cannot debate at all," as Jefferson said.

There is small difference in the essence of Morris's plans for a French Constitution, written for Lafayette or Talleyrand, and that of Jefferson, written for the former on June 3, 1789:

The desirable object being to secure the good which the King has offered . . . the King in a *séance royale* should come forward with a charter of rights in his hand to be signed by himself and every man of the three orders . . . [as a quid pro quo for the continuance of the monarchy].

Jefferson did not show this to Morris, who noted, however, that "Mr. Jefferson was out of hopes with the States General. . . . This comes of having too sanguine hopes."

It may almost certainly be said with accuracy that Morris, in France, perceived from the first a practical incapacity and inexperience in all the upper classes which, though they saw "the abuses of their monarchial form of government," left them unable to reform it.

It must be remembered that in his *Autobiography* Jefferson laid the whole responsibility for the French Revolution on Marie Antoinette.

"I have ever believed," he wrote, "that had there been no Queen, there would have been no revolution," and he would have put her in a convent and kept "the King in his station with limited powers."

This assumption that one person, whatever her vices, could be responsible for so mighty a change is surely a faulty one for so great a man to have made. Yet even John Adams, with his equally long experience in France, wrote Rufus King after the September massacres that jealousy in the Duke of Orléans for the Noailles family accounted for most that had happened.

While of course neither of these comments is all that Jefferson and Adams said or thought, they fairly state their opinions. They make Jefferson and Adams sound like those whom the poet Coleridge described as proceeding "with much solemnity to solve the riddle of the French Revolution by anecdotes." Certainly they are at profound variance with Morris's realization that the issues were enormous and the solutions almost hopeless.

We shall later consider what it is the adversaries of Morris feel he did not do which Jefferson would have done had he remained as minister.

Meanwhile they had much trivia in common. Jefferson had bought the watch for Madison which Washington admired and asked Morris to buy a duplicate of for him. Abigail Adams asked Jefferson to shop for china and mirrors such as Morris ordered for Mount Vernon. Morris got rouge for Mrs. Penn and Jefferson for Mrs. Adams. And all publishers' problems would be solved if all men bought as many books to send to Morrisania or Monticello as they did. Both, like all official Americans, then and thereafter, were constantly asked "to loan their carriages." Both, when they went home, were engrossed by the affairs of their universities, Morris succeeding Hamilton as a trustee of Columbia.

And in their friends in Paris they were not greatly different. It was in the house of Madame de Corny, the friend of Jefferson, in the little Rue Chaussée d'Antin back of the opera, that Morris first talked at length to the Countess de Flahaut, and he was with Jefferson in that house the night the Bastille fell.

There is an implication in several books that from 1784 until his death Jefferson lived in chastity and that there was something very noble in doing so. As to this, there is presumably no valid evidence but surely it is as unlikely as the charge that "he peopled his plantation with slaves" by intercourse with black women. There is no question, however, of his *trois amitiés* in France, Madame de Corny, Maria Cosway, wife of the English painter, and Madame de Bréhan, sister of De Moustier, then French minister in the United States.

Jefferson presented Morris to the first and gave him letters to Maria Cosway in London. It was to her Jefferson wrote with his left hand, after injuring his right, the thousands of besotted words of any man in love and her last letter came to him when he was eighty-one and she sixty-nine.

As to the Marquise de Bréhan, the situation was a most curious one. Her brother, the Count de Moustier, a year older than Morris, had arrived in New York with her the previous February.

Abigail Adams Smith had already met her in Paris and said, "Mr. Jefferson, for one, seems much taken with her." John Trumbull had also met them in France. "She was a most interesting little woman who had been married to an abandoned brute with whom it was impossible for any woman of delicacy or any sense of virtue to live."

Jefferson had written Madison: "Receive her as an acquaintance of a thousand years standing," and in quieter vein to Sally
Jay, as wife of the Secretary for Foreign Affairs. Lafayette
wrote Washington: "I have invited [De Moustier] in your name
to Mt. Vernon as well as mine."

The seat of the government was then in New York and of
course Washington was still a private citizen. For some reason
New York society did not seem to like the minister nor his sister, nor did they like New York and America.

In May '88, Lafayette wrote again to Washington: "I had a
letter from de M. who (between us) appears to me not too well
pleased. We must humor him a little."

De Moustier then took his sister on a tour of New England
but in October Washington wrote asking them both to stay at
Mount Vernon.

By then the letters for Morris to take to France were coming
in. Colonel Humphreys of Washington's household, "by the
sure conveyance of Mr. Gouverneur Morris," wrote Jefferson
that the marquise had distressed "and undervalued a considerable company" by dressing "in the fashion of the negro
women in the West Indies." Madison's letter said that "Moustier
proves a most unlucky appointment . . . unsocial, proud and
niggardly. . . . Such of their countrymen here *as are not under restraint make very free remarks*" (Madison's italics).

The last was Jay's official letter to Jefferson, "entrusted to
Gouverneur Morris":

These are things I have not said or written to any other person nor
is it pleasant to say or write them. But in the situation you are in,
information of this kind is essential. . . . It appears, whether well
or ill founded is not important, that they have created and diffused
an opinion that an improper connection subsists between him and
the Marchioness. . . . It was observed that travelling in New England they occasionally occupied the same room at hotels. . . . You
can easily conceive the influence of such an opinion on the minds
and feelings of such people as ours. . . .

As Jefferson read all this he must have wondered how much
Gouverneur Morris knew of it and where with his presumable
indiscreetness he would repeat it.

Morris must of course have known. The phenomenon of incest in Europe interested him a great deal. Had not Montesquieu found both monogamy and polygamy wanting and regarded incestuous love of brother and sister as the only unqualified solution? Morris's *Diary* records numerous instances of it. But neither then nor in his *Diary* at his six later meetings with the recalled brother and sister does he make any reference to their relationship even though on Christmas Eve, '89, "Madame de Bréhan as usual says much evil of Madame de Flahaut."

Nor does he, in his many references to Madame de Corny and Mrs. Cosway, ever refer to Jefferson's friendship with them.

For that matter he did not, it appears, ever mention Madame de Flahaut to any but one American, or to anyone else except to a fellow sufferer one day in final chagrin.

Perhaps the marquise was his hostage against Jefferson, and the countess Jefferson's against him. It is more likely that they were both gentlemen though adversaries.

CHAPTER FOURTEEN

A Pleasing Woman
Not an Enemy to Intrigue

(*March–July 1789*)

Morris had been in France a few days less than two months when he left his hotel in the Rue de Richelieu and walked around the corner to a stationer's shop in the Rue Neuve des Petits Champs.[1] There he bought, bound in apple-green vellum, the first volume of the diaries he was to keep for the rest of his life.

Still pasted in the cover today is the sticker:

Marquis, Marchand, tient Magasin de Papiers de France et de Hollande, Papier à lettre, doré, glacé, et à vignettes. Encre de la Chine et autres de toutes couleurs. Boites, Plumes, Registres, Ciré d'Espagne, Ecritoires de Bureaux, Porte-feuilles en maroquin fermant à clef et de toutes façons. Il fait la bonne encre double et lisante.

There are twelve volumes of *Diaries,* running from 1789 to 1816. Ten are uniform with the first in size and paper, but the vellum binding of all but the first is pale ivory. One is a cheaper notebook, evidently used before Morris could secure a duplicate of the original.

The ink of China, or the good ink, *double et lisante,* is scarcely faded at all today, and the paper of France or Hollande is firm and tough to the touch. But this is true of most of the

[1] The Rue des Petits Champs today running from the Avenue de l'Opéra to the Place de la Victoire.

diaries and letters of that enlightened and elegant period when craftsmen made things by hand.

Diaries were fortunately a fashion of the time and, with his sense for history, Morris must have expected that if his was saved it would be eagerly read. He of course did not know of Pepys's *Diary* or of Boswell's but, like Boswell, writing twenty-six years before, he may have had "such an affection for this my journal that it shocks me to think of burning it. . . . I put down all sorts of little incidents in it . . . there is nothing too little for so little a creature as man."

A man's reasons for keeping a diary are not mysterious. He wants to record, so that he may recall, everything he has done and seen. The unique fascination of Morris's *Diary* is that each page might, as it were, be a collaboration by James Boswell and John Quincy Adams.

As literature, or philosophy, the *Diaries* have no standing, except as so revelatory a record of human behavior is the stuff of literature and philosophy.

Morris is seldom in doubt as to the rightness of his judgments of persons or events. It is quite clear that he felt sure that, had the French Revolution been entrusted to him, the result would have been benign. But it is also evident that he would have called in the Americans to help him with whom he had worked and argued, and that while he believed in greater force than the nobles or the King were capable of, he would, as he wrote De Moustier, have the King proclaim "that every barrier should be thrown down which time or accident may have opposed to the general felicity of his people."

In reading the *Diaries*, it must be remembered that they were written in a great rush after hours of business letter writing, conferences with bankers, and all the visiting characteristic of the time. He may not have asserted his views so provocatively as the curt entries indicate, and perhaps his frequent mental cruelty to one person was less than he makes it appear.

The *Diary* begins on March 1, 1789, when Morris was "employed in writing all morning" after a conference at breakfast on how to proceed "with respect to the tobacco." That night he saw Molière's *The Misanthrope* acted "inimitably well."

On the fifth Jefferson took him to Versailles to meet Montmorin, the Minister of Foreign Affairs, who was not so cordial
as he would come to be and Morris realized "he already has
had more trouble than he desires with strangers." That day he
met the Duchess of Orléans, for whom he was to do so much;
saw D'Estaing, whom he had known as commander of the
French fleet in America and who would go to the guillotine like
Montmorin. Jefferson introduced him to the Count d'Angivilliers, Administrator of the King's Building, older brother of a
Count de Flahaut, of whom Morris had never heard.

Jefferson had him to a family dinner at the legation in the
Champs Elysées with his daughters and Crèvecoeur's and
General Greene's sons on the eighth. Martha, one daughter,
would marry the heir of Morris's friend, Colonel Thomas Randolph, the next year and be a sister-in-law of Anne Randolph.

It snowed "very fast" on the thirteenth and he was all morning at the "agreeable amusement" of writing. Sociable and gre-
garious as he was, he rejoiced all his life at the times when snow
or rain kept him to his writing or his books. In the thaw two
days later he had his first "cursed fall" in the Paris mud while
visiting and was kept "till late to get my clothes cleaned."

There can be no question how much these malign mischances
hurt his pride. They were always recorded, but his mind was
too healthy to become morbid about them, though they may
have been compensated by other compulsions.

Malesherbes, the Minister of Marine, "that excellent old
man," heard that Morris was in Paris and, remembering his
paper on the commerce of the French West Indies, asked to see
him. Morris sent word that he did not wish to talk on public
affairs with ministers: "I had rather leave our affairs in the
hands of our minister."

Madame de Chastellux, widow of Rochambeau's chief of
staff in America, tried to tell him "the history of M. de Lafayette and Madame Simien" but was interrupted and it is interesting that Morris, with all his curiosity about such things,
made no effort to hear more, nor even mentions it again. He
was particularly careful to avoid mention of the love affairs of
men he had little use for.

Then at Versailles on March 21 he was at the house of Cabar-
rus when Madame de Flahaut entered. She was twenty-eight
years old, with chestnut hair curled under its powder and
brown, heavy-lidded eyes. The count, her husband, was sixty-
three. She spoke English, as her husband did not, and was "a
pleasing woman . . . not a sworn enemy to intrigue," Morris
calmly noted.

A week later Madame de Corny, Jefferson's friend, told him
Madame de Flahaut had asked her to have them to supper together the following Thursday.

Sunday, the twenty-ninth, was a fine day and Morris, going
to walk all morning in the gardens of the Tuileries, "met by
accident" Madame de Flahaut. One wonders whether it was an
accident, or whether Morris did not think he might be seen
from the Louvre, where Madame de Flahaut lived. He took
great pride in his ability to "walk" on his wooden leg. Was it
not possible that a maid would say, "Oh, madame, the big
American with the wooden leg is making his promenade.
Everyone is talking about him. My friend in the De Ségurs'
household heard them asking him about his gallantries in
America"? And so perhaps her mistress hurried out by accident
to join him. Like a good Parisienne, she offered to show him
the paintings in Paris. Then the count, her husband, appeared.
But enough had been said to make Madame de Corny's supper
too far away to wait for.

On the last night of March, Morris went to the Louvre for
the first time and found "an elegant woman and a snug party."

So began their long affair. At times the torments of romance
between them seem almost unbearable, and again their passions seem almost to have nothing to do with love. They go
on for months after March '89, speaking their stylized, seductive
lines as though they were in a play. And then it is as though
two gifted, wonderfully attractive persons said, "Time and
place and people have never had such dramatic possibilities.
Let us be lovers in this play. Who knows on what the curtain
will fall?"

The Louvre, with its tortuous stairs, its innumerable doors,
had become "a vast caravansery," cut up into rooms and apart-

ments for persons attached to the court, for whom there was
no room at Versailles or who were without means to have
houses of their own.

Residence there was a sign of that queer, pensioned poverty
of nobles like the De Flahauts, who had lived there—his rooms
on the floor below his wife's—for ten years on a sinecure of some
eleven thousand francs from the Crown. There was a pension
of four thousand more from the Count d'Artois and "generosi-
ties" from D'Angivilliers. Through his brother De Flahaut had
been appointed "director of the gardens of the King," which
with the salary gave him residence in the Louvre. He had succeeded the naturalist Buffon in the post. They bought his furniture from the estate "*à bas prix*," and even so owed almost two
years' salary on it.

In the family there was now a little boy of four, Charles de
Flahaut. Madame's rooms had become a salon, not in the grand
manner, but full enough of their witty, worthless friends, who
came to talk endlessly and to gamble.

There was peasant's blood in the lady's veins and with it an
extraordinary mingling of shrewdness and intelligence with
sweetness and gaiety, soft yet ruthless, wanton but decorous,
with at times a revolution and all but a Terror in her own life,
like that which would engulf France.

In 1747, Irène de Buisson, of noble blood, had married
Charles Filleul, son of a wood merchant in Normandy, where
the name Filleul is like Smith in London. Probably the reason
for the marriage was an indication of pregnancy. Six hundred
francs had just been paid by the King of France through Pompa-
dour to the Demoiselle Irène de Buisson de Longpré, doubtless
for her virginity. It was not, however, until July 15, 1751, that
a daughter, Julie, was born but even then the father was presumably the King, Louis XV. Before 1761 two sons were born
who died, but on May 14 that year Irène Filleul bore a
daughter, Adélaide. Her father was believed to be one Bourret,
with whom her mother was living. The mother of Adèle de
Flahaut is thus seen to have been a very immoral woman. But
it is agreeable to record that she left the pleasantest of memories

among those who knew her. Adèle wrote of her that "each morning she awoke smiling" and Marmontel that she was neither a dupe nor a cheat in life. While she was living with Bourret, in the days of his wealth, she amiably got him the thing he most wanted. He had built a hunting lodge which cost him three hundred thousand francs and his great desire was to have Louis XV come to lunch there with Irène and him. So it was done and he was able to say to himself for the rest of his life, "The King of France and I lunched with our mistress," which brought him great content and harmed no one.

Adèle's mother, Irène, died in 1767 and Adèle at six was sent to a convent, possibly the one to which she later took Morris so frequently, and there she stayed, except for holidays at Longpré with her cousin, the Countess de Seran, and her sister Julie. Heredity, environment and education made a strange mingling of sweetness, innocence and precocity.

Her cousin De Seran was married to the aged and very ugly De Bullioud. He had spoken of his ugliness when he offered a marriage "of good and tender friendship" and the young countess, thinking it over for twenty-four hours, said she was persuaded that beauty and ugliness are things easily forgotten, and they married, living with mutual tenderness and respect.

Louis XV, with his taste for Seran beauty, had made the countess his customary offer while Adèle's mother was still alive. It was declined and there was a merry supper that night, with Marmontel there, and tough mutton to eat as a symbol of her virtue.

Adèle's later novels are full of descriptions of the trees and gardens at Longpré, where she "was carried away into the beautiful kingdom of dreams." In most of the novels a boy of her own age appears and they meet, marry and live happily ever afterward. This was denied her as it was most of the women of her class in France. Very rarely were a boy and girl, each of great wealth, born to friendly families at the right time. The arranged marriage, the sale of innocence to age, was the habit.

Julie, her sister, of exquisite, blond, blue-eyed beauty, had been married at sixteen, the year of her mother's death, to the *"haut et puissant seigneur François Poisson, Marquis de*

Marigny et de Menar," thirty years older. The marquis was wealthy, in terms of a King's pension, and without other attraction. The King gave his daughter Julie an income of twenty thousand francs. A daughter was born in 1771 and died in infancy and for Julie, with more beauty but less intelligence than her sister, nothing lay ahead but the familiar pattern of the court.

In 1778 the young Cardinal de Rohan, "delicate as a woman, handsome as an antique god," later the dupe of the Queen's Necklace affair, appeared and Julie left the high and puissant Marigny to live and travel with the cardinal in the clothes of a boy acolyte. She never returned to her husband, going to L'Abbaye-au-Bois for a time for asylum until the King raised her income to sixty thousand francs and she was able to have a house of her own and continue as Rohan's mistress.

There Adèle, seventeen, joined her and there came the Count de Flahaut, fifty-three, of ancient lineage and a friend of Julie's husband, and from there the next year Adèle married him. There was nothing else to do, and her mother and sister had done it and remained persons of great sweetness whom she loved.

But in her novel, *Adèle de Sénanges,* the one closest to her own early life, the bride weeps as she goes to the church and the author protests the handing over of an unhappy child to a man of whose qualities and faults she knows nothing.

As with her sister, and after almost the same interval, a priest of the Church came into Adèle's life, Charles Maurice de Talleyrand-Périgord, two years younger than Morris and seven years older than she.

Contemporaries speak of an effortless elegance and seductiveness about her. Her face has "complex defects," the nose too long, the lips *"inquiétantes,"* but the heavy-lidded eyes are kind and penetrating and there is that wonderful, amiable, feminine sweetness and vivacity, and her figure, with its share of peasant blood, is full and rounded.

All about her seems accounted for except one insatiable thing and of that we shall know more.

On April 2 the supper at Madame de Corny's took place as arranged and the hostess said to Morris, as he was leaving, "Well, I have had you to supper with Madame de Flahaut. Am I not a good woman?" The next day when he went to the Louvre to be taken to see the paintings he found Adèle in bed, apparently having forgotten the engagement, as he then thought, though he was shortly to learn that "*rendez-vous mal compris*" were part of the game. The count came in and they walked until Adèle dressed and joined them but "a scene which [my] imagination had painted very well turns out good for nothing. . . . Wind, rain and of course mud. . . . But this is human life."

On April 1, Morris saw the elder statesman, De Castries, on the plan to service the American debt, in part, by deliveries of tobacco, rice, flour and salt provisions. The marshal was doubtful about the last. Ireland could supply them and the Bordeaux wine trade needed the Irish business. The marshal told him to put the whole thing in writing with a margin for him to insert his observations. "He thinks the debt trifling against the great object of French commerce."

Morris goes on very busy with the Farmers-General on the tobacco deliveries and plans for the India trade. It was apparently in his mind that intimate relations were possible with any one of a number of the ladies he was meeting, but at Madame de Ségur's, with three of them listening to him, he decided "to avoid all farther folly for this day" and went home.

On the fourth he met General Dalrymple, whom he had not seen since the cartel meeting in '82, and was received "with great cordiality."

Adèle was just going out as he called on the sixth and had no time for him. He was in a bad humor, not helped by a tiresome business lunch of timeless familiarity. A French mill man from Sedan wanted to export fabrics to America and Morris, to please an acquaintance, agreed to "obtain some patterns from Philadelphia." It was altogether so frustrating that all the letters he wrote the next day he misdated the sixth, a lapse for his orderly mind equal to a major breakdown. To top this he went, after dinner with Dalrymple and Jefferson, to the Louvre because

Adèle had sent him a card asking him "to pass La Soirée." To his chagrin he found the soirée did not begin until nine and when he went back the lady sent down word she was not well.

That night Constable was writing him from New York: "Robert Morris wrote to me in his difficulties. I have paid £2000 for him and would do more had I the abilities," and then he adds, "I well know your first attention will be paid to our friend but I trust you will consider me also."

On the tenth Morris had two French officers, friends from Valley Forge days, to dine and "we drink like men who had spent part of our lives in America."

He went up to the Marne, where the rope-drawn ferry was not much to the honor of France, a result, perhaps, of "a government oppressive to industry but favorable to genius." He was annoyed by the people who were clamoring for "a Constitution," without any idea of what constitution, and with those who were against Necker and those who were for him; and with Lafayette who, for the most involved reasons, intended to oppose a motion that the Queen should not be regent in event of the King's death. Altogether it is not to be wondered at that on Saturday afternoon he got very drunk, to his own exasperation the next day.

He walked his hangover off Sunday morning and went for a long talk with Jefferson on American finances. At home a big American mail was in and one would like to know why it made him feel "better company for girls of sixteen than I thought it possible for me to be."

On Monday, the twentieth, he went to the Louvre, met Julie's second husband, the Marquis de Boursac, and in the evening went back and Talleyrand was there.

One must wonder what were Adèle's thoughts, as these two brilliant men, one a towering figure with a wooden leg, met the other of medium height, his bishop's vestments hiding his clubfoot except as he limped forward. The American's voice charmed all who heard it. The Frenchman's for all his silky manners and "quicksilver" personality had a *timbre rude.* He carried a snuffbox, *"une vaste tabatière,"* and the American did not use snuff at all. Morris's face and nose were large and mas-

culine, Talleyrand's face slightly effeminate at its best, almost
gnomelike at its worst. The French priest was a Mason, the
American Protestant was not. (It must tax the suavity of them
both if they are aware that the wooden leg of one is still preserved and the brace for the right foot of the other, "a block
with a steel rod extending up the inner side of the leg to be tied
to a loop below the knee," is in a museum.)

The nature of Adèle de Flahaut was like the Maytime in
which she was born and these men were born under the cold
wintry stars of Aquarius. Both loved books and women. She
had known Morris a month that day and Talleyrand for ten
years, and her little boy was his son.

Morris left the Louvre almost at once to go to his correspondence, and two days later Lafayette came by appointment to
Jefferson's to get their advice.

Morris told him the Swiss Guards should be removed from
the King's person and, as a compliment and expression of confidence, the national troops be substituted. "Mr. Jefferson does
not seem to think this important." It was important. The Swiss
were a provocation to the country until they were massacred.
It was the sort of practical detail in which Morris excelled.
Afterwards Jefferson and Morris went to have their profiles
done and to get the watch for Jefferson to take home to Washington. Beau Dillon urged Morris to write Washington to hurry
along his Croix de Cincinnatus.

At the Invalides, a Frenchman told Morris he heard the
veterans saying what a pity it was so fine a man should have
lost a leg. Morris noted that the man had not seen him give
them a crown or he would have appreciated their compassion.

He went to the Louvre Sunday evening the twenty-sixth and
after supper Talleyrand read aloud a Protest of the Nobles and
Clergy of Brittany, during which Morris "uncivilly [fell]
asleep." Adèle was "unwell and has besides met with something . . . which preys on her spirits," perhaps the first cold,
mocking question from Talleyrand about Morris.

Monday morning the shops were closed and there was a
bread riot in Paris. Castries had shown Necker the debt plan

of Morris's and Necker had said he could only accept cash or tobacco. Troops with fieldpieces were moving along the Rue St. Honoré. Settlement with the Farmers-General hung on a small difference in price and "if it cannot be resolved [they] agree to go to arbitration."

As April ended Morris wrote Washington at length on the political situation: "The materials for a revolution in this country are very indifferent . . . one fatal principle . . . pervades all ranks. It is a perfect indifference to the violation of engagements. . . . The great mass of the common people have no religion but their priests, no law but their superiors, no moral[s] but their interest." It was written as Washington was taking the oath as President in New York.

On May 5, Morris saw the great spectacle, when the King, with the Queen, came to address the States-General. With his sense of history, it had, as he wrote, "the pang of greatness going off." Much has been made of the tears he said came to his eyes as the King was interrupted by the cheering, but they are as surely understandable as those of anyone watching a deeply moving play. And as to his wishing, amidst the cheering for the King, that someone would raise their voice to wish well to the unhappy Queen, what more in keeping with his attitude toward women and his magnanimous nature? "The pang of greatness going off" touched another great lover of human liberty.

I tell you again [Edmund Burke wrote] that the recollection of the manner in which I saw the Queen of France in 1773 and the contrast between that brilliancy, splendour and beauty, with the prostrate homage of a nation to her, and the abominable scene of 1789 did draw tears from my eyes and wetted my paper.

That the tears or the generous wish indicated Morris believed the inept royal tyranny should continue is absurd. It was a spectacle of "state and ancientry" and normal men would be moved by it. As the Majesties went out there *was* a "*Vive la Reine*" and the Queen curtsied low to the assembly and still lower as they cheered.

Morris had watched the parade bareheaded and came back ruddy with sunburn.

Adèle was at tric trac (backgammon) when he next called and he went to the De Segurs' and played with the children. At Madame de Chastellux's he noticed that the exquisite Duchess of Orléans had the finest arm in France and was always touching some part of her face to show the arm to advantage.

Then on May 12, while he was discussing with Jefferson the sale of some lands around the Falls of the Potomac, which Washington had written them about, another American came in. Their lives were to be strangely linked even after Morris was dead, and in a way they were to know more about each other's secret lives than any other man did.

The man was William Short, Jefferson's secretary from Virginia, then thirty years old, one of the founders of the Phi Beta Kappa. He had come out with Jefferson four years before. Morris remembered that he "had seen and known [him] in America" and, seeing him two days later at Madame de Tessé's with Jefferson, observed that "Mr. Short . . . is a great favorite."

Business was going badly and Morris's frame of mind was "melancholy," an unusual thing for him. He complained of a luncheon menu of "a mackerel, a pigeon, fresh eggs and asparagus," talked viniculture with Jefferson, saw a play with "vile Italian actors." He was having a "limonade and ice" in the Palais Royal Gardens when a waiter told him two ladies were outside, wanting to speak to him. One was Julie de Boursac, Adèle's sister, and he was puzzled to know what it was all about. He went to see Adèle the next evening and she insisted that he stay as Julie was coming, which he did. They "prattled nonsense" and put their husbands out of patience and it did not occur to Morris that when he was gone Adèle doubtless said to her sister, "Well, now you have seen him twice, what do you really think?"

The Farmers-General now resorted to a familiar mercantile last stand. They said the quality of the tobacco had been bad.

Morris explained the nature of the Inspection Laws and the system of plantation management to prove that "knavery . . . cannot have so great an effect as [they suppose]," and saw his lawyers about the suit which now seemed inevitable. Adèle was not at home when he called, on the way back from the lawyers, and he sulkily notes it was fortunate "as I thereby escape spending the evening abroad."

However, the next day things picked up. He went to see Madame de la Suze and first saw a French lady undress and dress, "except the shift." Baths such as Franklin had witnessed would follow at the Louvre. And that night De Boursac, Adèle's brother-in-law, told him he had been elected to the Club Valois of which he, Talleyrand, Lafayette, De Biron, the Abbé Sieyès, and the explorer Bougainville, who left his name in the South Pacific, were members.

On the thirtieth Jefferson and he had a long talk on French politics and Morris felt Jefferson "does not form very just estimates of character, but rather assigns too many to the humble rank of fools, whereas in life the gradations are infinite and each individual has his peculiarities of fort and feeble."

On the morning of June 1 the bankers, Le Couteulx and Cie, sent their chief clerk to examine all the papers Morris had written in French for the lawsuit and the plan for the debt. There was but little to correct, and De Castries, reading the latter the next day, said he would send it to Necker himself.

It was the fourth of June at Jefferson's house in the Champs Elysées that a small thing happened which must have given Morris enormous satisfaction. They were waiting for Short to get back from Versailles, where the Dauphin was dying. The day was cold and rainy and Jefferson had a good fire going. As they waited Jefferson said the sculptor, Houdon, wanted Morris to stand the next day for the figure of Washington, which Virginia had commissioned him to make. There could be no more indisputable evidence of the magnificence of the bearing of this man with the wooden leg. Paris must have been full of hungry models. Lafayette and Jefferson were both big, but one was awkward with queer shoulders and there was something lank in the other's build. No wonder Morris consented to "the humble employment of a manakin" and after posing the next day paid "a visit of respectful enquiry to Madame de Flahaut" and went off to the Club Valois with its men of the world.

However, at ten o'clock supper at the Louvre the next night Talleyrand was of the company and Morris records that he is "an intimate friend of Madame de Flahaut . . . a sly, cool, cunning and ambitious man," adding, "I know not why conclusions so disadvantageous to him are formed in my mind, but so it is and I cannot help it." Doubtless he had learned the extent of the intimacy and the paternity of her child.

He stood until he was tired for Houdon three days later but at home came a note from Adèle asking him to take her that evening to her sister's. He was "literally *échauffé*" but went to find her also weary and there was "a good deal of chit chat with her" during which she told him he suited the taste of the country.

The Farmers-General talked compromise again the next day and Morris went out to Versailles to a service in the Chapelle, where two nobles, in a variation of the modern hotfoot, put candles in the pockets of different gentlemen and then lit them "to the great merriment of the spectators." Morris, though not a victim, was very critical of the impression made on the domestics and villagers at worship.

On the twelfth the Third Estate "called on the nobles and clergy to join them and proceed to business, which has thrown the [nobles] into a rage." Jefferson came to tell Morris about it, saying the situation was very critical. Jefferson had written a Charter of Rights for Lafayette with ten brief points: the States-General alone to levy taxes and make laws (with the consent of the King); habeas corpus; civil authority over the military; abolition of pecuniary privileges and exemptions. But it included "annihilations of distinctions of order and with respect to this nation I am sure it is wrong and cannot eventuate well," Morris said.

The thing was that "Jefferson and the leaders of liberty here" felt that a bloodless revolution could be accomplished through something similar to the federal Constitution. Morris contended that if that were tried in a country of illiteracy at the bottom,

and inexperience and corruption at the top, the results would
be those which occurred, butchery and terror. Every ingredient
which had made the American Constitution possible was
missing.

All the week that followed Adèle was sick and "invisible."
On the nineteenth the clergy by a small majority went over to
the Third Estate and Morris foresaw that the nobles were
doomed. De Boursac told him "the King has called a Council
on the present state of affairs in which each is to deliver his
opinion in His Majesty's presence." This will not produce any
effect whatever, Morris told him.

On June 21, Sunday afternoon, Morris went to see Adèle,
now recovered. She seemed inclined to make him her con-
fidant about her domestic affairs and asked him about certain
affairs of gallantry she had been told he once engaged in. He
said they were idle tales and he had a perfect respect for the
lady in question. He said, hoping to make the point clear, that
he never lost respect for anyone who consented to make him
happy by affection.

The tension in Paris made it clear that further negotiations
on the debt were impossible but that it could probably be
financed in London.

On the twenty-third Lafayette, sitting next to him at dinner,
took Morris to task for injuring the Cause. Morris told him he
was "opposed to the democracy from regard to liberty," that
Lafayette's party was going headlong to destruction . . .
"their views respecting this nation are totally inconsistent with
the materials of which it is composed. . . . He tells me he is
sensible his party are mad . . . but is not the less determined
to die with them." Morris must have shaken his head. He had
already reminded Washington that Lafayette's education in
America had been only half completed. He told Lafayette to
bring the party to their senses and live rather than die with
them.

After a minority of the nobles joined the Tiers and clergy
on the twenty-fifth, the Farmers-General came suddenly to
terms. The résumé in the *Diary* of that day is a textbook passage of business administration and sound trading practice, a

thousand words of it, and Morris was anxious to be off to London on the debt.

On the last night of June a mob broke into a prison and released some soldiers held for drunkenness. The next day, Morris, too busy to use their cipher, wrote Jay how hopeless the situation looked and that the Queen and the royal brothers, "hated, humbled, mortified," were intriguing to save some shattered remnants of the royal authority. If the King had any abilities or any firmness he "would have had the exalted honor of giving a free constitution to above twenty millions of his fellow creatures . . . [to] the unanimous applause of posterity. . . . [But] he acts from terror only."

The same day, leaving the Flahaut apartments, he fell down the stairs and tore the knees of his breeches so that he could not go to the club, an enraging thing for a man who had stood for Houdon.

On July 4, at the legation's traditional party, he urged Lafayette "to preserve . . . some constitutional authority to the body of nobles as the only means of preserving any liberty for the people," and wrote Carmichael in Madrid that night that the French "want an American Constitution . . . without reflecting that they have not American citizens to support [it]."

The food at his traiteur's did not agree with him and he was indisposed for several days, though he walked with Jefferson, worried about his departure and the troops massing around Paris.

On the eleventh, Adèle, feeling better, sent a note asking him to supper, a party of five.

On Sunday the twelfth at the Louvre they heard that Necker had been dismissed and there was commotion in the streets, and Adèle was alarmed that her husband's name appeared on a printed list of "furious aristocrats." Morris drove two of the frightened guests home and continued on to Jefferson's, seeing a troop of cavalry stoned in the Place Royale, now the Concorde.

Jefferson said Necker was banished and Montmorin, the Foreign Minister, had resigned. The next day there were no carriages and Morris, with a green bow in honor of the Third

Estate in his hat, walked to the Louvre and tried to allay Adèle's fears.

He was at Le Couteulx's on the fourteenth when a man burst in with the news that the Bastille had fallen and the governor's head was being carried through the city on a pole. Haskell, another American, writing Constable that night, said he was with Morris when the mob passed and Morris called it "the Liberty Pole of France." Jefferson with Madame de Corny heard it when her husband came in. Morris went to his banker's and then to the Louvre where Adèle was in much anxiety for her husband's safety. "The question is whether he should leave the city."

Then with his often incredible frivolity Morris took the writing pad from Adèle's lap and scribbled some of his "wretched lines":

> No lover I. Alas! too old
> To raise in you a mutual Flame.
> Then take a Passion rather cold
> And call it by fair Friendship's Name.

The count demanded a translation and "looked rather foolish at the declaration of being too old to excite a passion."

In the morning on the way to Jefferson's, Morris's carriage was continually stopped, searched and ordered to detour. A British officer with him said he was happy to be in Paris at the present moment and "So am I," Morris said.

At the Louvre, Adèle told him she must see the deputies come to town the next day, "that all women have the like folly." At the club, nobles in from Versailles told Morris of the night before—how the Queen and the King's brother got the Household Troops drunk, officers and men, and planned to take deputies of the Assembly prisoner and of how the Duke of Liancourt, galloping out from Paris, woke the King at two in the morning with the news of the Bastille, of how Talleyrand had been ordered to write a speech for the King, who would come in to Paris the next day at eleven.

The events of the fourteenth held up the final settlement with the Farmers-General, who went "out of town." On the

seventeenth with Adèle, in a window in the Rue St. Honoré,
Morris saw the King come by with the deputies, even the
household troops wearing the cockade of Paris. Later he heard
of the flight of the Count d'Artois and felt that "the folly of
[Adèle's] husband and the madness of his brother [in supporting D'Artois]" would ruin them both and went to the Louvre to
warn her.

On Sunday he asked Jefferson for his passport to England
and dined at the Flahauts' with Talleyrand and De Biron there.

At the club the man who was to be president of the New-
York Historical Society recommended "a subscription to collect the various papers found in the Bastille and then to employ
an able hand in writing the annals of that diabolical castle. . . ."

He saw Lafayette, who had sent the keys to the Bastille
to Washington by Tom Paine, the next day, the twentieth, and
Lafayette said he had had "the utmost power his heart could
wish and is grown tired of it. That he has commanded absolutely an hundred thousand men, has marched his sovereign
about the streets as he pleased, prescribed the degree of applause he should receive . . ." Morris wrote Washington there
may have been 80,000. From the Lafayettes' he went to Le
Couteulx's.

It is extraordinary to see how apparent was the still distant
but gathering bankruptcy of Robert Morris. As Gouverneur
came into Le Couteulx's one of their people was going out. Le
Couteulx said the man was going to the Farmers-General to
say that "tobacco now at Bordeaux should be received, according to the real taxe." But that isn't so, Morris said. This is folly
and will only alarm the farmers. But the man was already gone,
and Le Couteulx said, "Robert Morris has drawn for the freight
of the *Alliance* on [our] house at Cadiz."

Morris was surprised and shaken. It plainly meant that
Robert Morris was very pressed and had drawn by a familiar
device on a distant branch house, which would probably accept
and leave him time to cover and explain.

He told Le Couteulx it might have been done to reimburse
another bank and to keep it all in one channel. Le Couteulx
said severely if that was so he thought better of it. That he

would feel better about a hundred thousand francs "in a train of business" than "20,000 as a dead advance," and Morris felt "too much the force of all these observations to reply otherwise than by assenting."

People said he was a "bad counsellor" for Robert Morris. Far more likely, as the end shows, that without him Robert Morris was like a reckless gamester at a roulette table.

"With infinite coolness and seriousness" he told Adèle that he could not "consent to be only a friend . . . that I know myself too well. That at present I am perfectly my own master with respect to her, but that it would not long be the case. That having no idea of inspiring her with a passion I have no idea either of subjecting myself to one. That besides, I am timid to a fault. . . ." She thought it a strange conversation, or so she said.

He left Le Couteulx's, saw the Duke of Orléans at the club and was "as cold as an Englishman to him." Then he went to the Louvre on other business.

The next day, with Lafayette's pass, he took her and her niece, Mademoiselle Duplessis, to see the inside of the Bastille and spent the evening at the Louvre "instead of writing, as I should otherwise have done."

He was waiting for his carriage the next day when a mob passed with a man's head on a pike and his body dragged naked on the earth. The man was De Foulon, seventy-five years old, who had accepted a place in the ministry. The head was shown to Foulon's son-in-law, the intendant of Paris, who was then slain and the mangled fragments of his body added to the parade. "Gracious God what a people!" Morris said. This was the sort of thing his critics later apparently expected him to approve. In his *Letter Book* for that day there is a letter to an unnamed woman[2] in America where he says:

I was never till now fully apprized of the mildness of American character. I have seen my countrymen enraged and threatening. It has even happened that in an affray some lives were lost. But we know not what it is to slay the defenseless [?] who is in our power.

[2]Perhaps someone can identify the lady from the close: "Remember me affectionately to all your family particularly to the little Captain."

We cannot parade the heads of our fellow citizens and drag the mangled carcasses through the streets. We cannot feast our eyes on such spectacles.

That night he knew that the Morris monopoly with the Farmers-General was over, and wrote him "the present is so mighty that it swallows up all the past."

The next morning, the twenty-third, two notes came, one after the other, asking him to come to the Louvre for dinner. He went and the previous conversation was renewed, Adèle telling him of "a marriage of the heart," without mentioning Talleyrand's name. Morris said the name and she agreed, saying "she [could not] commit an infidelity to him. By degrees however we come very near it."

He dined at the Montmorins' at Versailles the next day, congratulating him on getting the Foreign Office back, but Madame de Montmorin, looking three years ahead, said "she wishes to be a great way off." He advised Montmorin to recall De Moustier as minister in New York and send out Luzerne and then he drove back to the Louvre "in pursuance of a note received" that morning.

Saturday, the twenty-fifth, he worked hard all morning, a member of the States-General having asked him "to throw together some thoughts respecting the Constitution of this country," and on Sunday Adèle asked him if he would go to Versailles, "to confer with the committee who are to report a constitution. She [has been] charged . . . to make this request." He showed her what he had written and explained it for her to translate and afterwards there "was a little wild chit chat."

He dined Monday with Jefferson, got his passport, and then went to the Louvre where Adèle was "at her toilette." The count came in and she dressed "before us with perfect decency even to the shift. Monsieur leaves us to make a long visit and we are to occupy ourselves with making a translation. We sit down with the best disposition imaginable but instead of a translation . . . [elided in mss.]" *Questo giorno non leggevemo più.*

Morris made his own translation later, but before her surrender, Adèle asked him to send a message to the King through Lafayette.

He dined with Lafayette the next day and told him, refusing the source, that there should be "an association to protect the prince." It is not clear precisely what is meant by the words "[I] propose a plan to get rid of the difficulty of the Assemblée Nationale, which is bound not to tax till the Constitution is compleated and which is pressed in consequence for time." Possibly a brief adjournment like that in Philadelphia, July 1787. Then Morris urged "strongly the danger of a Constitution too democratical and leave him (I think) much impressed."

The warnings against methods "too democratical" should be weighed with those similar ones of Madison, Sherman, Gerry, Hamilton and almost all the rest of the thirty-nine men in Philadelphia, two years before.

On the twenty-ninth Morris took platonic leave of Madame de Flahaut—"In this I do myself violence, but it is right"—but made arrangements for letters to and from London.

On the thirty-first from Dieppe, after dining on fish, fresh out of the sea, he wrote Washington a long account of the Revolution, while it rained outside and the wind was fresh from the southwest.

On August 3 he saw Beachy Head and the lads in the English boats "whose cleanliness, activity and silence . . . contrasts amazingly with the boats . . . at Havre and Dieppe."

Dover was the cleanest town since America and the crops and animals in the English fields were better than in France. "The tea, sugar, cream, bread, butter and cold ham are each in their kind perfect," but the roads lack the "avenues of trees which give an air of magnificence in the approaches to Paris."

CHAPTER FIFTEEN

Pleasures Don't Wear Men
Out in Paris

(August–December 1789)

Morris's month in London was that of any private banker visiting there then or since. The main object was to feel out the possibilities of an Anglo-American syndicate to speculate in the American debt to France. For this, Daniel Parker, an associate of Robert Morris and a slippery, ineffective promoter, had persuaded Gouverneur Morris to let him come to London in June. His reports, on Morris's arrival, were as enthusiastic and worthless as might be expected from a man of his type.

This plan, however, was a long-term one with profits, if any, in the distant future. Additionally Morris had to deal with a variety of correspondents of Robert Morris, most of whom were large and uneasy creditors. Beside which, he had his own cargo ventures with William Constable and Company. And London was full of friends and relatives—his half-brother, Staats Morris, with his wife, the Duchess of Gordon, and old David Ogden, his sister's father-in-law—and several people Jefferson had given him letters to.

He took rooms at Froome's Hotel in Covent Gardens, six shillings a day for himself and one for his servant, and hired a carriage and horses.

The day after his arrival there was a letter from Adèle, but no letters "from Holland, so that I cannot go to work for the

relief of R[obert] M[orris]'s affairs." They came very shortly
from the Dutch bankers refusing a loan on Robert Morris's
"Delaware Works," where he still hoped the national Capitol
would be built.

Peter Whiteside, another Robert Morris associate, was in
Fleet Prison for debt arising from their transactions. There was
the question of his release and also a verification of all his
claims. And statements had to be drawn up by four merchant
bankers of Robert Morris's tangled accounts for Gouverneur
to study.

One of the letters Jefferson had given him was to the young
Lord Wycombe, twenty-four, four years younger than Adèle,
heir of America's friend, the Earl of Shelburne, now Marquis of
Lansdowne. He was out when Morris left it and Morris must
have often wished he had never left it at all. That night he
gave Colonel John Trumbull (thirty-three) "letters for Paris,"
and Trumbull left, to paint Jefferson before he left for America.

Jefferson's other letter was to Mrs. Cosway, one of his three
amitiés. Morris found her "vastly pleasant," but however in-
quisitive he must have been about Jefferson's relations with her,
there is no mention nor speculation about them. He discussed
with her a little, though, the *"froideur Anglais"* but it had to do
with ranging "the ladies in battalia on the opposite side of the
room [from the men]."

Mrs. Damer, cousin of Horace Walpole, seemed anxious to
know him better but he "had no time for that sort of thing just
now," though he told her, apropos of English formality, that
"the French, having no liberty in their government, have compensated . . . that misfortune by bestowing a great deal upon
society [which] I fear in England . . . is confined to the House
of Commons."

It was at her house he first met the Duke of Leeds, the
Foreign Secretary he was to deal with the next year. One can
see the traditional English cabinet minister eying the voluble
American. "After some time the Duke of Leeds wakes up and
enquires of Mr. Adams."

The negotiations in the City were harassing, caught as he
was between two fires. He was bound to do all he could for

Robert Morris but he must not do so much that there could be any inference of William Constable being involved.

The London correspondents of Constable were Phyn, Ellice and Inglis and the partners were not strangers to America. Now a great City house, they had been founded in Schenectady, New York, after the French and Indian War, as intermediate commission merchants and bankers between New York, Montreal and the Upper Posts.

Ellice, now forty-six, had been a New York Loyalist and returned to London in 1780 to found that branch. All the great North American land and mercantile names were on their books: John Askin, Morris, Willing, Macomb, Edgar and Macomb, Constable, and individuals like the Johnsons and Daniel Claus.

Constable wrote him afterwards, "I have given my word of honour to Mr. Phyn that our affairs should by no means be complicated with Mr. Robert Morris's." He told Gouverneur that "all things considered I am satisfied with your terms with Phyn but it could be better expressed." How familiar in business the next line. "The right of doing business with other houses is a good clause." He adds that Phyn says "Robert Morris is always jealous. I have done everything in my power to serve Robert Morris, but as is too often the case by lending your money you lose your friend. He is dissatisfied because I cannot go farther."

Whiteside, in prison, begged Morris to represent him at his creditors' meeting which Morris reluctantly agreed to do—more accounts to read and verify—if he would "acknowledge the amounts due Robert Morris."

Gregory and Company wanted to withhold moneys due Robert Morris from them and with difficulty Gouverneur got them released under an agreement to arbitrate any difference. Puller and Company, whose help was needed on the tail of the tobacco deliveries in France, wanted "to keep clear of Robert Morris" and asked Gouverneur's personal guaranty of Le Couteulx.

The talk in the old bank parlor comes clearly through the *Diary* entries in words familiar to any businessman.

MORRIS: There can be no doubt of Le Couteulx's stability, but
if you like, you may have my guarantee.

PULLER: Even so, we shall expect 2½% on the whole business.

MORRIS: Such a commission is wholly out of line. I'd have no
trouble placing it any number of places for 1%. However, I regard Puller's name in it as worth say an extra
½%. I'll go to 1½.

PULLER: Well, we don't like cutting our rates. However, I
assume there will be other business coming along and
with your guarantee we'll do this for 1½.

When talks like these were over, Morris went to walk in Kensington Gardens or "in the square before the door of the French
Embassy."

He went to visit at Down Place, the estate of John Church,
husband of Angelica Schuyler, who had served in the American
Army. They took him to see the marvelous telescope of William
Herschel, who had discovered the planet Uranus, and Morris
noted in Herschel the "manner . . . peculiar to men of his
kind of greatness: simplicity, modesty, mildness." He also
noted the Churches' young French governess sent by Madame
de Corny. "She is young enough and handsome enough," and
he suspected that Church was trying to give her a lesson. There
is a familiar Americanism in his note that the drinking water at
Down Place was the only good water he had tasted in Europe.

He went to see the great shipyards and naval arsenal at
Woolwich and was deeply struck, knowing already the influence of sea power in history.

But there were "no letters from Paris which amazes me" and
when on September 8 Parker admitted "the purchase of the
American debt [here] is off," Morris left for Paris in the morning. Mrs. Penn gave him a guinea to buy rouge for her.

He reached the Rue de Richelieu at seven the evening of the
thirteenth, bathed, and "sent to enquire [for] Madame de
Flahaut." She was out of town and he supped at his club, hearing the Assembly had agreed on a single chamber and a suspen-
sive veto for the King. Constable wrote him that night he had
given Benjamin Harrison an export order for 20,000 bushels of
wheat and sold the carriage horses at empty Morrisania for

seventy-five pounds. He said that one of Morris's sisters had just come in "much distressed. She has not had a shilling from the money placed here by Staats. She has applied to Burr [who was practicing law in New York] who assures her he has never touched a farthing."

With frustrated masculine perversity Morris proceeded to get very drunk with a Pole and two Frenchmen and had a sleepless night after the debauch. Apparently William Short joined the party because he came with comic guilt early the next day "to see if he was mistaken last evening in supposing it was me whom he met."

But not all frightened Paris was drunk. He found the De Ségurs tense and anxious, wishing they could flee to America. The Montmorin family were grave and worried. At Jefferson's, Lafayette admitted the troops would now not mount guard in the rain but was fatuously confident they would follow him into action. He admitted to being worried about bread for Paris and the Duc de la Rochefoucauld said, with that incredible irrelevance of his class, that someone had just written a good book on Commerce of Grain. At the Club Valois, nobles admitted the King's "feebleness of character" was such that "nobody can trust themselves . . . or risque themselves in support of his authority."

Then early on the morning of the twenty-second a note came to the hotel from Adèle. Word of his arrival had reached her in the country and she had come ninety miles in fifteen hours in a wretched carriage to see him. He dressed and hurried to the Louvre to possess her and the next day she took him to the Convent of Chaillot to meet the old English nun to whom she was "indebted for her education" and her facility in English.

Who can say what was in the minds of these two people in the months that followed, each at times so completely recognizable, each so incomprehensible? Their behavior is wanton and flagrant, and one may say, well, this is simply the loose morals of the eighteenth century. But that is frequently not the case at all, when as so often they are as careful of what people may say as any conventional moderns.

On her side, it appears increasingly that Morris's appeal was
so great that other men and even Talleyrand, as Vivian said to
Merlin, were "as dull as arithmetic." Her conduct has all the
winsome tenderness and the intimacy of little things of a girl
truly in love.

On the other hand, she saw her whole ways and means of
life, a roof over her head and money to live on, disappearing,
and Morris was rich, famous and an American citizen. Yet
though there is a trivial avarice about her, it is very trivial and
not unattractive as when in the Louvre she tells him, after they
have been extravagantly shopping for other people in America,
that she has no "handsome sugar dish" for her tea service.

Her attitude to the Revolution is as though it were an intellectual game in which the brilliant men around her made
moves, wrote financial plans and constitutions and asked her
advice about them. There is never the remotest shade of hatred
or blame for the wretched peasants and common people of
Paris.

Of course there are those who say that the affair with Morris
was arranged by her and Talleyrand, so that she might be
Talleyrand's spy. This is an absurdity.

There was an intellectual vigor and self-confidence about
Morris obviously beyond that of any man she had ever met.
Intellectually the equal of any of them, his Western breeziness
must have been enormously stimulating. We know nothing of
the intensity of her physical passion for Talleyrand but toward
Morris it was evidently insatiable until that August day in 1792
when the Tuileries was stormed. She all but says to Morris the
lines of Madame de Merteuil from the *Liaisons Dangereuses:*

> *Séduite par votre réputation il me semblait que vous manquiez
> à ma gloire. Je brûlais de vous combattre corps à corps.*

She used many feminine wiles on him, and seldom has it been
done more winsomely. But who will not recognize the girl in
love, when, after their first reunion, she irrationally takes Morris
to be shown off to the *religeuse* who had brought her up?

As to what Morris was thinking of, the answer is more
obscure. His conduct toward her is often calculating and

abominable. He is revoltingly careful not to say he loves her in those words. It would be easy to conclude it was merely a fascinating game to him, the cuckolding of a noble husband and a noble priest with a beautiful young woman. But there is much more to it. He thinks well of his own mind, but when he reads a letter of hers to Talleyrand he "bows to superiority." He assumes indifference "to keep her passion alive," but he goes back and back like the moth to the light. Conceding all his practiced skill in seduction, it must be remembered that for three years, with much temptation, he never practiced it elsewhere, and underneath it one senses the "aggression" complex arising from the inferiority his amputated leg gave him.

It is of course remarkable that both of Adèle's lovers should have been cripples. With their mental superiority to other men, it may have appealed to the maternal in her. Little but real fulfillment was missing in their intimacy. Mentally stimulating to each other, mutually sensual, they go happily shopping, to the theater and opera. They have their private jokes about languor after love, light lewdness, quarrels, tears, confidences, verses left by him when she is out—"Come lovely Woman, why so long delay?"—little troubles of the day, incessant demands from her for his carriage, or "to be called for," and the inevitable concern as to whether she is pregnant which, amazingly, they each hope she will be "when her husband returns."

It was four days after Adèle's return that Morris first met the famous Germaine de Staël, five years her junior, wife of the Swedish ambassador, daughter of Necker, one of the greatest heiresses in Europe, and mistress of Talleyrand's friend Narbonne. There had once been a plan for her to marry Beau Fersen, when he came back from Yorktown. There is little reason to doubt that Morris could also have had Minette, as her father called her, had he so desired. They were friends for many years afterwards, long after the link to Adèle was broken. Like Adèle, she became a novelist. She was not a beauty, though her rich breasts and her passions and her money appealed to many men.

Aside from anything else, the reason she had no amorous

appeal to Morris must have been that she was not "a sensible woman." Everything about her was fantastic and often grotesque, qualities wholly absent in the two women most important in his life. Whatever sins they committed or whatever disasters struck them, they remained well-organized, "sensible" people.

Edward Gibbon, who had wanted to marry Minette's mother, saw her at eighteen and wrote Lady Sheffield she "was wild, vain but good-natured." Benjamin Constant, once her lover, said twenty-five years later, "[She] is a serpent of ferocious vanity," and someone the previous year told John Quincy Adams, who put it in his *Diary*, that "talking to her is the same thing as if you had been talking *avec une folle*." Fanny Burney said that "with all her wildness and blemishes [she] is a delightful companion." Jefferson told Daniel Webster she was "nervous and fidgety. Got up from the table at dinner 5 or 6 times and walked up and down."

All this bears on Morris's personality. The complete libertine would certainly have wanted the body of Madame de Staël, if only for the experience of such variety.

One must wonder how a characteristic question of hers at their first meeting affected him. She asked him if he had written a book on the Constitution. He said he had assisted in its formation. Then she asked him how he lost his leg. Unfortunately not in the service of his country, he told her and wrote in his *Diary* that in the Falstaff's Leer of invitation she gave him he saw how easy it would be to stimulate her curiosity to the experiment of what can be affected "by the native of the new world who has left one of his legs behind him." There is no record that the amputation was ever mentioned to him by Adèle de Flahaut.

The next day he learned at Madame de Corny's that Jefferson had left for America, leaving William Short, three days before his thirtieth birthday, as chargé. No one knew that Jefferson had already been appointed Secretary of State.

Meanwhile, whatever the daughter might tactlessly say, there was much Morris had to say to Necker himself. Feudalism may have been "abolished," but food and cash for the nation had still to be provided and the government of a great continental and colonial power continued.

Wheat and flour, Morris proposed, could be brought quickly from the Hudson River Valley. On terms allowing a reasonable profit part of the American debt could be funded in Amsterdam with an inflow of cash to France and of supplies for the West Indies and the fleet. He gave Necker proposals for both.

It is wonderful to see the timeworn working of party jealousy and of the go-between, the five-percenter, follow. Lafayette, an opponent of Necker's, came at once to ask if Morris could not buy flour for them in London. It must have taxed Morris's usual urbanity to reply, "Yes, I could. Someone else could do it better. The trouble is England would not let it go"—without adding "as anyone else but you would know." And the same day "in typical fashion an intermediary, entirely ignorant of the business [came to say] such a contract can be obtained [if proposed through him]."

He had talked politics with Adèle the night before, and "this amiable woman shows a precision and justness of thought very uncommon indeed in either sex," and when she said, "Finally, my friend, you and I, we shall govern France," he conceded that "the kingdom is actually in much worse hands," and she made him laugh by saying that she was going to talk to Vicq d'Azyr, the Queen's physician, "and set him to work to remove some of Her Majesty's prejudices. . . . I would give her a man each night and a Mass each morning." It was a divine evening with the Count de Flahaut far away in Madrid.

But two days later, October 1, Adèle was *triste* and sure she had conceived. Morris talked to her "a long time. . . . If . . . nothing happens, we are to take care for the future untill the husband returns, and then exert ourselves to add one to the number of human existences. This is a happy mode of conciliating *Prudence* and *Duty*."

It is extraordinary that two such people should have contemplated her sleeping with her husband as a safeguard to their own passions, but certainly not unique in human experience.

Unlike those lovers, the National Assembly, Gouverneur wrote Robert Morris that night, "have no fixed system to get through difficulties but live upon expedients . . . they neither reason, examine nor discuss." He took Adèle to De Corny's, where she was very amiable to William Short, who was not a little pleased, and then left her at the Louvre "not without regret, on my part at least." She was going to Versailles in the morning but would write him from there, sixteen miles away.

At some date, and very probably this day, as the Flanders Regiment was being feasted at Versailles, Short and Morris became mutually aware of the other's love affair.

Madame de Corny was a close friend of Adèle's and there was plainly a telltale happiness about her and Morris coming in out of the "rainy, disagreeable" October evening. If Morris knew about Short, he had scrupulously avoided recording it, and never did so in *Diary* or letter in any but completely innocent words. So it was with anyone he cared for or disliked. The vices and secrets of the rest of mankind fascinated him.

Short had been twenty-six when he came out as Jefferson's secretary. Almost at once he had met Alexandrine Charlotte de Rohan-Chabot, known as Rosalie. She was a year older than he, married to her own uncle, the great Duke de la Rochefoucauld, twenty years older. Mother-in-law difficulties did not exist since hers was her grandmother, who had brought her up.

The tale of this diplomat and duchess is like an old troubadour's song. Short lived into his ninety-first year loving her. She ceased writing to him only after fifty years. Adèle yielded to Morris after four months. Short waited six years to possess the lovely Rosalie and then but briefly.

As Morris and he work more and more closely together in the financial and diplomatic affairs of their country, it is hard to realize the storms going on within them.

On the fourth Adèle was back from Versailles and Talleyrand and Morris both dined with her. It must have been exciting for her as the rivals "converse[d] about the public affairs." She said that if Talleyrand got in the Cabinet they "must make a million for her." Whereupon Morris with good condescending Americanism told Talleyrand "he must get men about him who understand work and who love work."

One can see Adèle's eyes turn to Talleyrand. "Well, what have you to say to that gospel?" Talleyrand replied calmly that he agreed but was "not willing to acknowledge that he does not love work himself," with which his severest critic would agree.

Morris probably thought to himself, I better make this a little more difficult, and set forth a shrewd but highly technical plan for the sale of the Church property. One feels that he expected it to be beyond the bishop's range, the sort of thing that Hamilton might understand but not a French prelate. However, Talleyrand of course grasped it at once, and agreed with one reservation. The quick grasp of it must have annoyed Morris very much, for he says in his *Diary, "I did not sufficiently explain it."* Altogether it was Talleyrand's night, because when he got up to leave them together he said he would "return and bid her good night."

The next morning Adèle told Morris of Talleyrand's "importunities" when he returned. Some of the manuscript is elided but the text seems to say that "if Talleyrand abandons her she is lost" and to ask if Morris will consent to some "sacrifice." He left her very coldly and at the Pont Royal he suddenly came on "a host of women [going] towards Versailles with some cannon," with aristocrats dragged from their carriages and compelled to join them in the "fine and pleasant morning."

Later in the day, with rain and a southwest wind coming up, even he feels deeply for Lafayette, "fleeing forward" before his troops going out to Versailles, "obliged to do what he abhors or suffer an ignominious death, with the certainty that the sacrifice of his life will not prevent the mischief."

At the Louvre, Adèle says "she will leave town without receiving the bishop. . . . She insists that she will be only mine."

The next day, with "Paris . . . all in tumult," they hear how the Queen fled in her shift, stockings in hand, and how the King and she are to be lodged in the Tuileries, and then for Adèle, the ominous news that "the inhabitants of the Louvre will be *dénichés* [expelled]."

How understandable her sudden anguished question asked in tears: "Why will you not marry me? It is because I have had a lover?" A storm of mutual recrimination followed—900 incoherent words in the *Diary*—guilt, honor, "a prior promise," remorse, "misery planted in her bosom for amusement," conscience, eternal fidelity, a gold ring in symbol until they are both free, "I will go with you anywhere" said by her.

From Morris: "Will you go to England next Monday?" From her: "I do not think you capable of ruining me but if you command I obey. I am yours."

Then the storm within abates in intercourse, as the gale mounts outside, and Constable writes him: "I am pained by your silence. Have I deserved it at your hands?"

The next day Washington wrote in his *Diary* that he had discussed with Chief Justice Jay "the propriety of taking informal means of ascertaining the views of the British court with respect to our Western Posts in their possession and to a commercial treaty." Jay approved the plan and "Colonel Hamilton highly approved . . . [and thinks] Mr. Gouverneur Morris well qualified." The day after, Washington talked to Madison about it. He thought it best to wait Jefferson's arrival, and "thought with me that if Gouverneur Morris was employed in this business it would be a commitment for his appointment as minister. . . . He thought with Colonel Hamilton, and as Mr. Jay also does, that Mr. Morris is a man of superior talents, but with the latter [Jay] that his imagination sometimes runs ahead of his judgment."

As they talked it over in New York, the candidate was kissing in the Louvre, "teach[ing] my lovely scholar all I know," and when the kissing was over he took her to the Petit Dunkerque to buy the ring.

Then he went to Lafayette's, where the marquise, Minette de Staël, and "Madame de Simien, [Lafayette's] friend," were "*en comité*." Lafayette, naturally keyed up by the events of the fifth, and about to head the government, said he would have a Cabinet of one minister from each party. (One wonders if that was the beginning of all the coalitions France has been burdened with.) Morris told him "he must have men of talents and firmness"—certainly not Mirabeau among them—"and for the rest it is no matter."

Whence he went back to the Louvre and asked Adèle to send for Talleyrand across the river in the Rue de l'Université to "pledge himself to support Lafayette."

At eleven that night Adèle sent a note saying Talleyrand had arrived and Morris went back to the Louvre to confer "on the arrangement of a ministry."

Talleyrand gave him "every assurance I can wish respecting Lafayette," saying, however, that getting rid of Necker is a *sine qua non* for him and that he, Talleyrand, should be Minister of Finance. Morris was "indeed . . . of the same opinion."

The *Diary* continues:

After arranging the new ministry we come to the Finance, the means of restoring credit etc. Consider his plan respecting the property of the Church. He is bigotted to it and the thing is well enough, but the mode is not so well. He is attached to this *as an author*, which is not a good symptom for a man of business. However, our friend insists with him so earnestly that she makes him give up one point. She has infinite good sense.

It must have been after midnight when Talleyrand left, and Morris and Adèle "close as lovers what we had commenced as politicians."

Narbonne, "much hurt," told them in the morning that Talleyrand, his closest friend, had come between him and his mistress, Minette de Staël. Adèle had doubtless thought that, with his ego satisfied by the Cabinet post, Talleyrand's "importunities" would cease. He would owe it in part to Morris's advice to Lafayette to take him in. They would be freer. The Louvre apartments might still be hers. But now she was sure Narbonne would intrigue against it, and while she and Morris talked the commissary of the district "comes to take possession of [the] appartment." Some delay was contrived but the picture of Narbonne, "with infinite wit [and] an *assez mauvais sujet*," makes her too tense to let Morris have her, and he left to "go early to bed, tired and vexed," though John Adams had observed that "Pleasures don't wear men out in Paris as in other places."

In New York that evening "the visiters to Mrs. Washington were respectable, both of gentlemen and ladies," and the next day Washington went to Morrisania, where he was disappointed "in Gouverneur Morris's barn of which I had heard the latter speak so much."

In the Assembly, Talleyrand moved the transfer of all Church property to the State "to nationalize and maintain," and the speech worked out at the midnight conference in the Louvre strengthened his position.

Morris went to see Necker on the debt and told him directly that he would not "engage in a purchase without such a view to profit as will save me from risque, and that he [Necker] must make a sacrifice." The funding could run between sixteen and twenty-four millions, and the cash portion would greatly relieve Necker. He was responsive. They would talk further, and Morris got to the Louvre as Adèle was going out.

"Here, read this. I shan't be long," she evidently said and gave him Voltaire's pornographic *La Pucelle*. She came back, though, too "much fatigued for Love's Disport."

At nine the next morning, Sunday the eleventh, he saw Lafayette and warned him that he must not try to be minister and soldier. He must concentrate on getting in the Cabinet "men of talents who have principles favorable to liberty." As to Lafayette's objections to the morals of some of them, "he must consider that men do not go into administration as the direct road to heaven. That they are prompted by ambition or avarice and therefore that the only way to secure the most virtuous is by making it [to] their interest to act rightly." Besides, it was preposterous to talk about morals, while insisting, as Lafayette did, on the utterly depraved though brilliant Mirabeau.

He dined at three with Adèle, much refreshed, and "After dinner we join in fervent adoration to the Cyprian Queen, which . . . conveys to my kind votary all of mortal bliss which can be enjoyed. I leave her reclined in the sweet tranquillity of nature well satisfied."

He felt so well himself that he went to Montmorin's, the Foreign Secretary's, broke up a "dully serious" conversation with his gaiety and thought what a pity it was "these people have not the needful abilities."

Talleyrand was at the Louvre and Morris told him that the parties to the new ministry must, as a unit, announce themselves as candidates to the people and tell the King it was all or nothing. Then he lectured Talleyrand on "general principles tending to the wealth and happiness of a nation . . . founded on the sentiments of the human heart." Talleyrand was very responsive and Morris thought what a relief it was not to have to make "dreadfully tiresome" explanations of first principles "for one of those half way minds which see just far enough to bewilder themselves." He left them together with "every confidence in my mistress."

It is not unlikely that had the ministry of talents been formed, after an appeal to the people, and had it brought efficiency into the food and currency supply, and been minded to tell the King and Queen to cease and desist from intrigues at home or with Austria, a gradual and benign revolution would have been possible.

Morris, after telling Lafayette not to try to be minister and army commander, sent him a letter setting forth the objections, urging him to stay with the army, and certainly not to go in the Council with Mirabeau or "even about the same time." He said he knew "the folly of offering opinion which bears the appearance of advice but a regard for you . . . and this kingdom" pushed him further than "one of less ardent temper [would go but] I do not wish you to consider this as an apology." It is a letter of great practical wisdom, warning Lafayette of his "too strict connection with the court" and based on Morris's realization that, whatever Lafayette's many virtues, balance of mind and the ability to bring men together was not one of them.

While Morris was writing this letter Adèle was writing Talleyrand a letter which she showed to Morris. It was evidently intended to take advantage of Talleyrand's entering the Cabinet, and so wisely and amiably end their understanding. Morris said it had "a deep knowledge of human character, an acquaintance with the world, which arises from reflection on the hearts of those who live in it, and the most just conclusions for the regulation of his conduct, enforced by the tenderness of female friendship. . . . I thought well of myself but I submit frankly to a superiority which I feel." It is interesting that the next words in the *Diary* are "She told me some days ago, after seeing Jefferson's countenance, '*cet homme est faux et emporté.*'"

When he took her from the La Bordes' supper that night "she nearly consents that I should go upstairs with her but I do not press the matter because, as she well observes, we certainly have no necessity for anything at present." They were both, he says, very tired and sleepy.

Two days later Morris had one of his few Boswell-Pepys disasters. The Duke of Orléans had left suddenly on a mission to England. No one seemed to know the purpose. It was not on behalf of the administration and unlikely to be on behalf of the King, since "no man in France is more personally disagreeable to the King of England." At the Club Valois no one seemed to know and Morris went to see if General Dalrymple knew anything. He found the general, with Colonel Gardner, two Frenchmen, and a prostitute, having a party. "In about five and twenty minutes I swallow a bottle of wine and depart." He went to Madame de Chastellux's, where he found he was drunk. "I am very absurd," he said in unconscious plagiarism from Boswell, "[and] in attempting gaiety," with Short, Rosalie de la Rochefoucauld and Madame de Ségur listening, "I am almost brutal."

Like a homing drunkard he headed for the Louvre. There he was sentimentally overcome at the sight of her "entrenched with her little chair . . . and the stand with candles etc."

Adèle was furious with him and at that moment Talleyrand came in and coolly looked him over. "At going away [they make] something like an appointment, I know not what. [Adèle] desires me to go away *for fear of Capellis.*" One can almost hear his maudlin speech in the *Diary* words "I insist that this is not the true reason." To get rid of him, she said he might call for her at the convent alone the next day.

He was up early the next day and wrote until noon and evidently in considerable repentance went to the convent. The repentance sufficed for Adèle to relent, though vexed at his conduct, and she said, "I tell you that I love you because I love

you. If I did not it would be very easy to get rid of you." They
went to the La Bordes', where her "countenance glows with
satisfaction in looking at [Talleyrand] and myself as we sit
together agreeing . . . and supporting the opinions of each
other. What triumph for a woman!"

Simultaneously Washington, "having resolved to write to
Mr. Gouverneur Morris to request, as a private agent, that he
would sound the intent of the British Ministry with respect to
their fulfillment of the treaty," sent his instructions to Morris
"to get a right judgment of their disposition and views."

Almost all the rest of October the Indian summer in Paris
was as soft and peaceful as in America, the city's riots and fears
in tragic contrast. On the debt, Necker said to Morris that he
dared not propose a sacrifice to the Assembly unless he was to
receive ten million francs annually for three years. Morris said
he could not go beyond twenty-four million gross with far
lower installments. Necker, pressed by French shipowners,
asked if he could not send ships in ballast to bring back wheat
and flour. Yes, Morris said, but it will run your costs up far
above the market. Necker said he must have more than thirty
days to turn around on the debt and the flour. Morris said he
could have sixty days but twenty-four million was the limit on
the debt. Then Necker sent "someone on the side" to ask Morris
the price of flour. He already knows. I told him, Morris said,
"30/ per bbl." Mirabeau, in evidence of the Cabinet's complete
disunity, urged the Assembly to send its own ambassador extraordinary to New York "to desire payment of the debt in
corn and flour," apparently blind or indifferent to Necker's need
of cash.

Meanwhile, amidst insatiable intercourse, often in tears,
Adèle told him, "You may wean me from all regard for Talleyrand," telling him the next day that Talleyrand tried to come
to dinner with her every day. At the Louvre on the eighteenth,
Morris met Julie's lover, the Cardinal de Rohan.

The next day Adèle heard, as she must have expected, that
her pension from the Count d'Artois, then in Germany, was
finished and that "friends, hopes, everything" must be abandoned. Her boy had come up from the country and she had

cried about him, "sexual mingling with maternal affection." She let Morris have her and "in random chit chat [played] the mocqueuse upon my bad French."

Morris saw Fersen, the Queen's lover, "for the first time . . . in Europe. . . . He has the air of a man exhausted." What a contrast these distracted men all were to what they had been going through Philadelphia, "ruddy and handsome" in Rochambeau's army.

On November 1, Adèle heard that the economist Vandermont (Vandermonde) had said Morris was a partisan of the Duke of Orléans, with whom he had hardly spoken, and that he should go to the lanthorn, "in other words to have me hanged." She begged him to appeal to Lafayette for protection. Morris said he had met Vandermonde almost a month ago and facetiously contradicted something he said about "Paris maintaining the kingdom of France." He quieted her by saying that if the man spoke disrespectfully of him again he would kill him.

On the ninth he dined at Necker's on the flour deal. Necker said Morris should post a compliance guarantee to which he agreed provided Necker was similarly bound. After getting Necker's agreement to "the binding of the King," Morris, like a shrewd trader, waived the point, saying he was satisfied with the honor and integrity of the minister.

Necker's son-in-law, Ambassador de Staël, "inveigh[ed] bitterly against the manners of this country and the cruelty of alienating a wife's affections." Morris had the impudence to agree that it is the "prostration of morals which unfits them for good government," the ambassador's wife having previously told Morris that she was receiving Talleyrand because Narbonne made her miserable by his conduct. She intimated that it was a help to Morris with Adèle. Adèle had just told him that Talleyrand was "so urgent last evening that she was obliged to get angry before she could send him away." It was a day of variety in which at tea he introduced rye bread toast "which is found to be excellent."

A settlement on the American debt, whether in thirty or sixty days, however helpful, would not produce cash enough to run the government and Necker was forced to turn to paper money with the radical vice of being unrepresented (having no backing). The proposed issue would, Morris heard, bring the French exchange down twenty-five per cent. However advantageous this would be to him, as a private banker, it must be said that he opposed it most strongly, as disastrous to the country.

Montmorin, the Foreign Minister, sent for him and belittled Necker and proposed that Morris and he handle the flour and wheat import. Now there were three, Necker, Mirabeau and Montmorin. It is wonderful to contrast these tangled factions and jurisdictions, of one of the oldest governments in the world, with the administrative skills at work in the new republic in America.

Morris told Adèle about it that night and she pathetically asked him whether, as a solution of everything, her husband might not be sent as minister in place of De Moustier and she go out with Morris. "I had already told her that it could not be, at least for the present," and then, perhaps thinking of the De Moustiers, in the languor after an embrace he asked whether Narbonne was the child of an incestuous union between the late King and his daughter Adélaide. She said it was the general opinion and she believed it.

It is curious to compare the story with Nattier's portrait of Madame Adélaide at the time, a blue-eyed, curly-haired girl, brimming with health and smiles. Morris expressed his horror and she replied, "Count de Montmorin, for whom you express so much esteem, lives with Madame de Beaumont his daughter."

The next day she let him see her in her bath, tinted with milk, and told him it was usual to receive visits in the bath. "I suppose it is," he noted, "for otherwise I should have been the last person to whom it would have been permitted. Appearances are scrupulously observed between us."

The debt negotiations looked sufficiently favorable for Van Staphorst, the Dutch banker, to come to Paris. He told Morris "the business was agreeable." The next day Lafayette suddenly told him that in fourteen days he would be "generalissimo with all authority. . . . This man's mind is so elated by power, already too great for the measure of his abilities, that he looks into the clouds and grasps at the supreme."

It must have almost choked Morris to have Madame de Chastellux liken Lafayette to Washington, and to hear from Van Staphorst shortly that Lafayette wanted him as a spy on the aristocrats. It was the week Lafayette threw a cordon of 6000 men around the street where Marat was bringing out his underground paper, *The Friend of the People*. He walked through Lafayette's cordon and was off to England.

Adèle was ill with a cold and the internal trouble she had had since the accoucheur had badly torn her at her delivery. Morris was suffering with great pain in the stump of his amputated leg. On her tenth wedding anniversary Morris saw her but she was ill.

Short and he, as well as Parker, back from London, were sanguine of meeting Necker's terms on the debt. They all talked to Talleyrand and agreed that he would propose it to the Assembly, if Necker declined it, and Morris urged him to deal much in predictions of the fatality of paper money. They all were worried about Talleyrand's attachment to the literary value of his speeches. De Tocqueville wrote later on the incapacity of literary men "who undertook the conduct of a tremendous crisis upon mere literary methods."

On the fifth of December at his house, Necker said he was prepared to go ahead but he must have security. Morris told him that no single house in Europe could be sufficient for security for so large a sum. Necker stuck to his point and Morris said "First, is the offer good? If not, there is no use talking about security. Besides, it's ridiculous to ask someone to secure a bargain that hasn't been made."

Necker replied that if he gave his promise Morris would only use it to negotiate and go around knocking on doors. Morris angrily said he would knock at no doors which were not already open to him, and their voices rose, so that Minette, in the other room, called out to her father to come there. Afterwards they agreed to sleep on it.

Adèle and he went to see the play *The Barber of Seville*,

which had "the merit of gaiety," but at a conference at Montmorin's two days later, De Moustier and Ternant, who was to succeed him as minister in America, came in to say that the distress of France made it necessary to put off all further negotiations.

The Duke of Orléans sent an emissary to see Morris on the best method of transferring some of his wealth to England, and Talleyrand asked Adèle to have Morris correct a paper he had written on the working of the sinking fund, which Morris did for him after relaxing with her. A few days later the same sequence followed on Choiseul's memoire on commerce of grain.

There was a brief scene at the Louvre the night of December 20, painful doubtless to the moralist, yet tender and familiar to ordinary human beings.

Montmorin had told Morris that Necker now once again favored the debt plan, provided there were European backers of sufficient property, as the Dutch financiers concerned were. Morris must have felt, Well, the delays have been exasperating but it looks as though the end of the year would see it settled. And he went to the Louvre.

Talleyrand and three other men were in the small salon. In the manner of the jealous lover he told Adèle he would not stay and took his leave. She followed him out to the dark, dirty staircase, down which he had once fallen and, as never before or after, said that if he would come back later in a hired carriage he might stay all night with her. The thought of hours, where there had always been hurried moments, must have been terribly appealing, but after a moment, in the silent darkness, he said no and left. It is hard to believe that anything but the thought of his arm and leg persuaded him. Even he was abject afterwards at his coldness and came back to "explain the causes, which principally relate to her."

As Christmas Week began he took her to the theater, played with her son, took them driving and went to Short's to read the *Journals* of Congress. At Madame de Chastellux's an abbé said the Assembly had been bribed by the bankers to pass a finance bill. Morris, annoyed and practical, said it was absurd, and the abbé, to show how little a sense of shame operated in Paris, told an incident of some flagrant homosexuality which had just oc-curred.

The next day, while driving with Morris, Adèle casually pointed out one of the men and Morris expressed his revulsion. She mentioned a woman they knew who always received her lovers as though she were a boy.

Christmas Eve, the Marquise de Bréhan said much evil of Adèle to him and Morris on Christmas Day noted how "all [of Paris's] gayness and her gilt [were] all besmirched," and how much the great city was fallen through the Revolution. They made love Christmas afternoon and afterwards took her son to parties, as news reached her of a further cut in her pension.

She was very shaken on New Year's Eve afternoon when a great dog outside the convent almost killed her son. At mid-night afterwards at the Louvre, everyone kissed everyone else, except Morris.

On the same day Richard Randolph married his cousin Judith Randolph and took her to his plantation at Bizarre in Virginia.

Morris had written in his *Diary* a comment on a note from Adèle, *"C'est bizarre, cela."*

CHAPTER SIXTEEN

Adieu—Un-Dear December

(*1790*)

ON NEW YEAR'S DAY the Count de Flahaut returned and Lafayette assured Morris that the French Constitution was better than the English. Tom Paine added that the French Central Bank, the Caisse d'Escompte, was more worthy of credit than the Bank of England. Both items were news to Morris as was Necker's announcement that the debt proposition was now too small.

On the fourth the National Assembly stopped all pensions, putting Adèle in despair, though her devoted maids said they would live on bread and water. The decision was of course called for, and in the public interest, but Morris felt there might well be some compensation such as England had given the Loyalists. Adèle, "with youth, beauty, wit and every loveliness . . . must quit all she loves, to pass her life with what she most abhors." The cover for a table she went with him to buy for Washington cost two thousand francs, two thirds of the pension she had had from the King.

Constable sent him an accounting on Morrisania that day. The dairy alone had cleared £103.12.0 without, however, charging "the dairymaids' wages" as a direct expense. Colonel Thomas Mann Randolph had returned the "little bay mare with a young colt. The other he kept."

Morris was very impatient with Lafayette, who asked him how to meet disobedience from district administrators. There is no way, Morris told him. You have said so much about liberty that you will have to leave this and other defects to time and experience. He tried to make it clear that the American Constitution was a "plain, calm, sensible appeal to the interests, feelings and common sense of our country. It must by its own intrinsic weight bear down all opposition." Lafayette's following remark, that he wanted to consult Paine of all people on the judiciary, must have shortened Morris's life!

With it all, he climbed 160 steps at the Louvre, "stinking of [the] ages," to a children's party at Madame de Chastellux's and heard Rohan, with "weakness," talk to Adèle and him about the Queen's necklace, a far-off, unhappy thing. Adèle asked him if another new plan for an issue of a billion paper francs, redeemable over twenty years, at fifty million a year by lottery, was any good. He explained the fatal consequences, while they made love, and they went to buy more things for Washington and wrote him to be glad they had not run him into more expense as two dozen cups and saucers for Mrs. Washington had been very appealing, with 3000 words more on French politicians.

On Morris's thirty-eighth birthday the Dutch bankers suddenly withdrew from the debt plan, and both Morris and Short, who had supported it, had to write the whole story to Hamilton. To Necker, Morris reported that he would go himself to Holland in the hope of reopening the matter.

The business of Constable was being neglected for Adèle and Robert Morris. On February 1 he acknowledged "19 letters" from Constable "barely mentioning their receipt and without referring to any part of them," as Constable with understandable annoyance wrote him.

On February 4 the King went to the Assembly and took an oath to support a Constitution which was still to be made. Morris commented, "It is a very strange thing that men who have lived in the world fifty years should believe that opposition founded on strong direct personal interests can be instantly calmed by a few honied expressions."

One is at a loss to understand how this wise and balanced man could see so clearly the political issues and apparently have no feeling, except of drift, with Adèle. They were, he says at the time, making use of every means to have a child and their ill-success was a great pity. He sat at the opera next to the Countess de Carro, a fine, unwashed country girl, and thought what a contrast she was to his much-bathed Adèle. He dined on red partridge which De Flahaut had brought and heard from Adèle how vexed her husband was that she refused him her bed, and coming back from the convent the next day, she yielded to Morris in his carriage.

She weeps at the thought of his departure for the Low Countries and when he tells her it will be brief, she says, "Not long for a husband because a wife can follow him, but very long for a lover [who] may be detained."

Minette de Staël asked him to bring her a good novel from London, and after a last embrace in the Louvre, Adèle following him to the stairs, he left for the north with spring in the air on the seventeenth. He climbed six hundred and sixteen steps to the steeple in Antwerp on the twenty-fourth, as Jefferson's daughter married the brother of Nancy and Judith Randolph.

On March 4 he was in Amsterdam telling the great banking house of Hope and Company that there was danger, however profitable it might seem, to Holland in being nothing but a broker in Europe. Profit without the production of wealth added nothing to the general mass. The partners listened and told him it was unlikely they could do anything on the American debt, but like prudent men added that if "anything likely to interest us comes up, please come back."

On the sixth John Paul Jones arrived from the court of Catherine the Great, via the Hague. The gallant sailor, now forty-three, whose life, except on his quarterdeck, always seemed to stammer like his speech, "commended" the French ladies, Abigail Adams had said, for their "neatness" and their much bathing, as Morris might have. He had been in Holland for three months since his dismissal at Petersburg.

It was strange to think that Jones had reached Nantes, December 2, 1777, with news of Burgoyne's surrender for Franklin and that General Riedesel, who had been in the surrender, should now be living in the same house with Morris, so that all three had a drink together and discussed Burgoyne.

Morris was a good deal of help to Jones thereafter, both in London and Paris, but found his stammer of speech and ideas very trying. Jones had an idea that he and Kosciusko—how they all stuck together—might get some sort of an offer of employment from Sweden and he had a wilder idea of sailing around the Cape of Good Hope, levying tribute on the places subject to the Turks. And he had some speculation on with Dr. Bancroft, the former spy in Franklin's household, to "supply wool dyers with quercitron bark."

The news from France that all payments had been suspended for a year, and that the presses were pouring out paper money, again stopped the debt redemption plan. At the house of the Jew with the wonderful name, Cappadocia, the daughter-in-law, "the wealthiest, handsomest and most accomplished Jewess of [the] city," almost made Morris forget his fidelity to Adèle. On the nineteenth Morris saw Sara Cappadocia, the fair daughter of Sion, again and there is a brief elision in the *Diary* page, but a letter came from Short complaining of Jefferson's official silence and telling Morris that his silence "displeases your fair friends here—they complain."

With Constable's correspondents, Van Staphorst and Company, Morris did clean up some matters. They agreed to take a silk cargo from India to liquidate a £3000 advance. He set them straight on the different standards of tobacco inspection in Maryland and Virginia. They wrote Constable the day after he left, "At last, we have been gratified with the visit of your Mr. Gouverneur Morris with whom we have laid the foundation for a connexion between us."

He left, with the violets in bloom, for London by way of Scheveningen on the twenty-second of March and five days later was at Froome's Hotel in Covent Gardens, coming up through a countryside of primroses, violets and fruit blossoms.

With him he carried Washington's instructions for "feeling [the] pulse and soothing [the] pride [of England] a second time," as Madison later described it. It is interesting to note

that in October his friend Jay had recommended Bancroft, the
former spy and present speculator, as more suited for the mission than Morris. It is also curious to note that on arrival Morris
made the mistake against which in 1781–83 he had so strongly
advised Jay. He told Luzerne, the French minister, all about his
mission, "thinking it best the French should know." He was
strongly criticized by his friends for this and by Monroe, who
three years later, though, condemned Jay, then in London, for
not doing the same thing.

Leeds, the Foreign Secretary, a year older than Morris, received him with outward cordiality on the twenty-ninth, saying he was happy to have the credentials, in the President's own
hand, and that he and the rest of His Majesty's servants wished
to cultivate friendship and commerce with America. He said
they were trying to get the right man to go out as minister. "My
Lord, you cannot want [for] men well qualified," Morris told
him. Leeds said they would talk further but a month's silence
passed.

Bancroft appeared with his side of the John Paul Jones
partnership and Morris told him they had better dissolve it.
American Loyalists borrowed money from him; he began to
hear more about Robert Morris's debts.

Luzerne criticized Jefferson's qualifications to be more than
governor of Virginia and Morris disagreed. Short wrote that he
had ordered payment of a beaver hat, to settle their bet. Jefferson was not returning. Why, Short asked rhetorically, does
Hamilton think we can borrow money at four per cent? He
adds that more aristocrats are constantly going into hiding.

Somewhat restless, Morris eyed the pretty *gouvernante* at
the Churches' whom he had seen the year before but he turned
his eyes away, as he did from Mrs. Phyn, the banker's wife, in
whom "beauty, sense and softness joined [because] I have
vowed fidelity on another altar."

When Sir John Sinclair, who was to head the first Board of
Agriculture, talked to him, as men talked a hundred and fifty
years later, of "plans to develop Africa," Morris omnisciently
told him at once what to do. Two parties should be sent out,
one to the headwaters of the Senegal River, one going south-

west from the Barbary Coast. They should meet on the Niger
and pursue its course, thus telescoping a hundred years of
Anglo-French exploration and development.

In mid-April he was very much cheered by his nephew,
James Morris, telling him of a mechanic who made wooden legs
"able to take the benefit of the knee joint [but] less solid than
the simple stick which I now use." He hoped a good deal of it
and had made a plaster of Paris cast of his right leg, by which
"to make a left leg of copper," and a model of his stump to
avoid fittings.

Washington was writing him that the surtout and plateaux
had arrived safely—they were "very elegant, much admired and
do great justice to your taste"—on the night that Morris was
eating oysters at the Mount Coffee House with James Boswell.
How wonderful it would be if either had asked the other if he
ever kept a journal.

Franklin had often called on Boswell in Half Moon Street in
'68 and now, twenty-two years later, Franklin died on April 17.
Madame Helvétius, whom Morris had just seen, in her ravaged
age, had written Franklin: "We shall meet again with all those
who have loved us, I a husband and you a wife—but I believe
you have been a rogue and will find more than one."

Lord Wycombe, back from the Continent, came to see him
and Morris was taken to the trial of Warren Hastings, hearing
Burke and Fox speak. The latter's mind appeared "like a clouded
sun." He went several times and often in the audience sat Fanny
Burney, born also in 1752, with a ticket given by "my royal
mistress very late overnight."

On April 28, Leeds wrote him that he had understood he was
in Holland but that in any event there must be a delay "until
redress is granted to our subjects." The note was cold and curt,
and Morris replied, ". . . it becomes my duty to ask of you my
lord, the nature and extent of the redress expected. . . . I trust
that I am mistaken [in understanding you do not want a commercial treaty]. . . . I should be very unhappy to convey a
false interpretation . . . your Grace will have the goodness to
set me right. . . ."

Both men of course understood all this. There was redress

to which England was entitled. "Not a day has passed since the treaty [of Paris] was put into effect when it has not been violated by one [American] state or another," Jay wrote Adams. But England held on to the Northwest Posts in equal violation and continued to impress American seamen.

As to the Posts, Morris told Leeds and Pitt, England would have the fur trade with whoever had the Posts, but they were a symbol of national honor to the United States. He urged trifling compensations on both sides and he pleaded that they give up impressment, though they pressed their own subjects, saying "this is the only instance in which we are not treated as aliens. You know, my lord, when a wound is recently healed it is easy to rub off the skin."

It is almost incredible to think how blind the British Government was to what they were losing in gaining the trivial advantage of unruly American sailors for their fleet.

The Posts, the payment for the slaves carried off by Cornwallis—thirty of them from Monticello and to a total of thirty thousand elsewhere—even the British intrigues with Kentucky and Vermont and trade with the Indies could be settled without war, but not impressment.

With all this, in their private talks, Leeds and Pitt, the Prime Minister, were cheery and cordial with Morris but they were in a strong position to wait. "There never was a moment," John Marshall quoted Morris as saying, "in which England felt herself greater; and consequently it is the most unfavorable moment to obtain advantageous terms from her in any bargain."

Morris knew, though he could not say so, that the immediate and prime cause of delay was the question of whether England was going to war with Spain. If she did, she would concede every point in order to bring America in as her ally, or pay a good price for neutrality. If there was no war, then she would drive the hardest bargain she could.

Spain claimed jurisdiction over the Pacific Ocean and there had been a brief naval brush with the British at Nootka Sound near Vancouver. England had announced she did not recognize any Spanish sovereignty in the Pacific, and while Pitt was talking to Morris, Miranda, a South American patriot, was in London seeking his backing for revolutions against Spain throughout South America.

The talks went on all summer, swinging from fair to foul with the Spanish question. Morris saw Leeds for the last time on September 15. Leeds said they hoped now to send a minister out very shortly. Morris left a grave warning as to holding the Northwest Posts.

Washington had written ominously in his *Diary* in July that he heard "that the traitor Arnold was at Detroit . . . leading to the conjecture that Britain had some design on the Spanish settlements on the Mississippi and of course to surround these United States."

In parting with Morris, Leeds offered to communicate with Washington through Morris in France. One can think of a great many men who would have eagerly agreed, but Morris told him to send his answer direct by his own packets.

In later answer to all the criticism of his alleged ineffectiveness, his confidences with the French ambassador, and particularly to the story spread by the British agents in America that he was personally too intransigent, Morris wrote one of his wisest and perhaps wittiest letters to Robert Morris:

I will suppose it to be a very good reason to be given to America for not conferring a *favor* on her that the man sent to ask it was disagreeable, no matter from what cause, but I trust that they will never avow to the British nation a disposition to make sacrifice of their interests to please a pleasant fellow. . . . If you mean to make a good treaty with Britain, support your pretensions with spirit *and they will respect you for it.* You must give them *visible reasons* because they will have *to justify their conduct:* and it will not do to say to a House of Commons *the American minister was such a charming fellow that we could not resist him.*

The summer in London was as frustrating and joyless to Morris personally as it was diplomatically. During the last half of July he was ill and largely confined to his rooms.

John Paul Jones and Thomas Paine were a plague of bother. The former, coming over to settle with Dr. Bancroft, was mobbed at Harwich on May 4 and in danger of his life. But the next day Morris got a settlement of fifty pounds out of Bancroft for him, only to have Jones send an emissary to say he would not sign an unconditional release. Morris was furious at a sailor's questioning his judgment as a businessman and asked the emissary if Jones thought he was a fool.

It was a very hard day for him. Beckwith, the British agent in Philadelphia, who had spread the story there that Morris was getting nowhere with Leeds, because of his obduracy and his taking the French minister into his confidence, had him to dine. It was after dinner that Mrs. Beckwith told him of the death of Elizabeth Plater, with the effect on him we have already seen. Paine was a frequent caller, his object being "to get rid of himself"—that is, to inflict the boredom of being with himself on Morris. He borrowed forty pounds on June 12 and on the thirtieth came back with a bill on Lewis Morris for almost the same amount. It was unpleasant for Morris to comply or refuse, since he knew nothing about it, so he let him have forty-nine pounds more.

In August, Paine came in with a draft on Lombard Street and asked Morris to cash it, to save him the walk to the city. Morris did so and told him he was a troublesome fellow. A week later he was again too tired to walk to the city and Morris loaned him three guineas.

Perhaps Paine had heard that great sums were going to Morris's credit from his private business with William Constable and Company.

The hapless Parker came with a new proposal for running privateers out of Cadiz to which Morris said no. Very quickly a bill of Parker's for six hundred pounds went to protest and Morris went to see the bankers, told them Parker was ill and asked them not to dishonor it.

Even Washington's bankers said they were not in cash to pay for some "high-priced wine-coolers" Morris had gotten for him and preferred not to advance. Morris paid the bill.

The new leg was ready for a try-on the night in May Lord Wycombe asked him to dine with his father. It turned out to be well made but useless.

Ogden and Wilkins matters were troublesome and, troubles
not coming singly, he had to write his nephew, James Morris:

> If your father's road carries up the gorge of the hill northeast of the
> upper end of my lane [at Morrisania] I cannot consent to it. This
> would indeed derange me most terribly besides giving [the public]
> a very crooked, hilly and rocky road.
>
> Your affectionate friend etc.

On September 15, as he was about to leave London, he met
Boswell again at the Piazza Coffee House and went to the
theater. There he thought "the herd of prostitutes . . . and the
open, shameless conduct of those who handle and converse with
them" was a reflection on the taste and manners of the country.
If he said that to Boswell it must have been a shock.

Meanwhile in France the situation had worsened. In May,
Danton had said Lafayette was the eunuch of the Revolution,
and in June, Lafayette put down the mutiny of the unpaid army
at Nancy with numerous executions, his education in America
having indeed been only half finished.

The identical situation had caused the mutiny of the Pennsylvania Line in New Jersey in 1781 and Lafayette had seen
how it was handled. The mutineers killed one officer, wounded
several others, and started for Philadelphia under a British de-
serter and their own sergeants. Lafayette and two other officers
were driven off and emissaries from Sir Henry Clinton reached
the mutineers.

On January 7, 1781, Anthony Wayne and Joseph Reed, Morris's adversary, went out alone to meet and talk to them. When
they were through, the troops paraded and turned back to join
the army. There were no executions and no reprisals.

Short had written Morris on June 20 that all titles and coats
of arms had been abolished and that Lafayette had been the
prime mover of it. He added that he was not enclosing Mirabeau's oration on the death of Franklin because the postage was
too heavy. There was an amusing side light on the abolition of
titles. Twenty-one hundred "girls" of the Palais Royal addressed

the National Assembly, demanding that "the dishonorable titles" such as "*garces, putains, toupies, maquerelles*" be abolished.

Short said he believed Madison would get the Paris Legation and that he had just sent Jefferson's furniture home. In London, Luzerne told Morris that he would be the next minister.

Lord Gower, thirty-two, was named as the new British ambassador and went out with long instructions from the Foreign Office. "Be extremely attentive in making yourself master of the interior state of the court of France, studying the passions and the interests . . . as to war or peace." Morris was to become the close friend of Lord Gower and his lovely wife, Lady Sutherland, twenty-five.

On July 14, Talleyrand celebrated High Mass in the Champ de Mars in the presence of the court and a great crowd of unarmed, restless people. The King and Queen were there. Someone wrote Lord Lansdowne "she looked well, but fat and sulky." Everyone was wet to the skin from the rain as Talleyrand celebrated the Mass.

There is a letter said to have been written by him to Adèle afterwards. Its tone is of flippant moralizing on the "*anarchie politique et morale.*" It says she was the "Supreme Being" whom he addressed and asks at the end whether Charles is to have a brother or sister or whether it is "*une fausse alarme.*"

On September 25, Morris left from Dover for Flanders, "a fine fair breeze from the north west and a charming moon light so bright that I see plainly in mid channel both the French and English coasts."

At Dunkirk he heard that "for 20% any article will be delivered [to any house in London] free of all risques." At Ghent he saw Rubens's *Dying Magdalene* and a *Thundering Jehovah* and thought the latter "degrading to the Omnipotent." At Mannheim he heard that the Elector's library had 70,000 volumes. "Of course there must be many bad books in it."

Washington wrote him October 13 that he was anxious about "sanguinary punishments" in France. He said "great temperateness, firmness and foresight are necessary [in the revolution].

To forbear running from one extreme to the other is no easy matter."

Morris, for a civilian, made an astonishingly acute observation on the sixteenth, with the opening strategy of two World Wars in it, saying in substance:

If the Emperor can get free passage through Liége with 20000 men, 10 to watch Namur and 10 to push by Charleroi, there is, I think, nothing from the citadel of Liége to the citadel of Antwerp which could delay the advance of good troops, well commanded, for 24 hours . . . the extensive and strong lines at Tirlemont require a great army to man them and they (may be) rather pernicious than useful

—and made it after writing at length to Constable on speculation in teas. The ledgers of Constable and Company all that fall credited him with large sums—fourteen thousand dollars on "furred fat skins"—for his shares in cargoes of curry, pepper, Bohea tea, and charter parties handled by Phyn, Ellice in London.

He was forced, though, to tell Robert Morris that he had had no success in selling lands in Flanders. "You tell me [that Mr. Joel Barlow] has given assurances that he can sell . . . but my dear friend, this same Mr. Barlow, after all his sales, sends back under protest a bill for 100,000 livres [fractionally more than a franc]." He says, however, if Robert Morris is not satisfied by all means to place the lands with Barlow.

On November 6, leaving Meaux at six twenty-five in the morning, he reached Paris at a quarter of eleven, bathed and dressed, and was off to the Louvre. Adèle was out but when she returned she seemed glad to see him, though Lord Wycombe was with her, seeming very *enniché*. She said she had been faithful. Talleyrand was also shortly in evidence.

She appears in the next few days to have been telling him that her relations with Talleyrand had been resumed but that Morris may, if he pleases, possess her. He agreed to do so "for the last time." Afterwards she told him she would keep his ring until she was in fact unfaithful. So that she appears to have said several conflicting things and there is no way of knowing which was the truth.

It seems incredible but true that Morris with his strong sexuality had been faithful to her during his absence. If such could be his control, presumably a woman, more delicately made, could have been equally chaste. On the other hand, she must have felt abandoned by him, and the importunities of husband, Talleyrand and Wycombe almost overpowering. And she may have been chaste but felt some anxiety on Morris's part about her was long overdue.

There is no question of his anxiety. "I think I had never in my life so many different things agitating my mind as at present and I cannot commence one affair because another is constantly obtruding." *And like a man to double business bound!*

Short dined at the De la Rochefoucaulds' on the thirteenth. One wonders what went on in those lovelorn but sensible minds of Morris and Short when they visited the Rochefoucaulds in the very house where Adrienne Lecouvreur had died with her lovers, Voltaire and Saxe, the victor at Fontenoy, beside her. Even as unhappy lovers, both Morris and Short must have been anxious about which would be named to the legation. Wycombe had told them Montmorin, the Foreign Minister, had asked for Carmichael from Madrid.

The next day Adèle said that she did not want to make love so that she could meet Talleyrand with a heart more at ease. Morris drove her to Chaillot and inside the convent she suddenly assented. When they got back to the Louvre the husband was waiting and asked for a lift. In the carriage he begged for Morris's help in getting named minister to America and to prevail on Adèle to agree. Then at the theater that night Morris saw Adèle with Wycombe, and the lackeys stared at his wooden leg.

He heard with alarm on the nineteenth that the Austrian armies were advancing to restore the *status quo ante* and wrote Washington of the hopeless situation.

The sovereign, humbled to the level of a beggar's pity, without resources, without authority, without a friend. The Assembly at once a master and a slave, new in power, wild in theory, raw in practise [taking] from this fierce ferocious people every restraint of religion and respect.

Constable wrote him that night that Robert Morris simply did not have the means to remit the debt of honor of two thousand pounds to Van Staphorst, and months later, "I hope you may find it convenient to return in the spring for unless we can have some better understanding I will dissolve this connection [with Robert Morris]. The constant and heavy advance . . . I learn you were at Paris the 20th November."

It had been a day of many business conferences for Morris with Van Staphorst and with Le Couteulx, with the latter complaining "bitterly of R.M." Morris also saw Lafayette and warned him that neither the American nor English Constitution fitted France. "England is surrounded by a deep ditch and being only assailable by sea can permit many things at home which would not be safe in different situations."

On November 28, Adèle drove Morris almost mad with her contradictions. Wycombe had been with her from ten till two, telling her, she said, that she was in love with Morris. She said she would not see him again, if Morris desired it. He said no, he did not and they embraced. Whereupon she told him she had given Wycombe the blue cup she had once given Morris. Perhaps the circumstances of his giving it back were the reason.

He arose December 2 after a night of sleepless anxiety, most rare for him, and went to the Louvre, telling Adèle that every mail was bringing him afflicting intelligence.

The new crisis had to do with Parker, who had been working with him on the debt scheme. He regarded Parker as "a devilish, slippery fellow," who was highly regarded by Robert Morris.

Word had now come, though still in vague terms, that Parker and a man named Rogers had committed a great fraud in London and that Constable was the victim.

We have said that a sense of guilt never oppressed Morris, whatever he did. This was the exception. He evidently knew that too much time had been given to his love affair at the expense of his business, and that, having resisted, out of old friendship, Constable's desire to make a complete break with Robert Morris, he was responsible for the very thing Constable had foreseen. "I told you so," Constable could say. "What else could you have expected?"

Still he took Adèle's niece, Mademoiselle Duplessis, home and realized on the way that he could have her. But he said to himself it would be "detestable" and set her down unharmed, his "bosom torn with anxiety." Strangely, perhaps psychosomatically, he said there was "a physical sense of grief" in his arm. In the morning he begged Adèle for the picture Talleyrand had of her.

On the seventh word from London that he must return made him incapable of business. He told Adèle but not the *Diary* the cause and she burst into tears and with pathetic tenderness offered him all her money, said she did not love Wycombe and let Morris have her.

The next day he went to his bankers for cash and a letter of credit for London. And then to the Louvre and gave her twelve hundred francs to redeem some jewelry she had had to pawn. He left for London the next day.

How incredible must have been his relief on his first morning there to have Lord Wycombe walk in. Afterwards he read his mail until 2 A.M., dining with Lansdowne on the fifteenth, the December fields of England being still green and pleasing.

On Christmas Eve he relaxed enough to get very nearly drunk at Penn's, with Boswell and young Franklin there.

"Adieu—un-dear December, adieu and away forever," Fanny Burney wrote in her *Diary*.

CHAPTER SEVENTEEN

Whether I Shall Engage
in a New Partnership

(1791)

IN LONDON at least he was at grips with the Parker disaster and able to do something. Parker and Rogers were in hiding from the sheriff's men. They would not meet him by daylight but at nights in taverns in the city. Nonetheless, when Morris met Parker he gave "vent to as little reproach as possible." They talked about salvage and Morris saw "he forms a design to take some advantage of me in the very moment that I am trying to serve him. I do not blame him, for it is his nature, and certainly I should see his situation more composedly if my own interest were not at stake."

He had some oysters and olives at the Mount Coffee House and wrote Constable with his usual optimism:

It appears that the moneys [Rogers] has received from the disposal of stock have been applied to the private use of himself and Mr. Parker . . . the acceptance of your bills to the amount of £15000 remain unpaid and that the value of the remaining stock is not equal to the discharge of that sum. . . . This is a most unfortunate affair but I pray you to be of good cheer for I yet think to extricate ourselves tolerably.

When Constable received it he wrote somewhat wryly to Robert Morris, "Our friend, G.M., philosophizes very handsomely and tells me that 'Tranquillity is better than risks.'"

Morris arranged his own appointment as trustee for the secured creditors, with Phyn, Ellice and Inglis as his surrogate, and left for Paris on January 16. Constable's debit balance with Phyn, Ellice and Inglis was then forty thousand pounds, and though cargoes were coming in to offset it, it seems evident that, in the course of ordinary business prudence, Morris should have stayed longer in London, and would have done so if no one had been waiting in the Louvre.

He left Boulogne at nine-thirty Monday night, the seventeenth, was in Paris at six-thirty Wednesday morning and at the Louvre at ten. They embraced at once, though she was soon in tears about Talleyrand's gambling and cruelty and her husband's misconduct in money matters. "He is a wretch and the best thing he could do would be to die." In addition Julie, her sister, was in great need and Adèle had had to send her money out of "her own misery." The King's aunts had gotten away to Rome. Ternant had been made minister to America.

One has perhaps to have experienced in modern postwar Europe such a call as De Flahaut made on Morris on the twenty-first, to appreciate its pathos.

The old, worthless aristocrat brought around "a friend" who wanted to export hardware to the United States. Presumably the "friend" told Flahaut there would be a commission in it for him. Morris sighed and told him that he would have to start by sending out samples and testing the market. The friend had neither samples nor prices and left disconsolately with Flahaut. Another stranger came shortly with a plan to ship "porcelain refuse" to America and get tobacco in return.

On February 16 at Adèle's, Morris met Madame de Nadaillac, who had come to see him. Adèle, her aunt by marriage, told Morris she was "virtuous, a coquette and romantic." Five years later he tried to find out about the first for himself.

When Morris brought Adèle back to the Louvre after dinner a week later, a blank envelope was handed her. Inside was Talleyrand's will, making her sole beneficiary. They knew he was in fear of death or assassination and Adèle wept all night. But when he was shortly safe for the moment, Talleyrand took back his will.

We have noted that there was one eighteenth-century vice from which Morris was free. He loathed gambling and hated cards. Part of the ruin of Adèle's life arose from her husband's reckless gaming. She had wept about Talleyrand's. She knew that Morris felt the influence of Lord Gower, the British ambassador, was vitiated by his gambling. Gower's mother had heard that his younger brother had gambled at the embassy and wrote him, "Your father was not present luckily [when I was told]."

In the face of this, after dinner at Morris's house on March 26 (a mob had just broken into the King's presence at the Tuileries and "courtiers with hunting knives and pistols" had defended him until Lafayette came in with the National Guard), Adèle proposed whist after dinner. She asked Morris to draw and he refused. She said unless he played she would never again set foot in his house. They were in ill humor with each other for several days and Morris retaliated with great coldness.

Guards, to ensure silence, were around the house where Mirabeau was dying as they passed on April Fool's Day and Morris was shocked at such honors paid to such a wretch, "never under the steady control of reason nor the firm authority of principle."

On April 7, Adèle suddenly asked him if he would marry her if she were a widow. He declined to answer, and when she wanted a yes or no, he asked her how she could expect a yes when she talked so much of Talleyrand's influence and had said his own six months' absence had cooled her affections.

Two days later she said, doubtless with a flounce, that her pride would never let her mention marriage again but that he must have a wonderful power over his own mind to love only to a certain point. Who would he recommend, if she became a widow? He suggested Talleyrand, to which she said no, she would then have to tell him about Morris.

Tom Paine now appeared in Paris, very much out at elbows and looking for a publisher for his *Rights of Man*. He went back to his dismissal by Congress in '79 and Morris told him frankly that he had urged it.

The week was varied. Morris saw Adèle twice in her bath.

There was another riot at the Tuileries, the National Guard paying no attention to Lafayette's order to clear the way for the King's coach. Lafayette resigned and fainted, and tried to enlist "as a private grenadier."

In London, Boswell's *Life of Johnson* was published. Morris had his first frog's legs, and with John Paul Jones in his rooms by chance, the heir of Lord Selkirk came in and met him.

During the Revolution, Jones had raided the Scottish coast and his sailors had carried off the plate from Selkirk Castle. Jones had later sent it politely back and now the heir thanked him. There was of course a story, some said only Jones's own, that he was the illegitimate half-brother of the heir.

On May Day, Morris saw Montmorin, who was very depressed and said he was going to resign. "England and Prussia were giving money to Orléans" and the King's brothers in exile. Morris told him that a foreign war appeared the only solution.

The next day Adèle told him that now D'Angivilliers, her husband's wealthy brother, had set off for Italy and the last means of financial existence was gone. She tried to be brave about it and was hopeful she might get a post in the royal household, one that two years before was eagerly sought and now gone begging. She told him on the tenth it was fixed but cried because he was cold to her.

William Short, depressed and anxious, came to see him. No word at all had come about the legation. Ternant had said Short was much below par but Morris told him Jefferson said Short was one of the ablest men in America.

Short now had even greater reason for wanting his future settled. He had just come from Roche-Guyon, to which Rosalie's mother-in-law had at last invited him. There he had evidently told Rosalie that he could stand it no longer without her. He was waiting for her answer. Unlike Morris, he was ready to do anything to marry her and, if she would consent only to having him as a lover, he must have the legation to be near her.

Her letter came on the twenty-seventh, like all of hers to him, exquisite:

A thousand reasons come to me to prevent my heart from responding to yours and you must not blame me for trying to stifle feelings that would be dangerous to us both. . . . I know that I am not speaking to you in the same language that you used to me.

Morris had seen Montmorin on the 24th and told him he was going back to England on the twenty-seventh of May. Montmorin suddenly asked him if he would be back in June and Morris said yes. One wonders whether the Foreign Minister had had wind of the flight to Varennes. He asked Morris for a memoire on the situation before he left.

In it Morris warned him that a crisis over currency was imminent and that the mob would blame the royal household. As the household's unpopularity increases, he said, its personnel should be changed.

Then he went to tell Adèle that he was going and had her in a profusion of weeping. He left to write Washington that he had dropped private negotiations on the debt on receipt of his orders to talk to the British ministers but that he strongly felt the value and propriety of them during a period when "we are not in a condition to pay our debt to France."

On the twenty-eighth he went to say good-by. There was only a half hour after dinner when she could send her husband away which they passed in a frenzy of mutual desire. He left at ten in the morning, passing Lady Webster, who was to be Lady Holland, on her way from London to Paris to "live discreetly even with prudery at first." She was a great heiress, twenty-one years old, and Webster, her husband, twenty-three years older, was shortly to lose by divorce her wealth, her long, merry face, dark curls and slim, high breasts.

On the Channel crossing there was a Frenchman with his daughter, just from a convent. "I never saw a little animal so salacious."

The Parker settlement was still the main order of business, and exasperating as the many meetings were, it turned out, as Morris had hoped, "tolerably well." Additionally he was able to do something concrete for Robert Morris.

Mr. Gouverneur Morris is here [William Knox wrote his brother, the Secretary of War]. He has made a great sale for Robert Morris in the Genesee . . . 40 or 50000 and another for [him] in Pennsylvania. [The Genesee price should help that of better lands.] . . .

Strange that McComb [R.M.'s associate] gave him full powers without priority of the joint proprietor [Henry Knox]. . . . G.M. made use of all that oratorical reasoning upon the subject which you and his other acquaintances know him to be very capable at. . . . I heard him very patiently. . . . He is going to Paris. . . . Either you have consented [to his power although I was your agent] or his procedure is highly unjustified.

William Knox was one of those timeless free-lance operators, with his office in his hat, who try to compete with established business. He was then living on a succession of small loans, a rather pathetic figure. Morris speaks of him in his *Diary:* "He seeks for elegant diction and forgets that there should be at least one idea in half an hour's talk."

However, wiser and more stable men than William Knox were annoyed at times by Morris's philosophizing and tendency to oratory in ordinary conversation.

In the same letter Knox writes "on the 24th [of June] a courier arrived at Lord Grenville's from Lord Gower" bringing news that the flight of the royal family from the Tuileries had been discovered at six in the morning of the twenty-first. Knox was with Dr. Bancroft, Morris and some others when the news came. Bancroft and Morris believed that "with good hunters (he is an excellent horseman) the King can reach Germany in 15–20 hours."

The flight to Varennes is one of the classic examples of the effect of chance on human affairs. The course of history was changed because "the cart of Drovet" stuck in an archway, stopped the royal coach and led to the King's arrest.

It is mentioned incidentally in the portion of Knox's eight-page letter, begun on the twenty-fifth and concluded on the twenty-seventh:

The King was known to the master of the post house at a place called Saint Merchould on the confines of Champagne and Lorraine within a few hours drive of the German territories—this man communicated the information to the municipality of Varennes. . . .

One wonders if Adèle, with all her sources of information, knew of the plan and listened at the Louvre for the sound of the coach leaving the Tuileries.

On the twenty-eighth Morris left for Paris. Aboard were Lord and Lady Sheffield and their two daughters, going out to see Gibbon at Lausanne. He arrived July 1 as the first of four issues of Tom Paine's *The Republican* appeared. The royals were back in the Tuileries and Lord Gower told his government he was uncertain what to do about their wish to see him, sent through Lafayette.

Morning and evening of the second Adèle and Morris made love, with Paris still ringing with the King's flight and the new decree forbidding emigration by the nobles.

Short, in spite of his unhappiness, gave the traditional party for Americans on July 4 and Paine was there, "inflated to the eyes and big with a litter of revolutions." Vicq d'Azyr, the royal physician, told them the Queen's hair had turned gray.

From the windows of the Russian Embassy Adèle and Morris watched the ashes of Voltaire carried to the Pantheon on the eleventh and Morris wrote to Constable that he had just heard that Lord Wycombe had left for America. "Show him all kinds of attention. He may perhaps wish to see Morrisania." The longer he stayed the better. With understandable vanity he took Adèle and Lady Sutherland to see Houdon's bust of Washington, for which he had posed.

On the fifteenth, Paris was in an uproar over the decree of the inviolability of the King and Montmorin spoke of the King's cruelties. When he told Adèle she said the King was brutal and nasty and mentioned one of his excremental habits.

The visible beauty of Paris touched him, the "fine moonshine, a dead silence and the river descending gently thro the various bridges between lofty houses all illuminated (for the sake of the police)."

On the twentieth Short took him to dine at the Rochefoucaulds' and Ternant asked him to advise Montmorin what Ternant's pay should be as minister in Philadelphia.

Adèle and he now became if possible more reckless in the time and place of their embraces, "in the passage . . . Mlle. is at the harpsichord . . . [Monsieur] downstairs . . . the doors are all open," and on the quai between the Louvre and the Tuileries, with the coachman staring straight ahead.

It is a matter of natural though indelicate curiosity to wonder what this lady wore, in a period of wide panniers, lacing and furbelows, to be able to behave so naughtily in so many places. Actually it appears that the daytime dress or street clothes were quite simple. English feminine fashions were popular, particularly the redingote, worn over a blouse and normal skirt, and the multiple petticoats had not yet come in. Neither the lovely Countess de Ségur nor the Duchess of Orléans in Vigée Le Brun's paintings is markedly out of date for a modern cocktail hour.

So on, day after day through early August, though Adèle worked with him on the translation of his plan for provisioning Paris which Montmorin wanted to give the King. His own attempt, she said, had "much of the foreigner in the stile." The extent of Morris's preoccupation is evidenced by Constable's letter to him of August 3:

I find to my great surprise that the term of our partnership ended the 10th June last . . . the question is not whether your business shall be admitted into the house of W.C. and Co. but whether as to me I shall engage in a new partnership. I am well advanced in years and wish for rest.

Constable and Morris were the same age, thirty-nine—but it was often "advanced in years" in those days unless there was robust health. And Constable was not without justified reservations concerning Morris. He had written him in June, "Since you have left us you have measured our resources by a European scale and have been as far wrong in all your calculations on our stocks as we exceed the old world in youth and vigour. Patience *toujours*."

They did not formally renew the partnership but Morris's principal capital remained with Constable and their joint-account trading was as heavy as before.

On the sixteenth Adèle told him Flahaut had written her formally insisting on his rights and that she had of course refused. Adèle's words are almost literally those in Madame de Lafayette's novel *Comtesse de Tende*, "*il voulait reprendre tous ses droites méprises* [he wished to take back all the rights he had given up]." There was a bitter quarrel with her husband on the nineteenth over her refusal and Morris and she wickedly "celebrated."

Lord Palmerston breakfasted with Morris, and noted in his *Diary* that his leg had been amputated in consequence of jumping from a window in an affair of gallantry. He adds, "Made an acquaintance with Madame de Flahaut, a very sensible, agreeable woman. Her husband and she have apartments in the Louvre where they live much at home."

There was a brief change in Adèle's frame of mind the first days of September and their meetings were full of quarrels, remorse, shame and longing for security. She broke through her pride to beg him again to promise marriage and he seems to have assented.

On the third the Assembly gave the Constitution to the King and the night it was accepted the Queen was cheered at the opera.

The days were trebly anxious for Short. Rosalie, from the country, had intimated that perhaps her virtue had softened. He consumed all Morris's morning on the fifth. Lady Sutherland cut him the next day and "his countenance decomposed" and his voice broke and Morris was afraid he would be blamed. But all the clouds briefly lifted for Short as he got his heart's lifetime desire.

It is strange to think Morris and he both saw Nelson's Emma, Lady Hamilton, that month. She was then thirty, Adèle's age, and Hamilton, sixty-one, was a trifle younger than Flahaut. Morris said she was "a very extraordinary woman of the town who went to Italy in keeping and there became so much the passion of Sir William Hamilton that he has married her." He thought her famous singing and acting were perfection but he had reason for humble gratitude, though he did not know it, that his affections had not fastened on her.

Meantime he gave advice to Montmorin and the King such as no one around them was capable of. He implored the King not to try to bribe the Assembly, not on moral grounds only, which the King might not understand, but "because they have too little consistency or even fidelity to be worth corrupting." Provision Paris, win the populace, not the Assembly. Give bread to the poor, he urged Montmorin. Let the price to other people find its own level.

Twelve million pounds of flour can begin to arrive in five months, with a daily ration of 200,000 pounds of bread to the people. I will arrange it. It is a great affair of state and I want no profit from it.

Montmorin exasperated him with petty questions—"make a small note on the subject to be delivered . . . with the memoire." On two different days Adèle had to revise the translation but they were both in tearing spirits again and she nearly fainted away from one embrace.

It is wonderful to hear him deliver a moral homily in an interval. A man came to him to invite him into a group speculating in the assignats, the paper money. Morris told him, "Gambling, ruinous to some, dangerous to all, is unfair when the bet is made with certainty of gain."

On the thirtieth, Morris wrote Washington, "[The King goes this day in about an hour or so] to close the session of the National Assembly. . . . [He has] accepted the Constitution and been . . . liberated. . . . [He must now] make himself popular." He adds that it is said De Moustier will succeed Montmorin as Foreign Minister, but that he doubts it. The King had actually approved, but changed his mind three weeks later when Montmorin appraised him of the "inconsequent conduct" of Madame de Bréhan.

There was a third lame lover in the Louvre that month. The young Lord Holland, eighteen, nephew of Charles James Fox, called on his way to Italy in pursuit of Elizabeth Webster.

Whatever the anxieties of others, all was well with one man. Lafayette resigned from the National Guard, telling his wife, "The Revolution is ended. The liberty of France is secured," and then left for Chavaniac.

In October, Adèle's family worries mounted. Julie was obliged to flee to avoid her husband's creditors on the seventh and a week later the pension of her niece, the shortsighted, pathetic Mademoiselle Duplessis, was stopped, and none of them knew what to do. Morris, with elaborate precautions, sent five hundred gold francs to the Louvre anonymously. Adèle knew it must have come from him and, much affected, melted away with desire for days afterwards.

In November, Morris had the Flahauts and Montmorins to dinner, hearing later that Madame de Montmorin accused him of many wickednesses. He talked mainly about provisioning the French West Indies and the fleet from America. Those aristocrats who were not already penniless were fearful that Santo Domingo would gain its independence and their properties in Port au Prince would be lost. Toussaint L'Ouverture, though, was ten years in the future.

In December, Narbonne, now Minister of War, called Lafayette back to command the army at Metz. The month went ominously on with Morris's and Adèle's meetings more frequent and more reckless. They seemed to delight in the risk of discovery and when Adèle dined tête à tête with Talleyrand one afternoon "to correct his work, an address to the King," Morris was undisturbed though he thought the appearance injurious. He did some notes for the King himself the next day on how to govern the country. While so engaged, a fanatic came in to tell him the American Constitution was good for nothing and he had sent one of his own for the United States to General Washington.

December 13, Morris was tempted to infidelity. He dined with Madame Foucault, with whom he corresponded late in life. Everyone left them. He says that she "desires it but when I propose to lie with her she tells me that friendship suits her better. . . . I feel no very strong desire," and he agreed. However, an hour later he had to wrestle with his conscience not to have Mademoiselle Duplessis, with her obviously Cinderella appeal, in the carriage taking her home. "But it would be wrong."

Two days later in Philadelphia, Alexander Hamilton began paying blackmail to Reynolds for his summer's folly.

It was on December 21 that Adèle first took him across the river to the Rue de Bourgogne to meet that romantic figure, Madame d'Albani, the widow of Charles Edward Stuart, the Young Pretender, who had died in 1788.

Louise d'Albani, a year younger than Morris, had married the Chevalier when she was nineteen and he was fifty, and eight years before his death had fled from the tragic drunkard with the poet, Alfieri, now still her lover.

She was comely and a bluestocking who read Montaigne an hour a day, Mann, the British minister in Florence, wrote at the time and Morris found her sensible and well informed. Adèle was plainly devoted and Lady Webster, who lived with her a little later, thought her delightful.

Writers about her found no such golden mean. To Vernon Lee she was the lamb at the sacrifice and to others the author of the precocious letter about her bed and body to Charles Edward.

In any event she was well fitted to understand the triangle of Morris and the Flahauts and she too had a now shaky pension from Marie Antoinette.

Adèle and Morris spent Christmas Eve afternoon in the "genial joy" of "repeated caresses," and Christmas Day they chose to dine and sup in a quiet little party of four—Morris, Adèle, and the Cinderella Duplessis and Madame d'Albani. The Abbé de l'Isle came in later and read some verses. On the twenty-seventh, reviewing the general breakdown in France, Morris wrote Washington: "America in the worst of times was much better because at least the criminal law was executed, not to mention the mildness of our manners."

Though they celebrated the Cyprian Rites on the twenty-eighth and twenty-ninth, Adèle was ill on the twenty-seventh and the last two days of the year, exhausted in part by worry over Flahaut's frightful debts and the northwest winds and rain.

In America the Senate was debating Morris's appointment as minister to France.

CHAPTER EIGHTEEN

Sir, We Stand on a Vast Volcano

(January–August 1792)

THERE WAS a group of powerful men in the American Senate who were determined Gouverneur Morris should not be minister to France.

Washington had sent up his nomination on December 21, with that of Thomas Pinckney to London and William Short to the Hague, and on January 3, Jefferson wrote privately to the latter:

A party in the Senate, against Gouverneur Morris, has joined with another party which is against all foreign establishments and neither being strong enough to carry their point separately they have been now twelve days in suspense.

Has the Senate the right to forbid a diplomatic mission? Washington asked Jefferson. "After mature consideration and consultation I am of the opinion," Jefferson replied, "that the Constitution has made the President sole competent judge as to which places circumstances render it critically expedient that ambassadors should be sent . . . and that it has ascribed to the Senate no executive act but the single one of giving or withholding their consent to the person nominated."

The argument went on for eighteen days when the Senate confirmed Morris 16–11. The ayes included Langdon (N.H.),

Ellsworth (Conn.), Rufus King, Dickinson, Robert Morris, and
Charles Carroll. The significant noes were Roger Sherman,
Aaron Burr, James Monroe, Lee of Virginia, and of course, remembering what Morris had said at the Federal Convention of
slaveholders in Georgia, Few and Gunning from that state;
Strong and Cabot, Massachusetts Federalists, voted no in protest of a legation in France as such.

Burr said he was opposed because "it has been asserted . . .
that Mr. Morris conducted himself so offensively in his intercourse with the English ministers that they were offended."

Roger Sherman said, "I bear him no ill-will. . . . I have personally known him for several years. . . . I allow that he possesses a sprightly mind, a ready apprehension . . . [and] I
have never heard that he betrayed a trust or that he lacks integrity [but] with regard to moral character I consider him an
irreligious and profane man. [Such men] might be men of honor
yet I would not put my trust in them. . . . Benedict Arnold
was cruel and profane. I am against such characters."

Monroe said Morris was well known to be indiscreet. "Upon
the grounds of character he was twice refused as a member of
the Treasury Board . . . [and] he is a monarchy man and not
suitable to be employed by this country, nor in France. He went
to Europe to sell land and certificates."

On the day of the vote Washington gave Jefferson the draft
of a personal letter to Morris. It is very interesting that Jefferson in returning it said that he had "freely used the liberty
[given him] in softening some expressions lest they should be
too much felt by Morris."

The letter is one of the finest of its kind ever written.

The official communication of the Secretary of State will convey
to you the evidence of my nomination and *appointment* of you . . .
at the court of France, and my assurance that both were made with
all my heart. . . .
Whilst your abilities, knowledge in the affairs of the country and
disposition to serve it were adduced and asserted on one hand, you
were charged on the other hand with levity and imprudence of
conversation and conduct. It was agreed that your habits of expression indicated *hauteur,* disgusting to those who happen to differ
from you in sentiment . . . that in France you were considered as

a favorer of aristocracy and unfriendly to its Revolution, that . . .
that . . . I will not go further into details. . . .

. . . that the promptitude with which your lively and brilliant
imagination is displayed allows too little time for deliberations or
corrections . . . and it is the principal cause of these sallies and
that ridicule of character which begets enmity not easy to be forgotten but which could easily be avoided if it were under the
control of more caution and prudence . . . it is indispensably
necessary that more circumspection should be observed by our
representatives abroad. In this statement . . . I give you a proof of
friendship. I do it on presumption that a mind, conscious of its own
rectitude, fears not what is said of it. . . . I have the fullest confidence . . . that you would find no difficulty, considering yourself
as a representative of this country to effect a change and thereby
silence in the most unequivocal manner your political opponents.
Of my good opinion, and of my friendship and regard you may be
assured.

The Senate had confirmed Short 15–11, all the noes saying
their votes were against a legation in Holland, not against him.
Apparently Jefferson was unaware of his "son's" desperate longing for Rosalie and his dread of transfer from Paris. He wrote
him not to worry about the Hague because if there was not an
appropriation Carmichael was coming home and Short could
have Madrid, six hundred miles from Paris. The blow was a terrible one to Short, who, hoping against hope, had been "buying
plate and employing a maître d'hôtel."

In London, Morris, hearing from Constable of his nomination, though not its confirmation, wrote guardedly but under-
standingly to Short. "I sincerely participate in any regret this
may occasion you."

Tom Paine, hearing of it February 13, wrote Jefferson:

[Morris's] appointment is a most unfortunate one and as I shall
mention the same thing to him when I see him I do not express it
to you with the injunction of confidence. He is just now arrived in
London, and this circumstance has served, as I see by the French
papers, to increase the dislike and suspicion of some of that nation
and the National Assembly against him.

He apparently said something to Morris ten days later when
he was "every hour more drunk with self-conceit." "He de-

clares that the riots and outrages in France are nothing at all,"
Morris noted.

Lafayette wrote Washington:

Give me leave, my general, to you alone to offer an observation
respecting the late choice of the American ambassador [sic]. You
know I am personally a friend to Gouverneur Morris and ever as a
private man have been satisfied with him. But the aristocratic and
indeed counter-revolutionary principles he has professed unfitted
him to be the representative of the only nation whose politics have
likeness to ours, since they are founded on the plan of a representative democracy. I hate everything like despotism and aristocracy
and I cannot help wishing the American and French principles were
in the heart and on the lips of the American ambassador to France.
This I mention for you alone . . . and beg this hint of mine may
never be mentioned to anybody. I add the tribute of praise which I
owe to Mr. Short. . . .

Three days before, Washington had signed a letter to the
King of France and Congress questioned it. Jefferson, though
he had softened the letter to Morris, wrote for his own record,
"This is one of the many proofs I have had of his [Washington's]
want of confidence in the events of the French Revolution. The
fact is that Gouverneur Morris, a high-flying monarchy man,
shutting his eyes and his faith to every fact against his wishes,
and believing everything he desires to be true has kept the
President's mind constantly poisoned with his forebodings."

While this is all rather damning, one must wonder whether
later either Jefferson or Lafayette felt that a different minister
would have prevented the Terror, or Lafayette's flight, or his
wife's imprisonment, or Napoleon's wars. Furthermore, it is
evident that Washington could have mollified a great many
people by another choice than Morris. He must therefore have
believed, on balance, that the choice he made was sound and
in the interests of the country.

Morris had written on February 4 at enormous length to
Washington on the French situation. Of the aristocrats he
said, "[They] burning with the lust of vengeance, most of them
poor, and all of them proud, hope that supported by foreign
armies they shall be able . . . to reestablish that species of

despotism most suited to their own cupidity," scarcely the
words of a blind supporter of them.

Relations with Adèle had on the whole gone well during
January. He of course did not know then of his appointment.
She had told him on the sixth that Talleyrand was going away
but she could not say where. On the eleventh Morris heard it
was on a mission to England, without official status, to secure
the neutrality of England in event of war between France and
Austria.

Adèle was in bed ill the night Talleyrand came to say good-
by and Morris stayed him out, telling her later that he had
never heard more absurdity from a man of sense in his life than
Talleyrand had talked about fiat money.

On the twenty-first Le Ray de Chaumont and Morris agreed
on terms on which Morris was to buy the famous Macomb
lands in northern New York, presumably for Madame de Staël's
father. The next day Adèle bids him a tender farewell and
"renews to me her assurance that she will go with me to America."

The exact words of so precise a writer as Morris must be significant. It seems obvious from these that he desired her to go
with him, that he, unaware of the appointment as minister, intended to go home on the vast Macomb business, and that she
had *again* promised to do so. Who can say what their lives
would have been had the Senate's vote gone 16–11 against?

In London on the eleventh of February there were "unpleasant letters," possibly from her about his appointment, of which
Lafayette then knew, possibly, though, about the constantly
worsening affairs of Senator Robert Morris.

There is a somber fineness in the letter to Robert Morris of
April 10:

I cannot quit this subject without mentioning that when I think
of your various concerns, of the characters of many with whom you
have been connected, of the perplexity of accounts during the paper
money time and of the impossibility that your wife and children
should ever go through with the adjustment; when I join to this
apprehension that should you fall during my absence there is no
person I know of either able or willing to see that they have justice
done them, I say that very often when I think of these things it

makes me feel sick at heart. I am sure that it is of the utmost importance to you to wind up some concerns *even with a loss* rather than leave them to posterity. I wish that all accounts between you and I may be closed that I may with more clear propriety in case of any accident step forward to an adjustment, in which I should then have no personal interest.

A few days later he declined, to Robert Morris, Jr., any commission on a sale of Robert Morris's lands to Church or any other business he might do for him.

His letters to Washington, Senator Rufus King and Jefferson on his appointment are written with dignity and a manly sense of responsibility, stressing particularly that he must not aim at popularity with any single group.

He saw Mrs. Siddons as Desdemona on February 14, a date of great later significance in his life. That day Theodorick Randolph, younger brother of Richard Randolph, died of tuberculosis at Bizarre.

He stayed in London until April 30, busy with purchases to be sent the legation: malmsey, eight gross of porter, four gross of Burton ale, a coach and maps and books. His credentials from Jefferson had arrived, setting his salary at nine thousand dollars a year, with a year's salary for "outfit," and a quarter's for his ultimate return. A secretary of his own choice could be named at $1350 a year, and young Henry Livingston, twenty-four, was selected.

Lord Wycombe was in town, and at dinner with him, his father, Lansdowne, told Morris that peculation in ministries was a thing of minor importance, and that though he himself detested the practice it prevailed to a great extent even in "virtuous" America. Morris assured him "very seriously and very truly" that he was wrong. And so he was, though the distracted Hamilton was then doling out thirty, forty-five, fifty dollars to the wretched James Reynolds, while Angelica Church was writing his wife: "Tell Hamilton if he does not send my father [as] ambassador that I shall believe he has no influence at court and I will try not to care for him." At Lady Affleck's Morris saw and spoke to the forlorn Mrs. Benedict Arnold.

He says little of his talks with Constable, who wrote home to

Macomb on the failure to sell his lands, "I have endeavoured to throw the blame on Gouverneur Morris who had written so positively that he would sell the lands that you counted on that money."

And to Staphorst in Amsterdam, Constable wrote:

I am sorry that you should think Mr. G. Morris had acted amiss in authorizing Phyn and Co. to draw on you for £5000. . . . He would not have taken the liberty but that he authorized you at same time, in case you declined the advance, to redraw at maturity on Phyn. . . . I can only say that punctual provision shall be made for your reimbursement.

On March 15, Dumouriez became French Minister of Foreign Affairs instead of Montmorin, and in April, France declared war on Austria, the war which would go on for twenty-three years. England announced her neutrality.

There is a side light on Morris's private feelings in a letter to Hamilton. Luzerne, the French minister in London, who had been out with Rochambeau, was dead. At the auction of his effects Morris bought his Cross of the Cincinnati, "out of respect to that society, but *as I have not the honour of belonging to it* [I will forward it to anyone you name]."

On April 30 he left for Paris after inspecting the veterans' hospital at Greenwich and noting that bed sheets were changed once a month in winter, every three weeks in summer, and that the men got a clean shirt twice a week in summer.

At noon May 6 he was in Paris and when he had changed he walked to the Louvre, after waiting a long time for a fiacre. When the niece and husband left, Adèle and the American minister celebrated and she told him she had promised Talleyrand to visit him in London. She asked Morris for permission and approval. He gave the former but not the latter.

Short received him sadly and must have been filled with understandable envy as Morris set out house-hunting with Adèle.

May 11, with Adèle and the niece, he settled on the house in the Rue de la Planche at thirty-five hundred francs a year. It must have been a pleasant afternoon with the women telling the bachelor-minister where things should go.

From his *Diary* it is evident that he was now very careful
of all he said to the aristocrats. Dumouriez had not yet set a
date for his reception and Morris's colleague, Lord Gower, considered the affairs of France brought almost to a close, with
the armies in the north unequipped, hungry and mutinous.
Morris warned Madame de Tarente, in answer to her question,
that "Their Majesties should not only march in the line of the
Constitution but should not permit any person in their presence
to jest on that subject."

The fourteenth was Adèle's thirty-first birthday, and though
he does not mention the fete, they went to a goldsmith's for
some purchases and he spent the evening at the Louvre.

The next day Short presented him to Dumouriez, then fifty-
three. Morris asked leave, because of his leg, not to wear the
traditional sword when the King received him. Dumouriez said
there would be no difficulty. Morris then said he was naturally
frank and open and had not hesitated at the time of the Con-
stituent Assembly, as a private citizen and out of regard for
France, to try to effect certain changes in the Constitution
which seemed essential. He said he had been unsuccessful and
that now, as a public man, he considered it his duty not to
meddle in French affairs.

This is what he should have said to the Foreign Minister of
the Revolution. Assuming that Dumouriez accepted it completely, the critics of Morris never seem to realize that there
was a succession of foreign ministers to follow, each more to
the left. They seem to imply that Morris should have told
Dumouriez that he would not bother with what Dumouriez
thought: he would make his case with one of the many successors.

All through May he pressed Dumouriez for the audience
with the King which would seal his position as minister. There
was no reply and Short's passport for Holland did not come
through. Brief mention should be made here of James Swan,
one of the expatriate American promoters on the fringe of
French finance at the time. Like most such people, he always
had "inside" intelligence of which regular diplomatic officers

are unaware. He used to write Henry Knox about Morris's inadequacies.

He came to Morris on May 12 in typical fashion to tell him that the idea of his not being received "was started by Short" (out of jealousy). I do not believe it, Morris said.

It is interesting to know that in 1795 Swan got control of the American debt to France, but was in a French prison for debt from 1808 until his death in 1830.

Meanwhile Adèle and Morris went on their way through the pretty, pleasant days.

May 30, Morris said good-by to Short, who was to leave for the Hague June 1. It would be fascinating to know what these two men, so much unalike in looks and destiny, both then their country's envoys and each the lover of a French aristocrat, said to each other. Short with his troubled spinsterish face looking up at Morris, thinking he has had all the luck.

On June 2, while Morris was at breakfast, Short returned. His carriage had broken down and he had had to come back for another. "He complains heavily of the persecutions of fortune and indeed seems to be penetrated with the idea that Heaven has marked him as an object of desolation." Then Morris adds, "I cannot help smiling at this affliction." Perhaps it was not written callously but in thinking of his own arm and leg and the uncertainties in his heart about Adèle and indeed about himself.

The next day, as Lady Sutherland was delivered of a boy, Morris was presented to the King (and later the Queen, "who shews me her son") and handed the letter written by Jefferson, signed by Washington.

Very great, good and dear Friend and Ally.

I receive as a new proof of friendship to the United States, the letter wherein you inform me that you have accepted the Constitution presented to you in the name of your nation, and according to which it is henceforth to be governed. . . .

His first report as minister to Jefferson on the tenth runs to 4000 words.

The best picture I can give of the French nation, is that of cattle before a thunder storm . . . every member of [the government] is engaged in the defence of himself or the attack of his neighbor . . . some reason to believe the great mass of French population would consider even despotism as a blessing, if accompanied with security to person and property such as is experienced under the worst governments in Europe. . . . National bankruptcy . . . seems to be inevitable. . . . The dilapidation in every department is unexampled . . . the whole kingdom (Paris excepted) is interested in the non-payment of taxes.

Senator Monroe wrote to Jefferson at the same time:

The appointments of Gouverneur Morris and Wayne [to command the army] is so generally reprobated that no one appears to vindicate it in either instance. It is said it would have been difficult to have found more unfit persons even if some industry had been used to select them.

On the seventeenth the Jacobin Society petitioned the Assembly to suspend the King and Lafayette at Metz denounced them and set out for Paris.

Morris wrote Jefferson the brief dispatch with the fateful words, "Sir, we stand on a vast volcano," and wrote Constable that, as to Chaumont's offer, "I will not say anything for or against it . . . the lucky moment once lost will not present itself again [the moment of my offer to you in London]."

On the eighteenth Lafayette's letter, urging a coup d'état, the purging of the Jacobins and that "the power of the *revered monarch*" be left intact, was read to the Convention.

Morris wrote Jefferson that the end was beyond "the ken of mortal foresight," but his contemners evidently feel that there was some chameleon way by which he could have stood successively well with Lafayette and then with Dumouriez, St. Croix, Le Brun, Robespierre and the men who guillotined Robespierre.

June 20 a deputation of the Faubourgs of Paris filled the Tuileries, passed the unresisting Guards and forced the King to put on the red bonnet of liberty. One is reminded of Trotsky's mordant words written a hundred and twenty-five years later: "Revolutions are always impolite because the upper classes have never taught manners to the people."

In the lull Morris embraced "my friend, after which we go

together to Madame d'Albani's," and Lord Gower wrote his
government that Lafayette, by his letter, had passed the Rubi-
con, and took them to task for their ciphering. They had evidently used the "6th Octavo. I have the 9th."

All the last days of June, Adèle and Morris were very close.
On the twenty-ninth Lafayette and he met with "antient familiarity" and Lafayette, exhausted and tragically pitiful, kept
saying all he wanted was "the American Constitution [with] an
hereditary executive." Morris warned him to go back to his
army before he was sent to Orléans for high treason and Lord
Gower reported, "We are on the eve of a great crisis. M. de la
Fayette during his stay in Paris was not sufficiently bold and
energetic to affect the Jacobins with that degree of fear which
it was intended to produce and it has only served to make them
more active."

Morris tried to see Rosalie de la Rochefoucauld in vain on
the twentieth, perhaps with a message from Short.

July began quietly, "writing all morning," calling at the
Foreign Office, buying china and stationery for the legation,
with dinners tête-à-tête there or at the Louvre and a drive
afterwards in the Bois or to the convent at Chaillot, back to
the Louvre for an embrace and a translation by Adèle of a
note for the Foreign Office.

If there were other dinner guests at the legation, the count
usually came with his wife and her niece, but on Bastille Day
Adèle came alone to dine at half past five, "embrace and then
walk in the garden. At seven she leaves me." It was as though
they knew it would soon be over forever and that, like the King,
they fostered "a thousand empty hopes and vain expectations."

The next day John Paul Jones in his house at 19 Rue de
Tournon, which runs into the Luxembourg gardens, heard of
a plan to have him negotiate with the Algerian pirates.

Three days later he sent word to Morris that he was dying.
Morris went to him and drew his will, which named Robert
Morris as executor. Between four and five Morris left him to
dine with Lord Gower.

The biographers of Jones speak bitterly of the "social butterfly" who "hurried away from the dying man's side to attend a

dinner." It seems certain that Jones's mistress, Aimée de Tellison, was with him and that Morris or any man of feeling would
have supposed they wished to be alone. When the afternoon
dinner was over, Morris went to the Louvre to take Adèle,
with Vicq d'Azyr, the Queen's physician, to Jones's house.
When they got there Jones was dead.

It was singular, Morris wrote much later, that Jones "who
detested the French Revolution and all those concerned in it
should have been followed to the grave by a deputation from
the National Assembly . . . [and] I who during his life had
rendered him all possible service [should be reflected on by one
of the American gazettes for not paying him due respect]. . . .
Before I quit poor Jones I must tell you that some people here
who like raree shows wished him to have a pompous funeral.
. . . [I said] I had no right to spend on such follies either the
money of his heirs or that of the United States. . . . I have
since had reason to be glad that I did not agree to waste money
of which he had no great abundance. . . ."

When, in October, Jones's effects were auctioned Morris sent
someone to bid up the prices. He wrote the heirs, "The sword
given to him by the King of France was not put up but is reserved for you." A sword Jones had worn in the action of the
Serapis and, as with Luzerne, the Order of the Cincinnatus
were bought by Morris, who offered them to the heirs at cost
"or if you prefer the price I will keep them." They are now at
Annapolis.

The day before Jones's death there had been a dinner party
at the legation and Montmorin, the former Foreign Minister,
was one of the guests. After dinner Morris and he talked in the
garden and Morris told him that he thought the King should
quit Paris. It was plain that not to do so was to invite execution. But "to quit Paris" meant another flight to Varennes and
was of course "counterrevolutionary."

If Morris's critics believed that he was morally bound to
await the execution of the King, they were of course entitled
to condemn this advice. However, American legations have
not infrequently been the asylums of foreign heads of state or
the agents of their escape.

In any event Morris and Monciel of the royal household made a plan for the King's flight, but the King gave it up on the day set for it. On July 24 he asked Morris to accept custody of his papers and money. Morris said he doubted that the legation was any safer than the Tuileries but as "the money bore no distinctive mark of proprietorship he would consent to take charge of it . . . in case His Majesty could find no one else to trust."

Monciel brought 547,000 francs to him that day and by August 2 had converted all but 100,000 into louis d'or and distributed them to adherents in twenty-louis purses. More was brought later and the final balance, then safely in England, was handed on to the King's daughter by Morris in Vienna, December 1796.

Talleyrand had returned from London July 3 but Morris had been spared sight of him at the Louvre until the twenty-second. Even then Adèle made no mention of him but was wholly Morris's, as though they both knew their last summer days were going. And Talleyrand's thoughts of his own safety may have left no room, even in that powerful mind, for anything else.

On the twenty-eighth another lover, Fersen, wrote Brunswick's proclamation that Paris would be destroyed if anything happened to the Majesties. It reached Paris as the Marseillais came in singing their wonderful song and at Madame d'Albani's Morris found "them all terrified at a riot in which the Marseillais have killed one or two of the National Guard."

There were really only seven days left, days in which the Louvre was crowded and the embraces "hasty" or impossible or with difficulty "in my chariot."

The Montmorins were "a family in great distress," with a month to live, and on the fourth at the Tuileries they all expected to be murdered in the evening.

The cool, pleasant July weather had ended and August began hot and oppressive.

On the sixth the Flahauts both dined at the legation.

CHAPTER NINETEEN

Cold Words on the Red Page

(*August–September 1792*)

THE LITTLENESS UNDERLYING GREAT EVENTS has seldom had more ironic illustration than on the hot, dry seventh of August, when Paris was "in great agitation."

In the late afternoon Morris went to the Louvre and took Madame de Flahaut to drive. Her husband and she had dined with him at the legation the day before, and on the drive "my friend tells me that her husband has behaved brutally and threaten'd separation." How familiar the ugly sequence—the conventional dinner triangle, all outward propriety, and then some exchange between Morris and Adèle too mutual or too intimate to be borne, even by Flahaut. "How could you expect," Monsieur de Clèves had said to his wife, "that I would keep my reason . . . had you then forgotten that I was your husband?"

The following morning Monciel from the royal household called and Morris went to dine at Madame de Staël's. There those about to die "desiring to drink," he sent for his own wine and "let them get preciously drunk" while he went to drive again with his friend. He "set her down" and drove across the river to the British Embassy in the Rue St. Dominique. Lady Sutherland told him she would "be at court tomorrow."

It would be the day when no one else attended and she

would give the Queen some clean clothes, of her own little
boy's, for the Dauphin.

The morning of the ninth De Monciel came back, bringing
more of the King's money to be hidden in the legation. Then,
after a talk with Constable and Chaumont on their business in
North America, Morris went again to the Louvre and for the
last recorded time possessed his friend in "a happy moment."

They had been lovers for thirteen days more than three
years, during which he had been out of Paris one full year.
They had made love several hundred times and in that whole
half-lyric, half-frustrated, incomplete relationship time and
place had never let them sleep together nor lie naked in each
other's arms. One must wonder how much the seared arm, the
severed leg and all his suppressed sensitiveness had to do with
it and his strange behavior.

That night Louis XVI, walking for the last time in the Tuileries gardens, said, "The leaves are falling early this year."

The morning of the tenth was extremely hot. De Monciel
came again, more hopeful of the situation, but he had hardly
gone when Morris heard the guns across the Seine, as "the
Château, undefended but by the Swiss, is carried and the Swiss
wherever found are murdered."

In their rooms at the Louvre adjoining were the three
Flahauts. Talleyrand and Lord Wycombe were somewhere in
Paris.

The Count de Flahaut, sixty-six years old, went recklessly out
to the help of his King at the first sound of firing. The Tuileries
was already in the possession of the mob and the royals carried
off to the National Assembly. Flahaut found his friend Vios-
mesnil wounded in the garden and somehow got him along the
Rue St. Honoré to the corner of the Rue St. Florentin for
asylum in the Venetian Embassy. It was the palace where
Talleyrand would later live and die in splendor. Flahaut made
his own way to the home of his friend Bertrand, whence he sent
a note to his wife. They met but once again.

In the Louvre, Adèle was dressing a seven-year-old boy in
common clothes for his nurse to take through raging Paris to
refuge in the legation across the river. Later in the afternoon,

by herself, she somehow made her own way there in safety. A large company was to have been at dinner "but many of those which were invited do not come" and Morris passed a sleepless night.

"We are quiet here" the next day. The weather was very hot and De St. Pardou came in, "torn to pieces by affliction." One night in the previous January, De St. Pardou could not be got rid of at the Louvre by Adèle and Morris, impatient to be alone. De Monciel and his wife sought refuge before Morris was up on the twelfth and the house was full all day with aristocrats to seek asylum and Americans for passports. Madame d'Albani and her lover, Alfieri, came, "violently affected and afflicted," begging Morris to get them a British passport which Lord Gower, of course, had to refuse. Somewhere in Paris, Clementina Walkinshaw, now in her seventies, mother of the Lass o' Albany, Charles Edward's child, managed to escape to Switzerland.

Not until the fifteenth did Adèle dare to venture out when Morris drove her, in deep distress, to the Bois where they walked until she was tired.

It is almost impossible, from present sources, to establish what immediately followed for Adèle de Flahaut, and the three men, her husband, Wycombe and Talleyrand.

On August 19, Morris had difficulty even as minister getting a passport to take Adèle to Versailles to see her sister-in-law, Madame d'Angivilliers, but there "the municipality [was] very polite." The Venetian ambassador had been "very ignominiously treated" and Lord Gower, who had been ordered home and burned his papers, was "in a tearing passion" at the Jacobins' refusal of his passport. That night Morris was "very gay" and the weather was pleasant. Marat was crying in the streets, "Up, up and may the blood of traitors commence to flow," and it was the day Lafayette escaped from the command of the French Army to Luxembourg where, to his amazement, he was made an Austrian prisoner of war.

One hesitates to criticize what a man does, when he believes himself in mortal danger, yet there is something poor in spirit in the letter of Lafayette to young William Short in the Hague.

You will greatly oblige me, my dear sir, by setting out for Brussels as soon as this reaches you, and insist on seeing me. I am an American citizen, an American officer, no more in the French service. That is your right, and I do not doubt of your urgent and immediate arrival. God bless you.

Lafayette

As Lady Holland said long later, there were others for whom she had more compassion.

The air was full of terrible tension, though ominously quiet except for a few executions of little people. As will be seen later, Morris was working with terrific, effective energy all month on American affairs, wonderfully adjusting his position, though never too much so, to the change in government.

He bade "a long adieu perhaps" at the British Embassy on the twenty-seventh, and by the twenty-ninth of August, Lord Gower, and all the rest of the foreign diplomats, had quitted Paris.

Scarcely any account anywhere of Morris, favorable or otherwise, fails to mention that he was the only diplomat to remain in Paris during the Terror. While this is quite true, it is usually stated with a quite faulty inference. In justice to his *collègues*, it should be said that they did not leave because of personal cowardice but because they were ordered to do so by their governments, who did not wish to deal with the jailers of the King. Without injustice to Morris, it should further be understood that he did not remain out of personal bravery or audacity. He had no orders to leave. (How much his adversaries could have made of it, had he done so.) America was a month or six weeks away unaware of the situation. And in addition, Morris would be the first to assert that actual danger to his person, unless by accident, was of the slightest and that to him, as to any normal man, such danger as there was had its appeal, and the chance to be present in the great storm was something not to be missed.

The night of the twenty-ninth between ten and eleven some Commissaires de Section entered the legation with an order to search for arms said to be hidden there. With his home crowded with aristocrats, Morris fronted the mob, refused the search, and demanded they "seize the informer that I may bring him to punishment. I am obliged to be very peremptory and at length get rid of them."

They were scarcely gone when Ste. Croix, for eight days a minister of the Crown, came in flight from the house searches going on all over Paris and told Morris there would be another visit that night. In the morning an official apology was made to Morris and he wrote Jefferson that the commissary and he "parted good friends." As he was writing Ste. Foi came to say that the guns of the Duke of Brunswick bombarding Verdun could be heard in the city.

To Madame d'Albani, who had reached Ghent, Morris wrote *in English:*

The lady you mention is still where you left her, but talks of changing her position. She desires me to convey to you in the strongest terms how dearly she loves you, and how deeply affected she is by all your solicitudes. Her family are as yet both well and free, but how long they may continue to enjoy the blessings of health and liberty is uncertain. Fear and suspicion have ever made men cruel. . . .

There is some reason to believe that the "other visit" at which De Ste. Croix hinted when he reached the legation that night of the twenty-ninth was not from returning commissaries, but from his friend the Count de Flahaut, still in hiding. The count had, with appealing recklessness, slipped out to dine at the legation on the twenty-second. He may then have told his wife what he wanted her to do. Or all three may have made a plan at dinner which was frustrated by the events that followed.

In the early afternoon of August 31, Morris received "an insulting letter from the Minister of Foreign Affairs," aimed, as Talleyrand, who came in, said, at forcing him to an acknowledgment of the new government before his own could instruct him. Talleyrand came back the next day, one of the few aristocrats able, for the moment, to move freely, because at Danton's request he was writing a defense of the seizure of the King.

The morning of the terrible second of September came and Morris went "out on business. Madame de Flahaut takes the same opportunity to visit her friends."

If the apparently authentic story of her visit to Mehée de la Touche, Secretary of the Commune of August 10th, is true, it seems certain that it was made that day, under pretense of visiting her friends, and without the knowledge of Morris.

Whatever her own and her boy's peril, she must have been sure that between Morris, American minister, Wycombe, an English milord, and Talleyrand, *enniché* with Danton, she and her son would somehow be safe. Her husband's safety was far less important to men who loved her. Whatever the count's brutalities or her own infidelities, there was between them the loyalty at least of a common life and name for thirteen years. He was almost forty years older than Wycombe—eight years older than she was now when Wycombe was born—thirty-five more than she, twenty-six than Morris, twenty-four than Talleyrand, and she could not abandon him.

He had evidently sent word that his life depended on a passport which only De la Touche could issue and he was no doubt aware, as her lovers would be, that De la Touche would not give one for kindness or even money.

She found De la Touche in his dressing gown with his barber and when the barber was dismissed she said what she wanted. He said he did not dare, that it would mean the guillotine for him. Blank passports were on his table and he went in the other room to dress. Through the door he saw her take four passports and came back in the room. It is quite useless, he said, they are not signed. No one knows what more had to be said or done by her but she left with the blanks and one signed passport which she promised to return the next day.

Somewhere Morris picked her up in his carriage and on the way to the legation they saw a proclamation that the enemy was at the gates of Paris. At his house "she is taken ill, . . . affected for the fate of her friends," and about four or five o'clock that afternoon the slaughter of the aristocrats began and lasted unchecked through a week of horror, though the murderers were no more than three hundred men. The Count de Montmorin was among the slain and Morris wrote to Short: "Among the many scenes of bloodshed . . . you will lament the fate of the Duke de la Rochefoucault, kill'd in the presence of his aged mother." Like the Princess of Cleves, Rosalie was free.

To the credit of that often grotesque woman, Minette de Staël, it must be said that she went at the height of the butchery "in her chariot with six postillions" to Robespierre's house to save her friends and lovers. The wife of the Swedish ambassador, herself a Swiss national, was presumably safe but it was valorous and Robespierre held her for six hours in confinement, though she was eight months advanced in pregnancy.

During the night of September 2/3, Madame de Flahaut succeeded in forging De la Touche's signature to one passport and somehow sent it to her husband.

Bertrand, with whom he was staying, came to the legation on the fourth. "Madame had sent for him to give him a compensation for his kindness in saving her husband," Morris wrote in his *Diary*. She was absolutely penniless and the money must have come from him. Her name is not mentioned again in the *Diary* for over three years, all of the entries, as he later states, being made with care to compromise no one.

On the seventh Talleyrand told them he hoped to get his passport and urged Morris to ask for his. On the eighth Danton gave Talleyrand his, for services rendered, and he was off to England, leaving Adèle to Morris and Wycombe. But this was wisest and not to his discredit. Very probably he carried with him the dispatch from Gower's chargé, left in Paris, to Lord Grenville, saying that Mr. Thomas Paine is chosen one of the deputies of the Department of the Oise, and Robespierre for Paris and that Paine would come over from London on the seventeenth.

Adèle's situation was that so long as she did not pass the doors of the American Legation she was safe, though the safety would depend, in event of the Commune's demand for her person, on the personal force and prestige of Morris to refuse it. But she and a healthy boy of seven could not stay shut up there forever. Nor was there safety for any aristocrat, a former pensioner of the Crown, anywhere else in France.

Of ways and means for her escape Lord Wycombe and Morris must have talked carefully when Wycombe called on

the morning of the ninth and dined with him the next day, as
the prisoners at Versailles were slaughtered. Bentham, who had
been Wycombe's companion in Paris, wrote Lord Lansdowne
that night from London:

> Melancholy news, my Lord! By and by there will be not a single
> honest man left in that accursed country. Liancourt was to have
> dined here; instead comes news that Rochefoucault is murdered.

It was evidently the opinion of Morris and Wycombe that it
was best to wait a little, hoping that the first vigilance and
savagery of the Commune would have a reaction. It would appear that after dinner on the tenth, Wycombe crossed to England, probably to lay the lines and pay the bribes for Adèle's
later flight. He evidently let his father know that he was briefly
in England and Lord Lansdowne wrote to him in London on
the sixteenth, urging him to "take a manly part in politics, be it
Aristocrat or Democrat, or else a respectable, quiet part."
Certainly not that of a Scarlet Pimpernel.

In London, Wycombe presumably made Talleyrand privy to
the plan, since it was his son whom Wycombe would also bring
out.

On September 18 Talleyrand wrote Adèle a long, strange
letter. (Since it is in Villemarest its exact authenticity is in
question but its date and content carries the conviction that
he wrote it or something very close to it.)

It would seem to have been written from a conflict of ideas,
and of course without sentiment. They seem to have been
these: piqued at the power and resource of Morris and Wycombe, he wanted to eat and have his cake; he did not like
having these foreigners interfering and in Paris, or Switzerland,
if necessary, Adèle would be of great use; however, if she came
to London there would naturally be an arrangement with him.
It is an ugly letter but whether he wrote it the reader must
decide.

It goes on:

> How ridiculous is your fear and how ill founded your alarms . . .
> your sex, your services, your patriotism are your safeguards . . .
> you were never more necessary in Paris than at this moment. . . .

[He has written, however, to some people about a passport for her.]
To tranquillize your troubled imagination . . . Come if you wish
. . . you will not be able to reproach me for not warning you. . . .
Your husband is at fault in not dissuading you . . . a government
will be established strong enough to put an end to the scenes of disorder which you lament so bitterly. . . . If you persist in wishing to
leave France, I sincerely advise you to go to Switzerland. . . . You
could become of the greatest utility in propaganda [Grande utilité
en Propageant] from the other side of the Alps *the principles of the
Rights of Man* [author's italics] . . . I should continue to write to
you . . . however realize the vivid pleasure which I should have in
seeing you again. . . . Try to calm yourself enough before you
leave to discover the true situation in France . . . as to the Giron-
dins . . . are Robespierre, Danton, Marat simply using the Duke
of Orléans? . . . I have such confidence in your penetration and
your judgment when you are not frightened. . . .

Cold words indeed on the red page, and not those of Gouverneur Morris, words strangely like those Talleyrand wrote in
his *Memoirs* when Madame de Flahaut was in Altona, still a
refugee.

On the eighteenth, from the Hague, Short wrote to Morris,
as go-between, the first of his distracted letters about Rosalie.

. . . L'epine knows where she (an intermediary) lived in the Rue
Verneuil—will you let him carry the letter there and if there is anybody give them the letter as they will know how to send it—if there
is nobody will you be so good as to enquire and let L'epine carry
the letter to Alex de la R—. Be so kind as to let me know what . . .
has become of Mde de Flahaut.

"I will take care of your letter," Morris replied on the twenty-
third.

In Paris the National Assembly ended on the twenty-first. It
and its ministries had had authority without power. Six hundred
and eighteen new men took its place, back of them the Jacobins
with power but without authority.

September 29, Lord Wycombe was at the legation. The
weather was warm and rainy.

From a distance in time or place, the power of a Terror or
an Occupation seems as omnipotent and omnipresent as God
himself. Through some mysterious mercy it is never so, perhaps
because, as Adèle wrote long afterwards, "Ah, God does not

see everything." Darkness, swiftness, courage and good fortune always let some people escape. Thus Adèle, with or watched over by Lord Wycombe, made her way to the coast and crossed to England with her son, presumably on the last day of September.

In almost unbelievable synchronism that night, Anne Cary Randolph, aged eighteen, bore a dead child, out of wedlock, at Glenlyvar, Randolph Harrison's plantation in Virginia.

CHAPTER TWENTY

No Legitimate Government Exists

(*October–December 1792*)

EXAMINATION of Morris's dispatches during this period is essential to our understanding of his position on the new direction the Revolution had taken. From such a sweeping charge as Monroe's that he was its enemy it might be thought that the Revolution had occurred on one day, to Morris's displeasure, and that he had never forgiven its instigators. Needless to say, there was a series of convulsions, each sweeping away the predecessor rulers in blood.

Perhaps the first thing to consider, since so much has been made of it, is that in at least two notes of September 1 and 17 to Le Brun, the Foreign Minister, Morris used the phrases "representations to my court" and "awaiting the orders of my court."

The use of the word "court" for government is said to prove that "he was more royalist than the King." Actually even the Adamses' letters of the time so refer to Washington's household.

There are a number of possible explanations, first, of course, that it was used deliberately and provocatively to indicate he was a royalist, at home and abroad. Even allowing for the provocation aroused by Le Brun's letter, this seems most unlikely, as being wholly out of keeping with Morris's general

diplomatic decorum and the more so as no other example of
such a slip has been found, even by his severest critics.

It is possible, as only writers will understand, that under
the terrific pressures of that month, with young Livingston, his
secretary, gone to America, writing thousands of words to Le
Brun, Jefferson, Hamilton, Short, Pinckney, Rufus King, and
copying them all in his own hand in his *Letter Books,* Morris
unconsciously reached for the four-letter word *"cour"* instead
of the one three times as long, particularly as it was the common word in the French notes to him until that month.

A more likely explanation may be this. While he wrote good
and grammatical French, he was accustomed to clear his trans-
lated text with a French person, very often Adèle de Flahaut.

What more likely than that in those hot September nights,
with the refugees bedded down, and the legation doors bolted,
she helped him with his enormous correspondence? "Put this
answer to that cursed Le Brun into French for me, Amie, while
I break the news to Short that the Duchess of Rochefoucauld
is free, poor lady."

"I do not think she will ever marry *le petit* Short even so,
poor man, so many disappointments, *ni ministère, ni mari, ni
la légation, ni l'amour à Paris.* Give me the letter." Perhaps in
light vendetta she chose the word and he let it stand or did not
notice it.

The immediate controversy with Le Brun had to do with
an American payment on the debt to France.

One section of the debt service provided for payments to
French agents in the United States with which they purchased
American supplies for the French West Indies. A payment of
four hundred thousand dollars on that account was due in
America on December 1, 1792.

Le Brun, knowing that a large American credit was available
in Amsterdam for the other debt service in Europe, asked
Morris (1) to anticipate the December 1 payment, due in
America, by sixty days, (2) to make it in Paris and (3) to
double its amount. Morris said he had no authority to do this
and was insulted by Le Brun's saying his "insufficiency of powers" was "pretended." For the record Morris wrote the "court"

letter which the birds of the air, or Tom Paine, carried to every enemy he ever had. This is its crucial paragraph in English.

There remains sir, another fact to remind you of, very important, which is stated in this same letter from Mr Hamilton; that considering the extraordinary expense occasioned by our war against the Indians it was impossible for him to provide payment of the sum of 400,000 dollars any sooner than the designated epochs, of which the last is December first, 1792. You can judge sir, by this recital of facts, whether it be possible for me to go beyond my offer to you to make strong representations *to my court* urging it to grant the succor you ask. An offer which you have refused to accept.

A full book could be written on the correspondence between Short and him on the installment to be paid out of the Amsterdam credit.

The situation, put simply, was that although Morris was minister to France he had received no instructions as to this payment, the earlier arrangements having been made by Short, while still chargé in Paris. Short was then made minister to the Hague and arranged the credit out of which the installment would be paid. Both men were in honest doubt as to their respective powers, a situation made more difficult by the overthrow of August 10 and the resulting delay in communications. In all this Short deferred to Morris's greater financial experience, though it would appear at times he enjoyed raising questions and difficulties. In part he put them thus:

I really cannot help thinking there might and wd. be difficulty if this money was pd. and expended by the present reigning powers [after overthrow of King]. . . . You say the business is straight as to us—but dont you think if it were paid after the known suspension of the King and expended during the *interregnum,* that there might and wd. be difficulties with respect to it? For we shd. certainly have made the payments to persons whom we are not as yet authorized to acknowledge as the government of France to whom we owe the money. . . .

Because of the events of August-September, Short, Jefferson, Hamilton and the Dutch bankers were all opposed to the "royalist" Morris's views that the payment should be made to

the *de facto* government of France. Hamilton wrote to suspend.
Jefferson, "friend of the Revolution," wrote Morris (October
15):

. . . while no legitimate government exists, we apprehend we cannot continue the payments of our debt to France because there is
no person authorised to receive it, and to give us an unobjectionable
acquittal. You are therefore desired to consider the paiment as suspended until further orders. Should circumstances oblige you to
mention this (which it is better to avoid if you can) [make clear]
with the most friendly declarations that [this] does not proceed
from any wish in us to . . . oppose the settlement of their government in that way in which their nation shall desire it: but from our
anxiety to pay this debt justly and honorably, and to the persons
really authorised by the nation (to whom we owe it) to receive it
for their use; nor shall this suspension be continued one moment
after we can see our way clear out of the difficulty into which their
situation has thrown us.

The Dutch bankers also raised the question of the form of
receipt to be signed by France at the hand-over. Their lawyers
advised them they were liable to the United States unless it
was signed in the King's name.

To Morris this was all nonsense practically and unwise politically. Short did not want the payment made but wanted
Morris "to do certain things respecting [it] with those same
persons whose authority you deny." Morris's letter of September
20 is long and patient, though he does remind Short "that observations respecting the legality of a government should not
be committed [as Short was doing] to post offices subject to its
inspection."

His position was this. It was proper and advisable to pay the
government now by elections *de jure* because "the corner stone
of our Constitution is the right of the people to establish such
government as they think proper. In this country, reason may
perhaps say one thing and force another, but putting all that
aside I think it proper to adhere to the original nature and form
of . . . payment." As to the bankers' hesitancy about the form
of receipt, let it be signed by the Executive Council. Above all,
from a practical point of view, we hold the whip hand since
this installment is but a small part of the debt and in any final

payment, to any successive government, we can of course insist that this installment be duly credited.

The payment was finally made, in the form and with the receipt Morris recommended, against the views of Jefferson and Hamilton, and no successor to the Terror ever questioned it. It should be noted further that Morris's insistence allowed his country to have the advantage of a more favorable exchange rate than a long delay would have secured.

As to the payments of interest due on accounts of French officers from the American Revolution, Hamilton left Morris complete discretion and "Short is directed to subject to your order . . . one hundred and five thousand guilders [for that purpose]."

In the case of the imprisoned Lafayette, sensible men in America, including Jefferson and Washington, both of whom were devoted to him, were in agreement with Morris that nothing effective could be done for him. Short, less experienced, more excitable, was calmed by Morris from Paris and by Pinckney from London.

Morris wrote a long separate letter to Short regarding Lafayette on September 12.

I have long lamented his situation. His circle is complete. He has spent all his fortune on a revolution and is now crushed by the wheel he had put in motion.

I incline however to the opinion . . . that his future treatment will depend entirely on himself. . . . Be all this however as it may, he is in their power and they will do as they please. The reasons you urge for his liberation are cogent, and I hope they will be attended to; but power sometimes makes law for itself, and in such cases it cares but little for history or posterity.

Supposing that Monsieur de La Fayette were a natural born subject of America, and taken under the circumstances in which he was plac'd, I do not exactly see how the United States could claim him. He was not in their service. . . . Can the United States interfere in an affair of this sort without making themselves parties in the quarrel? Monsieur de La Fayette is a Frenchman, and it is as a Frenchman that he is taken and is to be treated. Again, supposing the right as clear as it is questionable, I presume that before the United States made such demand they would determine to go all lengths to establish their right in case it should be refused; for otherwise by advancing the claim and then receding they would sit down quietly under an insult. Consequently they would consider well before they plac'd themselves in a situation to be dishonored or else drawn into a war.

In such matters Morris did not set himself up as sole judge. He sent Short's letter and his reply across to Pinckney, saying:

My opinion is that the less we meddle in the great quarrel which agitates Europe the better will it be for us, and altho the private feelings of friendship or humanity might properly sway us as private men we have in our public character higher duties to fulfil than those which may be dictated by sentiments of affection towards an individual. I may view this affair thro' a false medium and therefore I shall wait with impatience for your opinion and listen to it with deference and attention.

Jefferson had already written the three ministers:

A claim of the rights of an American citizen to a person in the marquiss's circumstances appears to me to be claiming nothing, and it can only I fear at best serve as a testimonial of national gratitude, and may be a consolatory tribute to the feelings of a man of whose services and zeal for our country there is I believe but one sentiment in America. If a measure of that or any other nature should be adopted, it ought I conceive to be so conducted as to avoid involving any discussion of principle and should be the joint act of all the American ministers in Europe, if distance of situation will permit their uniting within the time necessary to render it serviceable.

Morris replied, "I perceive that our sentiments are coincident with each other at which I am much flattered."

As to the question of Morris's blind devotion to kings and courtiers, there are these September letters: to Le Brun, after a handsome apology from him for the annoyances "inseparable from a great revolution":

I had the honor to receive your letters of the 8th and 16th. In consideration of the explanations contained in the latter I will not again refer to yours of August thirtieth. . . . As to my personal opinions, sir, they are of no importance in so grave a matter, but you may rest assured that I have never questioned the right of every people to be governed as they please. For many years I have sincerely wished that France should enjoy all possible liberty and happiness, and I am certain of carrying out the intentions of the United States in assuring you that these wishes are shared by all my compatriots.

These were not written as fine words to Le Brun. A month before Morris had written Jefferson:

I am bound to suppose that if the great majority of the [French] Nation adhere to the new form the United States will approve thereof; because in the first place we have no right to prescribe to this country the government they shall adopt and next because the basis of our own Constitution is the indefeasible right of the people to establish it.

To Rufus King, now senator from New York, Morris wrote:

. . . the Court was involved in a spirit of little paltry intrigue unworthy of any thing above the rank of footmen and chambermaids. Everyone had his and her little project and every little project had some abettors. Strong manly councils frightened the weak, alarm'd the envious and wounded the enervate mind of the lazy and luxurious. . . . The palace was always filled with people whose language, whose conduct and whose manner was so diametrically opposite to every thing like liberty . . .

It is doubtful if the practical wisdom and sacrificial patriotism of his letter to Washington of October 23 has ever been surpassed by an American diplomat. He saw at once of course that after the overthrow of the French Constitution no one could be sure where the interests of America lay. The ordinary man, wanting to be sure he was never held responsible for mistakes, nor made the victim of others' wrong judgments, would have demanded to be told exactly what he was to do, and if he disagreed with it, could then clear himself with an address to Congress.

Morris wrote:

I have mentioned to Mr Jefferson repeatedly my wish to have positive instructions and orders for my government [conduct]. I need not tell you sir how agreeable this would be to me and what a load it would take from my mind. *At the same time I am fully sensible that it may be inconvenient to give me such orders. The*

*United States may wish to temporize and see how things are like
to end, and in such case, leaving me at large with the right reserv'd
to avow or disavow me according to circumstances and events is,
for the government, an eligible* [i.e., suitable, proper, desirable]
position. My part in the play is not quite so eligible, but altho I wish
the Senate to be sensible of this, I am from wishing that any precipitate step be taken to relieve me from it, for I know how contemptible is every private consideration when compar'd with the public
interests.

To Jefferson, September 27, he summarized in two sentences
that reproduction by cell division of the French Revolution:

. . . you will observe that in like manner as the Cleric and Aristocratic Parties considered the Assembly in 1789 as an usurper, the
leaders of that Assembly affixed on the Jacobins the same charge of
usurpation, and now the leaders of the last revolution are charged
by some of their brethren with *Feuillantism.* You will see by the
gazettes that there is the same enmity between the present chiefs
which prevailed heretofore against those whom they considered as
their common enemies, and if either of the present parties should
get the better, they would probably again divide, for party, like
matter, is divisable *ad infinitum.*

He wrote Pinckney:

I wish much, very much, the happiness of this inconstant people.
I love them. I feel grateful for their efforts in our cause and I consider the establishment of a good Constitution here as the principal
means, under Divine Providence, of extending the blessings of freedom to the many millions of my fellow men who groan in bondage
on the Continent of Europe.

Though it was not a fact, Colonel Smith, Adams's son-in-law,
leaving Paris November 9, was glad to tell Jefferson that "the
French ministers are entirely broken with Gouverneur Morris."
He went on, as Jefferson recorded it, "They shut their doors to
him and will never receive another communication from him.
They wish Smith to be the bearer of any message from the
President. . . . He said they are sending Genêt here with full
powers to give us all the privileges we can desire in their country. . . . [Ternant, the French minister] has given me extracts
complaining of both Gouverneur Morris and Mr. Short. . . .

[Smith said] that Morris at his own table in the presence of his company and servants cursed the French Ministry as a set of damned rascals. . . . Smith has mentioned the situation of Gouverneur Morris freely to others here."

As Jefferson was listening to Colonel Smith, Morris was writing Washington:

I could be popular but that would be wrong. The different parties pass away like the shadows in a magic lantern and to be well with any one of them would in a short period become the cause of unquenchable hatred with the others.

The *Diary* of November-December is scarcely more than the weather and the success of Dumouriez's army in the north. Tom Paine was helping write a new Constitution and the questioning of the King had begun. In America, on December 15, Monroe, Muhlenberg and Venable had called on Hamilton to hear the confession of his tragic involvement with Mrs. Reynolds.

Of the King's likely fate Morris wrote Jefferson:

I come now to the trial of the King, and the circumstances connected therewith. To a person less intimately acquainted than you are with the history of human affairs, it would seem strange that the mildest monarch who ever fill'd the French throne . . . should be prosecuted as one of the most nefarious tyrants that ever disgraced the annals of human nature. That he, Louis the sixteenth, should be prosecuted even to the death. Yet such is the fact. I think it highly probable that he may suffer, and that for the following causes. . . . The Monarchic and Aristocratic Parties wish his death, in the belief that such catastrophe would shock the national feelings, awaken their hereditary attachments, and turn into the channels of loyalty the impetuous tide of opinion. Thus he has become the common object of hatred to all parties, because he has never been the decided patron of any one.

He knew that Genêt had been chosen to succeed Ternant in Philadelphia and that Paine and he were well acquainted. He wrote Washington that his inquiries showed Genêt to be "a man of good parts and very good education, brother of the Queen's first woman, from whom his fortune originates. . . . At the overturn of the monarchy [pro-Revolutionary letters written as attaché in St. Petersburg] were so many credentials in his favor to the new government and their dearth of men has opened his way to whatever he might wish."

Small wonder Morris wrote complacently of "the dearth of men" in France, with 24,000,000 people, when he thought of the giants and the geniuses little America had had, to make a revolution and a solid government.

Short had continued to send him letters for Rosalie, saying in one, "I took the liberty before and hope you will excuse it. . . . The old ambassador of Holland has arrived here. He informed me of Mde de Flahaut about whom I wrote you. I was exceedingly happy to hear of her. . . ."

Sometime at the end of November, Morris had been able to send Short a reply from Rosalie at Roche-Guyon. Then Short received word that he had been transferred to Madrid. It was further than the Hague from Paris, but the road to it was through Paris.

On December 28 the *Diary* says "Mr. Short arrives this day from Holland and goes to Rocheguyon tomorrow." A week later he was back and imperishable things had passed between him and Rosalie.

On Christmas Day, with a "foul sleet" falling on somber Paris, Morris had written Madame d'Albani, "Our friend has gone away since your departure but I wait, hoping in a little while or soon she will come back."

Within a few days the friend wrote him from Half Moon Street in London:

Not a line from you and yet I write, and will even always write. Soon I shall be arriving, however, for my mind is made up and the end of next week will not see me in London. I have done all I should and even more than I should; I don't know whether you owe me any gratitude, but I don't feel guilty in the least for having abandoned you so long. I claim the right of sacrificing you as much as myself when serious misfortunes call me. I complain to you, and with you, but it seems to me there can be no question of excuses between us because, on my side at least, there can be no wrongs. . . .

Let this be your New Year gift, you who were separated from this little island by a true republicanism; I will once more make you a present of the lovely blue cup which I offer you every year with renewed pleasure; you will find it among the china sent to Martin's [his steward's] care. Good-bye, my dear and good friend; I am in the best of spirits at the thought of seeing you soon.

How like the lovely blue cup this exquisite letter.[1]

[1]There is a postscript which has baffled me. "Cabagne says she sends you a New Year kiss." Cabagne, not a known *prénom* nor *surnom*. A pet name for Mademoiselle Duplessis? Or Adèle's maid, the message sent in light mockery knowing Morris's love of kissing?

CHAPTER TWENTY-ONE

The Glare of Ice

(1793)

THE MELODRAMA of 1793 began with the King's execution and ended with the Queen's.

Morris's company was dispersed. Lord Wycombe was in America, Adèle in Half Moon Street, Talleyrand in Kensington, now and then going down for a night or two to Juniper Hall, where the exiles living on De Staël's money were to be immortalized by Fanny Burney.

Morris himself was in Paris until the spring came, when he took a house at Sainport, twenty miles away, where peaches, apricot, apple and almond trees were in blossom and, as he noted, a mile and a half away were the ruins of the baths Henry IV gave Gabrielle d'Estrées.

At Bizarre in Virginia, as the fruit blossoms came, Nancy Randolph waited, watching a murder charge gather over her and her lover's head.

On January 5, Morris had come into the legation "glad to get home. The streets are in a glare of ice. Horses tumbling down. Mine came off tolerably.—To continue this journal would compromise many people unless I go on in the way I have done since the end of August, in which case it must be insipid and useless. I prefer therefore the more simple measure of putting an end to it."

Diplomatically the streets of Paris were a glare of ice all year for the most sure-footed man. Genêt had dined with Morris January 3 preparatory to leaving. "He has I think more of genius than of ability," Morris wrote Washington, "and you will see in him at the first blush the manner and look of an upstart." Morris had seen through the brilliant young man's unusual good looks and most people would agree with his verdict of upstart (most certainly Washington did within eight months). He wrote Robert Morris that his advice might be useful to Genêt and "your civilities as a gentleman he will in course receive." A legend arose afterwards that Genêt's actual mission was to take the Queen to safety in America and that the American, Swan, was part of the plot.

France had decided upon war with England. It would be declared February 1, while Genêt was safe half across the Atlantic, and the aim of his mission would be to draw the United States into the war and to re-establish the French empire in North America, pushing Spain out of the Mississippi Valley. Thomas Paine and Joel Barlow then in Paris, hostile to Morris, subscribed to the plan.

Of this Morris was not fully aware until February 12, when, fearful of French censorship, he sent a letter by safe hand to Pinckney in London saying:

I think it well that you should be acquainted with a fact which it is very important to communicate to our Secretary of State as soon as may be. I am inform'd in a way that precludes doubt that the Executive Council here sent out by Mr. Genest three hundred blank commissions for privateers to be given clandestinely to such persons as he might find in America inclin'd to take them. They suppose that the avidity of some adventurers may lead them into measures which would involve altercations with Great Britain and terminate finally in a war. This appears to me (waiving all question of honesty) no very sound measure politically speaking, since they may as a nation derive greater advantage from our neutrality than from our alliance. But whatever light it may be viewed in as to them, it is in respect to us a detestable project.

. . . I have no late news from America and none of any date which you would wish to know. Our Secretary of State seems much attach'd to brevity.

The privateer commissions were of course a fact confirmed by Genêt's actions immediately on landing at Charleston, South Carolina. That the French Government did not like an American minister opposed to their plans was quite natural and the sort of complaints made to Colonel Smith were being carefully made in Philadelphia. Ternant wrote his Foreign Office that he had "*fait connaître à M. Jefferson les plaintes auxquelles a donné lieu la conduite de M. Morris en France.*"

The King was executed on January 21, the decision of the Convention very much less unanimous than is generally understood. The vote was 387 for, 334 against, even Paine preferring that he be exiled to America. Morris tersely informed Jefferson of it on the twenty-fifth, saying: "it would be needless to give you an affecting narrative of particulars. I proceed to what is more important. . . ."

On the twenty-seventh he wrote a characteristic letter to the bankers of America in Amsterdam:

I learn from the friends of Monsieur de la Fayette (who is now prisoner at Magdeburg) that altho kept in close confinement no provision is made for his comfortable subsistence. I own that I do not believe this assertion, but should it be true I think no moment is to be lost in administering relief. You will therefore be pleased to write to your correspondents at Magdeburg on the subject, and desire them to supply the sums needful for him. You can extend your credit to the sum of ten thousand florins, which you will please to charge as paid by my order, in your accounts with the United States. Observe also that it is not in my contemplation to furnish the means of escape, for I cannot enter into intrigues of that sort directly nor indirectly, because it is not becoming the dignity of the United States to act in an underhand manner; but they would hear with great concern that a person who has been eminently useful to them should be in want of those necessaries which it is in their power to bestow.

Meanwhile Madame de Flahaut was still in London. It is in keeping with her independent and busy life as an émigrée that she had no interest in the *fainéantise* of Juniper Hall. Of all the refugees, she seems most completely to have retained the sense to organize her own life and, whatever the duplicities into which she was forced, to have avoided ever becoming fantastic or grotesque. She obviously tried at different times to marry, but three of the men involved would each have been an appropriate husband and the fourth, De Souza, certainly was. Each possessed in his way the charm and renown to which any woman would be drawn. None was an absurdity such as the patroness of Juniper Hall chose—the neurotic Benjamin Constant or the boy Rocca, half her age, whom she married.

Villemarest has a letter of Talleyrand to Le Brun of January 26 saying that Madame de Flahaut is "jealous of some other acquaintances I have made there" and to write him no longer in her care. To pick and choose which Villemarest letters to believe is a dubious business, though it is hard to see why the Minister of Foreign Affairs should be writing to one proscribed exile in care of another. But in the letter Talleyrand speaks of Madame Grand, later his wife, whose friendship he says he possesses, so there may be something in it.

Adèle's "little lodging in Half Moon Street" was being paid for by Lord Wycombe and Bobus Smith, and Lord Holland told Wycombe's father that Talleyrand was "a constant visitor," ostensibly helping her with her book.

Grim poverty had taken away most of the graces they had known, but the exiles were all steadfast in their loyalty to the stylized, heartless habit of assuring or increasing someone's passion for them by being unfaithful to it. There may have been a hint by Talleyrand that always "scribble, scribble, scribble" was dull business. A retort by Adèle that Madame Grand, however sensual, looked as though she could not write even her name, and "O those eyes to heaven in Vigée Le Brun's picture. *Quelle supercherie!*" He may have answered that John Wycombe was "a handsome youth," or so his mother said, but not very bright, though well enough to pay the rent. Did he in fact ever read anything? To which she may have said, "He was taught to read by the marchioness, his mother, and by Joseph Priestley. He was not, as in another case I can think of, sent away from home at eight." Well, so it probably went and not in the sulky jealousy Talleyrand suggests.

But as the letter was written the Count de Flahaut was arrested in France whence he had never been able to escape. This

gambler, this spendthrift, this possibly brutal though often injured old man, behaved in incredible fashion. He was apparently offered his freedom if he would implicate his friend
De Molleville, and he refused. He then managed to escape, but
when his attorney was taken as a hostage he, like a great gentleman, immediately surrendered himself and was executed at Ar-
ras.

When he was first arrested there was little Adèle could do to
help him, but what there was, with pleas and a pathetic sum of
money, she did. His execution made it impossible for her to return to France unless to the same fate. There had been a time
when apparently both she and Morris desired her freedom by
divorce or death so that they might marry. One must wonder
what would have happened if neither exile nor execution had
so tragically separated them.

Morris's problems as minister in Paris might have been too
much even for the wisdom of a Monroe, as Washington wrote
later in a mordant marginal note. It was "impossible to be on a
friendly footing with [the] persons to whom he had traced the
intention to excite a seditious spirit in America." He must, however, maintain a series of protests to Le Brun against seizure of
American ships by the French, and secure agreements from him
"to prevent in future the vessels of our good allies from being
exposed to the attacks of our ships of war," while Le Brun complained to Ternant, about to be relieved, of such unfriendliness.
Ternant, who must now address the head of the French Foreign
Office as *Citoyen Ministre*, wrote Le Brun he had seen Jefferson, *"Je lui ai fait part de vos griefs contre M. Morris."*

There were American adventurers in France to deal with,
men employed and financed by Le Brun to outfit ships under
the American flag for the French service, making a parade of
their patriotism and demanding passports from Morris. He refused them, he wrote Pinckney, because "real American vessels
have their registry and other papers in proper order and consequently do not need any documents which we can give and
which in fact we are not authorized to give."

It would appear that Morris's critics at the time and since felt that it was to the advantage of America to become an active ally of France and fight against England and that Morris was a poor American and an unfaithful public servant because he did not disregard the Administration's proclamation of neutrality.

One hesitates to apply the term "lunatic fringe" to the American Francophiles and the supporters of Genêt. Yet it is hard to find a better one for men who saw war with England either as the obligation or advantage of their country. These people condemned Morris as an Anglophile and a royalist. The angry American ship captains interned at Bordeaux howled that he did nothing for them and appealed to Tom Paine, of all people, as their advocate. But there is nothing surprising in that, then or since.

The London gazetteers, perhaps inspired, reported in March that Morris's house had been burned and he killed. He wrote Robert Morris that "it was not true at the time of publication," adding:

You tell me that in my place you would resign and come home but this is not quite so easily done as said. In the first place I must have leave to resign from the President but further you will consider that the very circumstances which you mention are strong reasons for abiding because it is not permitted to abandon a post in the hour of difficulty. I think the late decrees respecting our commerce will shew you that my continuance here has not been without some use to the United States and as to the rest we must console ourselves with the reflection that whatever is, is.

Genêt arrived safely in South Carolina on April 8 to a thunderous reception, and with Governor Moultrie's help had a recruiting station for his privateers going in five days.

On the day before, the *Virginia Gazette* and Richmond *Chronicle* had published a letter from Richard Randolph of March 29, giving notice that he would appear before the April Cumberland County Court "to answer in due course of law, any charge or crime which any person or persons whatsoever shall then and there think proper to allege against me. . . . Let not pretended tenderness toward my supposed accomplice shelter me. That person will meet the accusation with the fortitude of innocence. . . ."

At the middle of May, Fanny Burney heard that Talleyrand had had to sell all his books to live, and Genêt reached the Capitol in Philadelphia, where a letter from George Rogers Clark was awaiting him with plans for the invasion of the Mississippi.

The objectives of his mission were "to foster the extension of the Empire of Liberty," and to "plant it in Louisiana and other provinces adjacent to the United States"; to send French agents, financed by America, into Kentucky and Louisiana; to insist that no American privateers be fitted out "unless for the forces of the French nation"; and with him he brought commissions for Indian chiefs to invade Canada.

He was still having an incredible reception. "Ten thousand people in Philadelphia, day after day, threatened to drag President Washington out of his house and effect a revolution or compel [him] to declare war in favor of the French Revolution," John Adams wrote later. It may not have been quite that bad, as Hamilton cut the numbers down to a hundred, saying that "a crowd will always draw a crowd." Still it was bad enough and Jefferson wrote an Introduction for Paine's *The Rights of Man,* supporting France against England, and Beckwith, the British agent, mildly protested to Washington's private secretary.

The attitude of the Administration is well known, Jefferson, the Secretary of State, pro-French, Hamilton pro-English, Washington for official neutrality but more concerned with danger from France than from England.

In Paris "the enmity between the present chiefs" was mounting. Wheels were working within wheels and at the end of May "the Insurrectionary of the Commune," headed by Marat, arrested Roland of the Girondists. Here, as so often, the question arises, if Morris was expected to have been completely *persona grata* to the Gironde, what would have been America's position when Marat and the Commune swept it away? Or, had Le Brun had "no griefs" against him, what his position would have

been when Deforgues, from the left, superseded Le Brun on
June 21?

Tom Paine, of course, had no trouble on "the glare of ice,"
and what the result of it was we shall see.

Morris wrote Robert Morris, "I suspected that Paine was
intriguing against us altho he put on a face of attachment . . .
he came to my house and being a little more drunk than usual
behaved extremely ill. . . . I am told he is besotted from morning till night."

On June 25, Morris sent Jefferson "a list of those, who were
ordered by their brethren to be arrested, the names of those
who have proclaimed themselves to be the prime movers of the
Revolution of the tenth of August, and fathers of the Revolution." He is pleased with Jefferson's advices that "our fellow
citizens are disposed to preserve an exact neutrality" and adds,
"I labor incessantly to keep things quiet [as to the frequent
violations of our neutrality by the French privateers] and I
think it likely that some of my countrymen may think me too
much attached to France. . . ." To Washington the same day
he says, "Should the present society be able to establish themselves, I think M. Genêt will have a successor."

A week after the letters were being written Genêt declined
to dine with the Cincinnati because De Noailles, brother-in-law
of Lafayette and a member in his own right, would be there.

From Chavaniac, the distracted Adrienne de Lafayette appealed to Morris officially to pledge the United States as security for certain debts of Lafayette's.

He acted immediately but said nothing even to Washington
about it for a year. In the dilemma (that he could not act as
minister, nor fail to act as a man), he told Washington, "I informed her it was inconsistent with the dignity of governments
to appear in such affairs; moreover, I had not any right to dispose of the public property, but as far as my own would go for
her relief, she might count on every aid in my power."

It took the form of a personal loan for one hundred thousand
francs, made, Lafayette's daughter Virginia said, "in the most
generous manner, [and he delicately added] that he ran no risk

for if the advance were under any circumstances lost he knew America would make it good."

In November a hundred and fifty thousand more was asked by the marquise "to complete some arrangements which they had imagined at Chavagnac." This Morris declined because he thought the arrangements unwise "and because I had not the money," but he sent word to the children *that the United States would take care of them* (his italics).

The Austrian armies were thrusting southward, as Marat was assassinated, and Mayence fell to them. There was a "Royal or Christian Army, as they call themselves, on the Loire" and only "Austrian inertia," it seemed, kept them apart.

Robespierre entered the Committee of Public Safety on July 27, and *incivisme*, making it as treasonable to do nothing as to engage in counterrevolution, became a crime. A girl was punished for "depreciating the value of the assignats" by selling two heads of lettuce for twenty sous. Deforgues, replying to a protest from Morris at more seizures of American ships, said that it was difficult, because of language, "to distinguish our allies from our enemies." Morris told four Americans, deputed by the ninety-two captured captains at Bordeaux to demand their freedom, that French laws did exist which held them, and though he strongly protested to Deforgues in their behalf, he added, "I do not pretend to meddle in the interior business of the Republic." The deputies went to Paine, who asked Morris "if he did not feel ashamed to take the money of his country and do nothing for it."

It must have amused Morris to have money made a criterion of conduct, particularly by Paine, who had so often borrowed it from him. As to his doing nothing, someone did write Constable that "G.M. is much at ease at his chateau." Still they worried about his safety. "Gouverneur was well July 30," William Constable wrote his brother on August 28, "which is the last advice."

All year the enclosures for Rosalie had come from Short at Aranjuez. "Be so good as to put the address on the inclosed letter and send it to the house in Paris desiring them to send it to the lady whom you know and whom I went to see in the country. . . . Sh'd you have any means of sending letters to England by the way of Ostend or any other . . . be so good as to send me by that means any letter that person may send to you for me. She will write herself by way of Geneva and therefore I wish to make use of any other for greater security. . . . I had the pleasure of receiving from Mr. Pinckney your friendly letter enclosing me one from a friend from whom I was exceedingly anxious to hear. . . . I had begun to lose all hopes. . . . I beg you to give me some account of the family to whom I formerly wrote. . . . I receive no letters and think it best not to write to them until I hear again from you . . . write me [even] a single line to let me know whether they be still alive. . . . Send your letter by duplicate one by way of Holland or England and the other under cover to Messrs. Aine Reguy, père et fils in Genoa. . . . Since my last I received three from the person for whom I enclose one at present . . . you cannot render me a more acceptable or friendly service."

Seldom, surely, has the mail of American diplomats carried more personal longing and heartbreak. The letters were written as the aristocrats went in constantly greater numbers to the guillotine.

How completely that month Talleyrand seemed to have disappeared from history, yet on August 24 in Berlin had been born to the Duchess of Courland a daughter Dorothea who would be with him, twenty-one years later, when he dominated the Congress of Vienna gathered to settle the whole business.

By August, Genêt's conduct in America had become so outrageous in its endeavor to reach "the people" over the heads of the Administration and bring America into the war that on the twenty-third Jefferson wrote Morris they were under "the painful necessity of asking Genêt's recall. If he perseveres we may be forced even to suspend his functions before a successor can arrive to continue them."

There was almost certainly unanimity among the entire Cabinet on the move by this time, yet one wonders a little, from a letter of Monroe's to Brackenridge the same day, whether Jefferson let his disciple understand he had only reluctantly agreed. "The monarchy party has seized new grounds against the French Revolution, thinking to separate us from France and pave the way for an unnatural connection with Great Britain," so Monroe wrote.

No connection with Great Britain more unnatural than amity and commerce was desired by Washington, Hamilton and Morris, and as to hostility to France, Jefferson, Hamilton, Knox and Edmund Randolph on August 31 went no further, in a Cabinet opinion to Washington, than that Morris be provisionally instructed to make representations to secure a revocation of the edicts of seizure. Morris had neither done nor tried to do more.

Far from such balanced moderation were the ideas of men who were under no oath of responsibility. "Admit," Madison wrote Jefferson September 2, "the apologetic influence of the errors in our own government . . . such as the refusal in the outset to favor the commerce of France more than that of Great Britain [and] the unfortunate appointment of Gouv. M. [sic]." One must wonder whether Madison would have preferred Paine as minister or approved Paine's letter to Barrère, of the Committee of Safety, on September 5,

Thomas Jefferson, Secretary of State, is an ardent defender of the interests of France. . . . Gouverneur Morris who is here now is badly disposed towards you. . . . The representations which he will make on his arrival [after his recall] will not be to the advantage of France. . . . Morris is not popular in the United States. . . . Congress [not Washington] will require a great deal of information. . . . If the United States captains need a convoy [to protect voyages from France to the West Indies] it will be to me that they will write and not to Morris. . . .

In the same spirit of littleness Genêt was having his final say to Jefferson—that Washington "did not speak to me at my first visit [except of] the friendship of the United States toward France, without announcing a single sentence on our Revolution . . . that this first magistrate of a free people decorated his parlor with certain medals of Capet [Louis XVI]," adding the charges that Mr. Morris "favored as much as he could counter-revolutionary projects of Louis XVI . . . [and] communicated to him memoirs [as Jefferson had done and in favor of magnanimity] . . . of having no connexions except with suspicious persons"—and then the surprising charge that Morris had *"been the channel of the counsels which conducted Lafayette into the prisons of the counter-revolution"*—and of course that he had used the words *"in the name of my court"* so shocking to republican ears.[1]

On October 16 the Queen was executed and Morris wrote Washington, "France must soon be governed by a single despot."

Morris was awaiting Deforgues's answer to his note of the thirteenth that "from every quarter my countrymen who have brought merchandise into France are complaining against the decrees fixing prices for it" and asking relief. The reply from Deforgues said the Council learned with "the liveliest indignation of the conduct of their agent in the United States" and would punish it. Genêt had been recalled and Fauchet would go out to succeed him. Deforgues himself was going out as consul general.

There was no limit to the ingratitude of the French Government. On December 28 they turned on their friend Tom Paine, now fifty-six, said he was an Englishman, and clapped him in Luxembourg Prison.

---

[1]As a footnote to French diplomacy, royal or revolutionary, Adet's protest to Pickering, Secretary of State in 1796, is of interest. "As French ministers have always enjoyed the precedence to those of England not only in the United States but throughout the world, France, as a republic, has preserved and will preserve the rank she has held in the Diplomatic Corps under her ancient regime. The French people look on all peoples as equal and brother but they will never suffer that distinction contrary to custom [of their having precedence] should be granted, directly or indirectly to any state whatever"—the demand was that a privately printed directory listing the British minister before the French should be suppressed.

Pickering's reply was short but magnificent. "But, sir, this is impossible. These are private proprietors who print as they please and in such order as their ideas of propriety or humor or accident may direct."

CHAPTER TWENTY-TWO

The Bizarrerie
of Human Amours

THE LETTER which Richard Randolph had published in the Richmond paper had been written because he could no longer disregard the crescendo of gossip in Virginia. All through the state, planters, overseers and slaves were saying that he and his young sister-in-law, Nancy, had murdered the child born to them at Glenlyvar on the last night of September '92.

In the woodpile by the house a slave was said to have found the fetus of a white infant and there was gruesome evidence that it had been born in Nancy's room, back of the one occupied by her sister Judith and her husband. It was said that Richard and Nancy had smothered it and that he had carried the body downstairs and hidden it in the firewood. Under the law, the Negro who found the body and the Negresses who had seen the bloodstained bed and stairs could not be witnesses.

On April 9 indictments were handed down. Randolph was jailed, Nancy left in the custody of their attorneys, Patrick Henry and John Marshall. On April 29 trial of the Commonwealth of Virginia against Richard Randolph and Anne Cary Randolph began.

Jefferson, who had signed the Neutrality Proclamation on the twenty-second, was in the courtroom. Among the witnesses was his daughter Martha, now the wife of Thomas Randolph, older brother of Nancy and Judith.

Testimony was given by many witnesses, friends and connections of the Randolphs, that they had been convinced, long before the event, that Nancy Randolph was pregnant. An aunt, through a keyhole, had seen her standing naked and plainly pregnant before a mirror and Nancy afterwards had refused to let her aunt examine her for proof of her virginity. She had been shocked by seeing Nancy and Richard kissing when alone, and others had seen "fond familiarities" between them.

Martha Jefferson Randolph testified that "about the 12th of September" Judith Randolph asked her for some remedy for Nancy's colic and that she had recommended gum guiacum.

Their cousin, Mrs. Randolph Harrison, mistress of Glenlyvar, was in the dreadful position of being called to testify against them. Judith had written her three weeks before the trial, "Oh my beloved friend what have I not suffered since I saw you; O what may I not suffer before I see you again. . . . I do not know at present positively, but I have very little thoughts of ever returning to Bizarre."

Now Mary Harrison must tell what had happened at her house on the last night of September. The Randolphs had arrived from Bizarre, Jack Randolph and another boy cousin with them.

From the moment of her arrival Nancy had complained of being ill and had gone to her room immediately after the mid-afternoon dinner. The only exit from that room was through one in which her sister and brother-in-law were to sleep.

Late at night the Harrisons, sleeping on the first floor, were awakened by screams which they thought were Judith's. Richard Randolph came to their door to ask for laudanum and said that it was Nancy who had screamed with colic.

Mrs. Harrison gave him the laudanum and herself went upstairs. Judith was sitting up in bed and told her Nancy had hysterics and that Richard was ministering to her. Mrs. Harrison went to Nancy's door and found it bolted on the other side. She knocked and Richard admitted her, asking her to leave her candle outside as the light hurt Nancy's eyes. In the room were two child Negress slaves. Nancy appeared quieter and Mrs. Harrison left on hearing one of her own children calling her downstairs.

In her own room a little later, Mrs. Harrison and her husband, half asleep, heard steps on the stairs, going and coming, and "from the weight of the steps" supposed it was Richard Randolph.

The next day Nancy remained in bed, tightly covered, but Mrs. Harrison and a Negress slave saw bloodstains on the stairs, some on the bed, and when the following day Nancy rose, at her sister's insistence, and went downstairs, they found evidence that a birth had taken place.

After a few days, in which no reference was made by anyone to the night's events, the Randolphs left and a Negro slave told Harrison that a fetus had been found in the woodpile.

Patrick Henry, cross-examining very carefully, drew the admission from Mrs. Harrison that the bloodstains in the bed could have been the result of innocent female causes. He had already, in a much lighter vein, been able to throw doubt on the value of keyhole vision in establishing pregnancy, and ascribed Nancy's refusal of examination to innocence and natural delicacy.

Without conceding Nancy's pregnancy, he brought out through Jack Randolph that she had been betrothed to Theodorick Randolph, Richard's younger brother, who had died at Bizarre of consumption 229 days before the alleged delivery. Only his death, it was said, had prevented their marriage.

Judith Randolph was the last witness for the defense. She swore to her complete belief in the innocence of her husband and her sister, both as to murder or any improper attachment. She contradicted Mrs. Harrison's additional testimony that she had heard, and her husband seen, Richard Randolph going down the stairs with something in his hands. She said that immediately after Mrs. Harrison had left Nancy's room Richard had returned to bed beside his wife and never left it until morning.

That this was perjury few doubted. But it sufficed for the acquittal of her husband and her sister.

Back to Bizarre, with its incredible name, the strange trio went to await the tragedies still to come. Young Jack Randolph went with them.

Jefferson wrote his daughter, "It is the moment of trying the affection of [Nancy's] friends when their commiseration and comfort become of value to her wounds. I hope you will deal them out to her in full measure, regardless of what the trifling or malignant may say."

Nothing had been proved, not even that a birth occurred. That it had, only Nancy herself admitted, twenty-two years later. There had been testimony that besides taking abortive drugs she had tried up to the last to conceal her pregnancy by the severest lacing. Presumably it would have been impossible in the ninth month to lace sufficiently to conceal her condition. It seems unlikely that a man dying of consumption was the father, and there is slight if any evidence that Nancy cared deeply for Theodorick Randolph.

Everything points to Richard Randolph as the father and her having conceived some time after Theodorick's death.

On May 12, after the acquittal, Judith wrote Mary Harrison:

. . . for better than a week before I met you at Cumberland Court House, my mind had been in the most perfect state of misery, which humanity is capable of enduring. I scarce know whether I should have suffered so much had I doubted my husband's innocence, for then, I confess my esteem for him would have been so diminished that I should not have felt what I did on his account, but perfectly conscious of that, as I have ever been, & still dreading the diabolical machinations of his & Nancy's unprovoked (but not less rancorous) enemies, words are inadequate to express what my weak mind endured. . . . My health is very bad, indeed so much have I suffered lately, both in body and mind that I much fear that a few *months* will put an end to my troubles in this world; neglected & thrown off by all whom I once fondly relied on. . . . Should I be so unfortunate as to leave another helpless babe . . . you alone, except my husband, I can call upon to befriend my dear little innocents.

It is a heartless business to dissect the writing of a lady so burdened and distraught. It is noteworthy, however, that Mary Harrison was also Nancy's cousin, and that, whatever Judith's sorrows, surely her little sister's were greater, and for them there is no feeling nor pity—nor thought of her as guardian of Judith's children. Her belief in her husband's innocence has the sound of self-persuasion, and surely the thought of returning to Bizarre, previously expressed, would not be so hateful if she thought the dead Theodorick had been her sister's seducer.

In 1815, Nancy wrote William Giles a cryptic letter, some of it in the first, some in the third person. There is a reference in it to charges against her of forging letters, but elsewhere in it she says, ". . . I found a torn piece of a printed letter, from my sister, to Judge Tucker in April 93. What remains is sufficient to prove the falsehood of Mr. R's [John Randolph] aspersions. . . ."

The "aspersions" included the accusation of murdering Richard Randolph. Is it not likely that "the torn piece" of Judith's letter made it clear she knew her sister and husband were lovers?

In the circumstances of the time, Nancy at eighteen by her unchastity had now lost all expectation of suitable marriage. *Pamela* and *Clarissa Harlowe,* which she had devoured, made clear, in Pamela's case, the happy reward of virginity. And the death of the ravished Clarissa, poor and persecuted, showed the price of unchastity, however unwillingly committed.

Presumably a girl who at seventeen yields her virginity to a lover is not undersexed. In Nancy's case the consequences were so horrible that her interest in sex may have been temporarily assuaged. But gradually and normally the anesthesia must have passed, possibly quickened by the attentions of men who would now regard her as a natural and willing subject of further amours, though not of marriage. There is a note of all this in the torn scrap of a letter to Mrs. Dudley at the time: ". . . left me amid the gloom allied to solitude. . . . I shall very shortly become a paragon of res[pectability?]."

It is startling to see how the life she was to lead at Bizarre is described in a textbook of sociology. Calhoun's *A Social History of the American Family* says:

The typical family included several adult, unmarried women, unpaid servants of their kindred [Nancy's own words later]. In many cases they labored bitterly in dishonor . . . "old maids" in the sense that made the term one of intense reproach [and] their presence gave grounds for the enforcement of the Mosaic prohibition of marriage within forbidden degrees. . . . It was not unreasonable that persons related even by marriage should have been prohibited from marrying each other.

A large measure of her shame arose from the fact that intercourse with her sister's husband was then incestuous and marriage to him, should her sister die, forbidden.

In this dreadful prison propinquity the three lived, two of them in debt for their lives to one whom they had injured and who stood between them. A social revolution would have been necessary to change it. Probably only a handful of single women in the whole world were then able to earn an honorable living on their own. "How forever fresh-springing are [a female's] *difficulties* when she would owe her existence to her own exertions," a music teacher says in one of Fanny Burney's novels.

Even abundant money, so scarce at Bizarre, would not have solved it all. There was almost no life possible for an unmarried woman alone, unless as a prostitute.

As Nancy faced all this one can imagine that her only comfort was that her child had been mercifully born dead. What provincial morality did to her was small beside what it would have done to the child. It gives one pause to consider the full and brilliant life awaiting the son of Adèle de Flahaut in a more careless, less censorious world.

CHAPTER TWENTY-THREE

An Order to Quit
the Kingdom

(1794)

VERY EARLY in January, Narbonne wrote Fanny Burney's sister:

Tuesday at 5 o'clock a messenger of state came to Talleyrand's house [in London] carrying an order to him to quit the Kingdom before five days. . . . All roads of the earth are impracticable for him but with that nothing equals his calm, his courage and almost his gayety.

The qualities of calmness, courage and gaiety, so common to both Morris and Talleyrand, may only have proceeded from something superficial in their brilliant but robust natures. But in what pleasing contrast they always are to the morose lamentations of the Lafayettes and the Paines and the sepulchral forebodings of the Monroes. Proscribed by France, while believed by England, doubtless with justice, to be a French secret agent, speaking no English, Talleyrand's choice of asylum was more or less limited to Denmark and America.

He chose America, and, like Morris going first to France, went with good introductions. Angelica Church wrote her sister, "I recommend to your most particular care, my dear and kind Eliza, my friends, Messieurs de Talleyrand and de Beaumetz. Make our country agreeable to them. I have for these persons the most sincere friendship, these interesting stran-

gers . . ." and while Talleyrand is slightly delayed in getting
away she finishes a kerchief for Eliza to wear "on your head
or neck" and in sisterly acerbity asks whether she *ever* received
"the hat with purple ribband" sent home by Franklin's daughter, Mrs. Bache.

To Washington, Wycombe's father, the marquis, wrote:

Talleyrand does me a great deal of honor in supposing a letter from
me may be of use to him with you. [During] three years in England
he has conducted himself to my intimate knowledge with the strictest public and private propriety. [He has] no asylum except that
country which is happy enough to preserve its peace and its happi
ness under your auspices. . . . I have the honour to be with the
highest respect and veneration . . .

The year was one of change and movement for all with whom
we are most concerned. Jefferson had resigned from the Cabinet and been succeeded by Edmund Randolph.

Robespierre was in great power, with Danton's strength waning and soon to end forever and, though Morris was still amazed
that "four years after the Convention 24,000,000 people have
brought forward no one either in civil or military life" fit to be
a leader, he wrote Washington that "Robespierre has been the
most consistent. 'He loves no play as thou dost, Antony.' There
is no imputation of corruption. He is far from rich."

He contrasts, as always, America with France in revolution.
With us "everyone cheerfully played his part; nor had we anything to apprehend but from the common enemy . . ." and
then with that insight into the future which his French friends
so often remarked he wrote, "They dread the moon of April
which is called la Lune Rousse, the red-haired moon." April
came and Robespierre sent Danton to the guillotine. He had
written the year before, "I love you more than ever and shall
love you till I die." Desmoulins, at whose wedding Robespierre
had been an attendant, died with Danton.

In February, Morris had realized that all the changes made
one for him desirable and he had written Washington, after
hoping "the Devil will [not] put it in your head one day to quit
. . . à propos whenever you think the United States can gain
anything by giving me a successor let it be done." He expressed

to Robert Morris the same willingness to leave, pointing out, however, that it should not be done as a concession to one faction in France. "[When] the government here [is] fixed on any permanent basis it would be proper to have here a man agreeable to the rulers."

Short had not yet heard, when he wrote Morris February 21 from Spain, that he had talked to Rosalie in Paris at the end of December.

I wrote to you on the 4th and 10th of December asking the favor of you to have my books & trunks of papers & clothes transported from my former lodgings to your house. I desire much to hear from you whether you have been so good as to have this done. It has been so long since I have had the satisfaction of hearing from you that I almost despair of it although it would be really an act of charity in you. If you did not write by so favorable a conveyance as that of Mr. Strobel, I suppose it cannot be the want of opportunities which prevents my hearing from you. If you were to address your letter to Mr. Pinckney or Messrs Aine Reguy père et fils at Genoa I should certainly get them one way or another.

I am exceedingly uneasy at not hearing from the family of my friends. The last letter was of the 17th of Sept. My uneasiness is increased by a report which has come here as far as I can learn from London. Although I cannot get at the source, or find any good authority for it, yet my anxiety is extreme. The report is that they are in arrestation, God knows why. As to their innocence in every respect I will pledge my life, though it is said that all of that class are in the same condition & that they are to be held as hostages until the peace. Mr. Strobel could give me no account of that family having never heard their names. I beg you my dear sir to let me hear something from you respecting them. If it sh'd be true that they are in this situation do let me know it, as it will then be out of our power. Whether it be so or not if you can be of any use to them I beg and intreat you to do it. My gratitude will be eternal.

To those who revere Tom Paine, it must be conceded that Morris did not seem to take his imprisonment too seriously. "Lest I should forget it, I must mention that Thomas Paine is in prison where he amuses himself with publishing a pamphlet against Jesus Christ," he wrote Jefferson. He discussed with Deforgues in February Paine's claim to liberty as an American citizen and said he considered Paine as out of his jurisdiction since he had adopted French citizenship. However, "reasons for his imprisonment should be communicated to the government of the United States."

Deforgues replied, "You reclaim the liberty of Thomas Paine as an American citizen . . . in occupying a place in the Legislative Corps [of France] he submitted himself to the laws of the Republic and renounced the protection [of the United States]. I am ignorant of the motives of his detention but I must presume they are well founded."

It would be contrary to Morris's whole generous nature to suppose he rejoiced in Paine's misfortune and absurd to suppose he wanted him executed. He may well have been given to understand that the less said the better and that nothing very serious would happen. He wrote Jefferson, not knowing Randolph had succeeded, "I might make things worse [by further intervention]. In the best of times he [Paine] had a larger share of every other sense than common sense and ardent spirits impaired the small stock he originally possessed."

To a "sensible man" such as Morris people like Paine and Lafayette, both devoid of common sense, choosing courses of conduct the end of which anyone could foresee, and then being not only unwilling to accept their consequences but wishing to reassume the loyalties they had abandoned, while at the same time being martyrs, must have been very trying to put it mildly. Nor was he alone in demurring at the hero image of Lafayette. Fanny Burney, on hearing that friends of Lafayette were saying her husband, D'Arblay, had been "second to Lafayette in America," wrote furiously even to her beloved father:

[Firstly D'Arblay] never was in America, secondly he never had any connexion with M. de Lafayette but as his equal except with respect alone to military precedence. Thirdly, having been an officer in the Royal Army from 12 years of age he had never served any man whatever but his King.

But in July when Madame de Lafayette was arrested there were no reservations in Morris's reaction except those her safety dictated. He told the Foreign Office, "The family of Lafayette is beloved in America . . . without examining his conduct in

this country my fellow citizens confine themselves to grateful
remembrance of the services he rendered . . . the death of his
wife might lessen the attitude of some to the French Republic.
. . . I cannot but think her existence of very little consequence
to this government and I am sure its enemies will rejoice at
their destruction of anything which bears the name of Lafayette."

It did not suffice to free her. Morris did not expect it would.
"I conceive," he wrote Washington, "by gaining time the present rage for executions must at length terminate."

So they did and Morris's successor had the pleasure of seeing
Paine and Adrienne de Lafayette at liberty.

In accepting the demand for Genêt's recall, it was ordinary
procedure for France, in due course, to ask for Morris's. In
America, as early as March 3, a now familiar conflict between
Congress and the President over the management of foreign
relations had begun.

Monroe, then senator from Virginia, wrote Jefferson March
3:

About 3 weeks past the Senate requested the President to lay before
it correspondence of Gouverneur Morris with our executive and
France. Two days past he laid before us voluminous correspondence, stating that he had omitted such parts as in his judgment
ought not to be communicated. The opinion of many is that his
discretion should extend to time only, but this asserts control over
the whole subject.

Back of the demand lay the strange desire of the anti-Federalists to go to war against England, and it became known that
the Administration proposed sending a special mission to England to try again for a settlement of the old issues, the Northwest Posts, payment for confiscated slaves, impressment and
the right to trade in the West Indies in American cottons.

It was clear to Washington that if Jefferson would go as spe-
cial envoy factional differences could be composed. Even
Monroe would not be likely to vote against Jefferson's work.
But Jefferson refused and Senator Robert Morris proposed
Hamilton. Monroe violently protested and said that John Jay,

the Chief Justice, would be no more acceptable, that he favored no envoy at all and certainly not a Federalist.

Meanwhile Senator Rufus King had secured Jay's acceptance. He was confirmed 18–8 on April 16, Monroe and Burr being among the noes.

On the twenty-ninth Washington wrote Jay, *Secret and Confidential*, "You are already informed that I am under the necessity of recalling Mr. Gouverneur Morris from France and you can readily conceive the difficulty which occurs in finding a successor." He asks Jay if he would agree, if it was so desired, to let Pinckney go over to Paris before Jay's arrival. "Let the transaction be confined entirely to ourselves," he concludes. At the same time he alternately asked R. R. Livingston if he would take the French post and in any event to reply at once.

Monroe was glad to let Jefferson know at Monticello that "arrangements are being made" to recall Gouverneur Morris.

Livingston, able but indolent (as Vardill told Lord Carlisle in '78), appeared reluctant owing to the necessity of an immediate departure, and on May 14, Washington abruptly asked him how long he needed to make up his mind. Morris long ago had said his friend was "too lazy."

The answer was unsatisfactory and on the twenty-sixth Monroe wrote Jefferson that both Madison and Livingston had declined and that Senator Burr was being considered "to lay the Republican party under obligation." Washington, in doubt of his integrity, ended that.

Later that night Monroe wrote Madison that the post had been offered to him. Should he accept? "An answer must be given the President immediately." His nomination was sent to the Senate the next day and confirmed the following.

During the jockeying and amidst the wrangling as to who was worse, France or England, Morris suggested a solution of the whole problem. He wrote Washington that he understood and shared the country's objections to a large standing army. There could be none to a navy. *"With twelve, perhaps 20 ships of the line no nation on earth will dare insult us."*

Randolph's instructions to Monroe of June 10 are interesting. They begin, "Nothing which has been forwarded to us relative to Mr. Morris requires any disavowal." They confirm that Jay's mission "is forbidden to weaken engagements between this country and France." They remind him that "Fauchet has said and you will hear that" there are two irreconcilable parties here, one republican and in favor of the French Revolution, the second monarchial, aristocratic, British, and anti-Gallican. You will deny this.

Fauchet wrote to his *"Citoyen Ministre des les Commissaires du Conseil Exécutif"* that Mr. Monroe passes *"pour un homme probe,"* but warns them that "that which could enfeeble the good will, not of the people but the government [toward France is] the influence of Beaumets and Talleyrand."

Angelica Church told Elizabeth Hamilton that those two wrote "in raptures to all their friends of your kindness and Colonel Hamilton's affability and manners." Jefferson noted disapprovingly in *The Anas* that "Hamilton and Talleyrand dined together and Alexander Hamilton drank freely." Burr gave a dinner "with orchestras and graces" and Talleyrand and Joseph Brant were among the guests.

Washington, however, wrote Lord Lansdowne:

It is a matter of no small regret to me that considerations of a public nature which you will easily conjecture have not hitherto permitted me to manifest toward [Talleyrand] the sense I entertain of his personal character and of your recommendation, but I am informed that the reception he has met in general has been such as to console him.

In April, Morris received a letter from William Constable, then in London, saying he was well, "as are your friends in Surrey Street." It seems likely that this was word of Adèle. Constable had been at the legation August 14, 1792, when Adèle was there, a refugee. This appears to be the only news Morris had had, though that, as we shall see, is a question. However, he did know that she was at least safe "from the rage for executions."

On the heels of it came a letter from the luckless Short. Morris's last letter had come

with a very cruel diminution, that which you enclosed for me having been taken out on the way. You will with difficulty form an idea of the pain which that circumstance gave me. I remain absolutely ignorant of all . . . since [her] letter of December 30 inclosed in yours of January 1. . . . I write a letter which I enclose herewith and put under your kind protection. You will judge from the circumstances at the time of receiving it whether and how to send it. My hand and heart almost fail me when I take up my pen to write. . . .

We know something of what Short and his faraway princess wrote each other. He told her that he would be content to be secretary to the minister in Paris, rather than minister himself anywhere else, to be near her. "I will resign to be with you. I am confident, as I have always been, that our vows have not been made in vain."

She tells him she has only two letters of his and had "burned the others when it seemed wise." How familiar to booklovers in love is it, when she says she has his copies and is reading Pope's works and Lyttleton's *History of England*.

"I also have a lock of your hair which I clipped off myself when I gave you mine shortly before you left for Holland [1792]. For more than two years I have been constantly wearing a little gold ring in the form of links, on one of which you had our two initials engraved."

There was nothing of reality to prevent their marriage. Short, though a diplomat, was independently wealthy and Robespierre's Terror would have softened even toward a duchess if she asked a passport to go to marry an American minister. Some intangible sense of guilt about her murdered husband's memory, some mistaken sense of duty to his mother, her grandmother, made it impossible for her to agree—the inability, almost morbid, to accept that "whatever is, is" so marked in Adèle, Nancy, Talleyrand and Morris.

Monroe reached Paris August 3, "having heard at Havre of the crimes and execution of Robespierre, St. Just, Cauthon and others of that party."

Someone has estimated that in Paris alone personal bereavement made ten thousand people desire Robespierre's death. Between April 17 and June 10, 3607 persons had gone to the guillotine and 8000 more were in Paris prisons with death hanging over them. All this and other vaster causes brought him to his end.

To a degree, however, the immediate impulse came from a "sprightly, naive, very beautiful woman" Morris had met, dining at Malmaison a rainy cold Sunday in July, five years before.

She was Therezia Cabarrús, whom Tallien had met and fallen in love with. Now in this July she was in the Carmelite Prison, with Josephine de Beauharnais and heard "*c'est demain qu'on me tue* [it is tomorrow that they are going to kill me]." She sent that word to Tallien and the next day he attacked the omnipotent Robespierre in the Convention, and then Carnot added that Robespierre was a ridiculous tyrant and the Terror was suddenly all over.

The "sprightly, naive, very beautiful woman" was to become one of the *merveilleuses* of the Directory in her gauze tunics slit to the hips, or her leopard skin worn with her breasts bare at the opera, a vision Morris was unfortunately to miss and Monroe, though "introduced to [the] bosom of the Convention," was unlikely to have appreciated.

On August 10, Morris took Monroe to present his credentials. Paine appealed to Monroe to secure his freedom, saying that Morris "wished to prevent my return to America that I should not expose his misconduct." He came out finally in November.

"As to my conduct," Morris wrote with his usual sunny felicity, "I will neither praise nor excuse it but confine myself to the sincere wish that my successor will act with more wisdom in a situation less critical."

The success or failure of his mission and the diplomatic propriety of his conduct are not to be settled by "proof" or argument. Paine, Lafayette and Genêt and their biographers are satisfied no one could have behaved in worse fashion. The weakness of their case is that it does not make clear what he was supposed to have done that he did not do.

Should he have become at once the avowed enemy of the King who had helped his country's independence? Should he have committed himself and his country to the first Assembly and Constitution? Should he have shifted to cheer for the Revolution of August 10, the massacres of September 2 and the Terror? They say he was a Francophobe and that the French ministers, of the Mountain, would not receive him, with his protests against their seizures of American shipping, and at the same time that he was close enough to these men to conspire with them for the executions of Paine and Genêt.

As to his aristocratic friends, are the records of Robespierre and Marat, Pétion, or Santerre, or Tallien, the butler's son, or Hébert so shining that Morris should have seen the light from the first and become their supporter?

The written advice he gave the King and Queen of France, or to Montmorin for them, in the twenty-five months between July '89 and August 31, '91, is in seven papers running to about 17,000 words.

The following excerpts while in no way a précis of the whole, which considered almost every aspect of government and policy, fairly represent the direction of Morris's thinking, and are essential in judging the criticisms of him.

In general the concepts from which his advice arose were "that the French have not those manners, which are suited to a free constitution [but] this is a reflection by no means dishonorable to that nation. . . . In a republican government those who wish to be great begin by obtaining the good opinion of their equals. For this purpose they must be virtuous, or appear so. . . . In free governments the laws being supreme, and the only supreme, there arises . . . a spirit of order, and a confidence in those laws for the redress of all injuries. . . . Those who [would rescue] their fellow creatures from slavery . . . must begin by instruction and proceed by slow degrees, must content themselves with planting the tree, from which posterity is to gather the fruit."

It was an incalculable folly, in his opinion, for the King to have called the States-General together, after three hundred years, and have no plan to put before them. It was all right for Americans to debate a Declaration and a Constitution. They knew how to proceed after almost a hundred years of town and provincial meetings.

"To talk to a multitude [illiterate] ungoverned and very soon ungovernable [about a Constitution] . . . you might as well talk about . . . the solar system . . . or refraction . . . of rays of light."

By May 1790 he told Montmorin, "In the present state of France, it is impossible to establish a moderate government." In effect the King must regain the means of preserving civil order or it will be over with him. Men are governed by force or by opinion—that is, either by the army or "the mass of good citizens who call themselves the people." There are now none of the second, only "a populace . . . which having nothing to lose, hopes to gain everything [by inspiring] terror . . . [therefore] the step to be taken is simple. It is necessary to have those [with you] who cause fear, not those who feel it. For this purpose you must give to the chiefs of the Jacobins [Danton, Robespierre] the hope of entering into the administration of affairs. You must promise it and you must keep your word . . . you must give these gentlemen places at a favorable moment, giving them all necessary confidence. . . . You must displace them likewise at a favorable moment. . . ."

In August, Morris drew up a Speech from the Throne with an analysis of the defects of the Constitution.

"It is no longer your King who addresses you. Louis the Sixteenth is only a private individual. . . . [I wish first] *to acknowledge the eternal maxim that all government ought to be instituted and exercised for the benefit of the people.* You have determined on a hereditary monarchy [and] a King of France can have no interest distinct from that of the people. . . ."

The advice goes into intricate details but says, "It is of the nature of absolute power to corrupt the heart" and "there is no check on the existence and action of the National Assembly except in its own majority's view, and the judiciary power [should not be] given to the Assembly. . . . The Assembly having reserved to itself the sole right of accusing judges for misconduct, timid and corrupt judges will decide in favor of those who have influence with the Assembly. . . .

"[It is unwise that] the legislative body has the right to make laws and decide on the application and execution of them . . . [and have] an existence dependent only on their own will [with] power to protect themselves from the pursuit of justice [and to] the command of such forces as they may think proper."

The idea that a council or committee of the Assembly shall, in effect, directly supervise all departments of the government will substitute vacillation, violate secrecy and utterly destroy not only ministerial accountability, since the committee will in the last resort decide, but all ministerial right to obedience from his subordinates.

The Assembly's reservation of war, peace and treaty-making powers compels the King to "a subordination to their will [but also leaves him] in uncertainty as to what that will may be."

The issuance of paper money by decree of the Assembly which may not lay sufficient taxes to cover, or let them be seasonably collected, will result in "that last stab to public credit [which] will perhaps prove fatal."

"Let then these important truths be duly considered. Where there is no authority [in the executive] there can be no accountability; where the executive power is feeble, anarchy must ensue, and where anarchy long prevails, despotism must succeed; *not indeed in the descendants* of your ancient kings, for they will probably be the earliest victims."

The speech faces boldly the sovereign's past errors. In Bolingbroke's ringing phrase, it says, "A patriot King cannot wish to be surrounded by needy dependents who first deceive and then betray him. . . . The excess of royal authority has . . . been also injurious, but the levity, the injustice and disorder of a government merely popular, must be equally subversive of public and private happiness. It is by a just combination of the three, each having an absolute veto on the others, that the general interest of the whole society will be best known and pursued and this great nation raised to that station of happiness and glory which nature seems to have intended. . . .

"[Say to your people] you require of me, and of every public functionary, an oath never to make any change in your Constitution. I will take this oath but I pray you to consider with me

for a moment the consequences it involves. My observation is
perhaps superficial and my fears vain. . . . But no one of us is
infallible . . . the seeds of evil may be concealed in the Constitution. . . . [If so] there will be no means of changing it
[unless by the sad alternatives of violating oath or duty]. . . .
Let us together make trial of your work; do not bind yourselves
not to change your decrees; for no one is too wise to improve
himself in the school of experience. If after this trial, the Constitution answers your expectations, you will place it with the
more confidence in the hands of your successors. If, on the contrary, you find parts of it to be feeble, or ill-adjusted, you will
have it in your power to amend them. . . .

"Whatever may be the result of your deliberations, I repeat
to you, gentlemen, that I submit to them unreservedly. Let us
then banish all suspicion. I give you my confidence and I demand yours. Let us labor in concert for the liberty and prosperity of the French nation. . . .

"I would have it permitted me to nominate as ministers of
the Constitution, those among you who have shown themselves
to be its most zealous partizans."

So much political wisdom had perhaps never been spoken
from a throne, but the King of France lacked the will and wisdom to speak it. And Morris warned Montmorin that with the
Assembly dissolved nobody would then be accountable but the
King. Against that he must be forehanded so that "when any
misfortune arises the people may say *'this is what our King has
warned us of, not in vague and indefinite terms,* but clearly and
pointedly.'"

Lodgings for Those Whom I Expect

(November 1794–April 1795)

THE ACTUAL INTENTIONS of Morris on leaving France, after Monroe had taken over, are so obscure that they led a biographer of Paine to assert that Morris was in fear of execution. Even the slight material then available made such a conclusion absurd, although all that is now available does not settle what was going on in that perfectly organized head.

John Jay was in London, the signing of his treaty two months away. On September 11 he wrote Hamilton, "You will receive this letter by the hands of Mr. Morris. He will also be the bearer of my despatches to Mr. Randolph [Secretary of State]."

In Paris, at the time, Monroe wrote the Citizen Commissary of Foreign Affairs, "My predecessor, Mr. Morris, finding it impossible to procure a vessel for some weeks wishes to go to Switzerland. Should it be agreeable to the Committee of Public Safety, will they . . ."

There was some delay, as Monroe explained to Washington later "lest this reaches you by any other channel." Morris had said that as he would have an idle interim he wished to go to see where "John James Rousseau lived." Monroe Americanized all French names: Maurice Talleyrand was Morris in Monroe's letters.

This apparently innocent wish rather shook them all. Monroe

reported that "the French Government said [Morris] might choose his route to leave France but they did not like to permit him to go into Switzerland where the emigrants [his connections] were and return back into the Republic. They were surprised he made such a request." Whereupon Morris abandoned the idea of returning to France and "without any difficulty" a passport was secured, though he wisely insisted on one from the Committee of Public Safety as well as Monroe's, visaed by the Commissary of Foreign Affairs. Still Monroe thought this "quite fair and said so."

Although the *Diary* is resumed in much of its frankness in October, it says nothing of this decision. There was no place to lock it away on his travels and security considerations had to be kept in mind.

He wrote Constable that his steward, Bromeline, was leaving with his books, and wines and furniture, "which I presume will be admitted free of duty."

On October 12 he left Paris for his house at Sainport, twenty miles away, writing in his *Diary* that if France would give up war for corn, oil, wine, silk, flax, hemp and iron she would have first place in wealth. "But she will be exhausted"!

The next day, while he was dining, Madame Simon, not previously mentioned, came to Sainport to say good-by. She had evidently been his mistress. "This ride [which she took] through bad weather is something and yet she will be *sage* which is very foolish." She spent the rainy night and they parted in the morning with "strong emotion which affects me much."

He passed the Swiss frontier at Morey on the nineteenth, with four hundred louis d'or in his pocket to the douanier's amazement, and the next day saw Lake Geneva and the Pays de Vaud. On the twenty-third he was at Coppet, dining with Minette de Staël, Narbonne and other émigrés in attendance, "constitutional mongrels" as the Swiss papers called them. Only shortly before Minette had met Benjamin Constant on the road between Coppet and Lyons, and her lover Narbonne would soon have to shift for himself, while she began her affair with Constant.

The *Diary* entries are largely impersonal except that Madame de Staël, who with her wealth maintained an escape organization and underground communication from France, told him that Madame Simon had gotten her passport and intended to set off soon. It was not particularly welcome news.

We know that Adèle de Flahaut had left London for the Continent in May, and that when Morris reached Coppet she was at Bremgarten, near Zurich.

It is impossible to say whether Morris knew this, though Madame de Staël must have known it and even Angelica Church in London knew, as she wrote her sister, "When you see Mr. Talleyrand tell him Madame Adèle is still in Switzerland and there likely to continue from the difficulty of travelling." It is possible and in keeping with her character that Minette de Staël knew but did not tell Morris. His *Diary* does not mention Adèle's name until six months later.

But it seems unlikely that so acute a man did not know. Certainly he must have been almost unbearably anxious to see Adèle. Perhaps he did and the itinerary, to the contrary, in the *Diaries* could be false. But this is unlikely.

He went, according to the *Diary*, from Coppet to Berne, and Berne to Basel, away from Bremgarten. At Basel he turned east through Rheinfelden, going toward Schaffhausen. At Waldshut on that road he was within a dozen miles of Adèle, and it had been twenty-five months since he had seen her. The *Diary* says he went on north to Stuttgart.

There seem to be two possible explanations. One, that for security reasons he did not turn off because the Chevalier d'Orléans was in hiding with Adèle, and Morris did not want to risk drawing the attention of the French police agents to them. Unquestionably known by the police to have been her lover, his failure to stop in Bremgarten might well lead them to reason that she was not there. This seems a valid explanation. But there is another which cannot be disregarded.

Sinner that she was, there was in Adèle a religious mysticism, not very profound, it is true, left over from her convent girlhood. There was a convent in Bremgarten, now an orphan home, and it is possible that after all the hurly-burly she was there, repairing her soul. It may be that she was not ready to see Morris again and forbade him to come.

There is no hint of a reason for these travels in the *Diary,* scarcely any names except those above. Still he was in good humor as they slid down the roads "in a glare of ice," while he admired the farmers' sheep and hogs. He became "very good friends with my postilion after I threatened to shoot him for being surly."

On the fifteenth of November as he was looking at the falls of the Rhine he first became aware of the malady of which he was to die, a week less than twenty-two years later.

Traveling magnificently in his own carriage, with his baggage wagon, his valets and outriders through Hanover and Lüneburg, he arrived "at the City of Petersburg Hotel at Hamburg at 10:45 in the morning" of December 10, dining that afternoon with John Parish, who was American consul and head of the merchant bankers, Parish and Company.

Parish, just ten years older than Morris, is always referred to as his "old friend." Actually the friendship probably began that day. The banking house, founded by John Parish's father, a Scot, in 1756, was part of the loose consortium, Hope and Company, of Amsterdam, the Barings of London, Le Couteulx of Paris and Constable of New York, and it was already a worried creditor of Robert Morris.

Vincent Nolte, whose memoirs became the story of *Anthony Adverse,* described John Parish "in a velvet cap trimmed with fur, cocked over one eye, wearing a velvet coat in the Polish style, a long Turkish pipe in his left hand and a silk leash holding two poodles in the right."

Because Morris came to Hamburg, John Parish's son David, then sixteen, and grandson George were to leave their names in the wild lands of New York, and the latter was to engage in a game of cards and a long amorous adventure there, the equal in recklessness of any of Morris's. It is extraordinary to think these two German-born Scots should be among the principal characters in two American historical novels because Morris changed his mind in October 1794.

Hamburg was the great neutral entry port for northern and central Europe. The London newspapers were delivered regularly from the packets bringing British diplomats and travelers to Europe outside of France. When Morris was ready he could board ship in Hamburg direct for New York.

The change in climate, the fatigue of the journey and the reaction from the long strain laid him up with influenza for the rest of the month, but though his cold was "still troublesome" on the twenty-ninth, he rode out to nearby Altona.

The next day he replied to the letter from Washington which had told him, "I assure you that my confidence in and friendship and regard for you remain undiminished, Always and very sincerely yours," saying, "I saw misery and affliction [in Paris] every day and all around me without power to mitigate or means to relieve, and I felt myself degraded by communications I was forced into with the worst of mankind in order to obtain redress for the injuries of my fellow citizens. Redress will come more from Jay's Treaty [with England] than Monroe's mission." He says he is delayed in going to London to which he would "have gone direct but the French would have harbored jealousies which I wished not to excite and so came by way of Switzerland and am weather bound."

Then he reverts to France and says, "In judging the French we must not recur to the feelings of Americans during the last war. We were in the actual enjoyment of freedom and fought not to obtain it but to secure its blessings."

We know of course of men whose right hands do not know what their left are doing. In Morris's case the hand that wrote the *Diary* was often kept in ignorance of the letters it wrote.

The January '95 *Diary* has little news. It notes that Madame Simon, who had arrived in Hamburg, had a Lesbian attachment for "Mademoiselle Renault, mistress of Walkier," and wonders on the eighteenth if "Martin arrived this day in Morrisania." John Quincy Adams, in his *Diary* for the twenty-fourth, learning that he might meet Morris in London, carefully recorded, "Morris shall not enjoy the smallest part of my confidence."

Then on the twenty-seventh from Bremgarten, Switzerland, Adèle de Flahaut wrote him her long letter in French beginning "Sir, I have seen in Switzerland the young Duke of Orléans [then 22]. . . ." She tells of his wanderings on foot among the mountains curiously like those of another Young Pretender, once husband of their friend Madame d'Albani. "He is melancholy, but gentle and unassuming and his whole ambition is to go to your America. But he has nothing in the world. . . ." She begs Morris to "render him the double service" of telling his mother of his veneration and asking where are his brothers "and any little details respecting them all."

The February *Diary* says nothing of the letter, but on the twenty-fourth he went after dinner to his new lodgings in nearby Altona. That day Adèle wrote him again, "A thousand thanks for your affectionate and consoling letter of the 6th. I shall depart as soon as possible. . . . *My cousin* [her cipher for the *young duke*] will go with me."

Morris's letter to her was not copied in his *Letter Books* and hers came to him without signature for security reasons. She warns him of the importance of the duke's incognito. "Hamburg is full of people to whom he is known. . . . As for me the smallest lodge far away from the town, will be most agreeable. . . . But above all things shun Altona." She says that the banker, Walkier, Mademoiselle Renault's lover, cannot possibly be kept in ignorance of the duke's moves, since he has made him small advances against his inheritance. She says that "it will be fifteen days before I shall be able to commence the journey. In that time I must send your bill of exchange to be negotiated at Basel [where he had stopped] for such a thing cannot be done in this small village. . . . Adieu, my excellent friend: I cannot find words to express how sensible I am of your goodness." With it was enclosed a boyish note of thanks from the young duke.

Morris wrote the dowager duchess the good news. The open heart and purse are characteristic of this generous man. Equally so his annoyance with himself for petty losses that night at cards, "because my mind was elsewhere."

There is no way of knowing exactly what these two people

still felt about each other, after all the hurricanes they had survived. Morris was forty-three, Adèle almost thirty-four. Someone has well said that people like them, after such passions, think of each other every day of their lives.

To Adèle now, as so frequently in the past, Morris must have symbolized strength and security. It was wholly natural, since money made little difference to him, for her to be able to ask him anything after what had been between them. She had survived through the wasting hazards and chances of the refugee by incredible pluck and ingenuity, not by her wits but by her novels and her millinery. There is little mercenary in such a person's seeking help, least of all from a man like Morris. And, aside from any love, such people must have been almost consumed with curiosity to see each other again.

Early in March, Adèle with "her cousin" started north along roads jammed with fellow refugees, passing signs of such poignant familiarity:

On ne laisse séjourner ici ni juifs, ni vagabonds, ni gens sans aveu, ni émigrés.

She spoke of those placards and those words in a letter to Monsieur Le Roi in 1823, remembering that bitter journey *"ni la Terre Sainte, ni la Terre Promise."*

On Thursday, March 19, "a fine morning," the *Diary* says, "we go to Newenstadt [Neustadt] to take lodgings for those whom I expect. The river presents a most wintry spectacle." There was no previous diary reference to those whom he expected, but on April Fool's Day the entry reads, "Made. de Flahaut arrives this morning. In the afternoon I place her companion, *Mr. Muller,* in the apartments I had taken for them."

The next day "the weather is fine and I conduct Mad^e. de Flahaut to her lodgings. It is cold." The next, "this afternoon I go to see Mde de Flahaut in her lodgings which are not convenient from the difficulties of subsistence." The next, "the weather is cold and disagreeable with a northeast wind so this afternoon to see Madame de Flahaut." There is room for much more on the rest of the blank page but perhaps masculine pride was too strong to let him write it. But from what follows it seems evident that what she said to him with the northeast wind blowing outside was something like this.

"There are many reasons why I cannot let you make love to me. I have a great *tendresse* for you, but the desire I felt for you at the Louvre is burned out by all that has happened. Life has been very hard. I know it has not been easy for you, but I am ill and weary. There was a sort of equality between us in Paris. Now I am a refugee and you are still a rich and powerful man. While I do not hesitate to accept the money you have given me to come here, or these lodgings from you, you must understand that I have my own integrity to think about and my own life. In other words, I will not stay here as a kept woman. My novel has come out. I am working on another, and I am a Parisienne. I can support myself by making hats for these gross German women. The good God knows they could do with some chic. So, dear friend, perhaps you understand. If so, you will let me say I simply cannot stay in this house because they will not let me cook for myself and you can't ask me to every meal. Do you understand that also?"

Morris doubtless replied, "Well, I don't know that I understand" (though of course he did). "I do agree that these lodgings are impossible. Still you insisted on shunning Altona."

At which there may have come a spark from past caprices and Adèle, with a flounce, said, "Well, I may have said that but you should have known better. You're always so sure you're right about everything. Why didn't you insist that I go to Altona instead of this loathsome Newenstadt, ugh?"

"Very well, will you come and stay at my house for a few days, while I find a decent place for you?"

"Someplace where I can cook, make bonnets and write?"

"Yes."

"But at your house, *tout à fait sage?*"

"Yes, under the circumstances."

"Yes, I will come. Would you like to kiss my cheek?"[1]

On April 6 he brought her to his own house at Altona. "Mad-

---

[1] It was long after I had written this that I came on the passage in *The Princess of Cleves* reading "*mais l'amour ce transport des sens, cette ivresse involontaire, cet oubli des tous les intérêts, de tous les devoirs je ne l'ai plus.*"

ame de Flahaut comes to dine and stay a few days. After dinner she is taken with a bleeding from the breast. A vessel formerly broken opens again."

The thought of cancer must have flashed through both their intelligent minds. Often in the past Morris had treated her with cold mental cruelty, and usually with more passion than tenderness. At the Louvre she had used all the wiles and caprices of a coquette on him. But in this crisis he behaved, in addition to material help, with all the charm of a boyish lover.

"On the south side of a steep hill going from the high plain down to the river" he found the spring's first violets and took them to her with his own light French verses:

> "Eh, bon jour, belle faiseuse, de romans et de bonnets
> Parfois vive et paresseuse, bonne et douce et sans apprêt.
> Quand vous ouvriez boutique, soit de modes ou d'esprit,
> Vous aurez grande pratique, L'amour même me l'a dit. . . .
> Au milieu des vos travaux, littéraires ou bonnetaires
> Je vous fais de lourds propos, qui ne sont que dinataires.
>
> Quittez gazes et romans, Bel esprit devenu sage;
> Menez-moi vous deux chalands, Manger mon petit potage.

He got her a house in Altona. He visited and walked with her. She told him the duke could get a loan if Morris would be his surety. "I think it over and tell her I will become surety." They both caught bad colds and were cross with each other.

Madame Simon, *sage* at their farewell in France, was ready to resume her liaison with him. Adèle, *sage*, was more desirable than Simon and the poor woman went back to Paris.

Morris never made any pretense about his ready surrender to any acceptable offer of passion. In the Paris years he was apparently completely faithful to Adèle, but from preference, not conscience. Evidently, as the *Diary* indicates, if Madame Simon had been able to find "a convenient means of cuckolding her husband here," Morris would have been nothing loath, but he could not be bothered with arrangements while his "mind was elsewhere." They "consulted together how best to procure five minutes of unobserved and uninterrupted conversation. I left it to her genius and it seems she found the thing impracticable."

On May 15, Adèle came to three o'clock dinner with him on a rainy afternoon with a hard wind from the south. She stayed late and they talked of "the rumor that the young King of France and his sister are escaped from the Temple."

The scene of the later novel *Eugénie et Mathilde* is set largely in these rain-drenched, ugly places, and the heroine, an émigrée, works and suffers as she did, on the monotonous banks of the Elbe, with the damp winds from the west, *"tout s'accordait avec les dispositions tristes de son âme d'exilée,"* and in the North Sea *"le roche d'Heligoland isolé au milieu de la mer."*

A week later he apparently could stand the platonic arrangement no longer and went on a cruise by himself in the Baltic from Lübeck, but coming back June 1 at five-thirty, he "went at once to see Madame de Flahaut."

Orléans and she dined with him the next day and the day following she came at one-thirty, "strongly affected by her situation in life." After dinner she had a second hemorrhage from the breast.

When he had taken her home he wrote his London bankers to advance Orléans "a thousand or fifteen hundred pounds . . . [and if] he should not be able, as we must all wish he may, to repay you, I hereby pledge myself to that effect."

Very suddenly forty-eight hours later he left for London, dining with Adèle before he sailed. The night was windless and his ship becalmed down the river. He sent back word to Adèle in the morning and she came down to dine with him again on board.

It was the day a Dauphin died in the Temple.

CHAPTER TWENTY-FIVE

By His Account
He Knew Everything

(June–December 1795)

ON JUNE 14, Morris was at the Great Hotel at Covent Garden in London.

The guest who first dined with him was a little boy of ten whose father was in America and whose mother Morris had just left. The *Diary* of the seventeenth reads "Mr. Smith calls with young Flahaut whom I keep to dinner and get Mr. Livingston to dine with him." The Mr. Smith was not a nobody. It was Bobus Smith—Robert Percy Smith—the older, "more agreeable, more cultivated" brother of the famous Sydney Smith. He was then twenty-five, reading for his M.A. at Kings College, Cambridge. He had been a friend of Wycombe and Lord Holland since Eton, where at twelve he had a fist fight with the future Duke of Wellington.

There is considerable likelihood that he had helped Wycombe in Adèle's original escape from France and contributed to her maintenance in Half Moon Street. Since '94 he had been looking out for her boy and it is wonderful to think that young displaced person had already seen Bowood, the great Lansdowne house he was later to know so well and where his daughter would be the marchioness.

Charles, Smith and Livingston came back the next day but one to dine again. One wonders what the precocious little boy

thought at table with the two Americans, hearing word of his
mother, remembering the *goutée*, the afternoon chocolate, the
big man with the wooden leg had taken him and his mother to
when he was "little," and the day of the massacres, three years
before, when she had sent him across the Seine with a servant
for refuge in the big man's house. Did he understand what
they meant when they said England was trying to re-establish
the coalition against France and had offered Russia a million
pounds a year for 50,000 men? Did Livingston ask the big man,
who used to come so constantly to see his mother at the Louvre,
"Is it true you are to be American minister to London?" Did the
little boy think, "Oh, when he was minister in Paris, he hid
Maman and me in his house. If he's minister here, perhaps we
can live with him together again"?

During the following week Morris saw the Marquise de
Bréhan, still with her brother, both exiles. He sent fifty louis
d'or to Madame de Nadaillac in Germany. He found that the
plate which Adèle's sister-in-law, D'Angivilliers, had entrusted
to him, the fatal tenth of August '92, had safely reached London and, melted down, produced 788 louis d'or on deposit at his
banker's.

July 2 he talked for an hour and a half with Lord Grenville,
the Foreign Secretary, on British policy to follow the Jay treaty,
which France was protesting as a violation of Franklin's treaty
with them of 1778. The talk went far and seemed to Morris to
go well, so that he said to Grenville, "I mention a business
which I have no right to meddle in . . ." and he went on to
show the inestimable advantage to Great Britain and America
if the former would cease the taking of our ships by their blockade and allay "the ill blood thereby excited. How useful it
would be to give immediate relief by a verbal communication
to the President saying Great Britain did not oppose our free
use of the Mississippi."

It is impressive to think of the saving of blood and treasure
and "the general oblivion of the past" that might have followed
swift acceptance of this advice.

On his way to dine with Pitt, on the fourteenth, Morris
stopped to tell Woronzow, the Russian ambassador, that if he

wanted to use Poland against Prussia, Kosciusko, who had fought with Washington, should lead the Poles.

Grenville and Lord Chatham were at Pitt's for dinner with him. The wines were good and the "conversation flippant," though a mob was stoning the windows of the house, over the price of bread, and Morris told the Prime Minister he had better send someone to the Count d'Artois, brother of the French pretender, the British favorite, "to help him from doing foolish things." Pitt had him back the next day for a long talk, after which Morris went on tour of southern England, where he saw them "plowing in a whole field of clover in blossom for the purpose of sowing wheat on it."

Lady Sutherland drove back to London with him from her country seat on August 18 and Burgess, "who had the American desk at the Foreign Office," met him to say Morris was to be minister. There seems to be no question but that he wanted the post though he told Burgess "a change of moon would change it."

At the end of August he left London for the north. Stopping at Burleigh House, he saw a painting in the great gallery where Elizabeth had been which deeply moved him. He had no knowledge of and small interest in painting, and his comments on what he had seen in France and Flanders were always trite. But Cardolici's painting "of our Savior blessing the bread and wine . . . occupies all my senses. I never saw such a countenance. Nothing human was ever so beautiful, so heavenly." A week later he was still thinking of "that wonderful combination of majestic sweetness, pity and resignation which I believe I shall never forget."

On his way north "there is a woman in the house with a nervous headache and I give her a mixture of laudanum ether as well from my particular attachment to the sex as out of general humanity."

In mid-September he reached Edinburgh, where the "evening effluvia" from the tall lands was as bad as Dr. Johnson had found them twenty-two years before. He dined well, with many lords, on oysters, turbot and mutton, and they took him to Holyrood to see the closet where Mary Stuart "was sitting with a lady and David Rizzio [when] this poor fellow was dragged out by the haughty, barbarous lords of her court and stabbed," and of course they showed the tourist the bloodstains on the floor.

He went on north, staying at Blair Atholl with the duke and going on to Inveraray, "the stronghold of the MacCailean Mhor," the fifth Duke of Argyll, now seventy-two years old. It was he on whom Boswell hesitated to call with Dr. Johnson, because he feared the duchess, the beautiful Elizabeth Gunning, "wife of two dukes and the mother of four," would find his company disagreeable.

"That, sir," Johnson said, "he must settle with his wife."

When they called, Elizabeth Argyll "took not the slightest notice" of them, but the duke showed them through "the place."

"What I admire here," Johnson said, "is the total defiance of expense."

The duke received Morris most cordially and Lady Charlotte sang for him, as he looked "at the fine view of Loch Awe" in the twilight, and in the morning Argyll, "who has a rage for husbandry," took him out to see "the immense barns which he built to dry the grain in the intolerably wet climate."

We shall never know what he thought of the Duke of Montrose, at whose house he stayed the thirteenth and fourteenth of October, the entry being heavily inked out.

He came on south through Derwentwater, and the country where Wordsworth was writing, through the grim Midlands, making a careful record of labor conditions in the mills.

He was in Birmingham the day the Directory was established in Paris and reached London November 22, "the roads from Coventry jammed with coal wagons."

There John Quincy Adams, twenty-eight, on his way to be American minister at the Hague, came to see him. Morris's *Diary* records it in five words, but we cannot blame young Adams for his longer entry.

"Mr. West proposed to take the same opportunity to visit Mr. Gouverneur Morris at the York Hotel, Covent Gardens . . . this is the first time I ever saw that gentleman who conversed with as much freedom as from his character I expected. . . . Mr. Morris by his account must be a very able negotiator for he gave us to understand that while he was our minister in France he knew everything that was going forward. It was his business to know it [and he did]. This parade of sagacity, these lessons on the theory and practice of negotiations so freely given, so liberally tendered—what do they mean?"

The next day Lord Grenville presented Morris to the King, who asked him among other things when Pinckney was coming back (as minister). Morris told him he did not know and the King ponderously replied, "They're very slow in that country." Morris noted that he could have told His Majesty of another country where they were very slow "on American subjects."

On December 5 at a great City dinner Morris sat between the Foreign Secretary and John Quincy Adams, and we see from his *Diary* the other side of Adams's entry of November 24. Adams, Morris writes, "is deeply tinctured with suspicion and sees design in everything. His mind has received early a wrong bias and I think will always go obliquely."

At dinner the toast to John Jay was heavily applauded and Morris whispered to Adams that news of it would hurt Jay at home, at which "Adams pricks up and his countenance (in general insipid) overflows with joyful expression . . . from this I conjecture his father and Mr. Jay are at political variance."

December '95 went quietly along. The Churches came to see his plans for Morrisania. Madame de Damas wrote her famous tribute to him. Full of Christmas spirit, he told Lord Grenville "it would be a pleasing thing to America if he procured the release of Lafayette" from Austria, England's ally. Grenville said the prejudice in England was too strong against Lafayette.

"Monsieur, I send you my son," the Marquise de Lafayette had written Washington. The namesake had arrived in September and Washington put him in charge of George Cabot in Boston.

"I am distrustful of my own judgment in deciding on this business," the President wrote Hamilton, "lest my feelings should carry me further than prudence (while I am a public character) will warrant."

There is a wonderful piece of humor in the *Diary* of the twentieth. "Walk in park. I never saw so many ugly English people together. They seem to have given each other a rendez-vous."

The walk was taken after a long letter had been written to Washington giving him the political atmosphere of London. It contains one of the many casually wise paragraphs which show how paramount in Morris's mind, under all circumstances, were the interests of his country. He had made suggestions to Lord Grenville of things which might well be done to please America and Grenville had said "something might be made out of it." But Morris knew nothing would be made of it because he was "a charming fellow."

Let me not forget to mention [he says in this letter], though it comes in here rather out of place, that nothing will so strongly affect the government of this country, as the view of an American navy, though in embryo. Wherefore I do most ardently desire, that something may be done this session toward its establishment. And I flatter myself, that, in the present temper of America, any taxes for that object would be cheerfully borne.

He says with wonderful foresight that it has not escaped Washington's penetration that "France is now a military government in the straight road to a single despotism . . . doubtless exhausted [but capable still of] convulsive struggles. But this country is still fresh as a youthful bridegroom."

Washington was writing him almost the same day a letter of great length approving what Morris had said to Grenville and suggesting the course of further talks. The letter was signed "Your affectionate friend."

On December 5, James, brother of John Marshall, had arrived in London with his bride Hetty, Robert Morris's daughter. He brought a letter from his father-in-law to

My dear Gouverneur
I perceive something in the contents of your letters which I dislike . . . you should not listen to the tales of the envious or malicious.

James Marshall had come out with a desperate scheme, this time to sell lands Robert Morris had in Virginia. One must wonder whether he had thought he was marrying a great heiress or knew how close her father's ruin was.

Behind the marble, which L'Enfant, the architect, was ordering for Morris's new house, the plaster walls were crumbling.
The great financier, writing Parish in Hamburg that he had
accepted his drafts "which I can't meet right away," told him,
"I have lately formed a plan for selling fifty to a hundred thousand acres [which will cover everything]. *This is not visionary.
This is certain as fate.*" But like a man going to pieces, he also
thought that "cotton samples" he had given Beaumetz, Talleyrand's companion, would turn out a great profit. He begged
Constable to pay two thousand dollars to Alexander Hamilton
for him. Constable said even he was pushed "but I will see
Hamilton and undertake for $2000, relying on your remitting
it."

The great fortune on paper was blowing away and at times
one feels Gouverneur Morris stayed in Europe because he could
not bear to see a disaster he was powerless to avert.

It has been said on Robert Morris's behalf that when he
made his enormous commitments for lands he could not have
foreseen the financial paralysis of Europe, arising from the
French Revolution and the Napoleonic Wars. The warnings
had gone early and often from Gouverneur, and from Constable, and it seems more likely that nothing but an illimitable
bull market could have saved him.

Morris told Hetty Marshall that he desired her "to consider
[me] as a father," and cautioned her husband against "that
downright assertion" in matters wherein if he was not ignorant
he was "at least not well informed. He has this fault in a most
eminent degree."

Marshall, probably forewarned that Morris would not let
himself be involved, told him that "Hammersley's House will
take him by the hand which I am heartily glad of."

On the last day of the year, De Moustier, now forty-four,
leaving the marquise, gallantly crossed to the royalist underground in Normandy, though, as Morris wrote Washington,
"the bringing back to the Vendée [of] that victorious army
[from Spain] obliged the royalists to disperse and conceal themselves."

In Albany, New York, Talleyrand had heard from Schuyler that through Madame de Staël his name had been erased from the proscribed exiles and that he might return to France.

No blue cup "which I send you every year" came from Altona.

CHAPTER TWENTY-SIX

Called by Indispensable Circumstances

(January–June 1796)

I N THE WINTER of 1796 the issues of American foreign policy were ratification of Jay's Treaty of Commerce and Amity with Great Britain, and the bitter French reaction to it. France in substance said that to have made such a treaty was a violation of Franklin's alliance with them.

America was familiarly divided between the extreme Francophiles and Washington's Administration, who primarily desired neutrality in the Anglo-French war, but who also believed that in the long run Britain would be victorious and that it would be folly recklessly to become her foe.

Although Morris, in his letters to Washington and Hamilton, overestimated the then, though not the final, extent of French exhaustion, his judgments on the whole were wonderfully sound. He had warned the French their paper money would fall to a hundred to one and it had done so and the guillotine had left no capitalists to bring it back.

A letter to Hamilton said:

You will naturally weigh, not only the naval forces, but also the financial resources of the opposed powers. The noisy folks with you will undoubtedly be loud in our obligations to France, and on the long list of our grievances from England. As to the former, I think we should always seek to perform acts of kindness toward those who, at the bidding of their Prince, stepped forward to fight our battles. Nor would I ever permit a frigid reasoning on political motives to damp those effusions of sentiment which are as laudable in a nation as they are desirable in a private citizen. But would it be kind to support that power which tyrannizes over France and reduces her inhabitants to untold misery? As to the conduct of Britain towards us, although I see as clearly as others the ground of which we have to complain, and can readily account for the resentments which have been excited, yet I give due weight to the causes by which that conduct was instigated and if in some cases I find it unjustifiable, I cannot consider it as in all cases inexcusable.

It is interesting to contrast this wise and judicious balance of mind—and the practical good sense which goes on to suggest how the issue of seizure can be focused successfully on a single point—with the capricious frame of mind which led John Quincy Adams to refuse to dine with Lord Grenville on January 18, after accepting, and makes Morris sorry again "for that suspicious turn of his mind." Adams visited Morris afterward, "convinced that Great Britain means ill to us. I think they only mean good to themselves except two or three vexed at our prosperity."

Adams came back and "in his wrath and indignation [seemed to Morris] absolutely mad" (as Franklin indeed had said once of the older Adams). He breathed "nothing but war. He blows up so easily."

It is always interesting to contrast the inner repose of men like Washington and Morris with the excitement and petty personal judgments of their adversaries.

At this time Adet, the new French minister in Philadelphia, advised his government that Jay, with "*son caractère difficile, ses caprices, sa hauteur,*" guided by ambition to be war minister, had thrown himself into the Revolution, forgetting his French origin, and that the Jay Treaty was the result!

How different Washington's sensible letter to Hamilton:

Now suppose they [the French] encouraged by influential men in this *court* send out an envoy to make strong remonstrance against the unfriendliness (as they will term it) of our treaty with Great Britain [a treaty not of alliance but to regulate commerce] we would know what to do except for unhappy differences among ourselves.

[And now as to the request from young Lafayette that I seek his father's liberation, I feel that] to facilitate their wishes as far as it can be done with any propriety on my part I would, as a private person, express in a letter to the Emperor the wish that he might be freed. If you and Mr. Jefferson see no impropriety send it to Pinckney to judge.

But so much, as Morris would say, for a tiresome subject, except that even he was staggered by the evidence of the British plans to land in force on the Continent. "Five thousand horses are to be purchased for the cavalry in the United States."

In March, De Moustier, back safely from Normandy, came to breakfast with his sister, and Sir John Johnson, the once hated New York Tory leader, called, and Morris took "my godson Alexander Hamilton Church to see the elephants and to buy toys."

Spring came in Paris and Napoleon married Joséphine. On the morning after the wedding they went to visit her children Eugène and Hortense de Beauharnais at their school in St. Germain. The headmistress was Madame Campan, once the royal governess, and the sister of Citizen Genêt.

The links of coincidence that day were several. Hortense, "a little girl, a trifle awkward in the uniform worn by the pupils, with pretty eyes, beautiful fair hair and a sheep's profile" would bear a son to the then eleven-year-old "young Flahaut." With her, or on tiptoe outside the door as she met the man who would be her stepfather and brother-in-law in one, was little Eliza Monroe, her best friend, the daughter of Morris's successor. Eliza would be godmother to Hortense's Bonaparte child.

The day before, Washington had been writing Morris that he had heard from Morris's sister, Mrs. Ogden, that he was leaving for home. He asked him "with affectionate regard" to get him some good English farmers for Mount Vernon. It again seems positive that Morris intended to go home. Robert Morris wrote him in March and early May, "I doubt whether this will reach Europe in time to catch you" and "I expect you are on the point of embarking."

The letter reached Morris May 16. The next day "I walk

out to Kensington. Madame de Graave tells me of an intended marriage between Madame de Flahaut [for ten months no mention of the name] and M. de Souza, also of a coldness between him and her respecting the Duke of Orléans. I presume that he [the duke] has been *un peu mystérieux* and she *un peu légère à cet égard.*"

That night he wrote to Washington that he was called by some "indispensable circumstances to take a journey into Switzerland and my sense of propriety induces me to make the long and inconvenient circuit of Hamburg in preference to the short cut through France." He has no time to say more than to urge Washington to accept another term or at least name his successor.

It would certainly appear that he had, as with Jay in '94, told his sister he was coming home and that the lure of Eve had again been too much for him.

It fits his whole story that before leaving he should have "dined with Mrs. Vassal[1]. Her son-in-law is Sir Godfrey Webster, whose lady is en route from Italy accompanied by Lord Holland, but the husband seems quite unsuspecting and unconcerned."

The lady was the famous and rich Elizabeth Vassall, Lady Webster, who had spent the winter in Rome with Morris's and Adèle's friend, Madame d'Albani. She was twenty-six, Lord Holland twenty-three, "horrid disparity," and she came back to "have my wretched marriage annulled" from Webster, her father's age, and to let her fifth child be born in wedlock to Lord Holland. All summer she would have to wait in "Hamburg, full of emigration."

On June 12, Morris was ashore at Altona, so crowded there was no place to stay for more than one night. He was forced to go into Hamburg to the King of England Hotel. It was a drizzly, damp day with a west wind and he called on Adèle, who had already been to his hotel while he was out. The Altona winter had been dreadful for Adèle, snow blindness causing a red bar across her vision, so that in working on her book she had left out letters in words and sometimes words themselves.

Apparently these two people, so incredibly drawn to each

other in all but final vows, said nothing that day of De Souza. As they were talking, Richard Randolph died in agony at his plantation, Bizarre, in Virginia.

On the eighteenth Morris moved from Hamburg to Altona, only to find that Adèle's "project of taking me in as a boarder is baffled." He supped at her house the next night, "where there is a party to play all night by way of getting into Hamburg as soon as the gates are opened."

On the twentieth Macon, an aide of Lafayette's, "calls regarding the project of getting Lafayette out of prison" and after dinner with Madame de Flahaut he took her for a drive.

In the imagined dialogue between them in April '95 there was one of two omissions. She may have hesitated, after saying she would not be his kept woman, and added "unless, as you once spoke of, you intend to marry me." Or waited desperately for this man, at once generous and so cold, to say it. Or it may be true that the brilliant José Maria de Souza-Botelho, thirty-seven, then Portuguese minister to Denmark, was already captivated by what he had heard of her and her novel and been in touch with her. And said enough to make her believe she could marry him and must no longer play with Morris.

In any event on the drive she told Morris for the first time "her whereabouts with her Portuguese lover, M. Souza."

Whether De Souza and she were actually lovers by then seems doubtful. More likely Morris could not resist the irresistible question and she said, "Why yes, what did you expect?" in equally irresistible retaliation for his cold fire.

How much to be expected is the next day's entry. "Dine at Hamburg with the Simons" and the string of days that follow "all day *chez moi* taking German lessons from Mademoiselle Matthiesen, the landlord's daughter."

And then, as so often, he can stand it no longer and calls on Madame de Flahaut and comes sulkily home to tea alone, since she has not asked him to stay.

On the twenty-eighth and twenty-ninth he goes back. Orléans is there and they talk finances.

As June ended Talleyrand sailed from America for Hamburg. He carried a letter to James Marshall in Hamburg from Robert

Morris, saying that Talleyrand would give Hetty "all the Philadelphia news. . . . I am still plagued with debts and protests."

The Robert Morris *Letter Book* that summer is pathetic reading, the letters of a man going to ruin, artificially hopeful and pretentious, trying to create the impression of confidence, promising the impossible, promising interest to a creditor who knows even a fraction of the principal is too much to expect, hoping for a miracle. "Suppose you make up a company to buy 50,000 acres. Give me $2 per acre and discharge Colonel Smith's mortgage." "If certain things I am working at succeed, I will pay you sooner than you expect in any event with interest in nine months."

"I will cheerfully comply with your request to remit $1500 in this envelope if . . ." and a most colossal device of putting off the evil day with a draft on James Marshall at sixty days sight in favor of "Harry Lee" for £8949.16.9½. He hopes that Marshall has the cash or will have it at the maturity of the acceptance.

On July 5, Morris calls on Adèle. "She has been ill" but, he comforts himself, "she told my coachman so, Saturday, four days ago and the fool forgot to tell me."

The sixth, the seventh, the eighth, he goes and each time she is "abroad," and this many-sided man, whom the greatest affairs of men could not daunt nor perplex, "plans to leave for Germany."

On the night before his departure Adèle relents sufficiently to dine with him and the next morning he gets away at 3 A.M., with only the landlord's daughter ("she could not sleep") to say good-bye as his carriage started along the sandy roads to "the great unpeopled town, immense but lacking solidity," of Berlin.

CHAPTER TWENTY-SEVEN

State and Ancientry, How Congenial to My Tastes

(July 1796–97)

THE LENGTH and frequency of the correspondence between Morris and Lord Grenville which followed has given rise to the conclusion by some that Morris made his tour of Germany and the Empire as the paid agent of the British Foreign Office. Later he brought a libel suit against Duane for making the charge. It is equally grandiose and erroneous to suppose, as has been alleged, that the journey was the result of a fixed plan to liberate Lafayette.

It seems entirely clear that Morris took it because, as he wrote Lady Sutherland, he wanted to see state and ancientry, so congenial to his tastes, because, in part of himself, as he wrote the same lady, he floated "like all light substances on the stream of time," and finally because he could not yet put an ocean between him and Madame de Flahaut. Certainly there is small record of the "business concerns" which some say kept him unwillingly away from home.

There is also an indication that he wanted, in petty fashion, to offset Adèle's rejection of him by becoming the lover of one of the most virtuous women in Europe, the widowed émigrée, Madame de Nadaillac.

On his travels the *Diary* has passages of almost Swiftian disgust with the grossness of German sexuality, from that of the Princess Hohenloe who asked him to come on a financial matter while her lover was there, to the woman selling pineapples below his window; the maids of honor in Berlin who went with the Queen after masked balls to brothels for the night "to take her chance of the public"; the habit of mixed companies of men and women visiting the Anatomical Museum "to see the phallus of Chevalier —— three inches wide"; and Lisette, the daughter of the landlord, with whom "I do not care to do it, though she is very handsome, for she takes snuff."

Of course his own conduct is far from irreproachable but it somehow preserves his stylized, amusing indecorum.

He does not feel for all the émigrés as he does for those in Hamburg. "These people," he says of the colony in Vienna, "lead me almost to forget the armies of the French Revolution and often the unforgiving temper and sanguinary wishes which they exhibit make me almost believe the asperities of their enemies." Almost twenty years before he had written Joseph Reed he would find him "a generous foe," if Reed did not wish to be his friend and told his calumners in Philadelphia his revenge would be forgiveness. Malice and vindictiveness were intolerable qualities in his eyes.

But this quality of mercy was not limitless. Kalitchkoff, the Russian ambassador in Berlin, asked him, "How can we save the chief of the House of Bourbon?"

"I tell him," Morris says, "in my opinion he has nothing left but to try to get shot."

In Berlin on July 25 he went directly in his indefatigable venery to Madame de Nadaillac's house. He had met her in February '91, "an aristocrat *outré,* handsome, virtuous, a coquette, romantic." He advised her to love him. She replied that "she has preserved herself pure . . . resisted the King of Prussia . . . it would be ridiculous to succumb to a voyageur who treats everything lightly and yet such a thing might happen," though the Baron d'Escar was in love with her and wished her to marry him.

They dined together at Lord Elgin's the next night, Morris took her to a party at Count Haugwitz's and she asked him to dinner on the twenty-ninth. It has to be admitted that in his hunting Morris always had the unfair advantage over ordinary rivals of his own coach and four.

The after-dinner seemed to be going favorably when D'Escar, like Talleyrand of old, came in. "Chance usually decides these things," Morris observed, undismayed.

Morris noted that Lord Elgin left the embassy early in pursuit of his own amours. Elgin evidently did not know of the lady in Altona or he might have said to Morris, "Yes, I have met the Countess de Flahaut and saw a very pretty tribute paid her. Coming out to Germany in '94, Lady Bessborough and I dined at our consulate in Utrecht. There were a number of guests and Henrietta Bessborough was offered the seat of honor, which she promptly declined. You will be interested to know why."

"Yes, why?"

"As we were going in she learned that the author of *Adèle de Sénanges* was of the company, and insisted that the honor must be hers."

In August, Madame de Nadaillac warned him that he was talking "too politically and that it was irksome to the Cabinet." He so disliked Prussia and the Prussians that he replied, "The so-called Cabinet are only clerks . . . fearful a stranger should penetrate the arcana of their humiliation," and as for Potsdam, "It looks like the vulgar expression of I would if I could."

He was so provoked that he took Madame de Fontana for a ride in the park, "*beaucoup de tendresse* but in a moment when according to the usual course of things she should be all abandonment, a whim of virtue takes hold of her imagination."

After this he decided to go hunting in Dresden and arrived August 19. There the émigrés touched his heart.

In the streets are many French émigrés who are travelling eastward to avoid their countrymen. They are allowed to stay only three days . . . serene and even gay. So great a calamity could never light on shoulders which could bear it so well. Their hope is in the kindness of that Being who is to all his creatures an indulgent Father.

As he arrived Monroe, angered and embittered, was being recalled from his post by Pickering, now Secretary of State.

Hundreds of American citizens were in French prisons and scores of our vessels seized.

On September 15, Morris reached crowded Vienna, as Washington's Farewell Address was being made. The best lodgings he could get were "two wretched rooms up two flights of stairs at the Three Axes Hotel," but the Prater was superior to any city he had seen.

Napoleon was now master of North Italy. Two French armies were across the Rhine. There were no British troops on the Continent and only in the Mediterranean, and the blockading squadrons off Brest, was there any check to the French power.

Morris warns Lord Grenville of the traditional British political unpopularity on the Continent. The talk is, he says, that Britain encourages the war against France, only to serve her own aggrandizement in the two Indies. He recommended a statement that "the principal object of English policy now is to protect the German Empire and the Low Countries; that the dearest interests of Britain are eventually concerned with that defense and protection." He takes note of the threats of war against England from Madrid and points out to Grenville the advantage to him, if there is war with Spain, "after dwelling on the unprovoked aggression of His Most Catholic Majesty [to] say it justifies you in demanding, as a condition of peace, that he shall open his American dominions to the commerce of all," meaning of course particularly Morris's own country.

From Madame de Staël came a characteristic command "to open the prison door of M. de Lafayette. You have already saved his wife from death; deliver the whole family. Pay the debt of your country!"

This matter was certainly much on Morris's mind but his judgment evidently was that Lafayette was in no danger, nor in too great distress, and that neither Morris nor even Washington himself had the open sesame.

Sir Morton Eden, the British ambassador, presented him to the Emperor on September 24, where Hue and Thierry, "anciens valets de chambre" to Louis XVI, saw him and came afterwards to pay their respects.

Eden and he got along very well together, although he thought Eden was "more devoted to whist than his country- men," but that was a first impression and he came to respect the ability underlying the outward indifference as he watched Eden leaning "quietly against the wall" during a long talk with the Empress. Eden presented him to the archduchesses and Madame de France, who bore "a strong resemblance to her father, Louis XVI, and I cannot help observing on the malignity which pursued her poor mother and would have persuaded the world that this was an offspring produced by her gallantries."

As for Morris, a damsel came to the Three Axes to "obtain her object," which he gave her but "got rid of her" when she came back the next day.

On October 16, as he put on a stocking wrong side out, he remembered he had done so the day his leg was crushed and amputated, and writes, in a bitterness he almost never reveals, "the mark of that misfortune to this hour." It was the day Lord Malmesbury arrived in Paris to try for appeasement. Spain, too, had declared war on England. Napoleon had just had his vic- tory at Arcola, and the French were gathering ships and men to land in Ireland.

Lest England rely too much on the Pope's intention to de- clare a Holy War on France, as Bonaparte neared Rome, Morris reminded Grenville that the papal military potential would not be more than "a detachment of monks, supported with a due quantity of bulls and such like ammunition from the Vatican."

In mid-December in that wintry city he met young Madame de Lita, who quite swept him away. He said to her at once that he must have her but before she could answer her husband and the Prince Sapieha came in. Even so she gave him a rendezvous for that night but when he came back "she finds it out of all rule to surrender the first day," but then she did in her drawing room. The next day he came back "and as soon as her husband is gone we performed the nuptial rites. 'Tis a pity I did not fall in love with her sooner." She set the next day to receive him again but the glimpses of the moon had visited her when he came.

One can almost see him standing in the snow outside by his carriage, thinking, as was his custom, "Whatever is, is." He told his coachman to take him to the Chancellery.

After acquainting Baron de Thugut, the chancellor, with the political state of Europe, "as much as was proper, I take out a letter I had received from Madame La Marquise de la Montagne, sister of Madame de Lafayette. . . ."

Thugut listened and must have sighed patiently as he contradicted the account of ill treatment of Adrienne de Lafayette, who had insisted on coming across Europe to join her husband in the prison of Olmütz. Thugut said he wished they had never had anything to do with Lafayette. His wife could leave the prison whenever she chose, but she could not keep going "backwards and forwards."

Morris "solicited his release in vain." Thugut said Lafayette would be liberated at the peace in any event, and if England would ask for him he would be glad to be rid of him. "They may, if they please, turn him loose in London." Morris asked Thugut if he would send a letter for him to Madame de Lafayette in Olmütz, and Thugut agreed.

At the Three Axes, Morris wrote Lord Grenville what Thugut had said, and urged Grenville to ask for Lafayette, saying, "You could then send him to America under such a weight of *notorious obligation* that he shall be incapable of disserving you. In any case you would do an act agreeable to America which would cost you nothing."

To Adrienne de Lafayette he wrote very sympathetically but very sensibly. He said he was assured that the marquis was well lodged and in want of nothing; that "far from entertaining the barbarous idea of depriving you of the assistance of art [medical], the physician of your choice will be sent to you." He tells her not to despair—"time will give liberty to M. de Lafayette"—and suggests, as tactfully as possible, the importance of prudently avoiding "exasperation . . . by odious reports . . . which might consequently postpone the moment of his liberation." In other words, that Adrienne herself and Madame de Montagne and Minette de Staël were not helping matters.

That done, he went to see Madame de Lita, who insisted on being *sage*. Whenever a lady, who had once yielded to him, refused to go on, he behaved in the most unreasonable and petty manner, usually leaving at once. It is so unlike his sweet reasonableness in larger matters that the question arises whether it is not the result of sensitiveness about his leg, "the mark of that misfortune to this hour," a sensitiveness usually masked, but still representing his only inner uncertainty and sense of inferiority.

So he told Madame de Lita that he was going away, and she replied that had she known it "we should not have been well together." He waited, evidently hoping. It is amazing to see the penetrating accuracy of his judgments of everything but his own oestrual desires. After he left the De Lita house a Polish noble in exile, Lanskorenski, came to tell him the Emperor of Russia had taken his son to see Kosciusko in prison and then released him "and 10,000 Poles confined in Siberia" with passports and money to bring them home. Lanskorenski told him with tears in his eyes, "They are all in ecstasy and that single trait does more (in my opinion) toward securing the Russian part of Poland than an army of twenty thousand men." Are they not the tears and ecstasy of that attractive race which ever since have most distressed their friends?

On the eve of St. Sylvester he sent a note around to Thugut urging that Lafayette be released for the New Year and reminding the Chancellor that "forgiveness granted to others is the only unobjectionable title of which we can avail ourselves before the King of Kings."

Madame de Lita was "abroad" when he called January 3, 5 and 6. On the eighth she received him but refused his advances and on the tenth he left Vienna for Prague. He did not know of the panic in Philadelphia, with 150 failures and 67 people jailed for debt, Robert Morris himself among them, his fortune of ten million dollars, Benjamin Rush said, shrunk to 2/6 in the pound, far less than his debts, estimated by some at thirty million dollars.

From Dresden, January 25, 1797, Morris wrote Sir Morton Eden, reminding him what he had said and written to Thugut about Lafayette, enclosing copies of the whole correspondence and asking Eden to follow it.

In Dresden he met some people he liked, particularly Hugh Elliot, the brother of Lord Minto, "a manly fellow," who wished to establish himself in the United States, "having half a dozen illegitimate children and their mother to take care of. . . . I wish he could come over. There is room for all his little ones."

Morris first liked Elliot because, when a man infuriated Morris by saying "it was wise of Washington to resign while yet in place [John Adams had become President], inferring that he could not have been re-elected," and then asked insultingly what "four million [Americans] can do," Elliot said he hoped the United States would join England to take and divide all the French and Spanish possessions.

Then he went on to Leipsig, where the Queen of Saxony "points out to me a young Mademoiselle Reidesall, who was born in America [when her parents were prisoners of war near Monticello] and christened 'America' [and] I reclaim my countrywoman." He was "all the time on my legs" at a royal ball at which the Grande Maréchale made the French Revolution clear to him by the statement that "France was overturned because the Queen laid aside etiquette"!

It was in Leipsig that "Madame Crayen desires to show her attachment. I caution her. She says 'I have but one idea. I care for nothing else. Why conceal my passion [for you]. I glory in it.'"

The lady was a court beauty "for whom the King of Saxony was so mad he waited on her bridal dinner in disguise."

On Washington's Birthday "in the Indian phraseology we brighten the chain together," and the next day in his carriage "we worship on the Cyprian altar. A perfect winter's day." She was sure "from the lively sense which it excited" that she had conceived, which Morris thought possible and the ardors continued. In an idle interim Morris went to hear Baron Munchausen "play on the harmonica which he assured me last evening that he excelled in and convinced me this morning that he was mistaken."

Madame de Crayen followed him to Berlin where the King

of Prussia had a new explanation of the French Revolution. He told Lord Elgin that Morris, in the service of England, had arranged it.

The Cyprian worship with Madame de Crayen was held almost daily until it came time for him to leave Berlin, March 14. They were both deeply agitated and she said to him, "I dare not ask, I cannot expect that you will love me but do not, I beseech you, quite forget me."

He was at the Hanoverian court at Brunswick on the twenty-first, disgusted with its gross homosexuals, men and women.

On March 31, Morris reached Hamburg and went after dinner to see Madame de Flahaut. He visited her the first three days of April, telling her particularly of all the books he had bought in Leipsig, and while they were talking Parish brought him the news that "my poor friend Robert Morris is ruined. A heavy stroke upon my bosom and I fear the account is but too true." The James Marshall mission had of course been a failure and Robert Morris had written him, "Having been so long accustomed to see things fail I begin to consider it as a thing of course."

In the early morning of December 19, 1796, Robert Morris heard that "Judge W—— was taken by the sheriff last night and notice was given me to take care of myself for unless cash to meet the crisis is produced this day or tomorrow, it will be my turn next. Where it is to come from I do not know. I am so beset on every side."

He hung on for a few days, writing Constable on the twenty-second, "I will pay you this money as it will be in my power." Then the end came and he went to the debtors' prison.

There was also news that Austria had had to sign an armistice with the conquering French armies within sight of Vienna.

The next day, April 8, Morris moved to Altona, near to Adèle. There was no mention by either of them of De Souza. But in Virginia the will of Richard Randolph was probated with its manumitting provision for his slaves "to make retribution as far as I am able to an unfortunate race of bondsmen over whom my ancestors have usurped and exercised the most lawless and monstrous tyranny . . . to impress my children with just horror at a crime so enormous and indelible," leaving his estate, except the slaves, to his wife Judith, but cautioning her against "too much maternal love" for their young sons, St. George and Tudor, born after his father's trial. Nancy Randolph, twenty-three, was living with her sister.

In Altona, Morris let the rainy spring and summer days pass in aimless idleness, seeing Madame de Flahaut several times a week, recording the fact but saying nothing of why he saw her or even stayed at all.

The previous August, Talleyrand, homeward bound from America, had landed at Hamburg. In his curious, rather ugly memoirs, published thirty years before his death, he said:

> I wanted before entering France to know what was going on there. . . . Madame de Flahaut who was then at Hamburg seemed to me hardly disposed to furnish me with the desired information for when I was still coming up the Elbe she sent me word not to land . . . her reason for doing so was that people were saying she had been on rather intimate terms with me and she feared that my presence should be an obstacle to her marriage to M. de Souza, the Portuguese minister. . . . I thought I could without any impropriety take no notice of the extraordinary reasons alleged and spent a month at Hamburg in the society of people who did no more than I did myself interfere with the marriage with the stupid [in that usage] M. de Souza.[1]

Vincent Nolte recorded that John Parish was particularly helpful to Talleyrand at the time and that his gratitude took practical form after the Peace of Amiens.

A man of the world and a diplomat like De Souza can scarcely have been unaware of Adèle's love affair with Talleyrand, or that her child was his. The insufferable French passage is only equaled by an Anglo-American one the following year.

At times in '97 it seems as though Morris had said to himself, "I cannot go until I have possessed her again." Again as though he hoped somehow to hurt her, as she saw him driving with Miss Matthiesen or her young sister, "who begins to feel the gentle hint from nature's tongue," or Miss Gehrt, their friend,

[1] *"C'est tout,"* his biographer Lacour-Gayet says, *"et c'est vraiment peu pour la mère de son fils."*

all three young girls of respectable bourgeois families who, after the drive, stayed, sometimes alone, sometimes together, for tea and taught him German or Dutch. Still, love-making with any of them in his rooms, "with a raw northeast wind blowing the house," bored him, and he would stop, after driving them home, "to call on Madame de Flahaut" and finding "nobody home so come back and read."

The nights were deathly quiet, she wrote in *Eugénie et Mathilde*, "not a single noise, neither the sound of carriage, nor the slightest motion. The silence caused the voice of the town crier to sound lugubrious as he went his hourly rounds through the town."

Even a request from Madame de Nadaillac in Berlin to buy chintz for her was a welcome relief. Perhaps no man of comparable force and intelligence has ever so completely wasted his time.

As he was buying the chintz Parish came in the shop and told him the Directory was issuing letters of marque to their privateers to seize American ships, and later in the afternoon another man told him Talleyrand was responsible and had advised the Directory that "the United States must fall." In America, Talleyrand had written Wycombe's father, Lord Lansdowne, that the "inclination was in favor of England" and he feared the bond of common laws and common language against France.

Adèle was out when he went to tell her about it, and at their next meeting, a few days later, told him that "Lord Wycombe is gone through to Switzerland and probably to treat with the French Government. His journey is quite a secret."

She may not have failed, in her own light malice for his strange behavior, to point out that while one of his rivals was a cabinet minister, the other was an envoy from his government, while Morris played with the flattered daughter of his landlord. He wrote in his *Diary* that if it was true about Wycombe it was ridiculous. Then Frazer, the British minister, confirmed that he had seen Wycombe but said no more, and Morris went off on a week's excursion.

June 9, in rainy, dirty weather, he "visited Madame de Fla-

haut on my return. She seems quite *en désordre*." She would
not see him that day, or all week, though he was sure she was
at home. And she must have been in almost unsupportable disorder, alone, poor, her eyes, by which she made novels and
bonnets, affected, asking herself, "How can these incredible
men, all four of them, Talleyrand, De Souza, Wycombe, Morris,
treat me so, doing nothing and yet not leaving me alone?"

One is not sure about De Souza. It seems plain that he had
talked about marriage. The answer may be that his father was
still living, and that though De Souza was thirty-nine, paternal
consent and assured inheritance were still necessary, and could
not be secured to marry someone without birth or fortune, and
not so innocent as the day she married the Count de Flahaut.

Off Morris went to nearby Denmark.

On July 3 he was back. There was a letter from the English
Duchess of Cumberland asking him to raise some money and
send it to her at Leipsig where she was without funds. He sent
her a draft on Freis and Company. Montjoie, an acquaintance
of Adèle's, was waiting to ask for a thousand francs, which
Morris gave him and hurried to Madame de Flahaut's.

De Souza, back from Berlin, was there before him and Adèle
listened while De Souza said somewhat cryptically to Morris,
"I have heard with surprise that you were a great democrat in
the French sense of the word." The two stags eyed each other
and Morris left to fetch both Miss Matthiesens and Miss Gehrt
to tea in his rooms.

The week that followed he acted like a man possessed. He
went to see Adèle on July 4 and 5, without recording what they
talked about.

On the seventh he "called on Mr. Parish to announce my
departure." He separately had Miss Matthiesen in for tea and
Miss Gehrt for strawberries and they were both suddenly shy
and said their parents were scolding them. He walked home
with one of them, wondering what had happened, stopped at a
bookbinder's to "fix the composition of an atlas" and walked on
to Madame de Flahaut's. She was abroad.

He spent the next day in Hamburg, coming home after dark
to find "Madame de Flahaut is again abroad." But the next

day, Sunday, rainy with a wind west-southwest, she came after dark and spent the evening.

He did not tell her that during the afternoon he had met Lord Wycombe, who had talked "with much warmth against his quondam friend. She had a design to marry him. He is of those men who go far in the way they travel and believes more than is just. At the time when I supposed their connection to be what I now find it was . . . she sent her servant to him with a letter full of all sorts of tenderness and dying sensibility. She had nearly caught him and he seems to be very angry at it."

The spectacle of these two rich and influential men talking thus together about a lady who by their testimony had allowed them what they wanted is the ugliest in all their lives. How Morris could have brought himself to write, "He [Wycombe] seemed a proper subject to work upon and she exerted herself to get hold of him," is beyond understanding, unless, hearing, falsely or truly, that Wycombe had been her lover when Morris was, or when she would not have him, his vanity was almost mortally hurt. Whatever he wrote in conclusion that night we do not know because he—or perhaps Anne Randolph—had the good taste to ink it out.

How psychosomatic again is the fact that afterwards he is home for almost a week because his stump was paining him badly and even Miss Matthiesen only came to borrow sixty dollars.

On the twenty-eighth and thirty-first Adèle was "abroad."

In America the aftermath of Hamilton's affair with Mrs. Reynolds had blown up again in Hamilton's outburst against Monroe, who wrote Hamilton that if his letter was meant to be a challenge, then "Colonel Burr will act for me."

One must wonder if it ever occurred to Morris to be grateful to Madame de Flahaut for all the outward decorum with which she behaved in relation to him or for her pathetically few demands on him. Hamilton had been disgraced by a common woman and another Hamilton, Emma, was, in Mahan's phrase, dragging a "man of Lord Nelson's masculine renown about England and the Continent till he was the mock of all beholders."

There seems no indication as the summer waned that Adèle told him anything of her future plans, though on September 21 she said while they were discussing the Directory that "they do not execute the decrees against the emigrants."

Actually her inventive mind, her ruthless independence and capacity to survive, had worked out a way to go back with her son to Paris, where her name was still proscribed. A more difficult obstacle to her return was that a passport could be issued abroad only to someone who was not, and never had been, an émigré and of that there must be documentary evidence.

During the week Morris kept to his rooms, with his paining stump, Adèle went to see Reinhardt, the French consular agent in Hamburg, who had been seeing her there for over two years. To him she presented a document, with all the necessary signatures and seals, certifying that from 1792 until 1795 she had lived continuously at 10 Rue des Postes, in Paris. It is a tiny "passage" on the Left Bank back of the Jardin des Plantes.

Reinhardt, of whom one would like to know more, of course knew the certificate was forged or bought, but it was quite "in order" and he gallantly issued a passport for her and her son to leave.

It is always possible that Morris, so secretive on occasions, knew of this and may even have helped to buy the papers. There is no evidence of it, however, and more likely she had said to herself, "Talleyrand will not help, nor Wycombe, nor Morris, I will do for myself."

Then, judging from an incident that followed, she may have said, "After all, Talleyrand is a Frenchman, he was a refugee— he will understand, as those big Anglo-Saxons cannot, that I can only be happy in France."

There appears to be no reference to her by Morris, in *Diary* or *Letters,* after September 21, 1797. He must have known of her plans to leave and omitted mention of it for reasons of security or the desire to try to forget.

She evidently reached Paris in October and found lodgings at 512 Rue de Lille, on the Left Bank, the next street beyond the Quai Voltaire, opposite the Tuileries. We know that Talleyrand, at the Foreign Office, then complacently "verified" Reinhardt's passport and the supporting certificate of non-emigration, though beyond that there is no evidence of any closer relation.

Small royalties may have been due on her books, conceivably some winnings from gambling in Altona, perhaps even something from Morris, but on the whole she was there without funds and almost without friends, after the guillotine, the small estate of Mesnil Bernard, inherited from her uncle, still sequestered. *"Les bestiaux et les ustensiles [là] ont déjà été vendus. . . ."* She needed its revenues to live, but application for them might reveal the fraud about her passport.

Still she had to gamble further with her little luck and wrote the Minister of Police that the sequestration was the result of a mistake in identity. "There were a thousand Filleuls [her maiden name] in Normandy." In what terrible anxiety she must have waited the police response. When it came it was *"accablant* [overwhelming]." Clearly the certificate of residence in Paris, given Reinhardt, was false. Her police dossier was full of erasures and changes in dates, *"altérées par une eau corrosive."* Some unwise perfectionist had even inserted a certificate of residence at Orléans during the first weeks of the Terror, when she had actually been spirited to England. The police brought her in. She denied everything. She said that what they thought was an ink eradicator used on the papers was a coffee stain where her little boy had upset her cup.

The police hesitated. After all, Talleyrand, high in the Directory, had certified the papers and she was released, while the inquest was continued.

Then at three in the morning, in police fashion, they came to arrest her in the Rue de Lille. She was quite ready for them in court later in the day, when they asked her name. She replied "Citoyenne Menars," the name of her sister Julie.

"La Citoyenne Menars? Qu'est-ce à dire? Vous n'êtes point la Citoyenne Flahaut? Que signifie cette supercherie [trick]?" She told them it was not a trick. They must have confused her with a proscribed widow Filleul, a cousin *"au centième degré."* She herself had only been in Hamburg *"pour les affaires de com-*

merce momentanément." She said she was not Flahaut, only Flahaut's sister.

"Le ministre ordonne l'information!" Who can blame him? She was warned she would be spared *"aucune démarche."*

Very quickly there came to the police a letter from Le Couteulx de Canteleu, Morris's bankers—and one may hope it was his doing—asking liberty for the widow Flahaut "who, far from being prejudicial to the Republic," is useful to it *"sous le rapport des moeurs,"* essential basis of our government.

Time for once was on her side. The severity of the proscription was waning and out of the melodramatic vaudeville gradually her freedom increased and revenues from Bernard Mesnil began to reach her.

It is rather wonderful to know that a record of one so indestructible should have survived perhaps the third greatest single destruction in history.

On the night of July 24/25, 1943, the Royal Air Force attacked Hamburg in great strength and the suburb Altona with its old town hall, customhouse, schools, hospitals, fish market and public authorities was practically destroyed: 3188 dwelling houses were wiped out and 1749 heavily damaged.

Inquiry was made of the authorities of Hansestadt Hamburg-Altona on March 10, 1951, as to the possibility of there being any record of Madame de Flahaut in the municipal archives.

On April 3, one hundred fifty-six years after she had first arrived, one letter was found. It had been written March 2, 1799, in French to President von Stemman of Hamburg by the Countess Charlotte von Schimmelmann and read:

I beg to recommend to the kindness of Your Excellency a matter which greatly interests me, although I have not had the advantage of knowing personally Madame de Flahaut. She wishes that V.E. would be so good as to give Mons. Texier the papers which concern her, which she has requested him to ask you for, and from which she is expecting matters which will help to give her back tranquility and happiness, perhaps in her country. I know that V.E. is animated with feelings full of humanity for an unhappy class which groans under the unfortunate circumstances of our times, this class of émigrés whose troubles are too often without remedy and without consolation. I, therefore, do not recommend the matter of Madame de Flauhaut to you, but I beg leave to bring her interests to your kind notice.

On October 14, Morris had been present when Lafayette was brought to Hamburg with his family, for formal release. He told Morris he chose to consider himself as freed by the influence of Great Britain, "and I did not choose," Morris afterwards wrote John Marshall, "to contest the matter because, believing my application at Vienna had procured his liberty it would have looked like claiming acknowledgment." He urged Lafayette to go to the United States and ask President Adams to make proper provision for him.

Then Morris left Hamburg for Germany. He saw Beau Fersen, his handsome face now haunted, and near Cassel "the landlord is an old Hessian soldier who worked very hard cutting down the wood at Morrisania and is very sorry he did not stay in America."

After Dusk
I Reach Morrisania

(1798)

Iᴛ ɪs ᴄᴜʀɪᴏᴜsʟʏ ꜰɪᴛᴛɪɴɢ that as 1798 opened there should
have been an outburst of unrelated personal criticisms of
Morris, Wycombe and Talleyrand from people who knew them
but did not connect them with Madame de Flahaut or each
other.

Elizabeth Holland wrote in her *Journal:*

Lord Lansdowne in old age, surrounded by dignities and wealth,
is helpless and more an object of pity than envy. . . . His son
[Lord Wycombe] is an alien to his country. . . . This extraordinary
son is still in Dublin where his conduct has procured him three spies
who watch every action of his life.

Wycombe was in Ireland, actually supporting the rebels who
had induced Talleyrand to land a French force. This strange,
familiar treason needs no comment, nor is Talleyrand of course
to be criticized for using any means to bring England down,
though Fanny Burney wrote her sister, "How like myself you
must have felt about Talleyrand . . . indignant, amazed,
ashamed. [How could he have done this after the asylum England gave him when] we became partial to him almost to fondness?"

On the same day Abigail Adams wrote her sister, "General

W—— used sometimes to give anyone an office of whom he was *affraid*. This was the case with Governeer Morris."

It was a red-letter day, for on it James Monroe also wrote John Taylor:

Mr. W. can trample the Constitution under foot, in rejecting the channel of publick ministers to intrigue with the British Government through Gouverneur Morris, a man without morality, an avowed royalist, with no traits about him but such as are infamous.

In Berlin the last day of the month John Quincy Adams wrote his father, the President:

Baron Alvensleben the first time that I saw him asked me several questions regarding Mr. Morris who he said had given much dissatisfaction here. I told him that Morris had long ceased to be in any sort of employment under the American Government and hinted that I had seen a newspaper paragraph pretending that he was now in the English service of which I was altogether ignorant.

Alvensleben continued in French that he believed Morris was *"un volontaire en politique"* who held powers only from himself. "His conduct," Adams continued, "has nowhere been such as to do honor or credit to his country. He is yet wandering about at some of the small German courts."

Early in the previous December, Monroe had published *A View of the Conduct of the Executive in the Foreign Affairs of the United States Connected with the Mission to the French Republic during 1794, '95 and '96.* It was a bitter 100-page attack on Washington and Morris and a defense of his own mission.

It seems true to say that Thomas Paine brought more misfortune to his benefactor, Monroe, than he did to Morris, who had seemed so indifferent to his fate.

Much praise had come to Monroe from the Francophiles and the anti-Federalists for his part in Paine's release. On the face of it the royalist Morris had let this American patriot and citizen languish in jail, if not, as Minnigerode would have us believe, sought to have him executed.

Monroe, a great democrat, succeeds the royalist, frees Paine and has the advantage of his wise and lofty counsel. And of course after Paine's prison term Monroe honored himself in having Paine as a guest in his house.

Morris would have sympathized, if with amusement, with what of course followed.

Monroe had written in some disillusionment to Madison about this uncontrollable man two years before:

Paine is still with me. He wanted to go in Oct '94 in Spain and even told the Committee of Public Safety he would go as courier *to help me*. The Committee of Public Safety said no, as he was a [French] deputy. I told [Paine] whilst in my house he would write nothing for the public either of Europe or America on the subject of our affairs, which he did not entertain a very favorable opinion of [Paine said he was accustomed to writing but I insisted and he finally agreed], but he wrote in cipher to Muhlenberg [of Pennsylvania] by Pinckney coming out of Spain, who (fortunately) returned it. [Monroe says he then went over the whole arrangement with Paine again and thought it was understood and agreed.]

Nonetheless Paine sent the *Aurora,* the anti-Federalist paper published by Bache in Philadelphia, an open letter to Washington, saying:

As to you, sir, treacherous in private friendships (for so you have been to me and that in the day of danger) and a hypocrite in public life, the world will be puzzled to decide if you are an apostate or an impostor, whether you have abandoned good principles or whether you ever had any.

Even Washington's ability to keep his temper was somewhat shaken, and Monroe's *View of the Conduct of the Executive* stirred him even more deeply but he waited 118 days to think it over. But in the *Aurora* there were further charges that he had granted Talon, a confidential agent of the French pretender, "a very particular audience before the arrival of Genêt." This roused Washington to a denial, in a letter to the Secretary of State on February 6, of "the impudent, wicked and groundless assertion. . . . With Talon I had no acquaintance. I pledge myself I never exchanged a word with him outside of the public rooms on public days. (Publish my whole letter to Gouverneur Morris and his to me and let the public pass on the charge—that either of us—was a derelict to France and the contrary to Great Britain.)"

To his friend Spottswood, on March 30, Washington wrote his 44-page reply to Monroe's *View of the Conduct of the Executive*. To those unfamiliar with it (Washington's *Writings*, Vol. 36, Fitzgerald) it will be another revelation of a different Washington from that of the statues. Original, supple, caustic but even-tempered, it is the work of a man enjoying the opportunity for once to indulge his own skill in controversy and rebuttal, taking Monroe's text and paralleling it with bright laconic comment or even more devastating new queries.

Monroe had begun with the fact that the appointment of Morris as minister to France "would tend to discount the republican cause there and otherwise weaken the connexion between the two countries."

As to that Washington notes, "Mr. Morris was known to be a man of first rate ability and his integrity and honor had never been impeached. Besides Mr. Morris was sent whilst the kingly government was in existence." Monroe had continued that "Morris was known to be an enemy to the Revolution and a partizan of royalty. Thereby the name and weight of America was thrown into the scale of kings against that of the people and of liberty."

WASHINGTON: France *was* a monarchy. Whatever may have been Morris's politics he pursued steadily the honor and interests of his country with zest and ability and with respectful firmness asserted its rights. Had Mr. Monroe done the same we should not be in the situation we now are.

MONROE: In May '94 I was invited by the President through the Secretary of State to accept the office of minister plenipotentiary to the French Republic.

WASHINGTON: After several attempts had failed to obtain a more eligible character. It has been noted already that Mr. Morris was appointed during the reign of Louis XVI. . . . Afterwards under the fluctuating counsels and changes which succeeded even the acuteness and wisdom of a Monroe might not have served.

Monroe said his instructions were to make a great deal of American gratitude and friendship to France.

WASHINGTON: Could it be inferred from thence that in order to please France we were to relinquish our rights and sacrifice our commerce?

MONROE: Upon my arrival in France which was August 2, 1794, I found work of alienation and disunion had been carried further than I had before even suspected.

WASHINGTON: If we had submitted to them without remonstrance we should have still been their dear friends and allies.

MONROE: I was opposed to Jay's going to Great Britain [to negotiate a treaty].

WASHINGTON: Did the then situation admit any other alternatives than negotiation or war? Was there an abler man to be found to conduct the former or one more esteemed?

MONROE: Had that treaty never been passed what might we not have expected from French friendship.

WASHINGTON: Nothing if she did not perceive some advantage to herself in granting it.

MONROE: It was intimated to me that [France] had imbibed an opinion that Mr. Jay was sent to England with views unfriendly to France and that my mission was for the purpose of covering and supporting his to England, contemplating on our part a close union with England and that the other was an act of policy intended to arouse and deceive.

WASHINGTON: Strange concept and want of information this.

MONROE: As Jay had refused to send me a copy of the treaty [to communicate to the French Government they and I] thought it extraordinary.

WASHINGTON: No one else will think it extraordinary.

MONROE: Such was my condition upon the above occasion.

WASHINGTON: And extraordinary indeed it was.

MONROE: Well satisfied I am that France declined taking Florida in her treaty with Spain from a fear it might weaken her connection with the United States.

WASHINGTON: Guess work this and not at all probable from that motive.

MONROE: My wish was to conciliate the French Government

[towards the Jay treaty] and most anxiously I looked toward the Administration for means of doing it.

WASHINGTON: What means is it he wanted? Did he expect to be authorized to declare that his government was in error in having made a treaty without first obtaining the consent of the French and to ask pardon for not having submitted Mr. Jay's instructions to the rulers of that country?

MONROE: In my first note, September 3, 1794, I combatted copiously the condition of France in harassing our commerce.

WASHINGTON: But finally told it that if it was not convenient to comply with these articles the government and people of the United States would give them up with pleasure.

MONROE: Much was said in that Address [Washington to Congress of the United States] of the advantage of our accord with Great Britain . . . without the slightest attention being shown to the French Republic.

WASHINGTON: To state facts for the information of Congress and not to write eulogisms on the French nation or conduct was the object of the then President. If Mr. Monroe ever fills the chair of government . . . he may let the French minister frame his speeches.

So it went on in this knockabout fashion and though, of course, Washington had the advantage of the last word for the moment, he displayed a not unpleasant ability to quarrel like a normal, angry but self-controlled man.

And in reply to Monroe's almost last question, "What would have been the condition of these states had France been conquered?" he asked, "In turn, what will be the consequences of France overturning so many governments? and making partition of so many countries?"

The troops of Napoleon had sacked Rome and invaded Switzerland. Morris wrote March 10:

The French are in Berne. From the German ocean to the head of the Adriatic, including everything round by the British Channel, the Atlantic and the Mediterranean, except Portugal and Naples . . . This empire is too rapidly and widely extended to put on a solid existence but there is every means of extensive mischief.

In the shadows of this great glare the conqueror of Rome had
banished Minette de Staël from Paris and the French at Rastadt
refused to sit at the same table with Fersen as the representative of Sweden. In shaken England, even after a vast tax bill
was passed, officials of the Crown turned back a fifth of their
salaries to the Treasury, and grandees like the Duke of Bedford
gave a hundred thousand pounds from their purses for the war.

Morris was on his way back to Hamburg from the petty
German courts. He was indisposed one morning, "owing to
water I drank," and adds one of those medical non sequiturs of
the times—"so I take pepper with my roasted chickens."

He arrived in Altona at the end of June. There were letters
of Constable mentioning the men whom Robert Morris had
dragged down with him "with nothing to show."

My whole fortune would be but a drop in the ocean [of R.M.'s
debts]. The world speaks hardly of him as they are apt to do of
the unfortunate and those who suffer think they have a right to
abuse those who cannot pay. . . . *Why do you not return?* Your
brother Lewis is upon the point of death. . . . John Kean to whom
you wrote has been dead two years.

Kean's descendants would live at Liberty Hall.

Constable's letter of May 27 was sent in quadruplicate to
London, Liverpool and by two packets to Hamburg.

I hope you are on your voyage . . . not hearing from you I was
constrained to hire Morrisania [Farm] to Gibson for one year. It
has never produced 1000 a year. . . . I would to God, my friend,
you were here. We want character in our public counsels of decision. Your sister is well. Samuel, I am told, is in better health.

There was no Madame de Flahaut to hurry to see and Miss
Matthiesen told him she was to be married July 5. He bought
her "a nuptial present" and had scarcely given it to her when he
met D'Escar, now the husband of Madame de Nadaillac, and
about to leave with her for France. He himself went with Parish
to inspect a ship to take him home.

There is an entry, the only one in ten years, that he went to
church and heard a good Protestant sermon and another that
perhaps says more than its brief words. He had driven out of
Altona, where he had so often gone with Adèle, or the young

and much impressed Gehrt and Matthiesens. "I send back my carriage and walk alone for three hours."

Lafayette came to ask advice. ". . . I take little heed as to the answers." To Madame de Lafayette, who came to talk about the practical matter of the money they owed Morris, he said he had empowered Mr. Le Ray de Chaumont to settle with her in France.

News that "Nelson has destroyed the French fleet in the Bay of Alexandria" reached him before he sailed on October 4. On the ship was the family of James Le Ray de Chaumont to go to the Wild Lands. While he was on the Atlantic, his horses dying on the stormy voyage, Pitt told Russia, Austria and Prussia that England would fight until "France was reduced within her ancient limits." Lafayette went over to London, where the Duke of Bedford, Lord Holland and a few others made up a purse of three thousand pounds for him.

Lady Holland thought it "shabby in the Americans not to do something for a man who deserves so well of them but I confess there are many whose situation excites my compassion much more." The same day's *Journal* says that "Lord Wycombe's behavior to his father admits of no apology."

December 1, in heavy snow and rain, Morris's ship entered the eastern end of Long Island Sound, but the storm and winds were impossible and from Point Judith Light they turned back to Newport.

Not until the twenty-third did he come into New York Harbor, where Church, Colonel Hamilton and "David Ogden my nephew," now twenty-three, met him.

New Year's Eve he sat in Mr. Low's pew in Trinity Church and at last, "after calls on the clergy and the mayor," on January 5, 1799, after dusk he reached Morrisania, where he dined, less than a month before his forty-seventh birthday.

CHAPTER TWENTY-NINE

Is Retirement a Possible Thing?

(1799)

MORRISANIA was leaky and ruinous." Books and papers sent home from Paris were in confusion and Morris first settled down in the greatest happiness to sort and arrange them. "Among my books," the *Diary* for January 13 reads, "Still among my books" on the fifteenth when an architect came to begin on the plans shown the Churches in London three years before.

Before long Morris would have "laid out $50 or $60 thousand dollars in buildings and alterations," including "a bath room $50" and be living, Rufus King said, "much to his own taste *en garçon.*" A chef and a huntsman would be brought from Europe, farmers settled on the place, and it is pleasant to record that when "James Morris sells me a negro for £80" he was freed before he had to work for a new master.

Morris liked to write with rather mock modesty to his European friends of his "farm," of his "pretty good house, not a castle," but of his beef and dairy herds and his orchards he thought very well. It was not a "great house" in the sense that Bowood was, or his friend Lord Gower's Cleveland House, where there were 282 paintings in the gallery. There were no such houses in America but Dr. Johnson would have liked "the total defiance of expense" at Morrisania, and the view over the sound from the "terrace roof 130 feet long" was delightful.

It took many months to bring Morrisania to such magnificence but he made "long mornings . . . to get far on with my business." The trifling idleness of the final years in Europe was gone.

One must wonder whether Morris purposely set the date of March 31, 1799, for the Chevalier d'Orléans to dine with him, four years to the night since he had come with Madame de Flahaut to Newenstadt. And what news Orléans, who owed to her his presence in America, gave Morris about her.

In late April, Morris went to Philadelphia to visit Robert Morris in the debtors' prison, dining with Pickering, Secretary of State, the night before. He heard from him that "Robert Morris has behaved very ill," and the names of some of the men ruined by their advances to him. Robert Morris owed Gouverneur "24000 exclusive of what he paid in Europe on my account, the amount of which I do not exactly know."

Many sentimental myths have been made about this man who "pledged his private fortune to save the American cause." Of his downfall William Graham Sumner observed, "It cannot be said that the United States were bound to guarantee him against his own speculations for the rest of his life."

In prison Robert Morris told Gouverneur that Samuel Ogden "owed him £12,000 on account of the Delaware Works." Gouverneur had seen Ogden on his way to Philadelphia, found him "much pressed" and "desired him to make out a state of his affairs."

It was perhaps natural that his sisters, their husbands, the nephews, David B. Ogden and young Wilkins, and the niece, Gertrude Meredith, should regard the return of the wealthy bachelor as the solution of their own financial problems.

The situation is still familiar enough in ordinary life. Morris was "a confirmed bachelor." Whom should he provide for if not his sisters' children? Familiar enough, but never pleasant and certainly never carried on more brazenly for fifteen years nor ending, on the part of heirs presumptive, with more vicious malice.

It is important and gratifying to note that the famous Morris head was again "perfectly organized" and that he was not deceived about the heirs during the entire time.

On May 21, "Ogden came begging for money. I advance $1000." The next day "Mr. Wilkins asks my consent to the marriage of his son, Isaac. I refuse. *I find they have made up their minds to lean on me as heavily as they can.*"

The question of the marital intention of this great catch interested several people to Morris's amusement.

John Dickinson, his old colleague from the Continental Congress, "talks to me about my supposed gallantries and seems desirous to know whether I intend to marry. Rutherford tells me Miss Dickinson's family wish me to espouse her. I answer in general terms it is not impossible." Two weeks later the Schuylers come unannounced, "bringing their unmarried daughter to dine." Morris had made a large loan to their son-in-law, Church, a few days before.

In reply to his letter about Lafayette at Altona, Washington wrote him May 26, ". . . it is unnecessary I hope to add that if either business or inclination should induce you to look towards the South, I shall be very happy to see you in this seat of my retirement."

The summer went on, "busy with workmen," fishing in the sound, walks and sailing, with the brilliant legal interlude at Albany where Morris was counsel for Gouverneur and Kemble in the suit brought against them by Le Guen for "alleged misrepresentation and substitution in cargoes of indigo and cotton."

Hamilton and Burr were the opposing counsels. Here were three minds unsurpassed in brilliance in North America, three men, alike in so many ways, unlike in more, Morris "with his commanding figure, his melodious voice and authoritative manner" towering over the other two. But as in all public debate Morris was "indiscreet" with "observations [so] injurious to my dear general" that the Court admonished him. Philip Schuyler wrote his daughter Betsy that Morris "felt it so sensibly that his amends pleased the judge. I hope he will profit by it for I very sincerely wish him well."

Hamilton's and Burr's client won his case.

Oddly enough for different reasons, Morris and Hamilton were as strongly against their fellow Federalist, President Adams, as was Burr, the associate and friend of Colonel Smith, the President's son-in-law.

It seemed essential to the principal Federalists that Washington be called back to the presidency. They did not perceive, as Charles Francis Adams the elder says, that "times had changed so that even Washington could no longer hope to stand as the type of the sentiments of the whole people." Evidently, by common Federalist agreement Morris was chosen to appeal to Washington.

On December 9, from Morrisania, he wrote him:

During a late visit to New York, I learnt that the leading characters, even in Massachusetts, consider Mr. Adams as unfit for the office he now holds. . . . You will easily conceive, that his predecessor was wished for and regretted, nor will you be surprised, that the doubt whether he would again accept should have excited much concern. . . . You must be convinced, however painful the conviction, that should you decline no man will be chosen, whom you would wish to see in that high office. . . .

No reasonable man can doubt, that after a life of glorious labor you must wish for repose, and it would not be surprising that a wish so natural should, by frequent disappointment have acquired the force of passion. But is retirement in the strict sense of the word a possible thing? . . .

. . . You stand pledged by all your former conduct, that when circumstances arise, which shall require it, you will act again. These circumstances seem to be now imminent and it is meet that you consider them on the broad ground of your extensive information.

Ponder them, I pray you, and whatever may be the decision, pardon my freedom. . . .

It seems certain that Washington never read the letter. He came in from his ride in the snowy dusk the evening of the thirteenth of December to die, as someone has suggested, by the act of James Monroe.

Word was waiting him that Monroe had been elected governor of Virginia. The news so shocked him that he refused to change, and sat in his wet riding clothes discussing it. The following day "the letter of Gouverneur Morris which would have forced him [to the presidency] found him on his death-bed preparing for other scenes than those disturbed by the stormy passions of men." So Charles Francis Adams put it with fine sonority. Washington died of pneumonia that day.

Word of his death reached Morris the nineteenth. With it came a request from the Corporation of New York for him to pronounce the funeral oration. "This request is distressing and I pray time till tomorrow to consider." As he had once said to Washington, "You must find more humility in me than my letters convey," and the great loss must have seemed beyond even his powers to deal with. The one man in whom his critical mind found no fault was dead.

Services were held in St. Paul's Church the last afternoon of the year. Morris reached the church at eleven in the morning, but the "grand civil and military procession" did not arrive until three and Morris spoke late in the afternoon.

Robert Troup, the deponent in Woodhull's death in '76, wrote Rufus King in London that Morris rose to speak amidst "awful grandeur . . . the heartrending notes of the musick . . . the tears which were constantly flowing from every eye . . . had ever an orator a sublimer theme? No—and yet I left the church a most mortified and wounded man. Not a tear was compelled to roll, hardly was a sigh excited. The oration . . . had the effect of a cold, historical narrative, not that of a warm, impassioned address."

It seems probable that Morris could not bring himself to the sort of Roman eulogy that the customs of the time and Troup expected. He realized the effect, curtly noting in his *Diary*, "Pronounced my oration badly."

On Christmas Day, Napoleon became First Consul and wrote in his own hand to the King of England.

So the wonderful century ended. It was all but a hundred years since Marlborough, sitting in the rain after Blenheim, scribbled the note to the Queen that the Grand Monarque's power was broken, and handed it to Colonel Parke to carry home. Now descendants of Parke were mourning Washington at Mount Vernon. It was over half a century since the Grand

Monarque's great-grandson stood at Fontenoy to see the British beaten, as he thought forever.

In Paris *Emilie and Alphonse* by Adèle de Flahaut was published. The subtitle read: *"The Dangers of Believing in First Impressions."*

CHAPTER THIRTY

You Would Have Been Chosen

(1800–2)

IN A STIRRING PASSAGE Duff Cooper points out that between two visits of Talleyrand to London the whole lifework of Keats, Shelley and Byron had been accomplished. America, in the ten years of Morris's absence, had produced no poetry much if any above the level of his own versifying.

Though Charles Brockden Brown was writing, Washington Irving was a stripling and Talleyrand had seen James Fenimore Cooper, now a boy of eleven, at Otsego Hall. The Connecticut Wits, The Pleiades, Trumbull, David Humphreys, Alsop, Theodore Dwight and Joel Barlow were scribbling Addisonian imitations, but a hundred and twenty-five years later Professor Beers of Yale said he was the only living man who had read through Barlow's *The Columbiad.*

It is doubtful if anything in America was being written superior of their kind to Burr's letters to his daughter, or at once so valuable and fascinating as the *Diaries* Morris brought home with him.

New York City had grown to over 50,000 people, still scourged every summer with yellow fever, and it was estimated that a seventh of its families were in the liquor trade. The city was filthy and noisy, from the cries of the chimney sweeps at dawn, those of the rusk and gingerbread vendors during the day, until that of the pimps calling "Hoboy" at midnight.

The composite picture of Gouverneur Morris from 1800 until his death in 1816, left us by previous writers, is of a mellow sage, remote from strife and strain, happy in the visits of "old friends," sitting out the sunset years in calm reflection, and dying at last painlessly at a ripe age. Such a sundown, twilight and evening bell is always dismaying to a biographer who would hold his readers' interest to the end.

Fortunately for Morris, and his biographers, the evening of his life was not, in Wordsworth's phrase, breathless as a nun at her devotions, but lit with lightnings and filled with night music.

The last sixteen were years of enormous physical and mental activity filled with the jangle of affairs, the toil of public service, human troubles and disasters, all met with his basic gaiety, generosity and good sense.

The Wild Lands of New York, north of the Mohawk, west of the Adirondacks, were the scene of much of this. There he and his friends left their names, their houses and their legends at Ogdensburg on the St. Lawrence and at Gouverneur, Le Raysville, Chaumont Bay, Parishville and Constableville. The house of Constable and Morris's own summer house are still standing. Near Watertown is the beautiful house of James Le Ray de Chaumont, whose father's house at Passy was occupied by Franklin.

The ten townships, 1000 square miles, of Macomb's Purchase of 1787 brought bankruptcy to some, ultimate wealth to others. Even a Dauphin, Eleazar Williams, was said to be there and the landowner James Le Ray to be only an agent of the French Government, set to watch him.

All the last sixteen years Morris traveled this wilderness. Halfway through those years, when he was six months in the North, he apparently asked himself, "Now what can I do to have the last act of my life live up to the standards of glamorous audacity I set long ago?" And having seen how to do it, he proceeded accordingly.

His brother-in-law, the Rev. Isaac Wilkins, had now become rector of St. Peter's Church, Westchester, near Morrisania and on the last day of March he came to see Morris, probably aware of his pending departure to serve out the term of James Watson in the American Senate.

We must remember that we see these Wilkins-Ogden brothers-in-law and their sons and daughters not only in the Morris *Diaries* and letters and those of his wife but in their own letters and the impression is not edifying.

The Rev. Wilkins now asked again if Morris intended doing anything for his son. Morris reminded him of what he had offered in connection with his St. Lawrence lands and of the son's refusal. Since he had refused, the son might find himself something more agreeable. He meant to do nothing for him.

A week later his appointment to the Senate was confirmed, and on May 3 he took the oath at the first session of the Sixth Congress then sitting in Philadelphia. The other New York senator had a familiar name as we shall shortly see. Morris's first official act was a motion to amend the compensation of our diplomats abroad, which was carried. He dined that night in jail with Robert Morris, *amici usque.*

On the fourteenth, he was of course in the noes who defeated, 14–5, "an act to permit in certain cases the bringing of slaves into the Mississippi Territory" and with the ayes who, 13–4, voted the prosecution of William Duane for his slander of Federalists in the *Aurora Gazette.*

The Senate adjourned that day for the last time in Philadelphia. When they reconvened in the early winter it would be in Washington.

Pickering was removed as Secretary of State by President Adams and John Marshall appointed just before the adjournment. Morris brought Pickering's letter about it back to Hamilton. The letter told how when asked to resign he had requested three months to do so. "In an hour I got a peremptory discharge."

Strange political rumors were afloat of a coalition between Adams and Jefferson and of an effort by New York Federalists to bring Aaron Burr into their fold, but "the thing which in my opinion has done most mischief to the Federal party," Morris wrote Rufus King, now minister in London, "is the ground given by some of them to believe that they wish to establish a monarchy."

The loss of Washington still seemed to some irreparable, but Morris added confidently to King, "*Nil desperandum de Republica* is a sound principle. Let the chair of office be filled by whosoever it may, the opposition will act as an outward conscience and prevent the abuse of power."

There is an interesting echo from the past in a letter of Morris's of that June to Charles Pettit found in the Gallatin Papers. Pettit, now sixty-four, had been in the quartermaster general's office during the Revolution and apparently some question had now arisen in regard to it and he had appealed to Morris for his recollection. Morris replied at once that he recalled it very clearly. He had drafted the letter to Congress on which the appointment was made. General Greene had refused to be Q.M.G., unless he could also retain command of his division in the field. He had felt forced to this because of wild civilian charges that he wished to leave the field because of cowardice, and he had also said unless he could have Pettit and Cox as aides he would not take it at all. How perennial are the slanders of politics.

Three days before it was written Adèle's boy, fifteen years old, "sat his horse through the long summer day at Marengo, when the smoke hung over the vineyards and Desaix came up, with the long shadows, from the south." To join the army he had overstated his age by a year to Napoleon and in Paris his father and Fouché were working separately on plans should Napoleon fail or perish.

There were other links to the past. Monroe wrote to Citizen Genêt what must be one of the very few funny if bitter remarks he ever made.

Porcelain entrusted to us by our esteemed friend, Mme. Campan, for you is unpacked at Alexandria. It would have been sent but I am afraid in the infatuated state of the public mind it might be considered proof of a conspiracy against the government and of treasonable correspondence with France.

Monroe closed his letter to Genêt: "as a friend of free government your name will be recorded in history." How could anyone believe that except Monroe?

And while Morris was at Lake George, Robert Troup wrote
Rufus King:

> Armstrong has lately published some of the most virulent and
> Jacobinical pieces against the Administration of the government
> and particularly against General Washington, Hamilton, Jay and
> Gouverneur Morris. I never have believed and I never shall believe
> after his attempt to create a mutiny in the army at the close of the
> Revolutionary War that he has a heart fit to be trusted with any
> important interests of his country. I allude to his celebrated address
> to the soldiers.

This was John Armstrong, now forty-two, and senior senator
from New York, married to Eliza Livingston. How amazingly
these people come back and back on the stage and how completely they always stay in character. It is interesting that Troup
should have been so sure that the heart of the author of the
Newburgh Addresses was not fit to be trusted with the interests of his country, but that with his improper drawings as a
Treasury official at the same time he could still be trusted.

In July, Morris started for the North, the lakes and Montreal,
the journey described in wonderful detail in a long letter to
Parish. It is the letter of the prophet-discoverer, and says, "The
proudest empire in Europe is but a bubble compared to what
America will be, must be in the course of two centuries." He
saw Niagara Falls and dined in Montreal with Sir John Johnson
who, twenty years before with his Tories and his savages, had
scourged New York to the very doors of Johnson Hall. After
dinner Morris "danced, that is hobbled."

In the fall Spain ceded Louisiana to France in return for
Tuscany and the election of a new American President went
into the House as Jefferson and Burr each received 73 votes
and Adams and Pinckney 65 and 64 respectively.

On November 11, Morris set out for Washington, the journey
taking eleven days with a stop in Philadelphia. He dined with
the President on December 4. It was dirty weather and a dark

evening within and without, when he dined with Elizabeth
Plater's son on the ninth.

On Christmas Eve in Paris an attempt was made to assassinate
Napoleon on his way to the Opera House, and Lord Wycombe,
who was in the street, went back to his hotel to tell Lady Holland about it.

Very shortly afterwards a busy little novelist wrote her publisher the letter that novelists always write their publishers.

First here is a letter for M. de Pesnay, translator of *d'Agathon,*
and I ask you to have the kindness to send it to him and to include
with it a *copy* of my book, *Charles and Marie.* Will you also be good
enough to send me the number of the *Gazette of France* which
speaks of my book and tell me to whom I am indebted for the nice
review. The sale has commenced? Does it go a little? I am going to
work to give you a book which will not be so short.

Adieu etc.
A. Flahaut

P.S. Please send 5 copies of *C. et M.* with that of M. de Pesnay to
[indecipherable] I beg you to make note of this.

It was followed shortly by another one, equally familiar:

I came up from the country two days ago and am leaving immediately which will prevent me from having the pleasure of seeing you.
I pray you to be good enough to send me what is left of my money,
as I have several hundreds to pay which much torments me. I enclose a receipt with the amount in blank as I do not know the exact
total.

Believe me etc.
A. Flahaut

P.S. Please be good enough to send me my money in a sealed
envelope. If I can find a moment before going to my little property
it will be to go to thank you and ask pardon for my importunity.

The immediate vital issues facing the Sixth Congress sitting
in its new Capitol were the choice of Jefferson or Burr to be
President and the new treaty with Napoleon, the First Consul.

Like their French brethren ten years before, the representatives of the great American people were not without thought
for the lighter side of life. When Jonathan Dayton, now forty,
Federalist senator from New Jersey, who had fought at York-

town and sat in the Federal Convention, reached Washington
he told his close friend Morris, perhaps with a sigh of regret at
being in Washington, that the morals of the women in Philadelphia were very corrupt. Morris said he doubted it.

He had just written his often-quoted letter to the Princess de
la Tour et Taxis in Ratisbon, saying:

We want nothing here [in Washington] but houses, cellars,
kitchens, well informed men, amiable women and other little trifles
of this kind, to make our city perfect; for we can walk here as if in
the fields and woods. . . . [It] is the very best city in the world for
a future residence.

As to the "amiable women," Dayton and he drank tea and
sat "near two hours" with Margaret Bayard Smith, something
she thought would make her sister smile. She was the new
bride of her cousin, Samuel Harrison Smith, then twenty-nine,
who had followed Jefferson to Washington from Philadelphia
at his invitation to publish a weekly and a triweekly paper.
There was a touch of a Paris salon about her house. A stranger,
his "countenance beaming with an expression of benevolence
and with a manner and voice almost femininely soft and gentle
[had called and drawn her] into observations of a more personal and interesting nature . . . there was something in his
countenance and voice that at once unlocked my heart." She
did not know who he was until her husband entered "and introduced the stranger as Mr. Jefferson. I felt my cheeks burn and
my heart throb."

The issues of the French treaty were briefly these: America
demanded indemnity for the destruction of property (ships
and cargoes) by the French Republic; the old treaty of alliance
was no longer binding and would not be renewed; and America
did not guarantee French possessions in this country. Napoleon
offered full indemnity if the alliance continued, or none with a
new treaty.

Morris wrote Hamilton:

The First Consul, if the dice run against him, will agree to our
offer. If they run in his favor he may reject it. . . . I think France

has pushed as far as reason will justify. [The Peace of Lunéville shortly gave her frontiers of the Rhine and the Adige and increased her population by one sixth.] Should she go further in Italy and eastward in Germany, the Austrians by rapid movements to a central position possibly may give the Consul a blow he will never recover.

As to who would be President—the candidates are "equal in worth . . . or equally void of it," Burr's "defects do not arise from want of energy and vigour." People believe "to courage he joins generosity . . . but they consider Jefferson as infected with all the cold-blooded vices . . . and the slave of Virginia." On the whole he believes Burr will win. It is a difficult choice for him. Jefferson, in his view, was a Utopian and Washington had rejected Burr, to succeed Morris in France, because of a doubt of the integrity of his character.

Balloting began February 11, with a heavy snow falling in the capital. By the fourteenth there had been 32 roll calls without a decisive vote.

Jefferson wrote that "coming out of the Senate Chamber [that day] I found Gouverneur Morris on the steps." Morris said the minority were opposed to Jefferson because they believed he would turn all the Federalists out, put down the navy and wipe off the public debt. He urged Jefferson to have his friends disavow this for him. Jefferson refused.

On the seventeenth Jefferson was elected, Adams naming John Marshall, his adversary, Chief Justice before the inaguration.

Morris replied to Jefferson's Farewell to the Senate, regretting, on their behalf, the loss of "that intelligent attention and impartiality [which Mr. Jefferson as our presiding officer has given proceedings and giving to him] assurance of our constitutional support of your Administration." A motion to alter the speech was defeated 19–9 and Jefferson in his Inaugural said as magnanimously, "We are all Republicans. We are all Federalists."

There was a great might-have-been to all this which Morris never mentioned.

His friend Robert R. Livingston had written him:

I learn with much regret that circumstances rendered it in your opinion inadvisable to become a candidate for the office of governor . . . your just claims are more than neglected. Had you run with Jefferson you would beyond all question under the present circumstances have been chosen by the [House of] Representatives to fill the first office of the Union.

Looking back over Morris's life for thirty years, one might well conclude that if he had married Kitty Livingston and "settled down" with that enchanting girl he might have been the third President.

All he said in reply was, "If, as you suppose, I had the helm of the ship, I should steer differently but whether better or worse it is not for me to say."

On the day after Jefferson's inauguration Morris wrote Livingston, "We have just now approved (unanimously) of your nomination to be minister plenipotentiary to the French Republic. Accept my congratulations. . . . I believe I can be of some little use . . . before you go."

We do not know what these two close friends said to each other. With whatever estimates of French political figures Morris gave Livingston, it seems unquestionable that he must have mentioned Adèle.

Information about her may be in the cipher portions of Livingston's letters or the letters which were not copied. Livingston did write Morris in June, "You told me when I left you that I should return an aristocrat. . . . I believe you were right."

Morris offered him a small "tho' a very beautiful service of plate . . . dishes, casserolles (or vegetable dishes), sauce boats and plates. [They] are more necessary than you imagine. Your French servants will knock china plates to pieces very fast and the servants of your guests will do the same thing."

Two years later the new Portuguese envoy in Paris with his wife must have dined at the American Legation. As the service was set before her, did she think, "But this is the very plate I chose with Gouverneur, *mon Dieu*, eleven years ago"?

Morris started home on the eighth, taking ten hours to go the twenty-four miles to Annapolis. There were "cash only" signs on all the inns and shops and appropriately Morris visited Robert Morris, still in jail in Philadelphia.

In May, as Jefferson wrote Monroe of his anxiety that France, instead of Spain, had Louisiana and Florida—"not so [as with weak Spain] can it ever be with France"—Morris was making his garden and Wilkins had sent someone to ask him to endorse a note. A coroner's inquest had acquitted a frail mother of infanticide, which he was glad of.

Morrisania was divine, "built on the shore of an arm of the sea six times broader than [the Danube at Ratisbon] and over which pass daily several dozen ships of all sizes." He says the landscape is *riant* (smiling, laughing, pleasant, the word most applied to Adèle).

He sailed to New York in his own boat, tying up at the foot of Wall Street to visit the Bank of Manhattan. Dayton and Burr came to dinner, Burr with news of Nelson's bombardment of Copenhagen. Benedict Arnold died in England. Morris wrote Le Ray de Chaumont to send him "a chasseur who understood fishing" and a cook. Both should be elderly or they could not be depended on to stay.

Young Isaac Wilkins, who had married without visible means of support, came to mollify him and was given a deaf ear, though a little later Morris sent him a thousand dollars.

Even a Lowell of Boston, young John, the Rebel, aged thirty-two, wrote his wife, Rebecca Amory, "Yesterday I dined with Gouverneur Morris, one of the most extraordinary men of our country. Few men of this nation exceed him in genius and no one equals him in good breeding. He is a perfect courtier, bred in the court of France, prior to the Revolution, or at least improved by it, having been our ambassador there in the most eventful period of its history. His house, furniture and style of living are all after the model and not inferior to that of the French nobility."

Lowell at the time was concerned in a piece of *curiosa* equal to any Morris had heard of in Europe, and it must have fascinated him, as such things did, if Lowell told him about it.

The first capital crime in a hundred and sixty-five years, an American tragedy indeed, had occurred in Dedham, Massachusetts. A strange boy of twenty, Jason Fairbanks, had murdered a girl of fourteen, Betsy Fales, and John Lowell had defended him. The defense was that the girl committed suicide. Ferris Greenslet wonders what the later Freudians would make of the fact that Fairbanks had been suckled by his own sister. He was found guilty, escaped and was caught on the shores of Lake Champlain, brought back and hanged.

During that summer the New York *Post* was founded by Hamilton as a Federalist opposition to the powerful and vicious Republican papers of Callender, Duane, Bache and later Thomas Paine. The Founders' List extant is not complete but there can be little doubt that Morris was one of them.

Yellow fever raged in the city into October, but failed to cross any of the New York rivers, and late in the month, with the Ogdens and Wilkins families at dinner, Morris had green peas and lima beans from his garden.

That week, in her then beautiful script, Nancy Randolph, still at Bizarre, wrote her friend Mrs. Taylor:

Your good husband occasioned me much chagrin by not calling when he was so near . . . you cannot conceive of my anxiety to see you. I have a considerable fever at this moment and my breast is entirely without skin. There was a blister put on it a few nights ago. However, I discharge all the family business and pay my constant attention to Mrs. [Dudley] and her child. Heaven surely assists me or I should sink. My breast is in violent pain and therefore you will pardon this hurried scrawl.

Yours ever A.R.

The preliminary treaty [of Amiens], "the truce of [French] exhaustion," had been signed on the first of October and Talleyrand had wonderfully outmanoeuvered Cornwallis, the English envoy, twenty years after Yorktown.

The first issue of the *Post* was November 16. A week later, with dreadful augury, Hamilton's boy, Philip, nineteen, died of a wound received in a duel in which he did not fire, fought because of a slur on his father. In December the paper carried three articles by Morris on the meaning of the peace to America. "No doubt can [now] be reasonably entertained," he wrote Jay, "of the prosperity, power and glory of our country if we preserve our union and form of government, in a word if we be not wanting to ourselves."

On December 8, Morris packed up and set off for Washington after more snug, pleasant days rearranging his books. On Christmas Eve he called on President Jefferson. The French Ambassador de Pichon, who had been Genêt's secretary, was there with his wife and they seemed to think the society of the capital was dull. Certainly three highly "intelligent men" were there, but perhaps two of them were thinking of "amiable women," like Adèle and Madame de Corny far away. It had been ten years since the little supper at the Louvre with Adèle and Madame d'Albani and the niece.

In the short period between Jefferson's election and inauguration, February-March, the previous year, the Federalists had pushed a Judiciary Bill through the Senate creating seven new district and sixteen circuit judges. President Adams had signed the bill and the places had gone to Federalist appointees.

In 1802, Jefferson's Administration and Senate majority proposed to repeal the bill, largely on the grounds of economy and lack of necessity. The Federalists held that the Republicans' only motive was rage that their party members had not been appointed. The move to repeal was a vital issue, and in large measure Morris headed the opposition.

On January 8 and 15 he made two powerful speeches against it, the text, for the first time reported "by a short hand writer on the floor," running to 40 pages, about 17,000 words. His points of attack were two: first, that repeal was unconstitutional; second, that the economies were unnecessary and absurd.

The first point, which in Theodore Roosevelt's opinion, as a young man of twenty-eight or twenty-nine, Morris exaggerated, had a good deal of validity at the time, and perhaps since, as efforts have been made to upset "the checks and balances."

Once inferior courts were established, as they were by the bill, Morris held the "power shall (not may) vest in them and their judges" hold office during good behavior. "If as a precedent, Congress could *ex post facto* destroy such courts, [then]

the people of America have vested all power incontinent in the
national legislature." With memories of his advice to Louis
XVI doubtless in his mind, he said, "They have not done so,
they have provided a check of the first necessity to prevent an
invasion of the Constitution by unconstitutional laws."

It must be remembered that the American Government was
only thirteen years old. There were still Federalists, as Morris
had told Hamilton, who wanted a monarchy, and there were
Virginians and men from the Western Waters whom the Federalists believed capable of any anarchy.

From a practical point of view, Morris asked whether, with
the increase of population and litigation, it was intended that
"six justices of the Supreme Court, men advanced in years, they
alone having [the necessary] maturity of judgment . . . shall
continually run from one end of the continent to the other,"
holding court. As to the added cost of the new circuits, it
amounted to one cent a man in the country. These "ostentatious
economies" were ridiculous. Was it proposed to abolish the
Mint because with expenses of $25,144.44 and salaries of
$10,600 it coined $10,473.29 in cents and half cents a year?

He closed with a good deal of rhetoric, it is true, but he is in
character as to moderation and good will when he says to the
Democrats, "Has [the measure] been passed in a manner which
wounded your pride, or roused your resentment? [Then] let us
join to remedy the defects. Have the magnanimity to pardon
that offense. I intreat, I implore you to sacrifice those angry
passions to the interests of our country. Pour out this pride of
opinion on the altar of patriotism. . . . Do not, I beseech you,
commit the dignity, the harmony, the existence of our nation
to the wild wind."

It was like the Paris days, after the first speech, to go to tea
at Jefferson's and see Dolly Madison come in with Mrs. Robert
Morris. He thought "Mrs. Madison has good dispositions [his
euphemism in France for likely acquiescence] which from the
shrivelled condition of the Secretary [of State, Madison] are
less to be wondered at."

There had evidently been no woman for some time and he
must have wondered about Mrs. Madison, with the rather silly,

good-natured face and very low round neck of James Peale's portrait.

There were two bars to any love affair between them, of which he was evidently unaware. Mrs. Madison was both virtuous and devotedly in love with her husband. But if this had not been the case there was an even stronger taboo. Aaron Burr wrote in his *Diary*, "Oh [her] unfortunate propensity to snuff-taking"! That propensity had saved several women's virtue from Morris.

After Morris's second speech, Vice-President Burr called, "disposed to go with us on the Judiciary." There was another link to the past in Paris. Jefferson and he had been at one in thinking that debate in the National Assembly was largely "bawling and hallooing." In Adèle's salon Morris had often sat as critic at Talleyrand's rehearsals of his speeches. It was therefore with pardonable pride that Morris, after these speeches had been printed, sent copies to Robert Livingston, the minister in Paris, with a note saying, "Send one of them with my compliments to M. Talleyrand who may perhaps recollect that we were once acquainted."

The repeal passed, however, in February and Morris, dining with Jefferson afterwards, found him, as in the past, "Utopia quite."

Morris's constituents in '79 had felt he neglected New York interests for national ones. In April 1802 he pushed through one piece of legislation of importance to his city and himself, "a light-house bill to provide security for sound navigation."

His gout was bothering him that spring, "squeezing my ankle and instep," he wrote Constable, who was also "harassed" by it. The letter is about a Constable-Le Ray de Chaumont sale of lands. Morris executes the necessary papers, observing that "the description of 'tracts of 10000 to 50000 acres' from running around them must be a piece of guess work."

During the summer Robert Morris was discharged penniless and homeless from jail. Morris brought him at once to his home. He wrote Parish about it later:

He came to me lean, low-spirited, and as poor as a commission of bankrupters can make a man whose effects will, it is said, not pay

a shilling in the pound. Indeed the assignees will not take the
trouble of looking after them. I sent him home fat, sleek in good
spirits and possessed of the means of living comfortably the rest of
his days. So much for the air of Morrisania.

It was not the salubrious air alone which revived the broken
man. Morris gave him an annuity "of a present value of $15000,"
though he did not tell Parish so.

Just before adjournment he had gone down to Mount Vernon.
"The old lady [seventy-one] is indisposed but as usual very
kind." Her life was drawing to a close and when Morris reached
New York it was to hear of her death and more poignantly that
of the lovely Sally Jay, leaving John Jay inconsolable. Madame
de Staël's husband, still Swedish ambassador in France, died
almost the same day but neither Minette nor Benjamin Constant was inconsolable.

Late that summer Lady Bessborough wrote a letter from
Paris to her friend, Lord Granville Leveson-Gower, with the
news that "Madame de Flahaut is married to M. de Souza. I
heard it before but did not believe it."

The lovely and indomitable "*faiseuse de romans et de bonnets*" had won her Seven Years' War.

José Maria de Souza-Botelho Mourão e Vasconcellos, six
years younger than Morris, a descendant of Vasco da Gama's
lieutenant, a distinguished diplomat and man of letters, had
been Portuguese minister to Denmark in 1795, when he first
read *Adèle de Sénanges* and went to meet its author. For two
years she had expected marriage would follow and then, like
Morris and Wycombe and Talleyrand, De Souza left her. There
appears to be no record of anything between them from the
April of 1797 to that of 1802. In the interval De Souza had been
ambassador at Madrid, but on April 8, 1802, he had presented
his credentials to Talleyrand as ambassador in Paris.

The story is, and doubtless true, that Talleyrand with unusual
considerateness arranged for Adèle to meet De Souza again,
though perhaps De Souza's is the undecipherable name to
whom she had asked her publisher to send *Charles et Marie*.

Talleyrand was now living in the palace on the Rue St.

Florentin, once the Venetian Embassy to which Count de Flahaut had taken his wounded friend, August '92. As this book
is being written, the Hotel Talleyrand is Paris headquarters of
the Economic Co-operation Administration. It is pleasing to
note that in a 4-page release of theirs describing the hotel this
grave body says it "has been the setting for history-making
intrigue, *world-famous love affairs* and crucial international
conferences."

"I have married you," De Souza told his wife, "in order that
you would make me laugh and I am grateful at having succeeded."

Lady Holland listed "those who dined with us from July to
September . . . Mme. de Flahaut. A volume would not suffice
[to describe her]. An agreeable adventuress who after failing in
various projects both upon Englishmen and Frenchmen at last
has closed her tempestuous career by marrying De Souza. She
has written some pretty novels—and her son, a fine and open
young man is handsome and uncommonly engaging in manners
and courtesy."

Finally Fanny Burney d'Arblay, writing to Miss Planta for
the English Queen and Princess to read, said "the second acquaintance . . . is a lady, Mme. de Souza. She soon found the
road to my good will and regard . . . she charmed and delighted me and we struck up an intimacy without further delay."

The news must somehow have reached Morris, though he
makes no mention of it and his many correspondents' letters are
not available. In the normal round of diplomatic dinners the
Livingstons must have dined at Talleyrand's, the Foreign Minister's, with the De Souzas there. Perhaps with his deafness
Livingston did not understand who Adèle had been. Certainly,
if from no other source, Morris learned it when William Short
came back toward the end of the year with his hopes of Rosalie
all but gone.

Or perhaps Tom Paine, who came home October 30 to stay
with Jefferson, told someone. He must have brought word that
Talleyrand, in defiance of Napoleon and the Vatican, had married and settled a fortune on the mistress, Madame Grand, he

had met in London in '92 when she "was little better than a woman of the town."

On the other side of Talleyrand's life, Livingston warned him in November that perhaps "we shall negotiate no further [about Louisiana] but advise our government to take possession."

CHAPTER THIRTY-ONE

Little Men May Succeed
Where Great Fail

(*1803*)

O N JANUARY 10, Jefferson wrote Monroe, "I shall nominate you tomorrow for an extraordinary mission to France." The appointment of this scion of "the Virginia House of Bourbon" to handle the Louisiana business naturally annoyed Morris. He wrote to Parish:

[Jefferson] by his appointment of Monroe is a true Christian [taking] special care that a stone which the builders rejected should be the first of the corner. . . . Jefferson believes in the perfectability of man, the wisdom of mobs, and the moderation of Jacobins. He believes in the payment of debts by diminishing of revenue and in the vindication of rights by appointment of ambassadors.

It is remarkable to see how this opinionated man almost invariably remembered Cromwell's adage, "Ye may be mistaken." He wrote to Livingston, "It is possible that I am unjust to Mr. Monroe but really I consider him as a person of mediocrity in every respect."

In brief Monroe's instructions were to offer up to ten million dollars for Louisiana, leaving France with the west bank of the Mississippi if nothing else would do. If Napoleon would not sell, then the right of deposit of American goods in New Orleans should be renewed. As for Monroe himself, if he failed he could probably have the legation in London.

Shortly before Monroe's departure Morris made his last speech in the Senate, having failed of reappointment by old Governor George Clinton.

He said he believed it was "the last scene of his public life" but he would not use a "pomp of words" about it. Speaking *against* the Federalist policies, he said that to avow peace and commerce as our policy was to leave us with neither of them. He outlined the sweep of Napoleon's domination and said moderation in dealing with him was a vain delusion. "When in any plan Napoleon fails, he falls [and] he will rule here unless by vigorous exertions you set a bound to his power." In his old biting and unpopular way he said he hoped "gentlemen [who] seemed afraid of information [would not] next be terrified at that other hideous spectre, common sense." And as to the violent controversy still raging over the judiciary, he said, "[Federal] judges will never be so wild, so absurd, so mad as to pretend that they are superior to the legislative power of America . . . the same sense of decency and self-respect will, I trust, prevent the Senate from claiming a superiority over the judges. I hope we shall not declare the Senate is superior to the law."

William Barry, then nineteen, later minister to Spain, reading it in Jessamine County, Kentucky, wrote his brother, "G. Morris has rung the alarm bell in the Senate and portrayed in a lengthy and eloquent speech the danger of delay [in leaving Louisiana in French hands]."

As in his past, Morris was still thinking of Paphian pleasures. His *Diary* records a series of calls on a Mrs. Morton and they are described with the light wickedness he has not used since the days in Vienna or Berlin. The lady is alternately receptive and "indisposed (this is *en règle*)" and pestered by the jealousy of her husband. At two of his visits she tells him a curious history, and at last in Philadelphia, on his way home, he secured from her most of what he wanted.

There can be little doubt that she was Mrs. Perez Morton, now forty-four, born Sarah Wentworth Apthorp, and that the strange history was that of her sister's suicide after Perez Morton had seduced her. Like Adèle, she was a writer. The *Massachusetts Magazine* had published the lyrics in '89 and the novel,

The Power of Sympathy, dealing with the tragedy had been published that year.

In Washington and Philadelphia in 1802 she had sat to Gilbert Stuart for three portraits, one of them perhaps the loveliest painted in America.

Dolly Madison's sister Anna wrote the following spring of dining at the Mortons' "extensive, pleasant place . . . believe me, had I her establishment, I would never quit it for anything in Washington . . . a handsome dinner and a pleasant party with a dash of Loo [shades of the Louvre] in the evening. . . . The Federalist party in Boston prevails."

When, in July 1803, Morris dined twice with the Mortons in Boston, "monsieur was cordial all things considered."

It seems likely that this beautiful woman felt some revenge on Perez Morton was long overdue.

As Monroe landed at Havre, William Short dined at Morrisania. How much they must have had to say to each other, not only of Monroe's mission, and Talleyrand, and the diplomatic difficulties they both knew so well, but also of whether, having loved the two French women they had, they would ever marry anyone else. Their destinies had affected them differently. Morris's face, even in Sharples's later portrait, is still that of an amused and serene man who knows, as he said, that "the art of living consists, I think, in some degree in knowing how to be cheated." By contrast, Short's small, troubled face is like that of the traditional spinster aunt of the 1880s.

Although the Louisiana Purchase was signed with Monroe present, his biographers have lamented that the actual bargain was struck between Talleyrand and Livingston just before Monroe's arrival, so that he signed a *fait accompli,* at five million dollars more than he was authorized to offer.

With a fellow New Yorker's pride in the city's mercantile tradition, Morris had said in his letter to Livingston, "I trust it will not be pretended that the application of money could not be as safely entrusted to your care and intelligence as to those of Mr. Monroe."

On Easter Sunday, Napoleon had hinted to Marbois that he was prepared to cede Louisiana, as beyond the French power to occupy or administer. Talleyrand at once asked Livingston what he would pay for the whole territory, intimating that he would consider twelve million dollars and the assumption by the United States of claims of its nationals against France of twenty million francs (four million dollars). Livingston, like a good trader, counteroffered with $11,250,000 cash and $3,750,-000 in claims.

When Monroe arrived he was deeply hurt by what had happened. A letter of his, in the recently opened Livingston Papers at the New-York Historical Society, reveals why he missed the bargain. He arrived in Le Havre April 8. "I have this moment arrived . . . the post sets out in a few minutes [and I hasten] to inform you of my arrival." His family and he are so fatigued by the voyage that "there will be a delay of a day or so before going to Paris."

Margaret Bayard Smith wrote her husband what they were saying in New York as to how it had been done:

It is said that when Mr. King [in London] expressed his uneasiness at the conduct of the Spanish intendant [in New Orleans] the English ministers assured him he need be in no ways anxious because war would soon take place, in which case the British would immediately take possession of Lous'na and as they would be our neighbors and friends, we need have no apprehensions about the French. On this information, Mr. King wrote the same to Livingston who urged ties to the French Administration as a motive for giving up that territory to us, thereby preventing their enemy from gaining such valuable territory . . . this proved effectual and the whole transaction was settled before Monroe arrived.

King came home from London two weeks after the signing. At the seaport he saw the recalled French and British ambassadors from London and Paris pass each other. He also saw Admiral Lord St. Vincent, and he appealed to him, as his last word, as Morris had to Leeds twelve years before. The appeal, in the interests of both countries, was to the British to give up impressment of American sailors.

In letters from Morris of May 23 and 24 to John Dickinson and Robert Morris there is an unconscious presage of events six years later. Morris's irrelevant use of connubial metaphors in political talks has been previously noted. He wrote now to Dickinson, "In adopting a republican form of government I not only took it as a man does his wife, for better, for worse, but what few men do with their wives, I took it knowing all its bad qualities." Then with his irrepressible lightness, whatever his age, he wrote Robert Morris:

If I should meet that enchanting Yankee [on my New England tour] whom you speak of I will endeavor to oppose the power of reason to the fascination of the enchantress. I have, you know, in my drawing room the picture in tapestry of Telemache rescued from the charms of Circe . . . marriage, especially at my time of life [fifty-one] should be more a matter of prudence than of passion. Good sense and good nature are of more importance than wit and beauty.

When the time came he lived up completely to his letter to Dickinson and threw the prudence, of which he had written to Morris, gallantly out the window.

John Rutledge, southward bound from Massachusetts, passed him on his way to New England and wrote a hilarious letter to Harrison Gray Otis of the encounter, July 17:

Thursday night at 10 o'clock I arrived in the dark and rain at Pomfret where I heard a chattering of French and upon entering the inn found Gou're Morris with two French valets, a French travelling companion and his hair buckled up in about a hundred papilliottes. His wooden leg, papilliottes, French attendants and French conversation made his host, hostess, their daughters and granddaughter with the whole family including the hostler and Betty, the cook maid, stare most prodiguously and gave me some idea how the natives looked when poor Cooke made his entree at the friendly isles [of the South Pacific]. When I arrive at a village where I the next day dined, the landlord, who proved to be a Federalist told me Governor Clinton from New York had passed by the day before in a coach by himself, *and his son in law, Mr. Genêt* in company in another coach and together they had three French servants . . . [another man swore] these fellows were not going to Boston for anything good, they were three devils. [When I told him it was Gou're Morris] he made many apologies (and regrets that he had not conversed) with the great man.

While no apology need be made for a man of the time who was expertly valeted, it was probably, in Morris's case, less than ordinarily an indication of vanity or foppishness. The "un-sighted" are taught today that they must, as a matter of self-respect, be several times as careful of their appearance as the "sighted." So with a one-legged man.

The day Rutledge wrote was that of the death of the wretched James Thomson Callender, author of the vicious personal attacks, first on Hamilton, then on his own benefactor, Jefferson, who had signed his pardon. Callender drowned, drunk and penniless.

Long ago Adèle had told Morris that Jefferson was *"faux et emporté,"* qualities hard to translate in conjunction. A two-faced fanatic? Deceitful and (yet) uncontrolled?

Certainly in the Callender case, in his smoothing down of Short's disappointment over Paris in '92, and his dangling of the Louisiana governorship before Monroe, Adèle was right about the great Jefferson, and he was *"emporté"* over Callender and very *"faux."*

Callender began in '96, with vicious attacks on Washington for sacrificing Monroe "because [Monroe] loved France." Jefferson loaned him money for further writing. In 1800, Callender was tried and found guilty under the Sedition Laws for an attack on President Adams, fined, with a prison term of nine months in Richmond. Justice Chase pointed out at the trial the difference between liberty and licentiousness in the press. Jefferson visited Callender in jail.

Upon Jefferson's inauguration, Callender asked him to remit the fine and set him free. Chief Justice Marshall refused assent and Callender wrote Madison a letter close to extortion and blackmail, saying Jefferson had done nothing.

On May 26, Jefferson wrote Monroe that he thought it best to avoid having Congress know about it and that the fine should be made up "by private contribution." He enclosed a quarter of it, fifty dollars.

Three days later Jefferson wrote again. He said he had given Callender fifty dollars personally but that he received it "not as charity but a due, in fact as hush money. So do not use the draft I sent you. It is long since I wished he would cease writing [on our policies] as he is doing more harm than good. . . . He intimated he was in possession of things he could and would make use of." How impossible it is to think of Morris in such a sly, unpleasant business.

There followed Callender's attack on Jefferson's morals, including the charge that he himself was peopling his plantation by intercourse with his female workers.

The *Diary* from August 24, 1803, to March 17, 1805, and covering the latter portion of the New England trip, is the only volume not in the uniform vellum binding. It is a cheaper book, though the paper is good. Perhaps the British blockade held up deliveries from Paris for the two years.

On August 25 there is a passage of Pauline simplicity and beauty. "We leave Tarrytown with the young flood and beat up against a north wind to enter the highlands where after sunset in a calm at the turn of the tide we cast anchor."

The trip went on overland to Lake Ontario, where with a great surf running, Morris himself took the helm from the pilot and "with no other resolution than my recollection of a former voyage" brought them safely in, later, despite a wooden leg, shooting the St. Lawrence rapids at Lachine.

It was appropriate that, when he got back, his election as honorary member of the Cincinnati, after twenty years, should at last have been received. There appears to be no comment on it by him in *Letter Book* or *Diary*.

Coming back, he began to think about a canal, "five feet deep and forty wide from the head of the Onondaga River to the Mohawk."

The year ended with what now seems incredible Federalist opposition to ratifying the Louisiana Purchase. All the balanced persuasion Morris possessed was used to secure it. He wrote Senator Dayton:

The ratification of the treaty and the subsequent acts for carrying it into effect appear proper. For admitting that Louisiana could have been obtained for less money, which remains to be proved, good faith requires that acts of this sort should be ratified. . . . I am prepared to pay my share of fifteen million to deprive foreigners of all pretext of entering our country. If nothing else were gained by the treaty that alone would satisfy me.

To Roger Griswold:

To blame the amount of the consideration paid might be imprudent for there are many reasons why Federalists should not use the little pretexts of economy, which their opponents so much vaunted formerly, and so much despise now.

It is interesting how his political attitude toward Jefferson on the question differed from his private one. He had said to Dayton, "The President is the organ by which the public will is pronounced, in transactions with foreign powers, and duty to ourselves requires that he be not disavowed, unless for reasons of the highest import." But to Livingston, half forgotten in France, he wrote:

I like well the treaty . . . it would have been generous and manly in the President to have told Congress that his minister in France had, before the arrival of his colleague with powers and instructions, in a manner highly honorable to himself prepared the way and seized the favorable moment to conclude an important negotiation in consequence of which they had in a few days not only realized his expectations, but exceeded his hopes. You have seen the communication actually made. When it was read in my presence, I was obliged to bite my tongue pretty hard to prevent it from telling the true state of that important action.

The Federalist lamentations went on long after ratification, not only over the price, but on the theory that for the United States to govern a territory not part of the federal Union was un-American.

Morris said, "I should indeed have lost all shame as well as pretense to understanding if I did not approve [the Louisiana Purchase]. A few millions more or less in the price [is] a fit subject for democracy to bawl about, but unworthy of notice."

It was true the country needed "a great man to step into the place of Mr. Washington but when I look at the course of events I am led to believe that little men may succeed where great men might fail," always provided the little men are not "a host of moody beggars starving for a time of pell mell, havoc and confusion."

There was one very amusing aspect of America's first attempt to govern a "foreign" territory where English was not the language. Even in 1804 the New Orleans balls were colorful and exotic occasions. The Spanish governor, in good Latin fashion, had preserved order at them by his own presence. General Claiborne, the new American governor, found this beneath his dignity and order was left to the police. It is moderate to say that hell broke loose.

In 1804, Morris came finally to the conclusion of the long correspondence with the Lafayettes over the hundred thousand francs he had personally advanced the marquise during the Terror.

To start with, the evidence of Morris's whole life is that in private money matters he was openhanded and generous to a host of people, those he liked and those he disliked. He was a rich man in 1804, it is true, and out of his wealth he had given large sums and endorsements to Robert Morris and Alexander Hamilton among many others.

Lida Rose McCabe, a biographer of the marquise, says that at the time "Morris had come to a testy and crabbed old age [fifty-two]. In the luxury of his Morrisania estate, with wealth assured, he had evidently brooded over the unsatisfactoriness of his efforts on behalf of the aristocracy. . . . In writing [to the Lafayettes] he seems to have made frequent mention of this loan. Furthermore he took pains to point out what extraordinary profits he might have made had he had the money to put into excellent investments. . . . The principal was 38,000 francs."

Unfortunately the 1888 *Diary and Letters,* edited by Anne Cary Morris, are not much more complete or accurate. They state that "the proposition of M. and Madame de Lafayette to take advantage of a law in France the letter of which made it possible for them to *avoid paying the interest* . . . disconcerted Morris."

The facts appear to be these. Morris gave the marquise a hundred thousand francs (twenty thousand dollars) (more than his salary for two years). By 1802 the Lafayettes were safe in France with enormous debts but with some assets to meet them.

Had Lafayette, like a man, written Morris a normal man's letter, assuming the loan to his wife, setting forth the state of his affairs and asking for its compromise, or even cancellation, there can be no doubt from the evidence of Morris's life that he would have received a handsome and generous reply. Instead of that Lafayette allowed, if indeed he was not the actual author, the lovely and utterly devoted marquise to write Morris on May 29, 1802, a letter, as though her husband had nothing to do with her debts. As with Morris, the whole evidence of her life with her extraordinary husband makes clear that it is a letter dictated to a distraught woman to shield an insipid husband.

One cannot blame her but only the unmanliness of the marquis.

She says that he has a few more resources, thanks to the government, than he has had for a long time. He would regard her debt as personal and pay principal, interest and the profits which Morris could otherwise have made (as he has several times pointed out) but Lafayette cannot take advantage of the handsome behavior of his own creditors.

Under the laws of France this may very well have been so. The trouble was that Lafayette did not write himself.

The marquise then says that the principal of thirty-eight thousand francs, the cash equivalent of the sum she received, with interest at five per cent, comes to fifty-three thousand francs and that can be paid.

She then says that Lafayette believes that the United States may concern itself with the affair and asks Morris to negotiate, with persons richer than Lafayette in America, to arrange for the government to pay him.

Although the letter is full of delicate sarcasm about Morris's "generosity," its general tone is one of distracted assumptions and anxieties.

Presumably the bland assertion that the principal was thirty-five thousand francs—a loss to Morris of thirteen thousand dollars, or, without interest, of over nine thousand dollars—without explanation, without saying "Would you agree that, against our wishes, we take advantage of the law as to the depreciated value of debts during the Terror, and let us settle on that basis, since it is all we can do?"—was too much even for Morris's good manners.

He wrote James Le Ray, his agent in Paris, "Mme. de Lafayette, then a prisoner, seemed very near being sent to the scaffold. To spare to her sensibility the grief of seeing the honor of her husband tarnished I advanced [a hundred thousand francs] for which they now want to pay fifty-three thousand."

"*Soit* [So be it]," he says in the French text, "I consent for I will not, by means of a noisy law suit, appear to be exalting myself at the expense of M. de Lafayette's reputation." To the marquise he wrote very temperately, saying, "You speak of a profit which I might have derived from a pecuniary service I was happy to render you in a critical moment. It was never thought of." No evidence has been found that prior to this time Morris had referred to profits which could have been made with the money (very likely Le Ray handling the matter for him, referred to them of his own accord). "The feeling which made of me your creditor forbade me accepting the mortgage-bond you kindly offered me at the time of your first stay in Hamburg. The same feeling, madame, allows me no observation at the present moment."

He goes on to say that his agent will give a receipt in full settlement and return the one of "seven or eight years ago." As to the United States paying Lafayette's debts, he adds, "You understand, madame, that, under the circumstances, delicacy forbids me taking any part in the deliberations concerning the matter. I can only assure you that in the case I should be paid here I will hasten to return to your husband the sum he shall have paid. *Dites, je vous prie, madame, mille choses de ma part à M. de Lafayette et soyez persuadée du respect et de l'attachement . . .*"

Finally in 1804 the portion was paid and Morris wrote his agent, "Unhappily they will ever bear me a sincere hatred."

On Christmas Eve, three years later, Adrienne de Lafayette died, her last words to the marquis being, "*Je suis toute à vous* [I am all yours]."

Eight years after Morris's death Lafayette was in the United

States and, with Jefferson in penury, was given two hundred thousand dollars and a township of land.

Brand Whitlock, Lafayette's biographer, disposes of his attitude toward Morris by saying Lafayette did not like Morris's "humorless eyes of porcelain blue. . . . Morris, in a word, bored him to death."

Of Lafayette, Anne Cary Morris quotes her ancestor as saying, "There is no drawing the sound of a trumpet from a whistle."

He Lives Literally
Like a Nobleman

(1804-5)

IN WALL STREET on a March day in 1804 a boy of fifteen asked someone the name of the man with the wooden leg he saw coming up from the river to the Bank of Manhattan. He was told it was of course Gouverneur Morris. The boy was John W. Francis, later the famous physician, and almost sixty years later he remembered the day and how Morris's "superb physical organization enlisted attention. Few men ever equalled his commanding bearing."

It is an interesting contrast to what the young Duke of Argyll, son of Morris's host at Inveraray in '95, had said on seeing Talleyrand the March previous—"the most disgusting looking individual I ever saw. . . . His feet are distorted in every possible direction. His having learned to walk steadily with such wretched materials is a proof that he is a man of considerable abilities." Hortense, the young Queen of Holland, mistress of Adèle's son Charles, remembered afterwards how Talleyrand always limped toward the first chair to hold on.

Few men, except the thirty-second President of the United States, and he for a shorter time, have overcome such handicaps to live so fully and magnificently as Morris and Talleyrand.

"Walk to tire myself and attend to the planting of my trees," Morris says in his *Diary* that March, as Talleyrand, hearing of

the ghastly execution of the Duc d'Enghien, perhaps his doing,
asks with his cold nonchalance, "What is there to make a fuss
about?"

But even at peaceful Morrisania there was "thunder and
rain," as another political storm was gathering. Dinner guests
told Morris in April that the Federalists to the north, and in
New England, had agreed to support Burr for governor of New
York.

Timothy Pickering, with his great, beaked nose and thin lips,
and Roger Griswold had begun to talk about a Northern Confederacy to include New York and to split off from the Union
because of the Louisiana Purchase. Hamilton and his wife, bitterly opposed to Burr, dined at Morrisania, and Livingstons and
Schuylers and Mr. and Mrs. Morton, and Lord Selkirk, coming
out to be British minister, whom Morris had not seen since they
had met with John Paul Jones.

Shortly afterwards Rufus King and Hamilton came, after
Burr's candidacy had been defeated.

It was May and Napoleon had become Emperor of the
French.

Jerome Bonaparte and his bride of the previous Christmas
Eve came to dine at Morrisania. She had been Elizabeth Patterson of Baltimore, forbidden by Napoleon, as long as he lived,
to enter the Continent of Europe. It must have been a sprightly
dinner party for a number of reasons. The bride, perhaps to
defy her imperial brother-in-law, continued to dress with the
daring of the Directory. "An almost naked woman," Margaret
Bayard Smith called her. And with them they brought "a young
Englishman of genius," the poet Tom Moore, twenty-five. He
had not yet come to the fame of Byron's farewell

> . . . before I go, Tom Moore,
> Here's a double health to thee!

or the night in Edinburgh when a whole theater audience rose
to cheer as Walter Scott brought him in. But Morris must have
had a peculiar pleasure in talking to him. Moore had just been,
with Lord Wycombe, on the fringe of Emmet's Rising in Ireland. Morris had him to dine again by himself in June, and

Moore from there went north with David B. Ogden to Ogdensburg. It was there he wrote *A Canadian Boat-Song,* preserved in so many collections. It is doubtful whether Morris himself ever wrote worse doggerel:

> Saint of this green isle! hear our prayers,
> Oh, grant us cool heavens and favoring airs.
> Blow, breezes, blow, the stream runs fast,
> The rapids are near, and the daylight's past.

On July 1, Morris went to Hamilton's office "to settle the affairs of William Constable and Company" for whom Hamilton was counsel. It is evident that Hamilton said nothing of Burr's challenge. There is no mention of any trouble between them until the night of the eleventh when Morris came into his house to find Wilkins waiting to tell him Hamilton had been killed by Colonel Burr in a duel that morning.

He went to New York early the next day. Martin Wilkins met him and said that Hamilton was still alive but when Morris reached his bedside Hamilton was unconscious.

Only the news of the death of Elizabeth Plater affected Morris's enormous outward emotional control as did the sight of Hamilton, dying.

"The scene is too powerful for me so that I am obliged to walk in the garden to take breath. After having composed myself I return and sit by his side till he expires." He nerved himself to attend the immediate autopsy and saw how the bullet had passed through the liver into the vertebra.

In the later afternoon, as a shower cooled the hot city, he promised to do the funeral oration the next day "if I can possibly command myself [but] I am wholly unmanned by this day's spectacle."

It has been noted previously that the importance placed at the time on long rhetorical funeral eulogy was one of the few customs of the age distinct from the present day. The funeral orations over the Athenian dead and Caesar's body were still the things men felt necessary. It is obvious that Morris felt strongly against such parades of sentiment and did them badly.

To his balanced logical mind an oration over Hamilton presented special difficulties. He must, as he said to himself, "pass over handsomely" Hamilton's illegitimacy, and forget how often he was "indiscreet, vain and opinionated." And that he opposed a republic and favored a monarchy, and that since Hamilton had "foolishly published the avowal of conjugal infidelity," in the Reynolds case, he could not dwell on the joys of his domestic life. With the whole city in agitation he must and "will not excite to any outrage on Colonel Burr," whom he "must consider in the same light with any other man who had killed another in a duel. All these points must be reconciled."

He felt the oration to be a failure, like the one for Washington at which Troup had said Morris had not drawn a tear, but he said, perhaps thinking of Plutarch on Marc Antony, "How easy it would have been to make them for a moment absolutely mad." As it was, the Francis boy, sitting on the altar steps at Trinity below him, saw Coleman, editor of the New York *Post*, crying, and that night Coleman came to Morris to ask for the oration, as he had been so overcome by it that his own notes were useless.

On one point there was no dilemma in Morris's practical mind. Means to provide for Hamilton's wife and six children must be found at once.

By the seventeenth Archibald Gracie had a form of public subscription ready, which Morris thought the wrong way to go about it. He thought "twenty intimate friends whose circumstances will permit them to do what their hearts might prompt [should] agree to pay his debts [of about $100,000]." With his wonderful grasp of the range of human feelings he pointed out to Gracie, Oliver Wolcott and Low that Gracie's plan would hurt the family pride. How were they to exclude small subscriptions or those of the indigent and how would it look to have a great man's family brought down "to the level of a beggar's pity" like Louis XVI? Besides, it might not be availing, considering the children had a rich grandfather, Philip Schuyler. And besides, there was property—the mortgaged Grange at what is today Clermont Avenue and 110th Street—which conceivably might pay the debts in time.

Oliver Wolcott wrote James McHenry, "[Morris has persuaded us] that it is in every respect fit, proper and necessary that a number of gentlemen of fortune should come forward to pay these debts and provide handsomely for the family."

This was done under a trusteeship with Rufus King and the others participating.

At the time the Duke of Orléans still owed Morris seven thousand dollars and Morris wrote Phyn, Ellice and Inglis "I hope it may suit the Duke of Orléans to pay but if not, it will be right to have the account settled and take a note for the amount." To the duke he wrote, "Payment must depend entirely on Your Royal Highness's convenience."

The Ogden-Wilkins relatives continued to press the rich bachelor for money, Wilkins coming for six hundred pounds. Morris told him he would endorse for such a loan and when convenient would take up Wilkins's note.

David B. Ogden, "the devoted nephew," told him he had sold his father's lands in the Genesee and that proceeds were already gone. Morris complained that no provision had been made for the money due him, and Ogden casually told him that if he bought a farm in New Jersey he would give his uncle a bond and mortgage on it.

Remembering Morris's letters to Hamilton on the insignia of the Cincinnati left by John Paul Jones and Luzerne, it was fitting that the society shortly called on him to write their letter on Hamilton's death, and equally fitting that the trustees of Columbia College elected him to fill Hamilton's place on the board.

As it turned out, it was to be expected that John Randolph of Roanoke would write his letter to his fellow Virginia congressman, Joseph Nicholson:

If [Burr's] influence were sufficient to divide us [Harrison Gray] Otis and Morris would tomorrow, ere those shoes were old in which they followed Hamilton to the grave, go to the hustings and vote for Burr.

It was written August 27, on the day Morris wrote a delightful letter to Jonathan Dayton in New Jersey telling him how to sail to Morrisania:

Embark at the point with as much of the ebb as will bring you to Staten Island Bay. Then stretch over and pass thro the Butter Milk

Channel, south of Governor's Island. Keep the main course of the
flood and running about 300 yards from Brooklyn Ferry keep around
Corlair's Hook so as to fall again within 200 yards of the Long
Island shore opposite to the Hook. Then stand diagonally across
the river so as to get within 300 yards of the York Island shore
between 3 and 4 miles above Corlair's Hook. Then stand on in what
is called the West Narrows (being 1 of 2 channels made by Blackwell's Island, keeping the midway till you have passed a great eddy
on the west shore about ½ mile above the entrance of the Narrows.
Then approach gently the York shore so as to be within ten or a
dozen yards when you clear the Narrows. . . . You will see on your
starboard bow a round rock . . . leave it twenty yards on your
right. Then the tide will shoot you through Hell Gate . . . discover
my house on your right . . . passing my nephew's house.

If you have any breeze you will be in my house three hours after
you leave your own. . . . I will wait dinner till four.

Four o'clock dinner! What a lovely hour to dine, looking at
the water, in August.

In the Print Room of the New York Public Library there are
two reproductions of interiors of Morrisania, as Jonathan Mason
of Massachusetts saw it that fall. In the hall is the tapestry of
Telemache resisting Circe and beyond a view of the "reception
room," with the first piano, across from the big ornate fireplace.
There are five rugs, many books and the chairs are comfortable-
looking. The library floor is dark, polished parquet imported
from France, almost as much a hazard to Morris as to Talleyrand, one would have thought. The bookcases with glass doors
are set close to the paneled walls and the whole impression is of
snug comfort.

There was a "great society and mirth added to splendor in
the extreme" when Mason stayed there. "My friend is a real
aristocrat and he lives literally like a nobleman. . . . He has
all this world can give but a good wife and amiable children.
. . . He also laments that he did not, twenty years ago, unite
his talents with some corresponding female mind to make each
other happy."

On June 10, 1796, the architect, Benjamin Latrobe, had rid-
den from Tuckahoe, "sixteen miles from Richmond on the north
side of James River," to a plantation with "another French

name [Bizarre] . . . not quite applicable to Mr. Richard Randolph's house at present." Surely no name was so applicable and it is strange so great an artist as Latrobe did not sense it. His *Journal* goes on, "I found Mr. Richard Randolph very dangerously ill of an inflammatory fever. . . . Mr. Randolph is much worse. . . . Mr. Randolph was visited about noon by a medical practitioner in the neighborhood, Dr. Smith. His opinion is against the probability of Mr. Randolph's recovery. . . . I dined with the melancholy family of my host."

John Randolph of Roanoke takes up the story. "I was told that an emetic (tartar) had caused his dissolution. Of his marked [alleged] aversion to Nancy I had not the most distant hint. . . . Did she mix or hand him the medicine? Had she the opportunity for doing the deed? The motive is now plain as well as her capability."

This letter was written twenty years later. After Richard's death the terrible women's-prison life went on, except that, in Nancy's words, hers differed "from any servant's only in this. I received no wages but was permitted to sit at table where I did not presume to enter into any conversation or taste of wine and very seldom of tea or coffee."

There is no way of establishing who gave Richard Randolph the medicine believed to have killed him, or whether it was given with guilty intent.

Nancy at the time wrote to Mary Johnston, "My presence now operates like a reproachful conscience on a sister and for that I am treated as a culprit. It is the last paroxysm of tyrannic power." The letter speaks of her despair, and of a previous ejection from Bizarre, "that dear sequestered spot," and says that even Randolph Harrison's "vivacity has failed to reanimate me."

The five letters to Mary Johnston—only two dated—are heart-rending. Nancy is sure she is "obnoxious to you." Their style is stilted and overelegant, the letters of a well-read person deprived of conversation and social intercourse, and scoffed at by "Judy" for her literary interests.

All of the times' venomous condemnation of a fallen woman, made more venomous by her sister's jealousy of her dead husband, was vented on her small head. Every trapping of Gothic horror was there, even to incest, as intercourse with a sister's husband was then regarded. Her sister's children were the malignant boy of eleven, Tudor, and the tragic deaf mute, St. George.

In and out came Richard's youngest brother, John Randolph of Roanoke, with his terrible angers, his dreadful physical ills and sexual impotency. Given time and place, and the characters involved, no balm in Gilead was possible. "Months in succession have been devoted to the needle (for Judy cherishes not a latent spark of affection for me) when my intellect absolutely languishes for a little indulgence." As often with the non-reading type, Judy associated reading with previous sin and saw to it "there never was an interval of leisure" for reading the books Nancy borrowed from neighbors. Relatives opened her letters. Her brother Thomas carried one off to Monticello. What right had a spinster to letters?

About New Year's, 1805, she had evidently been allowed to go for a visit to Williamsburg and one suspects from a letter to Mrs. Johnston of February 21 that she had had a proposal of marriage there. She says that Madame d'Yrujo "told me it was the most ridiculous thing in the world to dress in such a style and protested she would take away my cap and curl my hair or put on a wig. She possesses vast affability. . . . Someone asked Madame Yrujo if I retained my vivacity unimpaired. 'Oh heavens!' she exclaimed 'the most serious moralist of the age.'"

Madame d'Yrujo was obviously one of the most charming young women of her time. She was three years younger than Nancy Randolph and had been born Sally McKean, the eighth child of Thomas McKean, a Delaware Signer, and later chief justice and governor of Pennsylvania.

During Washington's administration the English, French and Spanish envoys had each married a Philadelphia girl, the Marquis de Casa d'Yrujo, young and handsome, marrying Sally McKean, and by this time they had a girl, Narcisa, and a boy, Caros.

There is a letter of Sally's to Dolly Madison, written in 1812, after D'Yrujo's quarrel with Madison over the Louisiana Purchase and his recall as minister, which is a feminine counterpart of many of Morris's: "I am just as giddy and full of spirits as ever. Indeed I am for the French principle, never to let anything trouble me much, unless it is absolutely necessary."

It is delightful and natural that she should have sensed that the unhappy, unwanted "drudge" from Bizarre, eager and fitted for the life Sally was leading, needed "to be brought out," have her hair done and her clothes changed and have some fun.

Gilbert Stuart painted three portraits of the marquesa and it seems doubtful if for once he caught the real likeness. Her pose is conventional, the face "nice," but the portrait as a whole is nowhere near so "stylish" nor animated as Sharples's later portrait of Nancy. We shall see what happened to the cap Sally wanted to get rid of.

Nancy adds that "had some of my principles been sufficiently flexible to offer homage at the shrine of wealth I might have averted this tissue of injustices by bestowing my hand when my heart *revolted* [her italics]."

The end of the letter is damaged but says "A.C.R. or rather Nancy . . . have relinquished the name of Ann."

Obviously her relatives thought she was in no position to refuse any marriage and to remain "a burden" on them.

On a winter night in 1805, John Randolph talked alone with his sister-in-law Judith and then, going to find her sister, said, "Nancy, when you do leave this house, the sooner the better for you take as many liberties as if you were in a tavern." She was poor, she was dependent and she "replied with the humility suitable to my forlorn condition 'I will go as soon as I can.' [John Randolph] stalked haughtily out of the room [and I sought] the relief of tears." Not till later did Randolph make his foulest charge that she had to go because of "intimacy with one of the slaves, your 'dear Billy Ellis'—thus you commenced your epistles to this Othello!"

She set out for Richmond. The malevolent relatives she left may have thought she could make a living as a seamstress, but one must wonder whether they did not expect and desire her to live as a harlot.

In Adèle's exile it was accepted by the world that she would

be a courtesan and small, if any, obloquy attach to it. Her child
had lived and Nancy's been born dead. Adèle's only punishment arose from being an aristocrat. It is wonderful to consider
how these two women managed to survive and triumph over all
the puritan and political forces against them.

The Murrays of Grovebrook took Nancy in and there, Randolph said, her advances to a Dr. Mead became so immodest
she had to leave. It would have been small wonder if the years
of chastity, in one of her affectionate nature, at thirty-one, had
made her recklessly "immodest." The wonder is that she could
have kept her senses at all, the object certainly of every man's
masculine curiosity and complacency. Her letter from Grovebrook of July 3, while happy at meeting people freely, speaks
of her humility over "that most recent charge," but says "I shall
rally again."

We do not know what happened but the Murrays allowed
her to leave and she went to Richmond, writing, "My memory
rejects all traces of unkindness [but] I shall during the present
year avoid those members of my family. . . . What a life of
penance."

In Richmond she got a room at "Prior's, a public garden"
where she "rested on a blanket spread on sacking," and Randolph sent her a hundred dollars in her sister's name. "You
returned them by bearer, Tudor, then a school boy because
sent in the name which you covered with obloquy." Then Randolph himself went and, finding her "fastidiously neat and so
was the apartment," saw "why the bank note was returned," the
inference being of course that she "was associating with play-
ers" and that it was a prostitute's room.

There she was, alone, related to all the great families of Virginia, as Jefferson, her brother's father-in-law, had his Second
Inaugural.

Later in the spring Lord Wycombe succeeded as the second
Marquis of Lansdowne, married now to a Lady Gifford, "a vulgar Irish woman near fifty and larger than Mrs. Fitzgerald. She
(had) lived with him publicly as his mistress for some years
past."

In New York, Madame Bonneville, a French emigrant, rather than émigrée, was keeping house for Tom Paine. He spoke no French and she no English. She could not cook and, their relations having no sexual aspect, one must wonder what was the common sense of the arrangement. It was the next year that the poor fellow's citizenship was challenged as he registered to vote. Morris was in no way responsible, though the challenge arose from his not claiming Paine as an American citizen in France. Paine, in confusion, wrote Vice-President Clinton, "The case is [Morris] did reclaim me but his reclamation did me no good."

Toward the end of the year Robert Livingston felt that Morris should return to public life and Morris, not without some natural hurt at two defeats for electoral office, and a diplomatic recall, wrote him, "[In the latter I was succeeded] by a gentleman who was, I presume more worthy of the public confidence. It becomes me, in submitting to the will of my fellow countrymen, to doubt of my talents for I cannot, neither can they, doubt of my integrity."

The Motto: I Must Be Sought

(1806–9)

IN FEBRUARY 1806 a pamphlet of 76 pages called *An Answer to War in Disguise* appeared anonymously in New York and was shortly afterwards reprinted in England. The author said he did "not affix his name" in order that it might be impartially considered. It had been written in answer to one published in London called *Frauds of the Neutral Flags or War in Disguise*, which within a year ran to five editions.

The London pamphlet set forth the British position that for neutral nations to insist upon "free trade" with Napoleonic France, in their own ships, was only war in disguise against England.

There was a flurry of questions among the Federalists as to the identity of the author of the reply. "There is merit in it," Uriah Tracy wrote Rufus King, "I regret that more time was not taken to increase its merits."

Pickering thought the trouble was that it was by one of those "authors who have a clear and competent view of their subjects [but] are apt to presume too much on the discernment of their readers." King told him the author was known to him and that he had thought they would all recognize him. To which, when they realized it was Gouverneur Morris's work, Tracy said he always supposed so and Pickering that he, too, had been sure it was his work, adding that "with a brilliant and cultivated mind [Morris] has a coarseness of sentiment which is incompatable with dignity."

If Morris had not been a Federalist there was probably no one of whom Pickering would privately have more disapproved. Reading the Pickering letter, one might suppose that for once the gifted, felicitous pen, which moved so fluently, had descended to Duane-Callender scurrilities. The pamphlet, however brilliant, incisive and telling, has no discernible "coarseness of sentiment." Pickering probably meant the flippant jibes at Sir William Scott, the legal pundit quoted in it.

The Federalist position, as put by Pickering, was that "the independence of the United States [is] absolutely dependent on the ability of England to maintain herself against all the efforts of Napoleon." But this did not mean, in the words of Morris's answer, that "a neutral, weak and unarmed, and from motives of fear or pretexts of policy [should] submit to outrages from an armed and powerful belligerent. [No] right rests on such submission [and] a wrong unresisted [does not] become a right."

The *Answer* is a plea to Britain to see that her own advantage lies in American good will, and that "no minister, however splendid his talents [and] no prince, however great his power must dictate to the President of the United States," whatever the Federalist opposition may think of him.

"We disdain to join with Barrère in stigmatizing as hucksters a gallant nation but we feel a right to expect a reciprocity of candour and decency."

Simply because, as the author of *Neutral Flags* contends, Britain is championing the liberties of mankind against the tyrant, "ought we, in aid of her exertions, submit to the [tyrant's] doctrines [when spoken by England]?"

Sir William Scott, Morris says, begins, "The general rule is" —the general rule of what? By what right does he accord to British prize courts jurisdiction over American vessels? All Scott is actually saying is, "My will is law, my advocate is power and I myself am judge," and it is not "a general rule" at all. "Will the British Government with its ex parte assertions of jurisdiction agree that the United States can rightfully make a prize of a British smuggler on the Spanish Main, taken in the breach of Spanish law?

"Napoleon said at Boulogne no trade with the United Kingdom as I am going to capture it," and Britain said the same thing about the French island of Martinique. "If threats could acquire rights the greatest bragger would be the richest man.

"Scott complains that we diminish the profits of sugar refineries [in England by shipping refined sugar]. In other words we by our industry diminish the benefits of monopoly and our rights must be invaded and our property must be plundered that refined sugar may become dear in England. And this argument is addressed to the good sense of England!"

Scott says "hostile treasuries are fed with a copious stream of revenue [which might] be turned into our coffers. How a revenue could be turned into the coffers of Britain by leaving articles, [which] neutrals now export, to perish in the colonies of her enemies, we are not so happy as to comprehend or conjecture. . . . Scott asks with what intentions did the enemy open the ports of his colonies to foreign flags? . . . certainly [Morris says] not out of any regard for us but solely with a view to his own interest and advantage. And what then? Must I, to defend my right, prove your enemy was actuated by pure love and kindness toward me? Since when have states been governed by the dictates of a stark-naked benevolence?"

To sum up, the British case that they, by right, are the sole masters and judges of the sea because they are defending the liberty of mankind, is wrong, unfounded and hypocritical. "Like Lord Peter in The Tale of A Tub [the British say] this is clear reason and you all be d—d for a pack of rascals if you pretend to dispute the conclusion."

The British blockade of the Continent tightened. Banking business in Marseilles was closed down and the man who was to be the novelist Stendahl was out of a job and reading the poetry of Alfieri.

In April, Congress passed the Non-Importation Act in retaliation, against British manufactures, for the seizures at sea and the blockade.

In London, Monroe received a letter from John Randolph of Roanoke, telling him that Monroe, not Madison, must run for President in 1808. Almost simultaneously William Pinkney of Maryland arrived as special envoy to make a new treaty with England, restoring to America the right of trade with the colonies, indemnifying her for captures and repudiating the right of impressment.

Pinkney brought a letter from Jefferson offering Monroe the post of governor of Louisiana and warning him against John Randolph's intrigue to upset "the two pillars [Madison and Monroe] of my happiness." It is curious to see how Randolph's not unusual political letter was remembered with other things which later gave evidence against his soul.

One can imagine the eagerness with which Morris that year opened the first volume of Talleyrand's *Memoirs*. There is no mention of Morris and only the one already quoted of Adèle, asking him not to see her at Altona. Morris wrote Parish, "I have just read the memoir of Talleyrand in which I find some truth with a great deal of falsehood. Everything is exaggerated even his wealth of talent."

It was the year of Robert Morris's death and the annuity had more than sufficed for his comfort. Toward the end of the year Jonathan Dayton wrote to Gouverneur Morris for money and Morris accepted his draft for $1020, writing him, "If you can avoid selling the land to pay, try to keep it."

A ship from France brought some lambs to Morrisania from Le Ray de Chaumont, as Napoleon, in Berlin, issued his decree shutting off the British Isles to commerce.

In January 1807, General Moreau, who had fled from France after his plot to assassinate Napoleon in 1804, dined at Morrisania. He had been a friend of Leclerc, the first husband of Pauline Bonaparte, now the Princess Borghese, and he added another story of incest, this time imperial, to the many Morris had heard.

In June, John Marshall sent his *Life of Washington* to Morris, who wrote his thanks for the mention of him, saying, "Few men of such steady, persevering industry [as Washington] ever existed and perhaps no one who so completely controlled himself. Thousands have learned to restrain their passion though few among them had to contend with passions so violent. . . . [He could] at any moment convert the energies of his mind to a cheerful exertion."

On August 7, Morris was evidently feeling lonely and his gout was bothering him. He wrote to Madame Foucault, for whom Adèle had accused him of too much fondness, a light bantering letter telling her to write to him. All he does is exist and think of her. He loves her always. Their friendship had commenced with a trying interlude one afternoon in the Bois, sixteen years before, with the lady in a predicament which Morris said no American woman could have survived. And he wrote the same day to Minette de Staël, urging her to come to Morrisania the next year to live on a milk diet, pluck peaches and write verses and novels, and as for love, *"vous n'avez qu'a l'y mettre* [you have only to put it there yourself]."

Madame de Staël, had he known it, re-exiled from France by Napoleon, was having a brief affair in Vienna with young Pedro de Souza, Adèle's stepson.

One letter led to another and he wrote Lord Gower, now the Marquis of Stafford, that it was seventeen years since Morris had said to him that "if the French Revolution was not arrested it would be fatal to the liberties of Europe. *The United Kingdom Stands alone* [author's italics] and those who ought to side with you keep aloof or are awed and subdued. If [only] your affairs with this country had been well managed we should now in all probability be your firm and useful ally."

On October 14 news reached New York of Napoleon's victory at Friedland, making "Europe [his] subject from the British Seas across prostrate Germany to the distant verges of the Russian Empire." The news shocked the Federalists, aware that there would be war with England as soon as the Administration could bring the public to it.

Whatever Canning said of "ancient usages" or Lord Grenville of "the right of visit and search," Jefferson and Madison appeared blind to what it would mean if Napoleon brought these men and their country to their knees.

It seems incredible that Jefferson should have written, almost sycophantly, to Livingston in Paris, "I think upon the whole the Emperor cannot be dissatisfied at the present state of things between us and England and that he must be rather satisfied."

Life at Morrisania was not all politics and correspondence. In October Mr. Walton from Ballston Spa dined there. In words reminiscent of businessmen in the first excitement of air travel in the 1930s, Morris wrote, "By means of the steamboat he can leave his own house on Monday morning, dine with me on Tuesday, do business in New York on Wednesday morning and be home Thursday evening."

But the year ended ominously for America and Europe. In November the British Orders in Council closed all European ports under French control to neutrals, though if a neutral entered a British port a navicert might be issued. A month later Napoleon countered with a decree that any vessel submitting to English search or sailing to or from an English port was a French prize.

On the same day Jefferson drafted "an immediate inhibition of the departure of any vessels from the ports of the United States" and five days later the incredible measure was passed and signed as the Embargo Act.

To Simeon De Witt, then fifty-one, who was to serve altogether for fifty years as surveyor general of New York, Morris wrote:

That we the people of America, should engage in a ruinous war [as Madison and Jefferson intend] to support a rash opinion that foreign sailors in our merchant-ships are to be protected against the power of their sovereign is downright madness and the attempt to frighten England by combining a non-importation [and exportation] law with a mosquito fleet of gunboats is truly absurd.

He wrote less farsightedly to De Witt Clinton of another idea "that can never occupy the attention of considerate men . . . the idle project for making bridges across North and East Rivers." He wished that such a thing were possible, as the city of New York began to push into the countryside, demanding roads through wooded Morrisania, which a hundred years later was destroyed, house and woodland, by the railroad.

Bridges to open up Long Island could only be built, he said, at an expense infinitely beyond the advantage, and only, if at all, by private enterprise. The result would be that the city would then take them over for a million dollars, whatever the cost.

As to politics, he felt the Virginia dynasty was so entrenched as to be for the time invulnerable and all that prudent men could do was wait for the "infatuated Administration" to wear itself out.

He left Morrisania on March 7, 1808, for Philadelphia and there on the eleventh he sat for his portrait. The *Diary* mentions the sittings, lasting until the thirty-first, speaks of Robert Morris's widow, "beautiful as ever and as elegant," and tells how he sat "with a parley of gay young bucks till late."

It does not mention the serious purpose of the trip, his lawsuit against William Duane for libel. Duane wrote Jefferson on the twentieth, "Tomorrow Gouverneur Morris's suit against me comes on." In the *Aurora,* Duane had asked a question framed adroitly, as he evidently thought, to avoid libel. The question was "Whence did Mr. Gouverneur Morris draw his compensation for his services at Berlin [1795] after his *dismission* from the embassy to France for carrying on an *illicit correspondence?*"

Duane, or his advisers, had not perceived that Morris could find grounds for libel in the italicized words. If the question had stopped at the word "Berlin" there could have been no action. Its intent was of course the inference that he had been in the British pay.

Morris won the suit, and went home on April 6.

Madame de Staël, close now to the final break with her lover, Constant, had sent Morris her latest novel, *Corinne,* and he wrote her how much he liked it. So well read a man, and the buyer of so many books, must have known of Adèle's "masterpiece," *Eugène de Bothelin,* published at the same time, but there is no mention of it or her.

On April 17, Napoleon seized all the American ships in French ports, to a value of ten million dollars, on the grounds that they must be English in disguise since the Embargo Act prevented their being American.

The relative indifference of Jefferson and his colleagues to French injuries or the over-all meaning of Napoleonic savagery is hard to understand except as "infatuation." It is a wonder that they did not declare war on both England and France, as young Theodore Roosevelt, in his *Gouverneur Morris*, said they should have done!

Not many years ago the picture of Napoleon in American school textbooks was of a lonely genius, giving laws and roads to France, dying a martyr in cruel exile. It is well to realize, as Arthur Bryant has so recently written, that "the most terrible trait in Napoleon and the reckless, uprooted race of Revolutionary warriors with whom he scourged Europe, was their complete indifference to human life and suffering. . . . Outside Britain and the remote corners of Europe which her sea-power had protected there was scarcely a town of any size in Europe that had not seen the French cavalry enter wiping, in Campbell's phrase, 'their bloody hands on their horses' manes.' " In '96, Morris had seen some of the French refugees fleeing before their cavalry.

From his *Memoirs*, it appears that Vincent Nolte reached Philadelphia, after a shipwreck, on the same March day that Morris had. David Parish, as agent for the Baring-Hope-Parish group, had been established there for two years. Nolte now found him badly tied up by advances he had made on cargoes held under the Embargo Act.

It seems unlikely that Morris and Nolte did not meet but neither speaks of it. Nolte may have been one of "the parley of gay, young bucks." However, for March 11, 1808, Nolte writes:

Among the old friends of the Parish family in the beginning of this century counted Mr. Gouverneur Morris, so celebrated as the American ambassador at the court of Versailles. He was a clear-headed and talented man. . . . He was living on his estate called Morrisania on East River, 15 miles from New York. From there he visited David Parish in Philadelphia during the Spring of 1807 and spent a couple of weeks. [He borrowed thirty thousand dollars from Parish, mortgaging his St. Lawrence lands, and had now sold enough to repay Parish.]

Late in the summer there began one of those periods in Morris's life about which he annoyingly says nothing and where the subplots are so fascinating to follow. The summer was healthy and happy, "fishing off Fisher's Island," "directing the course of a stone wall," farming and haying. Late in August he went north to improve the farm and build a house for summer residence at "the Great Bend."

He returned briefly and some day in October, perhaps the one when it was so dark he needed candles at noon to write by and a billiard ball was scarcely visible from one end of the table to the other, he drove into the city and went to a boardinghouse in Greenwich Village owned by "old Mrs. Pollack."

Of this no letter or diary of his makes mention. We do not know how the visit came about, whether by surprise or arrangement. The great coach stopped and the French riders dismounted to open the door for the ruddy, handsome man with the wooden leg. Looking from a window, Nancy Randolph may have recognized him even after twenty years, or she may have been expecting him. She had seen him last at her father's at Tuckahoe, when her mother was slowly dying and she was a child of fourteen and Morris a man of thirty-six. Now they were thirty-four and fifty-six.

We know a little of what they said to each other. In October, another twenty-three years later, she wrote Joseph C. Cabell:

[Mr. Morris] visited me at old Mrs. Pollack's in New York in 1808 and expressed a wish that some reduced gentlewoman would undertake to keep his house, as the lower class of house-keepers of his provoked the servants to a riot in his dwelling. He went [then] to his lands where he remained six months. . . .

There had been a letter she wrote to John Randolph before leaving Virginia. It bore, he said later, no injunction of secrecy. Honour, she replied, would have known there are things the communication of which involves that injunction. The letter must have been the full confession of her sins of '92, written perhaps in some desire to start fresh in a new place. The letter is lost but there is record in another letter of that February 1805, written in a different vein, which strangely fits Morris's coming to find her. It was to Mary Johnston.

> When a girl I was captivated by an uncommon device on a compartment of a little vase. A modest violet immersed in leaves; the motto "I must be sought" (it was in French which language I have lost in the vortex of persecution).

She was still slim and enchanting, as her portrait three years later shows, with a happy mischief behind her gravity. It is unlikely that the fluent Morris had no more to say than what she wrote Cabell. Still, things had to be taken in their turn and he was off to his lands.

How she had gotten through, how she had lived in the three years since Jack Randolph turned her out, we do not know. We know that she went to Newport, Rhode Island, where her situation became so desperate that she had been driven to ask Randolph for fifty dollars. He "did not deign to reply [hoping] to drive [her] to prostitution to bear out [his] charges." If suffering, she wrote him later, "could have driven me to vice, God knows there was no want of suffering."

Her presence in Newport, not elsewhere referred to, has been puzzling and it has been suggested that she may have had a "protector" or been a "housekeeper" there. This is unlikely but the fact that Richard K. Randolph, her third cousin, had married Anne Maria Lyman of Newport, July 4, 1802, and was living on Broad Street, Newport, about 1805–6, does not fully clear up the mystery. It seems likely that she was invited to stay with them, but if so it is hard to understand why she needed fifty dollars so desperately as to ask Jack Randolph for it. Still they, too, may have been censorious.

When Morris went north, we know from Nolte that David Parish went along, with David B. Ogden, "one of the first lawyers in New York," in attendance. How fitting that these two marplots should have had the same name and how companionable they must have been. There is an evil distinction in Ogden's face but Parish's was fat and common, with a snub nose and the look of a meddler in other people's affairs.

Through Ogden and James Le Ray de Chaumont, Parish bought 100,000 acres, "including the whole borough of Ogdensburgh, [later] the seat of George Parish . . . for about $9000." Out of the proceeds James Le Ray began to build his beautiful Palladian house. To design his own house, Parish brought out the French architect Joseph Jacques Ramée, who would later design Union College in Schenectady.

It was in Schenectady, on the way back in January 1809, that Morris was taken very ill and on February 9, with the thermometer at 10° below zero and the ink frozen, he made a will which it later became evident was satisfactory to David Ogden and the rest of the nephews.

By the middle of February he was safely home at Morrisania. There was a letter waiting from Senator Pickering which asked Morris "to bring forward publickly [a] conversation which Mr. Jefferson had with me," presumably to the discredit of Jefferson and his party. Morris refused, writing:

Whatever may have been or may be his conduct towards me or my friends there is I think a sanctity of social intercourse among gentlemen which ought not to be violated. . . . Moreover . . . every man has a right and is in duty bound to change opinions when good reason occurs for the change and every man has a right to pursue a course different from what he intended when in the lapse of time and of events the existing circumstances shall be different. These observations apply even to those engagements which Mr. Jefferson took with the public by his inaugural speech. . . . I owe it to justice and to him to add on this occasion that I believe his professions were sincere. . . .

A fortnight before, Napoleon had reached the Tuileries from Spain and summoned Talleyrand. In a Hitlerian frenzy he ridiculed Talleyrand's lameness, called him a cuckold and a traitor and said that he was *merde* in a silk stocking. Talleyrand acted as though he had not heard a word but as he limped away he said as moderately as Morris might have, "What a pity that so great a man should be so ill bred." Now Napoleon had dismissed Talleyrand as Minister of Foreign Affairs and Madison was awaiting his first inaugural.

The night before the inauguration Jefferson's successor as minister to France was writing a letter to Nancy Randolph. It would appear from his letter that she had written to him since his return, asking for advice or help, and saying a good deal about the dreadful years since September 30, 1792.

His reply was addressed to her at Stratford, Connecticut. She had probably been living there when she came to New York the previous summer.

How or when Morris first learned she was there is as much of a riddle as Adèle's presence at Bremgarten. There is a vague reference by the authors of the 1831 and 1887 *Lives* and *Diaries* to Nancy's teaching at Stratford.

The trail of that small clue leads to two pieces of evidence which, though entirely circumstantial, lead to a reasonable possibility.

William Samuel Johnson (1727–1819) was a Connecticut delegate to the Constitutional Convention and on the drafting committee with King, Madison, Hamilton and Morris. That year he was elected the first president of Columbia, serving until 1800, when he retired to live at his birthplace, Stratford.

In the December before Nancy was driven from Bizarre he and others subscribed a thousand dollars for "an academy for older boys and young ladies" on Meeting House Hill in Stratford. The ensuing incorporation did not take place, nor the academy get under way, until May 1806, by which time Nancy had left Richmond and reached Newport, Rhode Island, where from later letters of hers we know she was ill and destitute.

Though her own education had been from tutors at plantations, the style and content of her letters are such as to indicate it was well above the average. News of the academy probably reached her and an application to teach there followed.

She must have been under great strain to hide her "past," with word of it, however, somehow reaching Stratford.

Meanwhile Morris had been a trustee of Columbia since 1805 and may well have had various occasions to correspond or confer with Johnson, a friend of twenty years. Johnson may well have said, "You went to Virginia after the Federal Convention. Did you ever know Colonel Tom Randolph?"

"Of course I knew him. I stayed at his house. I got Hamilton to handle a lawsuit for him. Why?"

"A daughter of his is teaching at the academy at Stratford, and there has been gossip about her," Johnson may have said. "We have been obliged to dismiss her."

Talk not of gratitude [the first letter of Morris's begins] but communicate so much of your situation as may enable me to be useful. I once heard but have no distinct recollection of events which brought distress into your family. Dwell not in them now. If we ever happen to be alone you shall tell your tale of sorrow when the tear from your cheek may fall in my bosom.

Her letter had evidently spoken, not only of old unhappy things, but of the drab, narrow world in which she was forced to live. She perhaps let him understand that with health and comparative youth—she was almost the age of Adèle when he last saw her—the manless world to which public opinion condemned her was dull beyond bearing.

His letter goes on:

Perhaps you go too far in supposing existence without genius and taste to be a world without a sun. No doubt it would be unwise to found our scheme of happiness on the pebbles of sensual gratification. The mind, of higher origin, partakes of purer joy. But it happens, from the connection of soul and body, that even intellectual pleasure is generally obtained by the aid of our senses. Let us not then quarrel with the order of nature. It is the order of God. . . . Health, of which you seem to regret the possession, is in so far the first blessing that without it we relish no other virtues, a word which I do not use in the tea-table sense that calls a woman virtuous tho she have the malice of a dozen devils . . . but to express a pure heart, a chastened spirit, fortitude, benevolence, charity, virtue and health or, if you please, a sound mind in a sound body, give the best chance for so much of happiness as may consist with our condition. The incidents of pleasure and pain are scattered more equally than is generally imagined. The cards are dealt with fairness. What remains is patiently to play the game; and then to sleep.

Perhaps you may like these notions better in the loose jingle of rhyme than stiff and stately prose.

Take then the scrap enclosed and believe me yours.

The jingle is not profound but the last verse reads:

> Then why dear Girl rejoice or mourn
> That men approve or disapprove
> See, far beyond This Mortal Bourne
> The God of Mercy and of Love.

All this seems to have raised his general spirits—"hark to the hunter's horn" as it were—for he wrote verses also to young Mrs. Macomb, who had sent him her sketches of his house, saying she knew he would not have enjoyed her society with indifference and sent with them "the works of that wicked, witty devil, Voltaire . . . that great apostle of infidelity," perhaps the very volume Adèle had given him one afternoon in the Louvre to keep him quiet while she was "abroad."

A letter to Nancy of the third crossed one from her, to which he replied on the ninth that he would have to be in New York for ten days. It seems evident that, in a letter which he did not copy, he had now proposed she come to Morrisania. In contrast to the somber tone of her letters as a widow, it appears that the effect of contact with Morris had excited her and that much of the contact's delight was in being able to flirt a little, tease a little and, with charming femininity, demand to know about this and that before she joined him as she was evidently going to do.

His letter of the ninth says:

You ask my sentiments on a subject about which I am not sufficiently disinterested, and you introduce it by an anecdote of Mr. D. R. calculated to alarm my fears. This may be ingenuously contrived to establish the native equilibrium of my mind: but alas! time in taking away the ardor has not wholly quelled the rashness of youth. I can only answer that I will love you as little as I can. Be assured of my respectful esteem and believe me yours.

"Mr. D. R." could be Dickie Randolph but the general gaiety of the letter makes this unlikely. Probably it is the censorious Mr. Dudley Randolph.

It must have occurred to her that he would want to sleep with her. But also that it might just be possible that with kindness and security she might so flower again that he would want to marry her. Nor need all this have been merely calculating.

Few women wanted to resist that combination of charm, strength, generosity and gaiety which Morris had.

His next letter indicates that she probably wrote him something like this:

What about the stories I have heard about a beautiful woman who has been your "house-keeper"? And what about her predecessor? What did you have with these women? And I must tell you that, though I have been a servant in my sister's house, and am now destitute, I am still a Randolph and a Cary and I will not be a servant.

She may have added "or a backstairs wife." To this Morris replied (the beginning of the letter has been torn from the *Letter Book*):

. . . that she was a tall well-made good-looking woman of low birth and education: assuming to have so much of vulgar dignity as to wound my servants. The numerous ladies who visit me have never harbored an idea injurious to the virtue, as they call it, of my housekeepers: and they are right, for certainly I have never approached either of them with anything like desire.

I have often exprest the wish to have, in that capacity, a reduced gentlewoman, because none other can command the respect of domesticks. Pride may exclaim "Miss Randolph cannot descend to the rank of a servant under whatever name, or however elevated and distinguished." Pride is such a wrangling disputant that I will not argue with him. I can only say that our real relations shall be that of friends. Your salary, which must be the same I now pay, because appearances are best supported by realities, will, if your brother continues your pension, make a provision for future storms, should I be taken away before some better shall present itself. If he does not, it will be necessary.

I cannot close this letter without telling you again that my esteem and affection are undiminished perhaps encreased. God be with you and comfort you and make you happy and blessed.
Yours.

Even as he was writing William Short was again in Paris en route to St. Petersburg, as American minister, still pursued by misfortune. Word reached him there that the Senate had not confirmed him and he came home, never to see Rosalie again. "That phantom of duty" was still between them and she, rendered unhappy by it, still deprived herself of sight of him, *"quelque violence qu'il m'en coute."*

As with the *Diary* of '95, when he was in correspondence with Adèle about coming to Hamburg, the 1809 *Diary* says nothing of Nancy Randolph until April 23 when he "drove to Armstrong's Tavern and after breakfast brought home Miss Randolph of Virginia who had arrived from Connecticutt." Physically he was ill at the time, but there is no question, in light of their gay and happy life together, that it was a meeting of excited anticipation.

The editor of the 1888 *Diary and Letters* says:

Since that time [Morris's meeting with her in 1788 at her father's at Tuckahoe] Miss Randolph's life had been a sad one. Obliged by her father's ill-advised second marriage to leave her home, she had struggled for some time with but poor success to support herself. Morris, the old and trusted friend of her father and mother, hearing of her reduced pecuniary condition, and that she was teaching in New England, proposed, in the most delicate terms, that she should accept the shelter of his roof, and take charge of his household. This offer was accepted by Miss Randolph in the spirit in which it was made.

One cannot quarrel with the pietistic reserve with which this was written, although Anne Randolph had then been dead for fifty years. Even then, however, there might have been some intimation that this must have been very delightful as well as decorous and not quite so humdrum, dolorous and benevolent as it sounds. Still Morris's attachment to Adèle de Flahaut was then, and for fifty years more, kept a dark secret.

John Randolph later wrote, "When I heard of your living with Mr. Morris as his house-keeper I was glad of it as a means of keeping you from worse company. . . . Considering him as a perfect man of the world who in courts and cities at home and abroad had in vain been assailed by female blandishments, the idea of his marrying you never entered my head, another course did." And then he adds with his vicious malevolence, "[You are] a vampire that after seeking the best blood of my race has flitted off to the North and struck [your] harpy fangs into an infirm old man." This last description would have amused them both, as they rode "to my harvest fields" that summer, "dined at home without company," and Morris was

out early fishing in the sound with a northerly blowing, or
crossing at Whitestone to Flushing to pick up Rufus King and
drive to Rockaway for dinner. And the "infirm old man" had
to be away at meetings of the Columbia Trustees and the
Historical Society, and when she had "a phlegm" he rode out
alone to superintend the upper farm. They "dined at candle-
light" in the early autumn, an innovation doubtless her doing,
and he bought a new boat for eight hundred dollars, 36 feet
long and 16 feet beam, and their own fig trees bore fruit until
November.

On November 14 the youngest of the principal actors was the
first to leave the play forever. Lord Wycombe, now the second
Marquis of Lansdowne, died without issue at Bowood, aged
forty-four. The title passed to his half-brother, whose son, the
fourth marquis, would marry the granddaughter of Adèle de
Flahaut and Talleyrand.

Two nights before, several men, including the father of
James Fenimore Cooper, had spent the night at Morrisania.
One of them was David Parish, in difficulties with Hope and
Company and the Barings, and anxious, Nolte says, at the
$360,000 he had spent.

With unbelievable impudence, Parish took Morris, twenty-
six years his senior, aside to talk to him about his domestic
arrangements, because of which, Parish said, Morris's friends
were "hurt." He went on to say a great deal of the necessity of
avoiding scandal by prudence. He may have mentioned the
harm done Morris's reputation in Hamburg-Altona by what a
German writer calls his "loving festivities" with "*einem schönen
Emigranten, die Grafin Flahaut.*"

Exactly what the "friends" wanted Morris to do is not clear.
He told Parish, "I will not carry my ass to market on my shoulders," whatever that may have meant.

Whether those men dined with him "*en garçon,*" as they
called it, with Nancy Randolph in the background, seeing to
the servants, or whether she sat at the table until the port was
passed we do not know. In either event men guests have
seldom been less edifying.

On December 1, Morris wrote Madame de Damas one of those pastoral letters of his which, when they refer to the grave, must not be taken too seriously.

We have not indeed the gayeties of Paris, nor the pleasures of France, but we breathe freely a wholesome air . . . my establishment is pleasant and though expensive not beyond the means which I ought to possess and which time will either bring or take away. My health is excellent, save a little gout. . . . I can walk three leagues, if the weather be pleasant and the road not rough. My employment is to labor for myself a little, for others more; to receive much company and forget half those who come. I think of public affairs a little, read a little, play a little and sleep a great deal. With good air, a good cook, fine water and wine, a good constitution and a clear conscience I descend gradually toward the grave, full of gratitude to the Giver of all good.

The *Diary* gives no inkling of what Morris and Nancy Randolph said to each other in the first twenty-four days of December, but the event of Christmas Day was obviously the climax of gay and laughing conspiracy, planned to the last detail for surprise and effect.

We may take it for granted that these two people were now in love with each other. After his long bachelordom, love did not necessarily mean marriage in Morris's case. The Comic Spirit, in Meredith's sense, of which Morris possessed so much, must have said to him, "Come, they say you are old and infirm, and that you are descending gradually toward the grave. Why not have the last act live up to all the glamour and surprise with which you have played your part? What will so confound the nephews and nieces, what will be a better answer to the concepts of bourgeois morality which you so loathe as for you, with your wealth and fame and distinction, to marry Nancy Randolph? And, Gouvero, what will make you so happy? Well, as to that, certainly nothing!"

Then in the snug, firelit library they must have planned the details. "We shall say nothing to anyone. . . . We'll have family guests for Christmas Dinner as usual, and when we've dined, you will rise from the table and we'll be married. You must get a wedding gown."

There his lovely fellow conspirator had a better idea. She

almost certainly said, "I will not be at the table for dinner. When you're ready, I will come down wearing my old brown dress with the patched elbows." She wrote Joseph Cabell, "I glory in stating that I was married in a gown patched at the elbows." Being sensible people, they also made a prenuptial financial settlement which, in one delightful clause, has surely seldom if ever been made before.

Christmas Day was on Monday, a fine morning after a rainy Sunday. Cooper, the patroon, who had been there the night of Parish's talk in November, was one of the nine guests, with the Wilkinses and some Morrises.

"I marry this day Anne Cary Randolph. No small surprise to my guests."

There are references to this delightful event, by three later authors, which one must regret this genial bridegroom was never able to read. Surely their brevity, though not their wit, would have delighted him.

Sparks wrote:

On the twenty-fifth of December, 1809, Mr. Morris was married to Miss Anne Carey [sic] Randolph, a lady accomplished in mind and person and belonging to one of the most ancient and most respectable families in Virginia. To this connexion, although formed late in life, he often refers in his private correspondence, as a source of continued satisfaction and happiness.

Scharf, the historian of Westchester County, achieves greater economy:

[Morris's] term as Senator closed in March, 1803, after which he resided at Morrisania. On Christmas Day, 1809, he married Miss Anne Carey [sic] Randolph of Virginia. Mr. Morris delivered funeral orations on Washington, Hamilton and Governor George Clinton.

The English writer, J. A. Lovat-Fraser, ended his study of Morris in 1932 with this paragraph:

He rendered great service in starting the progress of the Erie Canal and was chairman of the Canal Commission from their appointment until within a few months of his death. In December 1809 he married Anne Cory [sic] Randolph of the famous Virginia family and had a son.

CHAPTER THIRTY-FOUR

Conjugal Pleasures, That
Pure Felicity

(1810–11)

THE NEW YEAR opened with a very fine, almost a summer
day at Morrisania for the happy man and wife. It is startling to
see how immediate was the spiteful reaction of the nephews
and nieces.

Gertrude Meredith, in Philadelphia, apparently wrote at
once in protest. What she proposed be done about the accomplished fact we do not know, but we have Morris's polite, re-
strained reply.

I received your letter, my dear child, yesterday, and perceive in it
two charges; viz, that I have committed a folly in marriage and have
acted undutifully in not consulting you. I can only say to the first
that I have not yet found cause to repent, and to the second that I
hope you will pardon me for violating an obligation of which I was
not apprized. . . . If I had married a rich woman of seventy the
world might think it wiser than to take one half that age without
a farthing, and, if the world were to live with my wife, I should
certainly have consulted its taste; but as that happens not to be the
case, I thought I might, without offending others, endeavor to suit
myself, and look rather into the head and heart than into the pocket.
Perhaps it would gratify a laudable curiosity to say what I discovered; but that must be omitted, to avoid the charge of partiality
—and the rather as the step I have taken gives sufficient evidence
of my opinion. When we have the pleasure to see you at Morrisania,

it is possible you may approve my choice, and you will certainly find that I am,

As ever, affectionately yours.

When the reply reached Philadelphia, one may imagine that Mr. Meredith said to his wife, "You have done a very stupid thing. I will now write your uncle in a different vein." And he did so on January 15, at some length.

My dear Sir,
I should be guilty of a very blame-able forgetfulness of many benefits conferred, and of ingratitude for the uniform kindness and friendship which I have received from you, were I indifferent to any occurrence which promotes your happiness—in your marriage therefore I have felt a deep interest and, I trust, you will believe this assurance of my sincere wish, that every expectation which you have formed in relation to it may be fully realized. . . .

He goes on to say that the badness of the roads and the congestion of court calendars (he was a lawyer) will keep them in Philadelphia "until warm weather" but, all phrased with painful politeness, hopes that "Mrs. Morris will not occasion a disappointment to us" but visit them, and that the Merediths, with their new house, will provide "comfortable accommodations [and not have] reluctantly to acquiesce in your making your abode under another roof."

He enclosed a pamphlet on the French Government which Morris acknowledged on the twenty-seventh, without reference to his marriage or a visit to Philadelphia.

One cannot escape the feeling that the Merediths then held a family council. "She may give him a child," Gertrude Meredith may have said, "though it would seem unlikely. But there are the Wilkinses and the Ogdens right next to them, able to take advantage of every favorable situation and here we are." "Well," one of them evidently said, "write to Morris and tell him we want William to go to Columbia now, and have his great-uncle look out for him."

Their son William was then eleven years old and his mother wrote the proposal to Morris, who replied:

The question you put respecting your son, it is not easy to answer shortly if at all. I have however no hesitation in saying, that he is too young to be well employed in a good college. In such a college things are taught to which a young mind is not competent. . . . Nor is this the only evil, which attends the ungracious conversion of a fine boy into that miserable thing a little man. He is led to believe, as he goes along, that he knows what in fact he is ignorant of. . . . [Children of eleven] after a four years course, in which with the aid of good memories they may learn to smatter a little of everything . . . before they know how to button their clothes, and are the most troublesome and useless, sometimes the most pernicious little animals, that ever infested a commonwealth.

We are endeavoring to put Columbia College . . . on a more respectable footing. We shall require qualifications for admission as cannot be acquired at a very early period, and proscribe such a course, that, if students go through with it, they will at least learn to be industrious, if they learn nothing else. . . .

So nothing came of the plan, but the University of Pennsylvania gave the boy a bachelor's degree two years later when he was thirteen! For all this the Merediths, six years later, took a revenge of incredibly petty malice.

What all the Randolphs thought we do not know, but there seems to have been no flood of felicitations, perhaps because of other floods and rains in Virginia.

Tuckahoe, Nancy's old home, in the possession of her brother, Thomas Mann Randolph, was the only one, Jefferson wrote a friend, not ruined by the rains.

"[My son-in-law's] horizontal furrows arrested the water at every step till it was absorbed. Everybody in this neighborhood is adopting his method of ploughing, except tenants who have no interest in the preservation of the soil."

There were other marriages which worried people that winter, Napoleon's to an Austrian archduchess and Minette de Staël's at forty-five to the boy, John Rocca, half her age to whom she bore a child. But Morris, like any proud bridegroom, was showing off his bride and "riding about town with my wife to pay visits." It was not until February that he caught a slip in his own *Diary* and wrote thereafter that guests came to dinner or to tea, not "with me" but "with us."

On March 10 the New York legislature voted the need of an Erie Canal, through what was then still a wilderness, and appointed Morris chairman of the commission. For the time it was a daring and enormous project, requiring federal aid and great public support.

To be named as chairman would have gratified any normal man, though Morris, while almost its originator and strongest advocate, doubted that the public could be roused to its benefits. The simultaneous appointment of James Monroe as Secretary of State, though inevitable, must have made him gulp.

He was to start in June on a first official tour of the north. Before going he wrote and received a letter from Benjamin Latrobe. Morris's letter was an invitation to Latrobe to accept a post as engineer with the Canal Commission. Latrobe's reply is a refusal, because of his work in the capital, unless the offer is of life tenure, in which case he would be interested in considering it.

To read anything more than it says into the polite conclusion of Latrobe's letter is unfair to him, particularly by someone who has not made a thorough study of his life and letters. Having said that, let us be unfair for a moment.

The letter ends, "Should I come to New York, few circumstances will give me more pleasure than to see at the head of this family a lady whom I had known in Virginia, who may recall my visit to Bazaar [sic] in 1797 [1796]."

Latrobe was at Bizarre the night its master died of poison. Is he saying, Would it not, in view of that event, be wise to appoint me to the commission for life?

In any event the offer for life was not made and before leaving Morris disposed of two very different matters, both characteristic of him.

Rufus King and he agreed that the provision of the old charter of Columbia requiring the president to be an Episcopalian was outmoded and undesirable. On the other hand, a quick alteration by law would arouse an opposition with irrelevant issues. They therefore decided that the change should come about gradually, not by statute but by what, in a wonderful phrase of the time, was called "outdoor agreement." The next step was to elect an Episcopalian president and a vice-president who was not. This was done and the way prepared for more intellectual freedom.

The other matter, though less important, was a delightful one of love and springtime.

In New York were living the portrait painter James Sharples and his third wife, Ellen, just back from England. Sharples, a year older than Morris, had first come to this country in 1793 and there, among many, had painted Washington and his wife in Philadelphia.

On May 25 the bride and groom had them out to Morrisania and on June 2 the portraits of both of them were done. For the sitting, Morris wore the becoming white wig of earlier days and who will criticize this natural vanity? The previous portrait by Thomas Sully had in a way been unfair, and even as a likeness, John W. Francis said, "it needs a loftier front and a more vivacious and penetrating eye."

As for Nancy, the Sharpleses saw her "chaste, demure" with a look of quizzical mischief behind her grave expression. The gown is simple, with a low but dainty décolletage, and, in what must have been amused insistence, she wears the "cap" to which Sally d'Yrujo objected five years before, with the curls escaping from it. Now the violet had been found. Now the adored wife of one of the wealthiest and most distinguished men in America need dress only to please him.

Love is of course the greatest thing, but it would be a morbid martyr indeed who did not rejoice in the worldly satisfactions it brought this much-tried lady. Seldom has there been such a triumph. From "the level of a beggar's pity," the scorn of the strait-laced, the more unbearable arrogance of those on whose bounty she was dependent, to be the chatelaine of a house like a nobleman's. And soon to be asked for money by those from whom she had had to beg it.

How quickly, though, these same people in her family and Morris's began to say, "We must not let her happiness go on."

On June 22 they started north on an arduous journey over bad roads, staying at filthy inns, kept by insolent people, except where the houses of friends gave them hospitality. The journey exhausted Nancy, and they were often in bed by dusk. At many taverns only public sleeping rooms were available and

it took all of Morris's prestige and persuasion, and much of his
money, to get a room to themselves.

On August 30, *The Columbian,* the paper of Columbia College, published a satiric account of an alleged meeting on the
trip between the Morrises and the Jacksons, the British minister
and his wife. They were said to have arrived together at an inn
that had only one bedroom which both demanded. *The Columbian's* rhymster described what followed with the rude relish
some people have for others' handicaps:

> Jackson and Morris stopped of late
> At an inn-keeper's outer gate
>   And neither budged a peg.
> At length the mighty man of Gath
> So proudly great, so full of wrath
>   Put down his wooden leg.
> I'll have said he by Thundering Jove
> The room's prepared and so, My Love
>   Walk in and take the ground.
> . . . So wife, said J.
> Come let us go
> And leave the man with the timber toe
> To eat and drink and stay with Joe.

The western terminus of the trip was Fort Niagara and
Lewiston whence they turned back, reaching Albany to stay
with Van Rensselaer, the patroon, on August 30. From there
east to Lebanon Springs on the Massachusetts border. There
they saw the Divine Service of the famous Shaking Quakers.

Morris listened to the preaching, full of "the superstition
and enthusiasm which duped our ignorant forefathers seven
centuries ago." He was particularly struck by the urging of the
"poor creatures . . . to abandon worldly pursuits . . . more
especially conjugal pleasures for that pure felicity which attends celibacy . . . that unnatural and impious doctrine."

They continued down the valley of the Housatonic through
Litchfield and New Milford and were home a little after sunset
on September 7.

Two months later Napoleon revoked the Berlin Decrees on
the understanding that Britain would repeal theirs. President
Madison, in the face of the continued seizures of ships and

cargoes, declared his satisfaction with France, leaving the Embargo Act in effect against England.

Of this Morris wrote to Robert Walsh:

Let noisy dram-shop politicians roar out their adoration of our
divine system, their detestation of despots and their contempt for
the slaves of Britain. You, sir, well know that neither would a British
monarch suggest, nor a British Ministry propose, nor a British
Parliament dare to exact a statute so hostile to freedom as that last
supplement to the Embargo.

The winter and spring of 1811 were spent by Morris largely
in bed laid up with gout. Senator Pickering still pressed him to
reveal Jefferson's conversation, now eight years old, involving
it with the cession of West Florida. From Morris's reply it is
now clear that in the conversation Jefferson had agreed not to
dismiss Federalist officeholders wholesale. Pickering also tried
to drag up a story that Jefferson's party had promised President
Adams to support him for re-election against the hostile members (Hamilton, Morris, Pickering, *et al.*) of Adams's own party.

Morris denied he had ever heard this but only that the Republicans would support Adams's Administration.

But to Morris these were dead, forgotten issues, and even so,
whatever he had heard though "not expressly under the seal of
confidence [was] in that sort of conversation where among
gentlemen there is so much confidence implied that it would
be indelicate to cite facts unless perhaps to eulogize another
after his death."

In June he was recovered sufficiently to go to Albany by
steamboat, with Fulton himself aboard and the craft making
eight miles an hour against the wind. There were a hundred
passengers aboard, the food was good and his passage cost
seven dollars plus half fare for his valet.

Back on the twenty-third, he left July 3 for Philadelphia in
a heat wave in the 90s. To De Witt Clinton, mayor of New
York, who was working on the canal plan for submission to
Madison, he wrote before leaving, "Any draft which you may
make will, I have no doubt, be proper and of course have my
full assent."

When he got back and read it, however, he found it needed

"some corrections of clerkship [which I have made and] which will, I trust, lead our secretary to be more careful." The stylist of the Constitution was gently speaking. And then, when Clinton's final draft came in October, Morris said:

Compliment the President to any conceivable extent short of impiety and I shall not object. Let it, however, I pray you, be well understood that I do not, otherwise than officially, join in offering to him or any other man as compliment, a splendid display of advantages to result from a measure after expressing the conviction that they cannot escape his detection . . . [undecipherable].

While on his trip to Philadelphia Nancy had had a visit from a young niece and her husband.

On December 4 they set out for Washington for the first time together. It must have been an enormous satisfaction to her to be going as the wife of a great man, with all his wealth to serve her comfort. And Morris, as their visits show, was very proud to have her with him. The route, with their own carriage and horses and baggage wagon, was through Philadelphia, to York and Lancaster, down through Baltimore to the capital, which they reached on the fifteenth, in enchanting late Indian summer weather.

De Witt Clinton was to have been there ahead of them, but had not arrived and Morris, with his punctilio, was unwilling to see anyone about the canal until they had paid their respects to Madison, and not to do that without Clinton.

As a result he missed a "much-admired speech" by John Randolph of Roanoke in the House, in which Randolph, like Morris a bitter foe of war with England, attacked the plan of Clay and Calhoun to conquer Canada in four weeks, because, Randolph said, it would bring supremacy of the North "over the planting interests," a strange conflict of interests in this twisted man.

The Morrises were staying at Tomlinson's boardinghouse and Randolph must of course have known of their being there. We are not sure exactly what happened.

Randolph wrote later, in his famous letter to Nancy:

When Mr. Morris brought you to Washington he knew that I held aloof from you. At his instance, who asked me if I intended to mortify his wife by not visiting her, I went . . . to ascertain whether change of circumstances had made any change in your conduct. . . . I was led to hope you had seen your errors.

The implication of this, of course, is that the righteous Randolph examined a penitent Magdalene, but, as is later implied, that Nancy told Morris Randolph had been as attentive as he had in the past when (so he claimed) she had said he had offered her marriage.

That he was there neither to see whether she had mended her ways nor as an accepted admirer, then or previously, is referred to in a later letter of hers.

Neither my husband or self can yet call to mind my ever having said Mr. Randolph was particularly attentive to me at any period of life, so wholly unimportant to us both was the fact. Of Mr. R's friendly manner to me in Washington, Mr. Stanford could judge. He found Mr. Randolph spending the morning with me at Tomlinson's when my husband was out.

It must have taken great Christian forbearance to talk to the man who had driven her from Bizarre. But Morris, with his healthy-minded good sense, had evidently seen and she, equally healthy-minded, concurred that the thing was to forgive and forget and pretend they felt nothing against him. And they showed that to be the case not only with him but with Judy, her sister.

On the seventeenth, the day probably of Randolph's visit, Morris thought it impolitic to hold off further seeing Madison, and called then, returning with Clinton on his arrival, the twenty-first.

On Christmas Eve, very appropriately, they dined with Serurier at the French Legation, twenty years after the eve of Noël in the Louvre, with its two embraces. The young French attachés had then been in swaddling clothes, and no French diplomat would have the tactlessness to ask, *"N'étiez-vous pas un ami de la Comtesse de Flahaut? Je la connaissais bien. Et aussi son mari, le ministre de Portugal. Avez-vous lu son nouveau roman,* Eugénie et Mathilde? *Vous vous souvenez son fils, Charles? Je viens de recevoir les nouvelles que Sa Majesté, Hortense, la reine d'Hollande, l'a donné un fils."* The young

Morny boy, half-brother of Napoleon III, had been born in October just past.

Still, if the minister had been so indiscreet, Nancy had the wit to say they neither one had read the French novel, but they had read an English one, *Sense and Sensibility,* by Jane Austen and liked it and its title very much.

As to the canal, Madison said he feared the bill was unconstitutional but Gallatin, the Secretary of the Treasury, thought well of it, and on January 15 the House committee reported in its favor.

Dear, Quiet, Happy Home

(*1812–13*)

Morris passed his sixtieth birthday en route from Washington, with Nancy too ill that day to travel. They reached Morrisania on February 5 and he left almost at once for Albany about the canal legislation, not getting back until March 18.

There, in April, from his windows, the view of approaching spring exhilarated him and he wrote Parish: "Oh, my friend, had we also a renewed spring of life." So William Short, dining with them late in the month, must have wished, thinking of Rosalie "lontana, lontana, lontana." There was snow a week later at Morrisania.

The Countess of Bessborough, whom Morris should have met in his earlier years and who so admired Adèle, had a second spring again that year at fifty-one. "I am courted, followed, flattered, and made love to *en toutes les formes*," she wrote, "by four men—two of them reckoned sensible and one of the two whom I have known half my life."

In April, Morris's wartime governor, old George Clinton, father-in-law of Genêt, died at seventy-three, and the municipality of New York asked Morris to speak the eulogy. He could hardly refuse, with any grace, though a political adversary, and much as he disliked such business. When a friend "climbed in the phaeton" to dissuade him, Morris said he was bound to go through with it, as a New Yorker and a man—but that he would say nothing to dishonor the dead, since that would be cruel, and nothing to dishonor his own political views, since that would be foolish.

He went through with it in the Presbyterian Church in Wall Street on May 19. It was "coldly delivered and better received than such speaking deserves," the *Diary* says.

On May 28, Morris left for Albany alone to be gone a month. From there at the patroon's home on June 5 he wrote a letter to Nancy which six years later she allowed *The Columbian* to publish. It read:

My dear Friend,
Your letter of June 1 was just now received and went directly to my heart. The patroon was sitting with me and but for the sanctity of connubial sentiment, I should have let him see and feel the tender kindness which so much endears you. God bless and preserve you, my dear wife. Again I entreat you that you will be careful of your health.

As to other folks, their civilities or the want of them are of no consequence. Estimate such things and indeed all things at their worth. We shall not then be either way the dupes in the commerce of life.

What can be said of the day-in and day-out cold ill will of the Wilkins and the Ogden relatives and of the amazing arrogance in them which made it possible? Nothing more than John Trumbull said in his portrait.

The Canal Bill was passed on June 17 and the next day in Washington war was declared on England, far from unanimously, the Senate voting 19–13 and the House 79–49 with Daniel Webster among the noes. On the sixteenth Castlereagh, the Foreign Minister, had told the House of Commons the Orders in Council had been suspended but, on the theory that we should not have a minister to a government with whom we are at odds, we had none in London and the chargé lacked the knowledge and ability to foresee and report what Castlereagh would do.

Morris reached his home in the evening of the twenty-third and wrote in his *Diary*, "Dear, quiet, happy home," as he had never done before. It was probably the night Nancy told him she was pregnant, and they both must have been deeply moved, and secretly anxious that all would go well in February.

Beside his entry, there is another line in her hand, "How different [the dear, quiet, happy home] in 1817."

To the Federalists, war on England was a terrible tragedy. "Pray God enable me to know and do my duty," Morris wrote on June 30. What in fact is the duty of a patriot when he sees the country he loves plunged into war by a narrow congressional margin, sees it managed by men for whom he has contempt, sees them cheered by a mob who in their violence cripple Light Horse Harry Lee for life? Sees its avowed aims matters fit for negotiation and sees it opening the gates to the expanding torrent of Napoleon's tyranny?

Those were the things Morris thought about as "I walk in the meadows near my house before breakfast."

The right thing was not so clear to him as to young Theodore Roosevelt, writing Morris's biography seventy-five years later. To the young jingo "the war was justifiable and was of the greatest service to the nation. [But] it would have been better to have declared war on both [France and England] . . . the war was distinctly worth fighting although peace left things as they had been. . . . Morris found space in his letters to exult over the defeats of Bonaparte but could spare no word of praise for our own victories. . . . [He] agreed with Pickering that it was impious to raise taxes for an unjust war . . . induced Rufus King to move in the Senate for a referendum on supplies for war. [He was] a champion of treason and cringing subservience to a foreign power." With all this, young Roosevelt conceded, evidently with admiration, that Morris "kept lighthearted and good-humored," which shows that he did understand a great deal about his subject.

John Jay, Rufus King, Richard Varick, Clarkson and Mason were among those who dined at Morrisania that summer and "left the table to confer in Mr. Morris's library," on drafts of letters "Gouverneur had prepared which we all went over and corrected."

The substance of them was, in Morris's words, "We Northern folks will not submit to a French alliance; neither will we con-

tinue the war with England, unless indeed she should exact
dishonorable terms of peace. . . . We must insist that she give
up the right of search."

The novelist Stendhal reached Smolensk to act as Napoleon's
commissary general, as the public meeting to denounce the war
was held in New York, with Morris the principal speaker, John
Jay being too sick to attend. In Berlin, John Quincy Adams
noted in his *Diary* that the practical and ubiquitous Madame
de Staël asked him how she could get her rents and interests
from America while they were at war with England.

On October 28, when Rufus King wrote Morris, "Congress
should declare immediate war against France and make peace
with England," no one in America knew of the retreat from
Moscow though Morris prophesied it would begin October 20.
Caulaincourt wrote, "The Emperor and the Guard did not leave
Moscow until about noon on October 19. . . . We slept at the
manor house of Trotskoie where we stayed during the whole
of the 20th to rally our forces, for many men and transports
had again fallen behind."

In the retreat the hapless Joel Barlow, appointed by Madison
minister to France the year before, died near Cracow waiting
to see Napoleon.

It is characteristic of Morris that during these weeks of planning and prophesying he should also have been engaged on
other business. On October 26 the Corporation Council of the
city thanked him and John Rutherford "for performing gratu-
itously the arduous duties of laying out the streets of the city."

In December, Morris talked to the Historical Society for an
hour and twenty minutes "on a gouty foot," and Stendhal,
catching his breath, heard a Mozart opera sung in Königsberg.

On February 9, 1813, the son and heir, lusty and healthy,
was born to Morrisania. The delivery must have been reasonably easy because Morris that day wrote a long letter to Lewis
Sturges against Madison's last proposals. "The American
people," he concluded, "cannot fail to suspect a design to
plunge them, by engaging their passions, both in follies and
crimes, for the notable purpose of gathering soap-bubbles."

The birth was of course a terrible blow to the hopes of the

nephews and nieces and, in some cases, their children. "You no doubt have heard," Nancy wrote later to Joseph Cabell, "of [young] Martin Wilkins's [grandson of Isaac Wilkins and Isabella Morris] name for our son Cutusoff."

The name was a timely and witty reference to the Russian general, Kutuzov,[1] whose defeat at Borodino opened the road to Moscow.

The fallibility of "family recollections" is illustrated by a letter written by a grandson of Alexander Hamilton in 1885, which Scharf quotes in his *History of Westchester County:*

Mrs. Morris was the sister of the famous John Randolph of Roanoke . . . when the present Gouverneur Morris was born in the advanced age of his parents . . . John Randolph wanted him called Kutusoff, after a Russian, as the newcomer was "cutting-off" many expectant heirs in collateral branches.

In later conspiracy with Wilkins, and the other expectant heirs, Randolph may have heard the jest, but at the time his "friendly letter to my husband written in George Town contains the warmest congratulations on the birth of our son with 'cordial wishes for Mrs. Morris's speedy and perfect recovery.'"

The ailing John Jay could not be godfather at the christening, on Washington's Birthday, writing sadly that he expected "to remove to a distant country." And four days later Robert R. Livingston died. One wonders if there was any thought of La Kitty, now Mrs. John Livingston, as godmother. Ten months later she was dead.

Madison's second inaugural speech was received on March 6 and Morris wrote, "When I read [it] I supposed him to be out of his senses and have since been told he never goes sober to bed. [The pain in his teeth necessitating the use of wine and opium.]

"It avows the war aims as the protection of our commerce and seamen," he wrote David B. Ogden, who must have been more interested in other matters, "but it is really to conquer

[1] Tolstoy describes him in *War and Peace* at the council before Austerlitz "with his uniform unbuttoned to air his great bull-neck . . . sunk in a deep easy-chair with his little, fat, old man's hands laid squarely on the arms of it; he seemed to be asleep but at the sound of Weirother's voice he opened his remaining eye."

Canada and scatter millions among [Madison's] constituents."
Hope lay, however, "in the signal victory of Russia, demanding
our thanks to Almighty God," he wrote Otis, "[and because of
it] France will abandon Spain."

By December the Northern Federalists wondered ominously
whether it would be possible to preserve the Union at all. If so,
King said, "only by checks to outrages which are no longer to
be borne," and Morris replied, "Our rulers seem to suppose not
only that Great Britain is extremely fickle but that her pity
exceeds her imbecility . . . that [they] had not hitherto dared
to do the mischief in their power, fearing the opposition would
appeal to the good-nature of the English."

Gout and other sickness were troubling that year, though the
babe thrived. In October from the field of Stillwater, where
thirty-six years before he had stood, "hellishly frightened" but
confident, in the face of Burgoyne's army, he wrote a letter in
verse to Nancy.

> Kiss for me, my love, our charming boy
> I long to taste again the joy
> Of pressing to his father's breast
> The son and mother. Be they blest
> With all which bounteous Heaven can grant
> And if among us one must want
> Of bliss, be mine the scanty lot.
> Your happiness, may no dark spot
> Of gloomy woe or piercing pain
> Or melancholy ever stain.

It was sent to *The Columbian* by her in 1818 and on it written,
"After this was written Mr. Morris and myself were never absent from each other except one night."

Another Anne in America, almost two hundred years before,
had written her husband two lovely lines of wifely love descrip-
tive of the love at Morrisania:

> If ever two were one, then surely we.
> If ever man were loved by wife, then thee.

The Marketman with a Red Note

(1814)

THE ABILITY of Morris to perceive and assess the realities of international politics provides many lessons for those who came after him. Perhaps it was with a special gift of prophecy that he wrote Rufus King, in January 1814:

I believe the President to be mistaken in his notion that Bonaparte will be pestered by insurrection. Neither Frenchmen nor any other men are prone to rise against so severe and crafty a chief as Napoleon [or Stalin?].

How naturally today the next follows on.

The President is also mistaken in supposing that Russia is the greatest power in Europe and especially that she will exercise her greatness in our favor. Russia, acting on the defense is indeed a prodigious power. Her back to the Arctic Circle, her left covered by the Tartarian deserts . . . she is assailable only on the side of Prussia and Poland. . . . Circumstances called finance will begin now to render the offensive operations of Russia less dangerous to her neighbors than, from the mass of her force, might otherwise be apprehended.

Russia had tentatively offered her services to make peace between England and America and there had been a rumor that Morris would be asked to go as special envoy. In spite of his gout, it seems evident he would have liked the mission, even from Madison's hands.

Then Lord Castlereagh offered direct negotiations at Gothenburg—"it is lucky he did not happen to mention Peking," Morris observed—and John Quincy Adams, minister in St. Petersburg, Gallatin, James Bayard, a New York Federalist, Henry Clay and Jonathan Russell set out from various directions, to come together finally at Ghent in July.

The way to peace with England seemed "open and clear" to Morris, once negotiations were under way. It could already have been had by competent diplomatic representation in London. "Let the right of search and impressment be acknowledged as maxims of public law and leave them to say how the exercise of the latter right shall be restricted between two nations speaking the same language. I am morally certain that the stipulations they propose, as reciprocal, will be safe and satisfactory to us and the universe." But the capacity to do it did not lie in "men without talents [who] administer the powers of a conventional government over a community, which boasts of freedom, [but over which] they exercise a tyranny which would drive the slaves of Asia to despair."

With all this, his general exuberance was unimpaired and he wrote to Moss Kent to have a Presbyterian chaplain get him "typsy and send you in that condition into the House . . . where uncorked of its bashfulness you may pour forth the ideas which your patriotic zeal may have begotten on your imagination," and then with his taste for such metaphors he adds, "This I take it is a conjunction copulative against which there is no commandment!"

Paris fell to the Allies on March 28, and by mid-April, Wellington's infantry was embarking for New Orleans. Morris, not knowing of it, wrote Randolph Harrison, once master of Glenlyvar, now of Clifton, that if the war went on with a nation speaking the same language, having the same religion, the same manners and nearly the same laws, he saw no alternative but for New York to join New England against the states south of the Delaware, the Susquehanna or the Potomac.

He urged his nephew Ogden, a delegate to the New York

Convention, to consider the state of the nation, to "dare hold Great Britain, as she deserves, to general admiration as the shield of mankind against the oppressor's sword, as the nourishing nurse of nations, as pouring out her blood and treasure for their independence."

It should be noted here that Lord Liverpool, the Prime Minister, recognized that the American war was unpopular in England and that Wellington told Castlereagh, "I think you have no right to demand any concession from America," and that Castlereagh told his envoys to discuss but not insist upon such British terms as control of the lakes or independent Indian territory.

On June 14 the victorious allied sovereigns landed at Dover, and with his taste for state and ancientry Morris must have wished he could have seen the spectacle. A week later in New York City he was asked to make one oration about which he had no hesitancy. At church, on the twenty-ninth, "I pronounce an oration of triumph to celebrate the downfall of Bonaparte tolerably well written and in part well delivered."

John W. Francis remembered dining at Morrisania afterwards. He said he asked the boy, Gouverneur, if he knew about Jack the Giant Killer. Morris spoke up to say, "Ask him about Gustavus Adolphus or Charles XII and he can tell you about them." Francis's memory must have slipped. The boy was eighteen months old! Such are the recollections of family friends to historians.

It should be said that the oration often referred to as on the Bourbon Restoration saw more blessings and permanence in that event than there turned out to be.

In August came the shock of the British burning of Washington. Armstrong, of the Newburgh Address, lost his place as Secretary of War, the President moved to the lovely Octagon House, and the sea bathing of Mrs. Rufus King at Rockaway was interrupted.

Meanwhile at Morrisania had begun the series of malign events which filled the mind and correspondence of its mistress until she died.

On July 29, Morris, having heard of the growing unhappiness and irrationality of the deaf boy, St. George Randolph, his wife's nephew, wrote John Randolph of Roanoke that he felt it arose from the tragic situation of a young adolescent, possessed of the natural urges of his years, and deprived by his condition of all "amorous dalliance. He must have been doubly sensible of his past misfortune, poor fellow." He speaks also of Tudor Randolph, tubercularly ill at Harvard. He hoped that Tudor could stay with them, and that his "mother will come north to join him." He says "[Judith] will find a comfortable house, an affectionate sister and a good friend. You will both find a hearty welcome."

Surely hospitality and forgiveness have never been offered more simply. And so Randolph seems to have accepted it, replying August 13:

> Your very friendly and interesting letter of the 29th of last month demands my warmest acknowledgment. The cause to which you direct my attention as the immediate excitement of St. George's malady has not escaped our attention. It occurred to me on the very first view of his situation, poor fellow. He is now quiet and that is all I hope for him. If I can possibly effect it I will have the pleasure to see you at Morrisania in the course of this month or the next. . . . A neighbor calling on his way to Petersburg affords me an opportunity of scratching these few hasty lines. My best wishes to Mrs. Morris. . . .

The Morrises had been planning a brief vacation when, just after Morris's letter of the twenty-ninth of July, Tudor wrote his aunt from Harvard, asking her for money to come to New York. This was not a matter of simply writing and mailing a check on her own bank account. It would have to be done by Morris, writing a business correspondent or some banking friend, like Cabot, to pay it to Tudor, and draw a bill on Morris in New York.

Knowing the incessant demands of his own nephews on him, it was unpleasant for Nancy to have to turn to him, in spite of the devotion between them, on behalf of her own. Few things are more intolerable than the long-continued charity of another, however close. "I was mortified," she said, "because I had already paid all I owed [Tudor's] mother and my pride was wounded by facing my noble-minded husband again. However, the sum desired was sent."

On August 4, Tudor arrived at Morrisania, "fatigued and in slender health," to be put to bed and nursed by his aunt. The next day Bruce, "a friendly companion" of his, also arrived to stay, and Tudor's symptoms of tuberculosis became alarming.

Morrisania was a mixture of hotel and hospital in September, with Morris himself confined to bed, and many visitors coming and going, including another classmate of Tudor's.

On Septmber 25 the boy had "a copious hemorrhage" and the famous Dr. Hosack and Dr. Hofmann were at the house for two days in consultation. Though a small matter for Morris, it is to be noted that their fees were paid by him.

Apparently exhausted, as well as alarmed for Tudor's life, Nancy wrote his mother to come at once. John Randolph was managing her plantation, Bizarre, but she was obliged to ask her friend Judge Tucker for money for the trip. She arrived at Morrisania on October 20 and apparently Nancy and she met as loving sisters, without mention of the past. Money, like time, is a great healer.

On the twenty-second, Morris was up and able to take his sister-in-law for a drive and that afternoon John Randolph himself arrived. In coming through Philadelphia he had had a bad fall "down a steep staircase," which left him unconscious and with an injured shoulder, knee and ankle. It must be remembered that his physical organization throughout life was wretched.

When he entered Morrisania "he pressed [his hostess] to [his] bosom and kissed [her] on the lips." He found Tudor better and had "hopes of him," as he wrote Dudley, if he could get him south of the Potomac before the frosts.

That night, or in town four days later, Tudor, with a malignancy of mind equal to that of his body, told John Randolph that his aunt was clandestinely indulging in "lewd amours" and that his "first impression of her as far back as [he could] remember is that she was an unchaste woman."

During the night of the twenty-second and twenty-third, John Randolph said later, an attempt was made to strangle him. In the morning Tudor told him he believed his aunt had poisoned his father. He went on, Randolph says, "If ever Mr. Morris's eyes are opened it will be through the child, whom with all her grimaces in her husband's presence 'tis easy to see she cares nothing for except as an instrument of power. How shocking she looks!"

John Randolph left for New York the next day and the reason for the quick departure is not clear. Nancy's testimony is that when they rose from dinner Randolph gave Morris a note, in the etiquette of the time, giving his permission for Judith and Tudor Randolph to stay on at Morrisania. Randolph's evidence is quite different. He says that Nancy and he were at the door— "when at my departure from Morrisania in your sister's presence I bade you remember the past, I was not apprised of the whole extent of your guilty machinations. I had nevertheless seen and heard enough in the course of my short visit to satisfy me that your own dear experience had availed nothing toward the amendment of your life. My object was to let you know that the eye of man as well as that of God, of whom you seek not, was upon you. . . ."

It is hard to believe that this scene of mental blackmail took place, yet the hatred, envy, malice of which it is composed are not unfamiliar.

On his way to his lodgings in New York, Randolph's coachman drove over a pile of stones in Cortlandt Street outside an unfinished house. The carriage was overturned and Randolph again painfully injured.

When Judith and Tudor heard of it on the twenty-fifth they drove to town to see him. The next day Morris, Nancy and their child went in to stay at the Ogdens', near Randolph, and to see what could be done for him.

It now appears, from the letters of Nancy, and other evidence, that a dreadful charge must be made against David B. Ogden. All that can be said against its validity is that he does not appear ever to have been heard in his own defense.

He was then in a desperate financial situation, with a large note maturing in a few days. He had, on his aunt's assertion, put an improper, if not illegal, and certainly undisclosed mortgage in favor of William Short on property already mortgaged to Morris. It appears that he had represented to Short, in asking for the loan, that he held clear title to the land, and that Short, very wealthy and relying on family friendship, had made the loan without search of title.

Pressed as he was, Ogden apparently saw as his only hope revelations about his uncle's wife which would result in divorce and make Morris eternally grateful to him. Aside from misjudging his uncle's nature, he was not aware that no one is ever grateful for such information. It was Nancy's contention that Ogden had already talked about this to Tudor Randolph, and that during the twenty-fourth and twenty-sixth of October he had seen Randolph with the story of her current lewd infidelities and a plan even to poison Morris, as she had Richard Randolph.

John Randolph could hardly, in his brief twenty-four hours at Morrisania, have seen enough to assert, unprompted, that Nancy "made him [Morris] a prisoner in his own house, that there may be no witness of [her] lewd amours. [She has] driven away his friends and old domestics that there may be no witness of his death. . . . [Does she] mean to force him to Europe where he will be more at [her] mercy, and dropping the boy on the highway, rid [herself] of all encumbrances at once?"

He could scarcely have thought of all this himself, and his cordial letter of August 13 has no such thought, but his dreadful mind was good ground for such seeds. As to Ogden's guilt, aside from Nancy's assertion of it, William Leigh, testifying the following year in another Randolph case, swore that "Randolph said he had been persuaded to write [the letter] by Ogden."

On the twenty-sixth Morris visited Randolph's sickroom twice, and Nancy took their child there to cheer him up. The Morrises and Judith dined at the Ogdens' that afternoon and returned to Morrisania. The next day the little boy frightened them with a sudden severe throat and they went through the familiar anxieties of parents at such a time.

On the evening of the twenty-seventh, their marketman came to the door with a "red note" from John Randolph, asking Morris to come back to town at once to see him. Nancy says, "[My husband] requested me to write an answer stating that he and our little boy had taken cold and he could not leave home." It is interesting to note how the use of the marketman as letter carrier fits the customs of the times. The Westchester farmers sailed daily from around Morrisania with their produce in "market sloops" to lower New York, coming back at night. They were very useful postmen.

Father and son were both recovered by the last day of October, the weather fine but a little sharp, and the happy family took a long ride by Harlem Bridge to Manville and by Kingsbridge home. Fittingly, on the night of witches and warlocks, John Randolph wrote his terrible letter to Nancy but sent it addressed to her husband. It arrived on the cool, clear morning of All Saints' Day.

Much of it has already been quoted. As to the rest, it charged that Nancy's "hands had deprived of life that of which you were delivered in October, 1792, at Randolph Harrison's. . . ." It said that she had "instigated Mr. Morris" against Chief Justice John Marshall, who defended her, and "whom you know to have been misled with respect to the transactions at Randolph Harrison's." As to them, he goes on in filthy detail. The letter appears to say he believes his brother Richard, not Theodorick, had been her lover and to accuse her of being his murderer. He sends the letter only to save Morris's life and hopes to hear of her repentance and never see her more.

The planners and writer of the letter were, of course, incapable of understanding the type of man they addressed it to. "Mr. Randolph's communication," Morris wrote Randolph Harrison, "gave me no concern, for Mrs. Morris had apprised me of the only fact in his possession, before she came to my house, so that her candor had blunted the point of his arrow." But his heart was deeply touched for "the houseless child of want that I took to my bosom" and he realized there were those who would "hate her because she is happy [so long as] we have among us curious women and flagitious men."

These latter must have waited, with eager hope, all day the first and second of November for news of the disaster they had planned. They would have been amazed to see the undisturbed Morris, sitting in his library, writing very long political letters to Timothy Pickering and Rufus King.

By the night of the second Ogden could wait no longer and went to Morrisania under two compulsions—to see what Morris was going to do, and to get him to endorse a renewal of a note for ten thousand dollars Morris had signed for him.

Although, in her 4000-word reply to Randolph dated January 15, 1815, Nancy says that her husband has just shown her Randolph's letter, it is evident that he had done so as soon as he received it. It seems probable that in her wrath she wished to reply at once, but that Morris dissuaded her, until she had had more time to think. She did, however, lose no time in speaking her mind, perhaps unwisely and without consulting Morris, to his nephews. On their part they were not hesitant about finding out how they stood in the light of Randolph's accusations.

On December 15 young Martin Wilkins wrote his uncle, with intolerable impudence, about a letter Nancy had written him and apparently asked directly where he stood as a beneficiary under Morris's will.

Morris, in a very careful reply, began by saying that he read Wilkins's letter to his wife and then goes on to say that "your aunt" wrote as she did trying to account for the condition of a being (Randolph) whose only fixed principles were envy and avarice and she was astonished that Randolph had attributed his malicious inventions to persons so near and dear as Wilkins and Mr. Ogden. With unbelievable restraint but shrewd rebuke, he adds, "What my intentions respecting my property were it is useless to conjecture. What they are it would answer no honest purpose to communicate. I am not without hopes, however, that some of these may enable me to be useful to you while I yet linger on the stage of mortality."

Then there is a letter of December 20 to Ogden, begun, "My dear Sir," from which it appears that when Randolph's letter failed to loose the thunderbolts an anonymous letter was also sent to the Morrises, containing the Randolph charges with additional matter of the same sort.

Evidently both Morrises knew that Ogden was the writer because Nancy replied to it, addressing Ogden, who asked Morris if he had been aware of her doing so.

Morris now said he did not know the conclusion of the letter but was sure it contained nothing contrary to his understanding. And he says he is sure it was "written to you as being her friend disposed, from the sentiments you entertain for me, to defend the reputation of my wife."

The conspirators had failed in their purpose, except as they brought sorrow to a lady who had already had her share. This time the guests who dined at Morrisania Christmas Day all had the family name of its master and mistress. It was sharp weather. The winter cattle-killing was over and on the twentieth they had commenced to fill the icehouse.

CHAPTER THIRTY-SEVEN

Go Tell This to the World

(1815)

A GOOD DEAL, by contrast to all this, is to be said for the tolerance toward sinners and the indifference to sexual lapses on the part of the "worthless aristocrats" Morris had known in France.

Two weeks after Randolph's red note was delivered the Congress of Vienna began. It was surely inexcusable that Talleyrand, at sixty, should have been "accepted" there, living with Dorothea de Dino, twenty-one, his nephew's wife, and the daughter of a former mistress. But who cared about that and when has a man done more for peace on earth?

As "curious women and flagitious men" brought unhappiness to Nancy, there was a party at Adèle de Souza's, now fifty-three, with Lady Bessborough there. "The wife of Marshal Ney, and Charles de Flahaut, now twenty-nine, sang several pretty romances. He ended with some old national song . . . which drove Adèle herself out of the room, really, or affecting to be, frightened, the latter perhaps, for she is not *en bonne odeur* at [the Bourbon court, since her boy was one of Napoleon's generals]."

There was political envy and malice of course in Paris. Three people wrote to ask Lady Bessborough if it was true "General Flahaut had sung the *Marseilles* and *Ça Ira.*"

Still, ten days later, November 24, 1814, after a round of parties, Lady Bessborough "ended at Madame de Souza's where there were some [allied] marshals, some savants and some singing. The gallant Flahaut sang, 'Dans le Camp des Danois,'" [and his mother told him not to sing the song of Napoleon's soldiers]:

> *Les guinées des Anglois dans nos bourses*
> *Les charmes des Angloises dans nos bras.*
>
> (O the English guineas in our packs
> And in our arms the English girls.)

The letter which Morris had written to Pickering on All Saints' Day began, "I now see that we are to be taxed beyond our means and subjected to military conscription . . . by the gentle spirits, who, for more than twenty years have lavished on Britain the bitterest vulgarity of Billingsgate . . . and shed . . . crocodile tears over the poor of that country crushed, as they pretend, by oppressive taxes to gratify royal ambition." He jeered at Monroe's idea that an expedition could after November ascend or maintain itself by the St. Lawrence, and he asked Pickering if Massachusetts was in earnest and "will be supported by the New England family" in throwing off the load of oppression. The letter was in reply to one from Pickering which said:

Let the ship run aground. The shock will throw the present pilots overboard and then competent navigators will get her once more afloat . . . the separation of north and south will be advantageous, and it will only be temporary. . . . As to the [Great] Lakes it would be a most desirable thing if Great Britain and the United States could agree to have neither armed vessels on the lakes nor any fort on their borders!

To King, Morris wrote that "a union of the commercial states to take care of themselves—and leave the war, the expense and the debt to those so eager to carry it on—seems to be now the only rational course."

All this was preliminary to the Hartford Convention which was to meet in mid-December 1814 to oppose continuation of the war and conscription, with a new federal Union as the menacing alternative.

The New England delegates had been named and Morris hoped to bring in New York. In the week of his letters to Wilkins and Ogden the "infirm old man," cut off from the world and his friends, wrote lightheartedly to Pickering that he felt he would ultimately succeed, saying, "A coy but willing damsel may for form and fashion require what the French call *une douce violence* but her embrace will not be the less ardent."

The twenty-five men going to Hartford were "high above the average in intelligence and public service," as Professor Morrison points out, but Jefferson called them "Marats, Dantons and Robespierres." George Cabot, the friend of Washington and guardian pro tem of Lafayette's son, was president of the convention. The uncle and father of Longfellow and of the historian Prescott, Lyman, the president of the Cincinnati, were delegates.

The platform, put briefly, was for peaceable dissolution of the Union or seven amendments to the Constitution, among them: abolition of representation of the slave population; only native-born citizens eligible for federal office; a declaration of war only by a two-thirds vote; no second term for a President and not from the same state twice in succession; admission of new states only by two thirds of both Houses.

Following the precedent of 1787, the meetings were held in "inviolable secrecy" and the charge of treason thereby laid against the delegates.

It is obvious from Morris's letter to Moss Kent of January 10 that he was confident that between Yankee good sense on one side and Madison's "dearth of ready 'rhino,'" the cash New England could provide, a compromise would be reached. Strangely enough, ready rhino was provided for Madison by Stephen Girard *and* David Parish. The latter's contribution, out of commingled English-Dutch-Hanseatic funds, was "international banking" at its worst.

The Hartford deliberations were not over until the end of January 1815, when a committee of three left for Washington with their proposals, not knowing that peace had been signed at Ghent on Christmas, the envoys dining together later on roast beef and plum pudding while they drank each other's

health. The treaty said not a word about the impressment of
sailors.

In Philadelphia, on their way south, the Hartford delegates
heard of Jackson's victory at New Orleans and two days later
of the peace. The news reached Morrisania February 12, Lincoln's sixth birthday, and Morris wrote in his *Diary*, "The news
of peace . . . may prevent a separation of the states, patch up
our tattered Constitution, and perpetuate the blessings of a
Jacobin Administration."

He had had too much experience of the world, however, to
suppose that all public virtue lay in one party or one nation. He
wrote Rufus King that day, "I am sensible, deeply sensible of
the difference of opinion between good men" and he added
that England, which he so greatly admired, "is guilty of the
utmost folly."

When, forty-six years later, it was proposed to dissolve the
Union, the descendants of the Hartford delegates rushed to fight
for its preservation "like men flocking to a feast."

Morris's buoyant assurance that all would yet be well with
his country did not extend to Nancy's situation. Their boy had
begun to prattle and to "exceed the promise of his earlier day,"
Morris writes with paternal pride, but to Randolph Harrison he
confided that his tenderest attentions were "required to soothe
his mother's anguish. Her health is sinking under wounds inflicted by relatives whom she believed to be friends," and then,
heavily underscored, he says, "She never deceived me."

It was his habit of life to take small notice of slander and it
seems evident that he counseled Nancy to make no answer to
Randolph's letter, now two and a half months old. The reply
which she did make on January 16, 1815, and of which she sent
copies to many people in Virginia, is so unlike what he would
have written that one must suppose she came to him and said,
"I must reply. This is tearing me to pieces and I cannot stand it.
It will lift some of the burden if I can write."

Considering the time interval and the nature of the reply, it
appears that her legal lord and master, with an enlightenment
beyond the times, said to her, "Very well. I recognize that you

are a separate and free individual and have every right to do what you want."

As with Randolph's letter, portions of her reply have already been quoted. Emotional as it is in part, its general tenor is logical, penetrating and effective. It begins:

Sir,

My husband yesterday communicated to me for the first time your letter of the last of October, together with that which accompanied it direct to him. . . . It seems, sir, as if you wished to apprise Mr. Morris and him only of circumstances important to his happiness and honour, though fatal to my reputation, leaving it in his power to cover them in oblivion, or display them to the world as the means of freeing him from a monster unfit to live. [Yet you told Mr. Bleecker and Commander Decatur of them.] . . . Did you believe these slanders? If you did, why did you permit your nephew to be fed with my bounty, and nursed by my care during nearly three months? Could you suppose him safe in the power of a wretch who had murdered his father? Does it consist with the dignified pride of family you affect, to have him whom you announce as your heir . . . dependent on the charity of a Negro's concubine?

. . . You say I confine my husband a prisoner in his own house that there may be no witness of my lewd amours, and have driven away his friends that there may be no witness of his death. . . . [Surely] if I wished to indulge in amours the natural course would be to mingle with the pleasures of the city [which I seldom visit].

. . .

When you kissed me on the lips [on arriving at Morrisania] did you then believe that you held in your arms, that you kissed the lips of a common prostitute, the murderess of her own child, and of your brother? Go tell this to the world. . . .

You not only charge me with the heinous crime of infanticide, placing [Richard] in the condition of an accomplice but you proceed to say that had it not been for the prudence of Mr. Harrison, or the mismanagement of not putting me first on trial, we should both have swung on the same gibbet and the foul stain of incest and murder been stamped on Richard's memory. . . . Who is there of nerve so strong as not to shudder at your savage regret that we did not swing on the same gibbet. . . . I remember when you threw a knife at Richard's head. . . .

There occurs her correction of his fixing her delivery as October '92 instead of the unforgettable last of September. Then, probably inserted by Morris, follows the reference to Randolph's first "entering the door of Congress [as] an outrageous patriot. Nothing in the French Revolution was too immoral or too impious for your taste and applause. Washington and Britain were the objects of your obloquy." (The alliterative phrase sounds particularly like Morris.)

There are references to characteristics in Randolph which had disgusted her in the past.

With all the letter's sweeping frankness, it never makes clear who was the father of the stillborn child. It ends coolly with the light assurance that "Happily you will not find my husband a headlong rash Othello."

"Just put that as the last line," Morris may have told her.

One wishes, for her peace of mind, that this catharsis could have ended it. If Morris had lived, doubtless it would have, but alone she seemed unable ever to forget it and at the time she made at least six copies of her 40-page reply.

On February 7 one went "in three packages" to William B. Giles, who had defended her "amid the fury of enemies long ago," which she asked him to show in Richmond. Giles, fifty-three, was serving his last term as senator from Virginia.

Poor St. George had meanwhile written her "a most affectionate letter." On the seventeenth she wrote Giles to see if her letter had been received or if more copies were necessary. She wrote again on March 14, as Randolph himself wrote to Giles, saying:

"I learn from authority that I cannot discredit that you have in your possession and occasionally shew to others a written paper which purports to be a letter from Mrs. Gouverneur Morris addressed to me, containing allegations against me of a nature highly injurious." He warns Giles, "I cannot consent that anyone under the pretext that he is not the author shall make himself the vehicle of calumny against me . . . neither will I suffer my family history to be raked up with the ashes of the peaceful to subserve the personal view of anyman. . . ." The end of the letter implies that he expects Giles will challenge him.

The day before, Morris himself wrote two letters, one coldly directed to Ogden, beginning, "I expected to have seen you before this day."

He encloses a letter he had received from Judith Randolph and his own reply which he asks Ogden to read, seal and post. He asks Ogden to show Judith's letter to "such persons within the circle of my acquaintance as may suppose she was a party to the plan for destroying her sister's fame." Ogden is then to send it to Dr. Mason, the rector of Trinity Church.

We do not have Judith's letter. Morris's reply is brief.

It is too true, my dear madam, that your son was a principal agent in those transactions which excite your indignation and abhorrence. The solemn assurances to which you have attested before an omniscient judge give me the pleasure of being able to prove that you did not participate in the scenes exhibited during your short residence at Mrs. Bradish's. I will omit no proper occasion to vindicate your honor from the imputation.

In agreeing with his wife that she must do what she thought best as to an answer to the Randolph letter, Morris evidently felt that thereafter he would not restrict its circulation. "Inform yourselves and be damned to you," seems to have been his attitude.

On September 7, 1815, David Parish, who six years before had had the insolence to "counsel" Morris on the "scandal" of Nancy's presence, wrote asking to be informed of the facts. Morris replied:

I annunciated this evening to my wife your wish to see her correspondence with her cousin. She tells me that my friend, David Ford, took a copy at Morrisania to confute and confound those who busied themselves in propagating slanderous misrepresentations. She will request him to communicate them to you.

During all this time, in addition to his private and political letters, he was carrying on his enormous correspondence about his Northern lands, a business for which a large staff would be needed today. The taxgatherer called to take an account of his furniture. "I desire him to set it down at the *highest* price that I may be subject to no malicious insinuations." And his interest in fish and game breeding, farming and roads was inexhaustible. One of his richest letters is the 8-page one of February 19 to

De Witt Clinton, acknowledging an address of Clinton's before the Philosophical Society, branching off into a discussion of timothy grass, the biology and breeding of eels, fish, oysters and native animals (with a paragraph on economic questions) —and the question of whether, since "our streaked bass" have "the shape, substance and manners of perch," they are not in fact perch.

There is a penetrating discussion of the incentives of private enterprise which, if taken away, will mean "all that action which moves the social machine would be taken away." Well, he says at the end, "I sat down to say a word about eels and somehow or other that slippery subject" has gotten away from me.

News of the escape from Elba reached Morrisania April 27, with the chestnuts and the peach trees and the apricots breaking into flower. Morris wrote that "Bonaparte will be quelled and his associated conspirators brought to condign punishment." High among them was Charles de Flahaut, now thirty, older than his mother had been when Morris met her.

Halfway through the Hundred Days, Napoleon sent him on a wild errand to see Metternich, the Austrian chancellor, and bring back Marie Louise.

Metternich and Talleyrand, with Wellington, had already left the Congress of Vienna to deal with Flahaut's master and he was turned back at the frontier.

At Pressburg, almost at the moment, Wellington and Metternich waited while Talleyrand went to kneel and beg forgiveness of another mistress, the aged, dying Madame de Brionne, cousin of Rohan, who had tried to get him a cardinal's hat thirty-one years before. She said to him, "So, you are there once more. I have always believed I should see you again. Deeply as I have disapproved of you, I have never ceased for a moment to love you."

Flahaut was closest, perhaps of them all, to Napoleon, in the afternoon at Waterloo, "sent to order up the massed cavalry, which made the last charge of the Empire," holding up the Emperor in his saddle as they rode off the field. "In the last scene of all, when a fallen Emperor sat waiting at Malmaison . . . Flahaut was still beside him," as Napoleon waited for the word that he might go to America, which never came.

In the room was Hortense, mother of Flahaut's boy of four, and Napoleon said his last farewell to her before he drove to the coast to surrender to Admiral Lord Keith.

When he was gone Hortense, of the laughing eyes, the heart-shaped face, the broad cheekbones, left, penniless, for refuge in Switzerland, with Flahaut following. She got across the frontier, but Fouché caught and held her lover at Lyons, despite all Adèle de Souza could do to help him.

Late in 1815 he escaped to England, a refugee again as he had been in September, twenty-three years before, and afterwards when, as a boy of ten, he dined with Morris.

At Morrisania, the week of Waterloo, there were wild pigeons in the cherry trees, and Morris walked a mile and a half with Nancy and the boy, twenty-eight months old, accompanying them. When they got back, in spite of the "long leagues," the babe "takes a little wine and milk and runs about the house frolicking till dinner upwards of two hours."

Randolph Harrison sent his son and daughter for a summer's holiday at Morrisania and Morris wrote him that his boy would be an ornament to the Bar and that if he were not a *Virginia Democrat*, people would think him a *New York Aristocrat*.

The visitors were gone and the Morrises were in the Mohawk Valley with their son, when young Mr. Low brought Morris a letter from David B. Ogden asking another renewal of the $10,000 loan "given for his accommodation," the loan about which he had called, the day after Randolph's letter had been received.

For the rest of the year the *Diary* entries are of single lines and the gout is very troubling.

A Little Frost Last Night

(*1816*)

THERE WAS much snow at Morrisania the winter of 1816 and Morris, between influenza and gout, spent his son's third birthday in bed, with only the parson and the doctor there to celebrate. Relatives in town had been told not to come.

It had been twenty-five years since "Paul Jones favored [him] with his company for a long time," until Morris had hurried off to the Louvre to find Adèle at tric trac with guests whom she got rid of to be alone with him.

There was no change in the power and industry of his mind, nor, it is splendid to note, "in the gayety of inexperience and the frolic of youth," which, as he wrote that summer, his friends would still find in him.

From his sickbed the letters on public affairs poured out, urging "internal but not direct taxation," protesting the proposed high tariff on tea, coffee, spirits and wine. If forty years ago, he said, spirits were smuggled to save a duty of ten cents a gallon, what profits would go to the contraband trade with a duty of one dollar a gallon? And this high tariff on manufactured goods to protect infant industries. Infant indeed, American hats and leather goods at the time of the Revolution sold in foreign markets against English exports. Low duties, which might seem to encourage foreign competition here, would stimulate "our mechanics to do more and better work."

And as to this thirst for American factories—well, he was not so sure of its absolute benefits. There was still little thought in America of the evils of the Industrial Revolution but Morris saw them in factories he had inspected "where poor children [are] pent up to march backward and forward with a spinning jenny till they are old enough to be drunkards and prostitutes."

He tells Moss Kent, yes, the "Federalists are generally [still] agreeable," but he himself will support Madison whenever Madison's measures have his approval, regardless of party.

How is this Erie Canal ever to be financed? Russell Atwater asked him. The method is quite simple, Morris wrote him. Let the state vest in the commission a great tract of land which, with auxiliary lands which interested parties will contribute, will be the basis for a loan of five million dollars, with interest at six per cent and charges of five per cent. Such a sum cannot, of course, be borrowed in the United States, nor at present even in Europe. However, the money markets abroad will soon settle down and be seeking outlets for capital.

The loan will be serviced by tolls sufficient to cover repair and maintenance plus seven per cent on the cost.

Additionally, like TVA, the commission will be authorized to use idle portions of the land *"in such manner as may be approved (by whom you please)"* for related purposes out of which profits, for the benefit of the sinking fund, can be made.

Morris was sowing his summer wheat in April when, as Hobhouse's *Diary* reveals, "Byron and [Hobhouse] went to Lady Jersey's. I was introduced by Flahaut to Benjamin Constant and his wife." Morris gave young Edward Everett, the other orator at Gettysburg, a letter of introduction to Madame la Baronne de Staëhl Holstein, so that he might taste "the sweets of your society."

In July, Nancy "rode to town to visit Mrs. James Monroe." The next year Harvard would give Monroe an LL.D. but not so Federalist Columbia. Mrs. Monroe was not a Virginian but Eliza Kortright, daughter of a New York merchant.

There was a voice from the long past that month, when Charles Carroll of Carrollton, now seventy-nine, wrote Rufus

King significantly, "I am glad to hear Mrs. Morris is well and happy. Remember me to Mr. Morris, Mr. and Mrs. Gracie and Mrs. King."

From Paris, Gallatin wrote to Monroe, "I have been told M. de Neuville had either given or received a note of the names of persons in the United States whom it would be agreeable to this government to see here [as minister] and that Gouverneur Morris was at the head."

Gallatin's letter closed with other news of all too great familiarity a hundred and thirty-five years later. "The cadres of the Russian Army . . . [are] made up of 800,000 men and the not dismissing [of them by] the Emperor [is] a subject of uneasiness to the other powers."

On July 6, Morris wrote his last letter to John Parish in Hamburg. David Parish was going home and the letter went by him.

Morris tells him, "Our little boy is generally admired, though the sentiments of a father respecting an only child render his opinion so liable to suspicion that prudence should withhold them even from a friend."

It is the letter with the reference to "the [still present] gayety of inexperience and the frolic of youth." Then, with disarming flatness, he says of Nancy—knowing what David Parish would pour in his father's ear—"The woman to whom I am married has much genius, has been well educated and possesses, with an affectionate temper, industry and a love of order . . . a kind companion and a tender feminine friend."

On October 8, Nancy took her son to town to get him winter clothing. There was a little frost that night. With those words, the *Diary* ends forever. In her beautiful full script, she has written below them, "Oh, my adored, my best of husbands, had I been told this was to be the last morning we should leave our chamber together, that equally the last night we should reenter it together I should have thought my heart would burst. I have traced the sufferings of your mind from the first detection of David Ogden's villainy. . . ."

By the twenty-sixth, it was obvious Morris was very ill indeed and that day he made a new will, naming Nancy and

Moss Kent as co-executors, with ten thousand dollars to Kent for his services.

The will's first provision is surely one of the most gallant a gentleman ever made for a wife. It confirms the ante-nuptial settlement of twenty-six hundred dollars a year, a large income for the time, gives her Morrisania, with all its stock and plate and furniture for life, with all improvements to be at the expense of the estate and "in case my wife should marry, I give her six hundred dollars more per annum, to defray the increased expenditure, which may attend that connexion." Has the *mort main* ever been so open?

Item, I give to my son, Gouverneur Morris, the whole of my estate, saving and excepting such bequests, as may be in this my will, and such as I may hereafter think proper to make. If it should please God to take him away, before he arrives at full age, or afterwards, not having made a will, I then give my estate to such one or more of the male descendants of my brothers and sisters, and in such proportions, as my wife shall designate; but in case she shall have made no such designation, I then give my estate to Lewis Morris Wilkins, son of my sister Isabella, on condition, that he drop the name of Wilkins, and bear the name and arms of Morris.

And the last provision leaves the legatee in no doubt as to whom he must respect and whose good opinion deserve:

Item, I give to my nephew, Gouverneur Wilkins, twenty-five thousand dollars, to be paid to him when he shall have arrived to the age of thirty, provided his conduct shall be, in the opinion of my executor and executrix, such as becomes a good citizen.

The jester of Kutuzov and "the great villain," Ogden, are not mentioned.

By November 4 he knew he was dying and that nothing could be done. He was in great agony. John W. Francis said afterwards that "his devoted nephew [Ogden]" was with him. In the entire 26-page letter Nancy Morris is not mentioned. She, however, said that her husband, knowing then of Ogden's villainy, told Dr. Hosack much against him from his deathbed.

On the fifth Rufus King wrote Christopher Gore, "We are

likely to lose if we have not already done so, one of our distinguished citizens, Mr. Gouverneur Morris."

On the seventh the *Commercial Advertiser* and the *Gazette and General Advertiser* carried the obituaries:

At 5 o'clock yesterday morning at his seat at Morrisania, the Honorable Gouverneur Morris, after a short but distressing illness, in the 65th year of his age.

The New York *Evening Post* had carried a brief editorial the evening of the sixth: "We are not sufficiently possessed of facts to attempt even a sketch of the illustrious deceased. He has filled a large space in the history of this country . . . the funeral tomorrow [Thursday] morning at ten o'clock at Morrissania [sic]."

It would be inappropriate to write somberly of this passing incident in the life of a man so seldom somber, so utterly without fear of death or the hereafter, so obviously at peace with God and himself. One may feel sure, however, that if there are Courts of the Morning he entered them with grace and good manners, and doubtless many great gentlemen rose to greet him.

Even the customary summing up or assessment of his character and life seems uncalled for. It is too many-sided, too contradictory for a single verdict.

Those who do not see for themselves the continuing magnanimity and genius of the man, through all his weaknesses, will never be persuaded to. The faults are never hidden, but it is doubtful that even those who see only the faults can find meanness among them.

CHAPTER THIRTY-NINE

A Volume Would Not Suffice

I N A WAY it would seem that the "Ogden villainy" was God's mercy to Nancy Morris. It supplied the "pressures" and tapped the energies without which, in her grief over Morris's death and the continuing shame of the Randolph letter, she might not have had the determination to survive.

Her childhood, after her mother's death, had been unhappy, her girlhood horrible, the next ten years an ugly dream. With Morris she had had five years of happiness before Randolph's letter came. Perhaps even in them she had been afraid the shadow of the past would come over her.

Now that he was gone, the very malice of her enemies became her weapon. She wrote to William Short on November 25:

When David B. Ogden purchased his father's Northern lands my noble minded husband became his security at the same time obtaining a mortgage on those lands. D.O. has since requested M.M. to endorse for him a considerable amount with solemn assurances that he was paying the principal of the debt for his father's estate. On discovering that all these assurances were made without a shadow of truth we sent the mortgage to be recorded. I now understand that D.O. has borrowed money of you on a mortgage upon these lands. Have the goodness to write me the extent of your claim on them. The interest of my lovely son alone animates me.

Accept the assurances of my great respect.

Before Short replied, the New York Historical Society "Resolved, that a portrait of the late Honorable Gouverneur Morris, deceased President of this Society, be procured at the expense thereof, and that the Recording Secretary ask Mrs. Morris to arrange it." She wrote at once to Thomas Sully in Philadelphia to make a copy of his portrait in the possession of the niece, Gertrude Meredith, who had protested his marriage so violently.

Sully wrote back, December 10, "I shall be very happy to comply with your request in making the copy mentioned whenever I can be provided with the use of the original portrait. At present Mrs. Meredith declines lending it."

"Read the enclosed," Nancy wrote De Witt Clinton, on the fourteenth. "My husband paid for the portrait at the request of his niece. If the Historical Society can obtain a sight of it for Sully, I will pay for two copies although I have been *threatened* with having my person seized for the *Ogden* debts."

The society intervened, naturally unable to believe it possible. Thereupon Mr. Meredith wrote them unctuously:

The portrait is peculiarly the property of Mrs. Meredith and as she has very lately felt herself obliged by reasons which cannot find a proper place in this communication, but which were entirely approved by me—to refuse an application for a copy from another quarter, with which I presume Dr. Hosack is acquainted—I cannot with consistency or self-respect yield to an endeavor to obtain one indirectly by using the liberal purpose of the New York Historical Society and weighty influence which on every occasion must accompany the request of its members.

Sully himself wrote Dr. Hosack, ". . . the true reason of his withholding the picture is to prevent Mrs. Morris from having a copy of it; for reasons which do not at all concern me. I think if after the lapse of time Mrs. M. would herself make the application, it would not be refused." The optimism was unfounded, and Ezra Ames made a portrait the following June.

Meantime, Nancy had sent Short, himself a Virginian, letters of condolence she had had from Virginia and which she said the Ogden family accused her of forging.

Have the goodness [she says] to give me the date of this loan to David O. Was it in June 1815? My beloved husband was torn from my bosom by the deep laid villainy of that swindler whose tissue of falsehood I had detected, all but the mortgage to you. D.O. calculated on winding up as executor. . . .

Mr. Jefferson wrote a charming letter to M. Morris in October.

It appears that the estate had been swindled of $100,000 and "$17,000 taken." Out of the rest, largely in wild land, must come taxes, the Wilkins legacy and the ante-nuptial settlement. Not until 1831 was this brave lady able to hand over to her "incomparable son" the estate free and clear.

We know from her that in the spring of 1817 she began to read the *Diaries* of Europe. One cannot suppose that Morris had been any less candid with her about the past than she with him. Yet with all her experience of sordid life, the facts written in Morris's own hand must have been more of a shock than her spoken words had been to him.

One can well imagine the irresistible curiosity with which she may have said to William Short, "Tell me, what was Madame de Flahaut like? You knew her well, did you not?" Perhaps he told her and also that he and Rosalie de la Rochefoucauld still wrote hopelessly to each other.

Perhaps it was Morris's death that waked the memory of old romance in Jefferson, in his seventy-fifth year that spring. He wrote to John Trumbull, "And Madame de Corny? What has become of her? Is she living or dead?" Trumbull sent her address and Jefferson wrote to her.

Trumbull himself had no such pleasant memories of lost romance. He wrote brutally the next year to his "nephew," John Trumbull Ray, twenty-six, "You for the first time address me as your father and Mrs. Trumbull as your mother:—you cannot be ignorant that your mother was Temperance Ray of East Haddam, a servant in my brother's house: where the looseness of her conduct left it uncertain who might be your father; but she swore according to law that I was:—I had no remedy."

It was the year De Souza published his edition of the *Lusiads* of Camoëns, and on June 19, in Edinburgh, Flahaut married "Meg Mercer" Elphinstone, the daughter of Lord Keith to whom Napoleon had surrendered. A month later Madame de Staël died in Paris. Short must have known of all this.

"*Bonne et riant* [kind and smiling]," Adèle went on, "*sa tendresse jointe à une indulgence souvent exquise et parfois excessive pour les faiblesses humaines* [with an indulgence often exquisite, sometimes excessive for human weaknesses]." Still, "I love all the sweet emotions," she wrote her old friend Le Roi.

Two more novels, and a play, *La Duchesse de Guise*, were still to be written. In 1824 a literary society in Lyons published the works of Louise Labé, the curious poet of the sixteenth century. For it Alexandre Dumas wrote an imaginary dialogue between Sappho and Louise Labé in which over several pages they exchange stilted, pretty compliments, as:

LOUISE: I cannot pretend to have equalled you, either in poetry or in love.
SAPPHO: . . . You are justly compared to me. Lyons in this respect need not envy Lesbos.

Halfway through, Louise speaks of Feminism, and Dumas adds a footnote in his hasty way. "Yes, Feminism [today there is] Flahaut, Souza . . . [as though they were two]."

Had Morris gone back to France as minister or traveled with Nancy, as Randolph implied they thought of doing, it seems likely that his two indestructible ladies would have had much in common. It should dismay the moralists that the greater "sinner" of the two had, over all, the happier life.

In 1820 the Duchess de Dino, then twenty-seven, bore a daughter, Pauline, to Talleyrand, in his sixty-seventh year. At Morrisania, with distraught valor, Nancy was still struggling against "curious women and flagitious men." The year before she had sent a copy of Morris's last letter to John Parish about her to *The Columbian*, asking them to publish it, which they did, saying, "Mrs. Morris states that *maternal duty* [their italics] impels her to the publication." Her son was now six, and who knew what people would soon begin to tell him about his mother and his father?

Moss Kent, her co-executor, had dismissed her agents, and

sold lands with no provision for unpaid taxes. She was forced to bring a suit in chancery against him, and hearing it, with John Jay's son Pierre as her attorney, Chancellor Jones gave her sole power. She had then to manage the estate through four land agents, and provide for taxes and legacies.

Her brother Thomas was now governor of Virginia, and her brother William, silent in time of need, wrote warning her "not to live in style."

A long summer's day was too short for all she had to do and her hope was only to live until her son's majority. "The voluminous correspondence of many great men, General Washington's letters from an early period of the Revolution until a fortnight before his death were read over and over," with her tired eyes in the evening.

There is a ghost story about her alone one New Year's Eve in the house "in the east limits of Gouverneur, New York." No novelist selects and then rearranges incidents of life with half the skill of the unknown, masked genius who gives ghost stories to an eager countryside.

The story is that Morris had brought "plate and costly jewels of the fleeing French nobility" to Gouverneur and hid them there in his house. His widow, sitting alone, suddenly heard a thunder of hoofbeats and horsemen reined up at the door, calling to her to bring out her husband's will. At that Gouverneur Morris stepped down from his picture on the wall, went to the door and drove the miscreants away (as he did with the commissaires at the legation in the Terror). Then he led Nancy through the house, showing her the treasure.

The Morris and David Parish estates were both forced to press claims on James Le Ray, and on Christmas Eve, 1823, he was obliged to deed all his property to his creditors and, like Robert Morris, go to a debtor's prison.

De Souza died of smallpox in 1825, and Charles Flahaut came with his English wife and daughters to stay at his mother's house. Within a few years Adèle's great worry, like any grandmother, was for the safety of young Morny, a lancer in Africa.

Then in 1831, with Morris's *Diaries* and *Letters* in Jared

Sparks's hands, Madison, forgetting the bitter war, paid his great tribute to Morris's work at the Federal Convention, forty-four years before. "A better choice could not have been made, as the performance of the task proved."

In May 1833, John Randolph was gone; and on April 19, three years later, at seventy-five, Adèle died in her house on the Rue St. Honoré near Talleyrand's palace on the corner. There Talleyrand said, "Love is a reality in the realm of the imagination." She is buried in Père La Chaise.

How Morris, Talleyrand and she would have delighted in one of the last scenes of the subplot.

George Parish, the grandson of John and nephew of David, lived in Ogdensburg. If neither Morris nor Talleyrand had known his grandfather he would probably have been a North German banker.

At this time "Prince John" Van Buren, the President's son, had as his mistress Maria Amerigo Vespucci, presumably the descendant of the forerunner of Columbus.

In the tavern at Evans Mills, New York, Van Buren lost five thousand dollars at cards to Parish and was quite unable to pay. He asked Parish if he himself was not in love with Maria Vespucci and if he would not like to have her. And Parish said yes, and they played one hand for her, Parish winning.

The lady was quite content with the change, and lived happily in scandalous and expensive sin at Ogdensburg thereafter as *Parish's Fancy*. Lucky for him his uncle David was not still alive. He had appropriately committed suicide, April 27, 1826.

On May 28, 1837, the weary lady at Morrisania died, her twenty-one years' trusteeship over and her "incomparable son's" lands, house and fortune clear. And they had seen him in Virginia, the Cabells, the Carters, the Carys, the Randolphs. Six feet one inch tall like his father, with "all the manly virtues which adorn human nature."

She was buried beside the spot where, in her words, "The best of men was laid until a vault could be created to receive his precious remains."

Less than a year later Talleyrand was gone at last after his long, wicked but magnificent life of eighty-four years.

Only William Short, so long alone, was left, still alone, until a winter day in December 1849.

In June 1841, after Gouverneur Morris, the younger, had given "The Church and Lands for the Glory of God and in Memory of His Mother," St. Ann's Church was consecrated.

Church and lands, a little hill with great boulders and trees, is today a lovely God's Acre in the midst of the most horrible of New York slums. Its light is indeed that of a good deed in a naughty world.

Under a grating in the east aisle is a stone in which are cut the words:

AND HERE BY HER OWN REQUEST
REPOSE THE REMAINS
OF
THE WIFE AND MOTHER
IN MEMORY OF WHOM
THIS CHURCH
WAS CREATED
TO THE GOD SHE LOVED
BY FILIAL VENERATION

Gouverneur   *Ann Cary*
Morris   *Morris*
Nov. 6, 1816   *May 28, 1837*
in his 65th year   *in her 63rd year*

Notes

The frequent custom of omitting all reference to sources seems to me as annoying as a parade of notes fixing every fact and document used. It is also unfair to reviewers and others working in the same period.

So far as possible I have indicated sources in the text itself and, where letters or documents quoted do not appear in the published writings of the patriot leaders, listed in the Bibliography, the notes give the manuscript collections where they can be found.

I do not believe there is any surmise in the book which is not either so labeled or recognizable from the language used. Weather and wind direction, for example, are habitual daily entries in Morris's *Diaries*.

After 1789, Morris's letters are from his *Letter Books* except as special collections are shown hereafter. Before 1789, they are in either Sparks, the published writings of their recipients, or special collections.

CHAPTER ONE

"The great lover with the wooden leg," a phrase of Greenslet, *Seven Worlds of the Lowells*.

Excerpts from letters and references to Detroit and Upper Posts, and letters on Pawnee and Negro slave girls, WEP.

Madame de Damas's eulogy in full, Sparks, I, 506.

I was anxious to know whether Morris and Boswell had a single, specific source from which they had drawn their many references to the sacrifice (or wars) of the Cyprian (or Paphian) Queen. Professor Pottle, editor of the Boswell Papers, replied that such "adjectives suit so perfectly the taste of the eighteenth

century for combining elegant periphrasis with classical mythology that any
educated man would have been likely to have used them." Professor Gilbert
Highet of Columbia University wrote that he believed "the type of phrase
came in with the 'libertin' of the late sixteenth and seventeenth centuries,"
adding, "for the Greeks and Romans these forces were real divinities, really
superhuman energies, and one did not simply 'sacrifice' to them by having fun."

CHAPTER TWO (1752–74)

Sparks, I, 4, refers to Morris family dissension.
G.M.'s letters to Kitty Livingston, MHS.
Liberty Hall, now a great house of fifty rooms, has come down through
the distaff side to its present owner, Mrs. John Kean. It is part of the extraordinary links of Morris's life that John Kean, a South Carolina patriot, a friend of
Morris, should have married a Livingston and the house be lived in today by
his descendants. From the house the stepdaughter of Sally's and Kitty's older
sister, Susan Symmes, left to marry William Henry Harrison (Tippecanoe) in
the Northwest Territory. The Livingston girls were in contrast to the swooning
lasses "with a delicate air" in the novels of the time. *Pamela's Daughters* should
be read in this connection. So were the Randolph girls in that regard, but
strangely like the gothic romances beginning to be popular. For that, *The
Haunted Castle* is well worth considering.
"Poor Reptiles" letter, Abbot, 106–7.
Livery Company to the King, Trevelyan, 239.

CHAPTER THREE (1775–76)

Moot's last meeting, *Republican Court*, 148.
Definition of treason, Rebecca West's in *The Meaning of Treason*.
G.M. to Lewis Morris, Emmet Collection, 723, NYPL.
For Wilkins at the caucus, Dawson, 69–72.
R. R. Livingston to his wife and all other letters of his hereafter, R.R.L.,
NYHS.
The excerpt from the William Smith *Memoirs* is apparently its only reference
to G.M. The 1769–75 volume is about 400 pages, in excellent condition but the
writing often undecipherable. A completely appropriate comment on "the dig-
nity of Gouverneur Morris" was lost when the hieroglyphic was found to be
Government, not Gouverneur Morris.
G.M. in Provincial Congress, Sparks, I, 36ff, and *Journals* of Provincial Con-
gress.
G.M. on Rivington case, Force, *American Archives*, Series II, 723–26.
G.M. to Charles Lee, Misc. Mss. (Morris), NYPL.
Jay on move to White Plains, Monaghan, 83.
G.M. to Washington on sick soldiers, Force, Series IV, Vol. V, 999.
Mathews and Coggeshall to G.M., Force, Series IV, Vol. VI, 1215.
G.M. to N. Y. Convention, Force, Series V, Vol. II, 1023.

CHAPTER FOUR (1777)

"Dear General" letter, HSP.
For Woodhull and Troup, see *Journals* of Provincial Congress, II, 410.
Memoirs L. I. Historical Society, Vol. II (1869), and John R.
Van Deusen article *New York History* (Cooperstown, April 1942).
William Whipple's "Notes of a Journey," *Pa. Mag. Hist. Biog.*, X (1886).
Morris's "scorched-earth" letter, Sparks, I, 131.
Jay to Morris on "paragraphs for the public" and his reply, Sparks, I, 132.

Sally Jay's reading, Monaghan, 100.
"Memorial" to Jay and Morris, G.C., II, 232. For what Washington should
have done, C. F. Adams, *Studies Military and Diplomatic.*
Morris-Schuyler letters, Sparks, I, 141ff.
The Silver Bullet, G.C., XI, 412.
Sally Wister's *Diary, Pa. Mag. Hist. Biog.,* IX (1885).

CHAPTER FIVE (1778)

Letters by or to members of Congress quoted all from LCC, unless other-
wise stated; letters to Governor Clinton from G.C.; Morris–Washington, G.W.;
data on committee membership and votes from JCC; all above readily found
by date.
Adams's preference for Gates, J.A., III, 47.
Laurens to W. Livingston, Sedgwick, 271.
General Varnum to Conway, Hughes, III, 246.
Lafayette's letters to Laurens, from Gottschalk, *Lafayette Joins the American
Army,* 112–16.
Pitt to Lord Shelburne, Shelburne, II, 9.
Stendhal on Lafayette's appearance, Josephson, 271.
Laurens to S. Adams on inexperience of Congress, Wallace, 341.
R. H. Lee to Arthur Lee on changes in Congress, *Letters of Richard Henry
Lee,* I, 408.
Vardill's brief to Eden and Carlisle, Stevens, *Facsimiles,* 438, 440.
For the pro-Gates case, see Bernard Knollenberg's *Washington in the Revolu-
tion.*

CHAPTER SIX (1779–80)

The original letter to Governor Clinton of October 10, 1779, MHS.
Morris's oblations to Venus, quoted by Monaghan, 276, from Iselin Mss.
Letters of Morris to Joseph Reed, Joseph Reed Papers, Vol. VI, NYHS. See
also Van Doren's *Secret History of the Revolution.*
Plan for commando raid to Franklin, LCC.
Adams to Marbois on Morris, *Diary,* III, 219.
Morris's "An American" letters, Sparks, I, 218; III, 219.
Correspondence in the Clajon matter, Gates Papers, Box XIV, 43, NYHS.
Jay's sympathy to Morris, quoted by Monaghan, 219, from Iselin Mss.
Morris's remarks at his amputation, John W. Francis Papers, NYPL.

CHAPTER SEVEN (1781)

Thacher's *Journal* reports the January attack on Morrisania.
Morris's letter to his mother in full, Sparks, I, 158.
William S. Livingston letter, G.C., VI, 680.
Morris's July 9 letter to Reed, Joseph Reed Papers, Vol. VI, NYHS. On
Cabinet qualifications, Sparks, I, 228.
All Finance Office matters from Robert Morris *Day Book.*
Benjamin Rush's estimate of R. Morris, *Autobiography,* 148.
Receipt for private legal services $4000 in HSP.
For the Haym Salomon incident, see Russell, 146, and Sumner, *The Finan-
cier and the Finances of the Revolution,* I, 280ff.
Fersen's letters from *Lettres d'Axel de Fersen à Son Père.*
The army going through Philadelphia from Thacher's *Journal.*
Morris to the Board of War for Watson's parole, HSP.
King George's remarks on Yorktown, Shelburne, II, 83.

CHAPTER EIGHT (1782)

The chapter title is a comment of Franklin on John Adams in Paris.
G.M. to R. Morris on commissioners, Sparks, I, 243.
Minnigerode found in the Genêt Papers how the Queen looked in bed, his *Jefferson*, 80.
Morris to Ridley and Morris to Knox and Wadsworth, HSP.
G.M. paper on coinage in full, Sparks, I, 273.

CHAPTER NINE (1783–86)

As to the Newburgh Addresses, there are many sources. The best are Hatch's *The Administration of the American Army* and Jensen's equally fine *Period of the Confederacy*.
I have no desire to condemn the work of a fellow writer but John Corbin's *Two Frontiers of Freedom*, which seeks to find in this incident a Fascist march on Rome (Philadelphia) led by "the two Morrises and Hamilton," seems to me fantastic. Readers may judge for themselves, though they should be aware that many quotations cited are out of context and out of time sequence.
Sturgis's *Members of the Society of the Cincinnati* (1929) lists past and present honorary members.
G.M. on West Indies trade, Sparks, I, 274.
For Hamilton's defense of the Tory, Waddington, Sparks, I, 125.
G.M. to Livingston declining an appointment, Duane Papers, Box 6, NYHS.
G.M. speech on the bank in full, Sparks, III, 437ff.
G.M. to Knox, MHS.

CHAPTER TEN (1787)

While I have treated the Constitutional Convention over Morris's shoulder, I have studied the *Debates* themselves and Madison's *Writings*. I do not pretend to have reviewed all the enormous secondary work on the subject.
I have carefully read Farrand (*The Fathers of the Constitution* [Yale Chronicles of America]) and Van Doren (*The Great Rehearsal*), the Beards, and Fisker (*The Critical Period in American History*).
There are two small books I particularly recommend to the general reader: *Fifty Five Men* by Fred Rodell, associate professor of law, Yale University, and *Constitutional Chaff* by Jane Butzner.
Colonel Humphreys's letter to Washington, Humphreys, I, 407.
The fishing trip, Washington's *Diary*, III, 226–30.
Madison to Jared Sparks, I, 284.
Madison on Lansing, MADW, IX, 459.
Lansing's death from DAB.
Abigail Adams on Morris, her *Diary*, Jan. 8, 1798.
Madison's expense account and payment to Morris, LCC, VIII, 694.
Montesquieu's *The Spirit of the Laws* with the long critical introduction by Franz Newmann of Columbia in the Hafner Library of Classics (New York, 1949) is invaluable.
Farrand, III, 236, quotes French Archives on G.M. "avocat célèbre," etc.
G.M.'s bank book, Papers, Library of Congress.

CHAPTER ELEVEN (1788)

The opening paragraph of the chapter is from a letter of David Thomas to Griffith Evans, MHS, Series III, Vol. 46, p. 371.

R. Morris to Gates quoted from Beveridge, I, 401.

Jefferson's duties in Paris, *Autobiography*, 96.

See Malone (1951), 162–76, for the naturally shifting views of Jefferson "far away from his native society and observing the perils of monarchical systems only."

De Warville's Mission, Jensen, 385.

Thomas Jefferson at Tuckahoe, BYJ, 11.

Data on Thomas Mann Randolph's family, *William and Mary Quarterly*, 1st series, XV, 119, and VIII, 120. Also throughout, Bruce, *John Randolph of Roanoke*.

William Constable's letters from his *Letter Book*, NYPL.

Morris's to Hamilton, Hamilton Mss., Library of Congress, Box XXXIV, 225.5348. This volume contains seven other letters from Morris on ratification by Virginia. See also Van Doren's *The Great Rehearsal*.

The interfaith participation in Philadephia, *The Republican Court*, 108.

Lafayette to Washington about Jones, Gottschalk, *Lafayette Letters to Washington*, 345.

Morris to Washington with geese and pigs, Sparks, I, 291.

For Perez Morton matter see *American Literature*, Vol. 4 (Jan. 1933), "The Author of the First American Novel."

John Adams to Abigail Smith on Cincinnati quoted by Roof, 205.

Perez Morton on Salem Poor, the gallant Negro, MHS, Series I, Vol. 6, p. 178.

American finances quoted in full, Sparks, III, 470ff.

CHAPTER TWELVE

Lady Shelburne's honeymoon reading from Shelburne, I, 268.

Lady Holland's, her *Journal*, I, 192.

Dimensions of Holland House library from J. Q. Adams's *Diaries*, June 2, 1816.

De Warville, Liancourt and Rochambeau quoted from *The Republican Court*, 90, 377, 380.

Blanchard from his *Journal*, Nov. 24, 1780.

Fersen from *Letters to His Father*.

The reluctance of the Swiss girls from Quennell.

Lord Shelburne's views on matrimony, Lady Holland's *Journals*, I, 210.

Examples of Hamilton's letters to Betsy, AMH.

Marshall to Monroe quoted by Cresson, 78.

Benjamin Rush, his *Writings*, 330.

Dr. Berkenhout's views from his *Journal, Penn. Mag. Hist. Biog.*, Vol. LXV.

Brooks Adams quoted from *The Theory of Social Revolution*, 9.

The King's bathing from Fanny Burney, Mar. 1, 1789.

For discussion of *Princess of Cleves* and *Les Liaisons Dangereuses* see Turnell.

CHAPTER THIRTEEN

The quotation in first paragraph is from Jefferson's *Autobiography*, 120, speaking of the patriot leaders. His comment on the nobles, the Queen, and the excerpt of June 3, 1789, quoted by Hazen, 42, 51.

John Adams on Orléans, R.K., I, 432.

On the Marquise de Bréhan and De Moustier: Abigail Smith, quoted by Roof, 197; John Trumbull, *Autobiography*, 118; Jefferson to Madison, MADW, IV, 460; Lafayette, Gottschalk, 332, 345; David Humphreys, I, 439; Madison to Jefferson, MADW, V, 281–82; Jay to Jefferson, quoted by Monaghan, 266, Iselin Mss.

Jefferson on the French Constitution, Hazen, 42.

CHAPTERS FOURTEEN–FIFTEEN (1789)

Quotations from the *Diaries* are all, I believe, fully apparent.

Morris's Mss. *Letter Book* is here used for the first time.

Material on the Louvre and the Flahaut family, Maricourt, 46ff.

Constable's letters, CPP. See references, John Askin Papers, Vol. I, for Phyn, Ellice & Company.

With good humor, I must quote two brother writers on Morris in Paris. In the magazine *Légion d'Honneur* for July 1938, Yvon Lapequellerie writes on "Two Americans in Paris" (Morris and Dr. Evans). He says of Morris, "Parisian customs, so new to him, hardly disturbed his Puritan simplicity!"

In *Lives of Talleyrand*, Crane Brinton says, "Morris was in love with the lady [Adèle] himself and paid unsuccessful court to her." Less amusing is an extraordinary surmise in Claude G. Bowers (BYJ, 439). He is, I think, very unctuous on the assumed chastity of Jefferson but says of Madame de Corny's having Morris and Adèle to supper, "the evil-minded may conclude that she had acted in the role of a procuress."

CHAPTER SIXTEEN (1790)

Bemis, *Jay's Treaty*, indispensable to understanding of Morris's talks with Leeds.

G.M. to James Morris, Morris Mss., NYPL.

Benjamin Vaughan to Lansdowne, Shelburne, II, 462.

Talleyrand's letter to Adèle that day, Bastide, 76.

CHAPTER SEVENTEEN (1791)

William Knox letters, MHS.

Wilcox, *The Mode in Costume*, discusses women's clothes of the time.

CHAPTER EIGHTEEN (January–August 1792)

Roger Sherman, Burr and Monroe on Morris, R.K., I, 420ff.

Paine to Jefferson, Conway, I, 336.

Lafayette to Washington, Gottschalk, 361.

Jefferson on G.W. and G.M., *The Anas*, 301.

All the details of Jones's death, burial and exhumation (1906) are set forth in *Commemoration at Annapolis* (Government Printing Office). General Porter, then ambassador to France, said in his speech that "In life [Jones] was perhaps the most conspicuous person on two continents." The volume and all biographies of Jones contain strong criticism from many people of Morris's alleged indifference to Jones. It seems to me quite groundless and factually incorrect.

Those desiring every necrological detail should see an article by Morgan Cunnington in *American Funeral Director* for June 1950.

Russell in his *Jones*, 275, says, "On a Sunday in July 1792, Morris . . . one of its chief social butterflies visited Jones, finding him in his backyard hammock. 'Mme. T. and two young ladies were with him. . . .'" It sounds true, and tends in a general way to confirm my belief that Madame de Tellison was at Jones's deathbed. The only trouble is that I did not find the passage in the Mss. *Diaries*, nor the editions of 1831, 1888 or 1938.

CHAPTER NINETEEN (August–September 1792)

The chapter title is a phrase of Maricourt who, reading the expurgated Morris *Diaries*, not knowing that Morris and Adèle were lovers, and apparently blind to Morris's regard for security, is amazed at his coldness.

Lafayette's letter to Short is in the Davenport edition.

Morris's letter to Madame d'Albani, Sparks, III, 34.

Madame de Flahaut's interview with De la Touche from Maricourt, 148–52. I have fixed the time from what seems to me the internal evidence of the *Diaries*.

Madame de Staël's visit to Robespierre, Nicolson, 124, and many sources.

Talleyrand's passport from Danton from the *Diaries* and many sources and told by him to Lady Holland in 1830, *Journals*, II, 36.

References to Lord Lansdowne, Shelburne, II, 393, 396.

Talleyrand's letter to Adèle from Villemarest, Tome II, 88–98. Without pretending to expert knowledge, or judging Villemarest as a whole, this letter seems to me to speak for itself as having been written by Talleyrand. The translation is the author's.

For Lord Wycombe's part in the escape see Lord Kerry's (a later Lord Wycombe) Introduction to *Secret of the Coup d'Etat*.

Short's letters, WSP.

The date of the birth of Anne Randolph's child is frequently given as October 1st, presumably during the night September 30/October 1, but she, in an effort to prove him wrong in every possible detail, herself corrects John Randolph of Roanoke in her letter of January 16, 1815. Her letter reads, "[You say that I destroyed] with my own hand in October '92 that of which I was delivered. You ought to have said the last of September."

CHAPTER TWENTY (September–December 1792)

On the question of payment on the debt after the King's arrest, Sparks, I, 390ff.

Colonel W. S. Smith on G.M., *The Anas*, 334.

CHAPTER TWENTY-ONE (1793)

The extreme pro-Genêt story is in Minnigerode's *Jefferson, Friend of France*, based on Genêt's Papers. See also *Washington and His Colleagues*, 118ff., for excellent summary; Bemis, 142ff.; Bowers, 227ff.

For the maintenance of Adèle in Half Moon Street, Shelburne, II, 394.

For Talleyrand and Madame Grand, Villemarest, Tome II, 115ff.; Maricourt, 158ff.

Ternant on G.M., Turner, 170–86.

The loans to the Marquise de Lafayette, G.M.'s *Letter Book* and, from her point of view, McCabe, 192ff.

Paine on G.M.'s alleged do-nothingism, Conway, II, 81.

Letters about Rosalie, WSP.

Madison to Jefferson on "unfortunate appointment of Gouv. M.," MADW, VI, 195.

Adet to Pickering on French precedence, Turner, 657.

CHAPTER TWENTY-TWO

The chapter title is a phrase of William Livingston's in a letter to John Jay (Monaghan) about Brockholst Livingston's marriage.

Bruce's *John Randolph of Roanoke* tells the story of the trial from the court documents in detail. Reviewing the book in the *Virginia Magazine of History* (Vol. XXXI), S. S. P. Patterson said, "It seems a pity that [Bruce] has deemed it necessary to go into the century-old misfortune of Anne Cary Randolph. What Theodore Roosevelt said of her in his *Life of Gouverneur Morris* is in much better taste. . . ." To which he adds the amazing falsehood "[Morris] was not very happy with her."

Originals of Judith Randolph's letters to Mary Harrison, VHS.

Nancy Randolph's letters, UNVA, except those to Mary Johnston, WML.

The typical family is from Calhoun.

CHAPTER TWENTY-THREE (January–October 1794)

Angelica Church's introduction for Talleyrand, AMH, 258.

Lansdowne's to Washington, Shelburne, II, 394.

Deforgues on Paine, Conway, II, 120. See also Woodward, 274.

Fauchet on influence of Beaumetz and Talleyrand, Turner, 186.

Paine to Monroe, as to G.M.'s fear of exposure, Conway, II, 80.

Morris's courses for the King of France, 6 Papers, Sparks, II, 472ff.

CHAPTER TWENTY-FOUR (November 1794–May 1795)

The Morris *Diary* resumes in October.

Jay to Hamilton on Morris's return, H.C.L., V, 27.

Monroe to Foreign Office for Morris passport, MW, II, 67 and to Washington, II, 112.

See Nicolson, 112–27, for Constant-De Staël meeting.

Angelica Church to Talleyrand, referring to Adèle in Switzerland, AMH, 108.

Adèle to Morris from Bremgarten, Sparks, I, 464–70. (Lucky Sparks. No one else, outside the heirs, has seen.)

Maricourt, 183ff., deals with Adèle's trip, with much primary material, but believes conversations between Morris and Adèle were to the effect that "Paris will soon be the scene of much action. "The placards' *ici ni juifs ni. . . ,*" Maricourt, 185.

Morris for letter of credit for Orléans, Sparks, III, 81.

CHAPTER TWENTY-FIVE (June–December 1795)

Beveridge, II, 203ff., deals with James Marshall's marriage and London mission.

For Bobus Smith see DNB and Greville's *Memoirs*, March 15, 1845, for his death. Lyte's *History of Eton College* for the fight with Wellington.

CHAPTER TWENTY-SIX (January–June 1796)

Adet on Jay, Turner, 888.

Eliza Monroe with Hortense the day after Napoleon's wedding, Aubry, *Private Life of Napoleon*, 89.

Lady Holland's trip to Rome and Hamburg and Madame d'Albani's pleasant society, *Journals*, I, 140.

CHAPTER TWENTY-SEVEN (July 1796–97)

Richard Randolph's will, *Virginia Magazine of History*, XXXIV, 73.

Memoirs of Talleyrand, I, 187, for incident with Adèle at Hamburg; Maricourt, 208–16, on her life there and her snow blindness.

Details of destruction in Hamburg and Altona from Air Ministry, May 29, 1951.

Letters from Countess von Schimmelmann from Burgomaster, Hansestadt Hamburg-Altona, April 3, 1951.

CHAPTER TWENTY-EIGHT (1798)

Abigail Adams letter in *New Letters of.* Monroe to Taylor in MHS, Proceedings, 3rd Series, Vol. 43, pp. 323–24.
Monroe to Madison on Paine as guest, MW, II, 440.
Washington's marginalia on Monroe, G.W. (Fitzpatrick), Vol. 36.
Lady Holland on Lafayette, *Journals,* I, 208.

CHAPTER TWENTY-NINE (1799)

Cost of improvements at Morrisania, R.K., IV, 326.
Scharf, II, 823, gives Morrisania boundaries as Union Avenue on East, Harlem River and Kills on south and west.
Le Guen vs. Gouverneur and Kemble, AMH, 169.

CHAPTER THIRTY (1800–2)

See Nevins, *History of New York Post,* and Van Wyck Brooks, *The World of Washington Irving,* for the physical and intellectual aspect of New York at the time.
Photographs of Constable Hall in *North of the Mohawk.* See the *Le Ray Mansion* (Watertown), Pamphlet, NYPL.
For Morris in Senate, Annals of Sixth Congress, First–Second Sessions, Seventh Congress, First Session.
Pettit incident, Gallatin Papers, Box 41, NYHS.
Monroe to Genêt on porcelain, MW, III, 195.
Adèle de Flahaut's letters, *Collections et Autographes,* Bibliothèque Nationale, Paris.
Mrs. Smith's (Margaret Bayard) observation from *First Forty Years of Washington Society.*
The Jefferson-Morris meeting on the Capitol steps, *The Anas,* 453 (see also Morris to Pickering, 1809).
John Lowell on Morris quoted by Greenslet, 150n.
Morris's speech on the Judiciary Bill in full, Sparks, III, 31ff. Beveridge says that to make the speech Morris got "to his *feet* as quickly as his wooden leg would permit"!
Adèle's marriage in G.L.G., I, 352; Holland, II, 155; Fanny Burney; and Maricourt, 226ff.

CHAPTER THIRTY-ONE (1803)

For Morris in Senate, *History of Congress,* Seventh Congress, Second Session.
Barry's letter on Morris, *William and Mary Quarterly,* 1st Series, Vol. XIII, p. 107.
Rutledge to Otis on Morris, Morrison, I, 278.
For Callender, Ford, *Jefferson and Callender.*
In characterizing Gilbert Stuart's portrait of Mrs. Perez Morton as extravagantly as I have, I was aware that all men and certainly all artists and critics would not be equally moved by it. I asked Theodore Sizer of the Division of Arts, Yale University, and my classmate, Gordon Aymar, himself a painter, for their comments. Sizer wisely replied that it would take several thousand words

to define beauty and that such an absolute statement about the undefined was offensively positive. He suggests it is "one of Stuart's most spirited female portraits." Aymar says, "If the accent is on the beauty of the *portrait* . . . consider Sargent's Miss Carey Thomas . . . if on the beauty of the sitter . . . Sargent's Mrs. Charles Inches . . . (and in early 1800's) Sully's Portrait of his Wife . . . (contemporaneously) Speicher's Katharine Cornell."

CHAPTER THIRTY-TWO (1804–5)

All quotations from Dr. John W. Francis are from his long letter to Henry B. Dawson, Francis Papers, NYPL.

The sailing instructions to Dayton are in Misc. Mss. (Morris), NYHS.

McVickar Snow, like Morris a member of the New York Bar, and a sailor, compared Morris's sailing instructions with charts of New York Harbor and his own experience. When he wrote me, two other men and he had just sailed a 57-foot schooner, *Pandora II*, on the course. In general the only changes in Morris's instructions are those arising from the dredging of the harbor since 1804. Snow comments, " 'From Brooklyn Ferry keep around Corlair's Hook'— still good advice; the deepest water lies opposite the Hook; 'stand diagonally across the river'—now better to favor the Brooklyn shore for 1.8 miles from Corlaers Hook; 'keep the midway' (of channel west of Blackwells)—now favor the New York shore, keeping no less than 100 yards from Blackwells Island until past the 'great eddy' (near Queensboro Bridge) and give it a berth of at least 70 yards further northward; 'approach gently the York shore . . . within ten or a dozen yards,' less necessary now because of dredging; 'on starboard bow a round rock,' since removed; water there now 90 feet deep; 'the tide will shoot you through Hell Gate,' at a speed of 4–6 knots; 'in my house three hours after,' starting at Buttermilk Channel, *Pandora II* ran it in somewhat less than an hour with a full flood tide and a 15-knot breeze on the beam." [1951]

Jonathan Mason's visit to Morrisania in his *Diary*, MHS, Series 2, Vol. II, pp. 7–8.

Latrobe's presence at Bizarre from published *Journals*. Professor Talbot Hamlin of Columbia University, who has now examined Latrobe's letters and series of diaries through 1810, advises me that he believes there is no further reference to Bizarre. As to my surprise that an artist did not sense the tragedy in the air, he says that the diaries are lacking in personal comments, and that with fevers so common in Virginia, Latrobe had every reason for taking the facts at their face value.

Incidents and conversations at Bizarre the night Nancy Randolph left, her letter, Sept. 7, 1831, UNVA. Her letters to Mary Johnston, WML.

Sally d'Yrujo's letter, "I am just as giddy," June 20, 1812, quoted by Cutts. See also Thomas McKean Genealogy.

Tom Paine and Madame Bonneville at New Rochelle, Conway, I, 374.

CHAPTER THIRTY-THREE (1806–9)

Duane to Jefferson on the libel suit, MHS, Series 2, Vol. XX, pp. 309–10.

Nolte on Parish-Morris, *Memoirs*, pp. 137–38.

Nancy Randolph describes Morris's first visit to her at Mrs. Pollack's in letter to Joseph Cabell, October 14, 1831, UNVA.

Her letter to Randolph, mentioning "honour," UNVA.

The "come and find me" letter, Feb. 21, 1805, WML.

The loan of fifty dollars asked of Randolph from Newport referred to in her letter of January 16, 1815, NYPL.

Originals of Morris's two letters to Pickering on Jefferson, MHS.

Morris's letters to Nancy at Stratford from his *Letter Book*. The *Letter Book* originally contained six letters to her. The short one of March 9 is on p. 59; the following page, containing the beginning of the next letter, has been torn out, as have been pp. 64 through 69, containing the other letters.

For Morris and the "schönen Emigranten, die Grafin Flahaut," see Ehrenberg, 44. Also Ehrenberg for portrait of David Parish.

For the academy at Stratford and Dr. W. S. Johnson, Orcutt, I, 422, and Dexter, *Yale Biographies and Annals.*

Mrs. Elizabeth Sammis, curator of the Stratford Historical Society, has the Academy's Secretary's book for 1805–65, but the Treasurer's Book which would list salaries paid has been lost.

CHAPTER THIRTY-FOUR (1810–11)

It is interesting to note that the 1888 *Diaries and Letters* quote in full Morris's letter to his niece Gertrude Meredith. Her husband's reply, HSP.

Bixby, 195, has the letter about Thomas Randolph's contour plowing.

A copy of Latrobe's letter, April 10, 1810, was given me by Professor Talbot Hamlin of Columbia University from the *Digest of Latrobe Correspondence* of his great-grandson, the late Ferdinand Latrobe. Professor Hamlin is unaware of the unfair question I have raised about it.

The New York *Columbian* containing the poem on Morris and Jackson is in the Morris Folder, Alumni Room, Low Library, Columbia University.

Letters to De Witt Clinton, DWC Papers, Box 4, Butler Library, Columbia.

The only known portrait of Nancy Randolph is that by the Sharpleses in the possession of her descendant, Miss Beatrix Cary Davenport. Miss Davenport has most graciously agreed to its reproduction in this book, for which I am most grateful. The portrait is so enchanting, so completely in itself a refutation of John Randolph's wicked charges, that the permission to reproduce it is particularly gratifying.

CHAPTER THIRTY-FIVE (1812–13)

Morris's letter to Nancy of June 5, 1812, was sent by her to *The Columbian*, August 3, 1818. Copy in Morris Folder, Alumni Room, Low Library.

Napoleon's leaving Moscow, Caulaincourt, *With Napoleon in Russia*, 167, and Josephson, 178–80.

Morris services in laying out streets, Stokes, *Iconography*, Oct. 26, 1812.

Nancy's letter, October 4, 1831, to Cabell regarding Cutusoff, UNVA. Scharf's *History of Westchester County*, II, 281, has the Hamilton version.

Nancy on Randolph's congratulation on the birth of her child in her letter to Carrington, March 22, 1815, VHS.

Jay's letter declining to be godfather, Jay Papers, IV, 370.

The whole of Anne Bradstreet's lovely poem to her husband in Percy Boynton's *American Poetry.*

CHAPTER THIRTY-SIX (1814)

Originals of the Randolph-Morris exchange about St. George and Tudor Randolph in Misc. Papers (Randolph), NYPL.

Nancy's payments to her sister Judith, her letter to Cabell, May 30, 1828, UNVA.

The course of Tudor's illness and his mother's arrival at Morrisania, G.M. *Diaries.*

The Manuscript Room, NYPL, has longhand copies of Randolph's letter from "Greenwich Street, Oct. 31, 1814," and Nancy Morris's reply of January 16, 1815. The letter transmitting them says, "They are in the handwriting of Henrietta Graham Youngs (1821–96), wife of Thomas F. Youngs (1805–83). . . . She was often at Morrisania where she most likely saw and made the copies. (For Mrs. Youngs' relationship to G.M. see Lefferts, *Descendants of Lewis Morris*.) It is also interesting to those who knew Mrs. Youngs to wonder why she with her singularly pure, upright Scotch character thought it worth while to copy these letters." This letter, written in 1901 by a member of the New York Bar, then thirty-eight years old, the son of one of the most distinguished scholars of the country, indicates how long the belief persisted that biography must be pietistic. In 1907 other copies of the letter were given the editor of the *Journal of American History* by the editor of the Roanoke (Va.) *Times* with the comment, "They would of course have to be expurgated if published." Mrs. Morris had sent a dozen copies to Virginia to be read.

CHAPTER THIRTY-SEVEN (1815)

For Adèle's gay party, G.L.G., II, 509–11.
Beirne is excellent on the Hartford Convention. See also of course Henry Adams, *Documents Relating to New England Federalism*, Chap. 8.
Nancy's 1815 letters, VHS.
Randolph to Giles, March 12, 1815. Misc. Papers (Randolph), NYPL.
Morris's letter to young Parish, September 1815, Misc. Mss. (Morris), NYHS.
His wonderful letter on "timothy grass, eels etc." in DWC, Box 6.
Young Flahaut with Napoleon at his fall, Guedalla's Introduction to Lord Kerry's *Secret of the Coup d'Etat*.

CHAPTER THIRTY-EIGHT (1816)

Morris's letter to Atwater in full, Sparks, III, 345.
Original of his introduction of Edward Everett to Madame de Staël, MHS. Perhaps Everett never used it.
Charles Carroll's reference to Nancy, Rowlandson, II, 311.
Gallatin's letter in Gallatin Papers (1816), NYHS.
Morris's will quoted in full, Sparks, I, 504.
His mention of Ogden to Dr. Hosack, Nancy's letters, UNVA.
On November 21, 1816, Charles Carroll asked R. King, "Is it known what disorder carried off Mr. Gouverneur Morris" (Rowlandson, II, 311). King had already written Gore (R.K., VI, 34), "There was a stricture in the urinary passage. Morris had himself unskillfully forced a whalebone through, [resulting in] lacerations and mortification. He did it some years ago with a piece of hickory."
There is a good deal of evidence that Morris did not have a high opinion of the medical profession, and, particularly in Europe, prescribed medicines for all and sundry, adjusted a valet's hernia, etc. This may in part have arisen from the unconscious feeling that his leg was needlessly amputated.
It is tragic to realize that such a death is one of appalling agony. He did not, as Henry Cabot Lodge said in the *Atlantic Monthly*, April 1886, die "without suffering and cheerful to the last."

CHAPTER THIRTY-NINE

The chapter title is Lady Holland's comment on Adèle, *Journal*, II, 155.
Nancy to Short on Ogden, WSP.

The Sully-Morris correspondence, DWC, Vol. 6, and Meredith's letter in *NYHS Quarterly*, Vol. XXXV, No. 1, January 1951.

Nancy Morris on Moss Kent, UNVA. The ghost story in *A Guide to Empire State* (3rd ed., 1947) under Gouverneur, N.Y.

Le Ray de Chaumont's bankruptcy, Kellogg, 13.

David Parish's suicide, Ehrenberg.

Madison to Sparks, MADW, IX, 447.

Maria Amerigo Vespucci and George Parish, *Guide to Empire State*, 523, and Kellogg, *Parish's Fancy*.

Mrs. Morris's name was Anne. The Ann of the church and tomb is ecclesiastical custom.

Bibliography

All that has previously been written about Morris has necessarily been without sight of the *Diaries* (1794–1816). Actually little has been written since the publication in 1938 of the unexpurgated *Diaries* (1789–92).

The full *Diaries* and *Letter Books* came to the Library of Congress under the will of Alfred Percival Maudslay, of Morney Cross Fownhope, Hereford, England, who died January 22, 1931, and whose first wife had been Anne Cary Morris, editor of the 1888 edition. The last item in the schedule of bequests in his will reads

Name of Legatee	*Address*	*Short Description of Chattels*
Library of Congress	United States of North America	All Journals, Diaries and Correspondence of Gouverneur Morris

Article 4 of the will, however, gave the executors the right to retain the *Diaries,* etc., to enable Beatrix Cary Davenport to make copies. The result was that there were restrictions on the *Diaries* until late 1950.

Unfortunately for historians, letters to Morris were not included in the bequest.

GOUVERNEUR MORRIS

MANUSCRIPT PAPERS

Diaries, Letter Books (Private, Land, Consular), *Bank Books,* Library of Congress

Letters: Historical Society of Pennsylvania (HSP); Massachusetts His-
torical Society (MHS); New York Historical Society (NYHS); New
York Public Library (NYPL); Old Tioga Point Historical Museum
(Athens, Pa.); Low Library, Columbia University, Morris Folder,
Columbiana; and in collections listed under general heading of
Manuscript Collections

MAGAZINES AND REVIEWS

American Historical Review, October 1937, by Elizabeth Brook
Atlantic Monthly, April 1886, by H. C. Lodge
London Quarterly and Holborn Review, July 1932, by J. A. Lovat-Fraser
Massachusetts Historical Series III, Vol. XLIII, 46; Series II, Vol. I, 20
New York Historical Quarterly, January 1951, by Irvine F. Cortelyou and
Theodore Bolton (on Ezra Ames)
Scribner's Magazine, January 1887, by Anne Cary Morris
Tyler's Quarterly Magazine, October 1920
Virginia Magazine of History, Vol. XXXIV

BIOGRAPHIES

Sparks, Jared. *Life of Gouverneur Morris,* 3 vols., New York, 1832
Morris, Anne Cary. *Diary and Letters of Gouverneur Morris,* 2 vols., New
York, 1888 (granddaughter of Morris)
Roosevelt, Theodore. *Gouverneur Morris,* New York, 1889
Walther, David. *Gouverneur Morris,* New York, 1934 (originally pub-
lished, 1932, in Lausanne, Switzerland)
Davenport, Beatrix Cary. *A Diary of the French Revolution,* 2 vols., Bos-
ton, 1939 (great-grandniece of Morris)

OTHER BOOKS

Akerly, Lucy D. *The Morris Manor* (Pamphlet), New York, 1916
Johnson, William. *Report of Cases Adjudicated in the Supreme Court of
State of New York* (*Jan. 1799–Jan. 1803*), New York, 1803 (for Le
Guen vs. Gouverneur and Kemble)
Lefferts, Elizabeth. *Descendants of Lewis Morris,* New York, 1907 (this
rather conspicuously omits dates of Mrs. Morris's birth and death)
Morris, Mrs. Gouverneur (Anne Cary Randolph): Letters in Library,
William and Mary College (WML); Alderman Library, University
of Virginia (UNVA); Virginia Historical Society, Richmond (VHS);
see also *William and Mary Quarterly,* 1st Series, Vols. VIII and XV

MANUSCRIPT COLLECTIONS

Clinton, De Witt, Papers, Butler Library, Columbia University (DWC)
Constable-Pierrepont Papers, New York Public Library (A marvelous
collection. Letter Books, Incoming Letters, Ledgers, Journals, etc.)
(CPP)
Duane, William, Papers, Box 6, New York Historical Society

Edgar, William, Papers of, in possession of William Edgar, Esq., Hewlett, L.I., N.Y.
Emmet Collection (Morris), New York Public Library
Francis, John W., Papers of, New York Public Library (26-page longhand letter of Francis to Henry B. Dawson "on appearance and character of Gouverneur Morris")
Gallatin, Albert, Papers, Boxes 41 and 138, New York Historical Society
Gates, Horatio, Papers, Boxes 14 and 43, New York Historical Society
Hamilton, Alexander, Papers, Library of Congress (seven letters from Morris)
Livingston (family) Papers, New York Public Library
Livingston, Robert R., Papers, acquired by gift in 1951 by the New York Historical Society
Morris, Robert, *Journal* and *Letter Books,* Library of Congress. Microfilms at Butler Library, Columbia University
Randolph, John, of Roanoke, Papers (Misc.), New York Public Library
Reed, Joseph, Papers, New York Historical Society
Short, William, Papers, Library of Congress (WSP)
Smith, William, *Memoirs* (Mss.), New York Public Library

The tragic death of William Jay Iselin, in an airplane accident, made it impossible for me to see the John Jay unpublished Papers at Bedford House. He had written me from South Carolina that I might "see any letters in the Jay Collection . . . the next time I visit [New York]." The next time was that of the crash which brought grief and a sense of enormous loss to all who knew him.

BIOGRAPHIES

Adams, James Truslow. *The Living Jefferson,* Boston, 1936
Anthony, Katharine. *Dolly Madison: Her Life and Times,* New York, 1947
Beveridge, A. J. *Life of John Marshall,* 4 vols., Boston, 1916
Bowen, Catherine Drinker. *John Adams and the American Revolution,* New York, 1950
Bowers, Claude R. *The Young Jefferson* (BYJ), Boston, 1945
Brinton, Crane. *The Lives of Talleyrand,* New York, 1936
Bruce, William Cabell. *John Randolph of Roanoke,* 2 vols., New York, 1921
Conway, Moncure D. *Life of Thomas Paine,* 2 vols., New York, 1892
Cooper, Sir Duff. *Talleyrand,* New York, 1932
Cresson, W. P. *Francis Dana,* New York, 1930
——. *James Monroe,* Chapel Hill, 1946
De Koven, Anna. *Life and Letters of John Paul Jones,* New York, 1913
Dodd, Anna Bowman. *Talleyrand,* New York, 1927
Fitzmaurice. *Life of William, Earl of Shelburne,* 2 vols., London, 1912 (Shelburne)
Ford, Worthington Chauncey. *Thomas Jefferson & James Thomson Callender,* Historical Printing Club, 1897 (42 pp.)

Garland, Hugh A. *Life of John Randolph of Roanoke,* 2 vols., New York, 1851

Gottschalk, Louis. *Lafayette Joins the American Army,* Chicago, 1937

——. *Lafayette, Letters to Washington,* New York, 1944

Greenslet, Ferris. *The Lowells and Their Seven Worlds,* Boston, 1946

Gwynne, Stephen. *Thomas Moore,* New York, 1905

Hamilton, Allan McLane. *Life of Alexander Hamilton* (for Angelica Church's letters), New York, 1910 (AMH)

Hughes, Rupert. *George Washington,* 3 vols., New York, 1926–30

Humphreys, Frank L. *Life and Times of David Humphreys,* 2 vols., New York, 1917

James, James Alton. *Oliver Pollock,* New York, 1937

Josephson, Matthew. *Stendhal,* New York, 1946

King, C. R. *Life and Correspondence of Rufus King,* 6 vols., New York, 1894–1900 (R.K.)

Langstaff, J. Brett. *Dr. Bard of Hyde Park,* New York, 1942

Loth, David. *The People's General,* New York, 1951 (Lafayette)

McCabe, Lida Rose. *Ardent Adrienne,* New York, 1930 (Lafayette)

McKenzie, Compton. *Prince Charlie and His Ladies,* New York, 1935 (for Madame d'Albani)

Malone, Dumas. *Jefferson the Virginian,* Boston, 1948

——. *Jefferson and the Rights of Man,* Boston, 1951

Minnigerode, Meade. *Jefferson, Friend of France,* New York, 1928 (containing Genêt Papers)

Monaghan, Frank. *John Jay,* Indianapolis, 1937

Morley, John. *Burke,* London, 1910

Morrison, Samuel Eliot. *Life and Letters of Harrison Gray Otis,* 2 vols., New York, 1913 (Otis)

Nicolson, Harold. *Benjamin Constant,* New York, 1949

Oberholtzer, E. P. *Robert Morris,* Philadelphia, 1917

Park, Lawrence. *Gilbert Stuart,* 4 vols., New York, 1926

Parton, James. *Life of Thomas Jefferson,* Boston, 1884

Phillips, Russell. *John Paul Jones,* New York, 1927

Pickering, O. *Timothy Pickering,* 4 vols., Boston, 1867–73

Pinckney, C. C. *Life of Thomas Pinckney,* New York, 1895

Reed, W. B. *Joseph Reed, Life and Correspondence of,* 2 vols., Philadelphia, 1847

Roof, Katherine Metcalfe. *Colonel William Smith and Lady,* New York, 1929

Rowland, Kate Mason. *Life of Charles Carroll of Carrollton,* 2 vols., New York, 1898

Russell, Charles Edward. *Haym Salomon and the Revolution,* New York, 1930

Sedgwick, Theodore, Jr. *Memoirs of the Life of William Livingston,* New York, 1833

Sizer, Theodore. *Trumbull's Trouble: An Omitted Chapter of the Artist's Life* (Pamphlet), Yale University Library, 1950

Smith, Ellen Hart. *Charles Carroll of Carrollton,* Cambridge, 1942

Sumner, William Graham. *The Financier and the Finances of the Revolution,* 2 vols., New York, 1891

Tower, Charlemagne. *Lafayette in the American Revolution,* Philadelphia, 1895

Trevelyan, Sir George Otto. *The Early Life of Charles James Fox,* London, 1891

Van Doren, Carl. *Benjamin Franklin,* New York, 1938

Wallace, David D. *Life and Writings of Henry Laurens,* New York, 1915

Whitlock, Brand. *Lafayette,* 2 vols., New York, 1929

Wiltse, Charles M. *John C. Calhoun, Nationalist,* Indianapolis, 1944

Woodward, W. E. *Tom Paine,* New York, 1945

LETTERS, PAPERS, DIARIES, PUBLISHED

Adams, Abigail, *New Letters of,* Boston, 1947

Adams, John, *Works of,* ed. by C. F. Adams, Boston, 1856 (J.A.)

Adams, John Quincy, *Diary of,* ed. by Allan Nevins, New York, 1920

Berkenhout, Dr., "Journal of," *Pa. Mag. Hist. and Biog.,* Vol. LXV

Blanchard, Claude, *Journal of,* ed. by William Duane, Albany, 1876

Carroll, Charles of Carrollton, *Journal of,* Maryland Historical Society, 1845

Clinton, George, *Papers of,* 10 vols., Albany, 1899–1914 (G.C.)

Cutts, Lucia Beverly. *Memoirs & Letters of Dolly Madison,* Boston, 1886

D'Arblay, Madame. *Fanny Burney, Diary and Letters of,* 5 vols., London, 1904

Deane, Silas, *Correspondence of,* Coll. of Connecticut Historical Society, Vol. II, Hartford, 1870

Fersen, *Lettres d'Axel à Son Père,* Paris, 1929

Gower, *Despatches of Earl,* Cambridge (England), 1885

Hamilton, Alexander, *Works of,* 12 vols., ed. by H. C. Lodge, New York, 1904 (H.C.L.)

Harrison, Benjamin, Letter of, to George Washington, University of Kentucky Libraries, Bulletin II

Holland, Lady Elizabeth, *Journal of, 1791–1811,* 2 vols., London, 1908

Holland, Lord. *Foreign Reminiscences,* London, 1850

Holland, Lord, *Trial of, for Criminal Conversation with Lady Webster,* London, 1797 (one of the most hilarious stories ever written)

Jay, John, *Correspondence and Public Papers of,* 4 vols., New York, 1890

——, *The Diary of, as Written during Peace Negotiations of 1782,* Bibliographical Press, New Haven, 1934

Jefferson, Thomas. *Autobiography* (containing *The Anas*), New York, 1914

——. *Writings,* ed. by W. C. Ford, 10 vols., New York, 1892–99

Latrobe, Benjamin Henry, *Journal of* (excerpts), New York, 1905

Lee, Richard Henry, *Letters of,* ed. by J. C. Ballagh, New York, 1911–14

Leveson-Gower, Granville, *Private Correspondence of Lord, 1781–1821,* 2 vols., London, 1916 (particularly for Lady Bessborough's letters about Adèle de Flahaut) (G.L.G.)

Madison, James, *Writing of,* 9 vols., ed. by Gaillard Hunt, New York, 1900–10 (MADW)

Monroe, James, *Writings of,* 5 vols., ed. by S. M. Hamilton, New York, 1898–1903 (MW)

Morris, Robert, *Confidential Correspondence of,* Philadelphia, 1917

Nolte, Vincent. *Memoirs,* ed. by Burton Rascoe, New York, 1934

Paine, Thomas, *Writings of,* 4 vols., ed. by M. C. Conway, New York, 1894–96

Palmerston, Lord. *Diary in France during July–August 1791,* Cambridge (England), 1885

Peckham, Howard H. *Kate, the Washerwoman's Daughter,* Lexington (Ky.), 1950. See Harrison, Supra

Rush, Benjamin, *Selected Writings of,* New York, 1947

Shippen, Nancy, *Her Journal Book,* Philadelphia, 1935

Short, William. "A Collection of Letters," *North American Review,* Sept.–Nov. 1926

Smith, Margaret Bayard. *The First Forty Years of Washington Society,* New York, 1906

Talleyrand, *Memoirs of,* 5 vols., Paris, Boston, 1895

Thacher, James, *Journal of,* Hartford (Conn.), 1862

Trumbull, John. *Autobiography,* New Haven, 1841

Warder, Ann, "Diary of," *Pa. Mag. Hist. and Biog.,* Vol. XVII

Washington, George, *Diary of,* 4 vols., ed. by J. C. Fitzpatrick, Boston, 1925

———, *Writings of,* ed. by J. C. Fitzpatrick, 39 vols., 1931–44

Webb, S. Blatchley, *Correspondence and Journals of,* ed. by W. C. Ford, New York, 1893

Whipple, William. "Notes of a Journey to Philadelphia," *Pa. Mag. Hist. and Biog.,* Vol. X

Wister, Sally, "Journal of," *Pa. Mag. Hist. and Biog.,* Vol. IX

Mention should also be made of the John Askin Papers (Detroit, 1928), which, though they do not refer to Constable or the Morrises, present a wonderful picture of part of the trade in which they were concerned.

ARCHIVES AND DOCUMENTS, PUBLISHED

Listing of State Department Papers and legislative records for the period of Morris's life would fill half a book. I believe these volumes contain the essentials.

Annals of the Sixth and Seventh Congresses of the United States in which he sat provide the congressional record.

Adams, Henry. *Documents Relating to New England Federalism,* Boston, 1877

Farrand, Max. *The Records of the Federal Convention of 1787,* 4 vols., revised ed., New York, 1937

Force, Peter. *American Archives,* Series II, Series IV, Series V, Washington, 1837–53

Hazen, Charles D. *Contemporary Opinion of the French Revolution,* Baltimore, 1897 (Jefferson, Morris and Monroe)

Turner, F. J. *French Ministers to U.S. (1791–97), Correspondence of,* Amer. Hist. Ass. Ann. Report, 1903, Vol. II

Journals of Continental Congress, ed. by W. C. Ford, New York, 1904ff. (JCC)

Continental Congress, *Letters of Members of,* ed. by E. C. Burnett, Washington, 1921–36 (LCC)

Wharton, Francis. *Revolutionary Diplomatic Correspondence of the U.S.,* 6 vols., Washington, 1889

Journals of the Provincial Congress of State of N.Y., 2 vols., n.d.

Debates in Federal Convention 1787, ed. by Gaillard Hunt and J. B. Scott, 2 vols., New York, 1908

Stevens, B. F. *Facsimiles of Manuscripts in European Archives,* 25 vols., London, 1898 (Dr. Johnson would have admired "the total defiance of expense" which went into the building of these magnificent volumes)

SECONDARY SOURCES, HISTORICAL (PARTIAL)

I have made no attempt to provide a complete bibliography for the American or French Revolutions. I believe I have read the best books on those subjects.

Abbott, Wilbur C. *New York in the American Revolution,* New York, 1929

Adams, Brooks. *The Theory of Social Revolution,* New York, 1913

Adams, Charles Francis (2nd). *Studies Military and Diplomatic,* New York, 1911

Beirne, Francis F. *The War of 1812,* New York, 1949

Bemis, Samuel Flagg. *Jay's Treaty,* New York, 1923

Bryant, Arthur. *The Years of Endurance,* London, 1942

——. *The Years of Victory,* London, 1944

——. *The Age of Elegance,* London, 1950

Burnett, Edmund Cody. *The Continental Congress,* New York, 1941 (Burnett)

Butzner, Jane. *Constitutional Chaff,* New York, 1941

Corbin, John. *Two Frontiers of Freedom,* New York, 1940 (for a theory on Newburgh Addresses)

Ehrenberg, Dr. Richard. *Das Haus Parish in Hamburg,* Jena, 1925 (in NYPL)

Farrand, Max. *The Fathers of the Constitution,* Yale Chronicles of America

Flick, A. C. *Loyalism in New York During the Revolution,* New York, 1901

Ford, Henry Jones. *Washington and His Colleagues,* Yale Chronicles of America

Fox, Dixon Ryan. *The Decline of Aristocracy in the Politics of New York,*

Columbia University Studies in Hist., Econ. and Law, Vol. LXXXVI, New York, 1919

Griswold, Rufus Wilmot. *The Republican Court,* New York, 1854

Hatch, Louis Clinton. *Administration of the Revolutionary Army,* New York, 1904

Jensen, Merrill. *The New Nation,* New York, 1950 (Jensen)

Johnson, Allen. *Jefferson and His Colleagues,* Yale Chronicles of America

Kerry, Earl of. *The Secret of the Coup d'Etat,* New York, 1924

Knollenberg, Bernhard. *Washington and the Revolution,* New York, 1940

Merlant, Joachim. *Soldiers and Sailors of France in the American War of Independence,* New York, 1920

Morse, Sidney. *Freemasonry in the Revolution,* Washington, 1924

Rodell, Fred. *Fifty Five Men,* Harrisburg (Pa.), 1936

Roth, Philip A. *Masonry in the Formation of Our Government,* Milwaukee, 1927

Spalding, E. Wilder. *New York in the Critical Period, 1783–89,* New York, 1934

Thomas, William Sturgis. *Members of Society of Cincinnati, Original, Hereditary and Honorary,* New York, 1929

Van Doren, Carl. *Secret History of the Revolution,* New York, 1941

———. *The Great Rehearsal,* New York, 1948

SECONDARY SOURCES, GENERAL

Calhoun, Arthur W. *A Social History of American Family,* New York, 1945 (Calhoun)

Cecil, Lord David. "The Whig Aristocracy" in *The Pleasure of Their Company,* New York, 1950

Dawson, Henry B. *Westchester County During the Revolution,* Morrisania, 1880

Ellet, Frances S. *Queens of American Society,* Philadelphia, 1867

Nevins, Allan. *The Evening Post,* New York, 1922

Orcutt, Rev. Samuel. *A History of the Old Town of Stratford,* 3 vols., Fairfield Co. (Conn.), 1886

Scharf, Thomas J. *History of Westchester County,* 2 vols., Philadelphia, 1886

Smith, Chard Powers. *The Housatonic,* Rivers of America, New York, 1946

Van Renesselaer, Florence. *The Livingston Family in America,* New York, 1949

Wharton, Anne H. *Salons, Colonial and Republican,* Philadelphia, 1900

Wilcox, R. Turner. *The Mode in Costume,* New York, 1942

Wilson, Henry. *Rise and Fall of Slave Power,* 3 vols. (Vol. I for early Abolitionism in New York), Boston, 1874–77

SECONDARY SOURCES FOR NORTHERN NEW YORK

Clarke, T. Wood. *Emigrés in the Wilderness,* New York, 1941

Hawkins, Richmond Laurie. *Mme. de Staël and the United States,* Cambridge (Mass.), 1930

Hislop, Codman. *The Mohawk,* Rivers of America, New York, 1948
Kellogg, Walter Guest. *Parish's Fancy,* New York, 1929
———. *The Le Ray Mansion,* Watertown, 1945
Merriam, Hilda Doyle. *North of the Mohawk,* Chicago, 1950 (photos of Constable house)
New York—A (WPA) Guide to the Empire State, 3rd ed., New York, 1947

SECONDARY SOURCES, LITERARY

In many ways these books are the most enlightening of the secondary sources and in themselves delightful reading.

Beers, Henry A. *The Connecticut Wits,* New Haven, 1920
Brooks, Van Wyck. *The World of Washington Irving,* New York, 1944
Ellis, Milton. *The Author of the First American Novel,* Durham (N.C.), 1933 (Mrs. Perez Morton)
Quennell, Peter. *The Profane Virtues (Boswell, Gibbon, Sterne, Wilkes),* New York, 1945
Raino, Anio. *The Haunted Castle,* London, 1927 (for discussion of Gothic novels, from which Madame de Flahaut's were a departure)
Turnell, Martin. *The Novel in France,* New York, 1951
Utter, Ralph Palfrey, and Needham, Gwendolyn Bridges. *Pamela's Daughters,* New York, 1936

FRENCH SOURCES

I do not pretend to any profound knowledge of the best foreign books on the French Revolution, though I have read a great many. There is a whole literature on Talleyrand, and Madame de Flahaut is the subject of enormous comment by her contemporaries and later writers. If the following sources are read they will provide the way to further reading.

Annales parisiennes politiques et critiques, Bibliothèque Nationale (very rare)
Bastide, Louis. *La Vie religieuse et politique de Talleyrand,* Paris, 1838
Goncourt, Edmond et Jules de. *Les Maîtresses de Louis XV,* Paris, 1860
Lacour-Gayet, G. *Talleyrand,* Paris, 1937
Loliée, Frédéric. *Talleyrand et la sociétè française,* 2 vols., Paris, 1910–11
Maricourt, André de. *Madame de Souza et sa famille,* Paris, 1907
Marmontel. *Oeuvres choisis de mémoires d'un père,* Paris, 1827
Sainte-Beuve. *Portraits de femmes,* Paris, 1882
Taillendier, R. *Lettres inédites de Sismondi, Bonstetten, Mme. de Staël et Mme. de Souza,* Paris, 1863
Vigée-Lebrun, Louise Elisabeth. *Souvenirs,* Paris, 1831
Villemarest, Charles Maxine de. *M. de Talleyrand,* 3 vols., Paris, 1834
Vivent, Jacques. *La Vie privée de Talleyrand,* Paris, 1940

Part of the fun and excitement of writing a biography is in the books which divert you from the main theme by their own fascination. There are others which fill you with pride in your own remarkable intellect and judgment. But there are many which say to you, "Look on my deeds, ye mighty, and despair." These are the great books of research and collation which, like the monasteries of the Middle Ages, keep the lamps of learning burning. One uses them with awe and humility.

Three such books are these:

Guide to the Diplomatic History of the United States, 1775–1921, Washington, 1935, by Samuel Flagg Bemis and Grace Gardner Briffin
Dictionary of Anonymous and Pseudonymous English Literature, 7 vols., Edinburgh, 1926–34, by Halkett and Laing
The Virginia Historical Index, Roanoke, 1934, by Earl Greeg Swem

Index

Index

480